Understanding Indian Society

Understanding Indian Society

A. M. Shah

UNDERSTANDING
INDIAN SOCIETY
PAST AND PRESENT

Essays for A M SHAH

Edited by

B S Baviskar
Tulsi Patel

Orient BlackSwan

ORIENT BLACKSWAN PRIVATE LIMITED

Registered Office
3-6-752 Himayatnagar, Hyderabad 500 029 (A.P.), India
E-mail: centraloffice@orientblackswan.com

Other Offices
Bangalore, Bhopal, Bhubaneshwar, Chennai
Ernakulam, Guwahati, Hyderabad, Jaipur, Kolkata
Lucknow, Mumbai, New Delhi, Patna

© Orient Blackswan Private Limited 2010
First Published 2010
First Paperback Edition 2011
Reprinted 2012

Photograph of A. M. Shah on frontispiece
Courtesy: Jagan A. Shah

ISBN 978 81 250 4264 8

Typeset in Adobe Garamond Pro 11/13 *by*
OSDATA, Hyderabad 500 029

Printed at
Yash Printographics
Noida

Published by
Orient Blackswan Private Limited
1/24 Asaf Ali Road, New Delhi 110 002
E-mail: delhi@orientblackswan.com

Contents

Acknowledgements   vii
Abbreviations   ix

Introduction   1
B. S. Baviskar and Tulsi Patel

PART 1   GENDER ISSUES   31

1. Assertive Voices: The Other Side of *Burqa*   33
   Mohini Anjum

2. Heart Beating with Fear and Eyes Filled with Rosy Dreams:
   Experiences of Poor Muslim Women in Rural Bangladesh   58
   Tulsi Patel

3. Towards a Conceptual Understanding of
   Female Infanticide in Modern India   93
   L. S. Vishwanath

PART 2   SOCIOLOGY OF RELIGION: 129
         BELIEF, PERCEPTIONS AND PRACTICES

4. Popular Perceptions of the Role of Catholic Priests   131
   Alphonsus D'Souza

5. Religious Cover for Political Power: Narratives from People
   and the Vernacular Press on the 2002 Riots in Gujarat   146
   Lancy Lobo and Biswaroop Das

6. This-Wordly Hinduism: A Case Study   172
   Ragini P. Shah

PART 3   DEVELOPMENT AND MODERNISATION   185

7. Grandmothers Hold the Key to Social Change   187
   T. Scarlett Epstein

8. Cooperatives and Industrialisation in Rural Areas:
   The Indian Experience   202
   B. S. Baviskar and Donald W. Attwood

9. Patidars as Metaphor of Indian Diaspora   220
   Pravin J. Patel and Mario Rutten

10. The Socio-Cultural Context of Informed Consent in
    Medical Practice   257
    Aneeta A. Minocha

PART 4   DISCIPLINARY CONCERNS   281

11. Empirical Meaning and Imputed Meaning in
    the Study of Kinship   283
    Andre Béteille

12. Gendering Sociological Practice:
    A Case Study of Teaching in the University   308
    Rajni Palriwala

13. Why Are Children's Voices Largley Unheard in
    Household Ethnographies?   331
    Shanti George

Epilogue: A. M. Shah—Man and His Work   352
N. R. Sheth

Glossary   362
Publications of A. M. Shah   364
Contributors   371
Index   373

Acknowledgements

This volume in honour of Professor A. M. Shah has been in the making for a long time. The proposal to prepare it was first discussed in a meeting of his students, friends and colleagues in Delhi in 1994. They decided to bring out a collection of essays as a tribute to him for his varied contributions to sociology and social anthropology as a dedicated teacher, competent researcher and eminent scholar. They decided to entrust M. N. Panini and the late Aneeta Minocha, both Shah's students, to work as editors. For various unforeseen circumstances they could not make much progress in the work. This task was then assigned to B. S. Baviskar and Tulsi Patel, both Shah's students and colleagues.

We approached most of Shah's students, friends and colleagues for contributions, and many of them readily agreed to contribute essays based on their ongoing research. After we received their essays, we took considerable time to get the essays revised and edited, since the contributors were scattered in distant places in India and abroad.

We would like to thank our contributors for their cooperation and patience. We are grateful to Dr George Mathew, Director of the Institute of Social Sciences, for his generosity to allow us to use all the facilities at the Institute to carry out our work. We would like to mention especially Ms Molly Bino of the Institute who single handedly managed to prepare several drafts of the essays, and conducted all the correspondence efficiently with a smiling face. We thank Orient BlackSwan for readily agreeing to publish the Festschrift, and their editorial team for cooperation and help in bringing out the volume with professional dedication. It was a pleasure to work with them.

It is sad that Aneeta Minocha, a favourite student and valued colleague of Shah's, passed away in October 2007 before the publication of this Festschrift. Apart from contributing an essay to this volume, she took an active interest in the project from the beginning. We will miss her forever.

Abbreviations

BJP	Bharatiya Janata Party
DSE	Delhi School of Economics
FGM	female genital mutilation
FLP	female labour participation
GS	*Gujarat Samachar*
GT	*Gujarat Today*
ICSSR	Indian Council of Social Science Research
JSR	juvenile sex ratio
KHAM	Kshatriya, Harijan, Adivasi and Muslim
MLP	male labour participation
NWP	North Western Provinces
SRBG	Selections from the Records of Bombay Government
SRG	Selections from the Records of Government
VHP	Vishwa Hindu Parishad

Introduction

B. S. Baviskar and Tulsi Patel

I

In an academic career spanning over five decades, Arvindbhai Manilal Shah (born 22 August 1931) totally dedicated himself to teaching, research, and other professional duties. This volume celebrates his varied and valued contributions while he was, at the same time, a teacher, researcher, and professional colleague. It contains fourteen essays on various themes, presented by his students and colleagues, as a modest tribute to him. It ends in an epilogue written by his close friend, N. R. Sheth, about 'the man and his work'.

We begin with a brief review of Shah's major contributions to development of sociology and social anthropology in India. His contributions may not be dazzling, but they are solid, original, and fundamental to the growth of the discipline. Given the constraint of space, we concentrate on his contributions to the study of the family, the caste system, Hinduism and its sects, village communities, and historical sociology. This does not mean, however, that his contributions are limited to these fields.

Shah challenged preconceived notions and popular beliefs about the family in India. To begin with, he criticised the indiscriminate use of the term 'family' and the tendency to move imperceptibly from one sense of the word to another. To avoid the confusion thus created, he suggested a necessary distinction between 'household' and 'family', for analytical purposes, and provided definitions for both the terms.

In his sustained writings on the family, which culminated in *The Household Dimension of the Family in India* (Shah 1973), Shah challenged several accepted notions: (i) that, in the past, joint households were commoner than nuclear households, (ii) that there is an inevitable evolutionary shift from the former to the latter, (iii) that joint households are characteristic more of rural rather than urban areas, and (iv) that urbanisation encourages formation of nuclear households. On the basis of historical as well as ethnographic data, he rejected the widespread notion that all villagers in traditional India lived in large and complex households composed of two or more married brothers. In fact, small and simple households were preponderant, and even among the complex ones the large majority was composed of parents and one married son.

Shah accepted the idea that there is some pattern in the developmental process of a household, for example, from simple to complex household and back to simple household following the break up of the complex household. However, this process was not cyclical in nature as conceived by Meyer Fortes and his associates, who believed that domestic groups (or households) passed through a set pattern in their developmental cycle. With convincing data and arguments, he also refuted the popular assumption that people lived in large joint households in pre-British India and that joint households were breaking up because of the impact of industrialisation and urbanisation initiated by British rule.

Shah's work on the family received widespread appreciation in the scholarly world in India and abroad. His teacher and lifelong colleague, M. N. Srinivas, said, 'Dr Shah's study is a milestone in the sociological analysis of the Indian family' (Srinivas 1973: xi). In a letter to Shah dated 22 January 1966, Louis Dumont said, 'Your study of the family is very useful. I have discussed it in a seminar with my students.' Marc Galanter, a sociologist of law, wrote to him on 17 July 1965, 'Your study of the family is very enlightening'. The eminent historian Tom Kessinger wrote a long review article, praising Shah's work. He said, 'The field is fortunate to have the contribution of A. M. Shah from the outset. An eminent sociologist with keen historical sense, his papers over the past thirteen years and his culminating work, *The Household Dimension of the Family in India*

(1973) have provided for us a set of carefully refined definitions, a sophisticated conceptual framework, and a constructive criticism of preceding work which should guide us around the pitfalls which have plagued the work on the . . . family' (Kessinger 1976: 2–8).

Shah's contribution to the understanding of caste system is equally original and important. In his *Division and Hierarchy* co-authored with I. P. Desai (Shah and Desai 1988), who was his teacher and colleague, Shah corrects the tendency among scholars, including Louis Dumont, to overemphasise the principle of hierarchy and to ignore the principle of division. Marshalling ethnographic data on caste from rural as well as urban Gujarat, he highlights these two basic principles governing the caste system. According to him, division (or separation) is as important as hierarchy. Division emphasises a sense of being different and separate rather than being higher or lower. However, there is a tendency in the literature to emphasise hierarchy as the primary principle. Caste in urban areas in particular, however, demonstrates division as the primary principle. Shah's research on caste covered both rural and urban areas unlike most other studies, which were limited to rural areas. He therefore pleads for the study of caste in urban areas in order to override the tendency to generalise about caste on the basis of studies in rural areas alone; the latter tendency distorts perception and hinders a balanced view. According to him, at one end, there are castes where the principle of hierarchy has free play and where the role of the principle of division is limited. The Rajputs, Kolis and Bhils in Gujarat are examples of such castes. At the other end, there are castes where the principle of division has free play and where the role of the principle of hierarchy is limited. The Vanias (Banias) of Gujarat are such an example. Dowry and bride price are characteristics of the Rajputs, Kolis and Bhils, where hierarchy is the primary principle; and their absence is a characteristic of the Vanias, where division is the primary principle. As Srinivas stated, 'Shah rightly points out the failure of scholars to take note of urban caste. Shah tried to fill up this gap'. Srinivas also noted that Shah's account of hypergamy in Gujarat is one of the best he had come across (Srinivas 1988: xi–xii).

Although Shah was seriously interested in the study of religion and enjoyed teaching courses on religion, he could not write on it as much as the other subjects. Nevertheless, whatever he wrote on Hinduism and Hindu sects is seminal. His joint article with Srinivas on Hinduism in *International Encyclopedia of the Social Sciences* (Srinivas and Shah 1968) is a masterly statement on the subject. Moreover, his recent paper, 'Sects and Hindu Social Structure' (Shah 2006: 209–48) is a path-breaking work. According to him, it is ironical that although there are literally hundreds of sects thriving in all parts of the country, there are hardly any serious scholarly studies about them. Scholars have paid exclusive attention to ascetics, monks, and mystics and very little attention to lay members of sects. There are excellent studies on monasteries, temples, and pilgrim centres but they are all inadequate in the treatment of sects. Sects are very important for the understanding of Hinduism, and a clear understanding of Hinduism requires us to distinguish between sect and non-sect configurations.

What is a sect? According to Shah, normally a sect has a definite founder, a definite deity or a set of deities, a set of definite sacred texts, and a social organisation. Herein lies the paradox: as sects grow, they acquire not only a complex organisation but also wealth and property, which need to be prudently managed. Thus, asceticism leading to monastic life creates a paradoxical situation for those who have not only negated but also renounced social connections and individual wants. In this connection, Shah highlights two important points. First, the renunciation of family and caste does not mean renunciation of the world. Second, sects composed entirely of ascetics need the support of lay sympathisers and followers.

Shah brings out two significant facts about sects. First, the founders of many sects had followers spread across regions other than their native places. For example, Shankaracharya, a Namboodiri Brahmin, was born in Kerala, but his teachings spread to many parts of India. Vallabhacharya, the founder of Pushti Marg, was a Brahmin born in Andhra Pradesh, but his sect spread mainly in west and north India. The founder of Swaminarayan sect was born in a Brahmin family in Uttar Pradesh, but his sect acquired a large following only in Gujarat. Ramanuja and Madhva did not travel outside south India, but they acquired a large following across the country. Dayanand Saraswati was born in Saurashtra, but the Arya Samaj founded by him acquired a mass following mainly in Punjab, Haryana and Uttar Pradesh.

Nimbarka, a Vaishnava *acharya* belonged to south India, but worked for a long time in the north, and his followers preached Vaishnavism in faraway Manipur. Chakradhara, the founder of the Mahanubhava sect was born in Gujarat, but established his sect in Maharashtra, and his followers carried it to Punjab. Second, Shah points out that even though most of the founders and *gurus* of various sects were Brahmins, most of their followers were middle-level non-Brahmins. Shah poses a number of questions for future researchers: with all the limitations of communication, how did the sects spread across the country? And what are the implications of such a pan-Indian spread of sects over the centuries? An equally significant question is: how is it that almost all sectarian movements were initiated by Brahmin gurus, but their following was mainly among the non-Brahmins? These are pertinent questions for historians, sociologists and anthropologists to ponder over and to seek convincing answers.

When Shah was just an undergraduate student, he had the rare opportunity of working as an assistant to Professor Srinivas, who was doing fieldwork in Rampura in 1952. This laid the foundation of his field studies of villages in Gujarat, in both nucleated villages in central parts and in dispersed villages in semi-tribal areas on the borders. His first sociological publication in the *Economic Weekly* in 1955 was an article on a dispersed hamlet in Panchmahals, just before he passed his MA examination. All this experience gave him valuable insights into village life and shaped his definitive views on the subject from both a contemporary and historical perspective. An article, written by M. N. Srinivas and Shah on 'The Myth of Self-sufficiency of the Indian Village' (1960: 1375–78) proved to be an eye-opener for those influenced by the prevailing ideas popularised by Sir Charles Metcalf in the 1830s and supported later by Sir Henry Maine and Karl Marx. Metcalf characterised Indian villages as little republics, socially and economically self-sufficient, and more or less immune to outside forces. Until recently, most writers on rural India took these ideas for granted. Shah challenged these ideas with wide-ranging historical and contemporary empirical data. He asserted that the village was always a part of the wider social, economic, political, and religious system. The appearance of isolation, autonomy, and self-sufficiency was an illusion. Shah provides many relevant facts to remove this misconception. He points out that the coastal areas of India had maritime commerce in agricultural produce with overseas countries since the beginning of the Christian era. It grew with the coming of the Arabs in the seventh century and Europeans in the sixteenth century. Besides, the villages also depended upon towns for certain goods and specialised services. The assumption that the village community was not influenced by and did not, in turn, influence the wider political structure is also facile.

Shah mentions that even in south India, in the preferential marriage system, the marriage field for a caste includes at least twenty to thirty villages. With the custom of village exogamy and absence of the preferential marriage system, the marriage field for a caste in north India includes at least two hundred to three hundred villages. Moreover, the pilgrimages take the villager beyond the village and occasionally into a different language area. Similarly, peasants visit fairs, which are held all over the country. All these facts reveal that the peasant's social and economic universe is much wider than the village. In addition, the pattern of landownership, tenancy, and labour frequently cut across villages. Thus, Shah is able to prove that the Indian village was always a part of a wider entity. Superficial observations gave only an illusion of self-sufficiency and isolation.

Around the mid-1950s, while engaged in fieldwork in a Gujarat village, Shah learnt about the caste of Vahivancha Barots—a caste of genealogists and mythographers who maintained records of genealogies of their clients spread over rural Gujarat. Shah made a systematic study of their role as record-keepers and as creators of myths and legends, that is, historians of sorts. The work was so fascinating that his paper on the Barots was published in the *Journal of American Folklore* (Shroff and Shah 1958) and reprinted in a volume edited by Milton Singer (1959). This paper created great interest and appreciation among scholars. Louis Dumont was all praise for it, 'This is the first report of its kind, it studies the genealogists in relation to their clients, Rajputs, Kolis and Patidars, and achieves a reasonable balance between fact and thought, description and analysis' (1961: 210–12). This was the beginning of Shah's interest and entry into the field of historical sociology.

Shah occupies a unique position among scholars as a practitioner of the craft of both the sociologist/social anthropologist and historian, working with equal ease and élan in both. He is, perhaps, one of the very few in India to be able to do this. The historian in him is reflected in all his writings, but the publication of his book, *Exploring India's Rural Past* (Shah 2002) firmly established him as a competent historical sociologist. This book was reviewed at length by a leading historian, Marcia Frost (Frost 2002: 2137–38). She begins by saying that this book is based on Shah's 1964 PhD thesis on 'Social Structure and Change in a Gujarat Village': 'It was a starting point for all researchers interested in a century of social and economic change in Gujarat. Since then he had been a mentor to innumerable Indian and international scholars over the years. That young scholar who authored the 1964 thesis matured into one of India's most eminent sociologists. *Exploring India's Rural Past* is a wonderful gem of solid economic and social history'. Frost goes on to say that with wide-ranging evidence, Shah shows that the myth of self-contained, autonomous village had no foundation in the reality of economic and social life. According to her, '*Exploring India's Rural Past* is an important contribution to our understanding of village life in the early 19th century and to the change—social, economic and political—which has taken place over the last two centuries. Shah is an astute observer of village life and kin and caste relationships over several decades'.

II

This section weaves a shared set of memories, some similar and some different, in an attempt to show the range of the varied areas in which Shah's students and friends worked and in whose work he took a keen interest. It is based largely on the experiences they shared with us. When his students, colleagues and friends thought of this volume, it was primarily to serve as a gesture of their fondness, admiration and respect for him. In recording their appreciation for him, they also provide a window to the vicissitudes of academic training in sociology at Shah's desk. By the time Shah retired in 1996, he had guided over twenty PhD students working in diverse fields and producing high quality theses.

Why is Shah fond of dissecting drafts so minutely and extensively? This is not an easy question to deal with, especially in times when this quality is becoming increasingly rare. It is in his thorough reading of drafts that, his presence remains in the minds of his students and colleagues and extends beyond his formal occupation of the professorship in the Department. The rigour he imposes on his students goes a long way in maintaining the high standards of the discipline. To be available to students for a no-nonsense, serious discussion on a given topic or on a draft was how Shah stood for his students. Serious scholarship and sincerity of purpose were what he communicated through his academic practice. Shah's unwavering contribution to academic work continues through his incisive comments on drafts given by his former students and colleagues. He gives his time selflessly. His expertise is not only enabling for his students and colleagues but it also helps to orient their minds towards a higher quality of contribution to the discipline. From 1967, he also liberally gave his counsel and time to the Indian Sociological Society, the only all-India association of sociologists. Personalities build institutions, and institutions build personalities. While persons occupying institutions come and go, the institutions remain. Arriving at about ten in the morning, leaving for lunch after one, returning for the second shift after two, and staying on until after five in the evening: that is how one would describe Shah's routine as a professor of sociology at Delhi University.

A few of the contributors in this volume have been Shah's MA and PhD students (Aneeta A. Minocha and Mohini Anjum); a few were his Master's students (B. S. Baviskar and Ragini Shah), and a few others his MPhil / MLitt and PhD students (A. D'Souza, Lancy Lobo, L. S. Vishwanath, Rajni Palriwala, and Tulsi Patel), having obtained their MA degrees elsewhere. His relationship with his research students did not terminate with obtaining their doctorates. Remarkably, he worked on the unfinished doctoral dissertation of the late Veena Dua on the Arya Samaj in Punjab. Her illness had kept her from completing her thesis. After Dua passed away, Shah took it upon himself to work on the two chapters she had submitted to him. Along with those chapters, Shah put together a few of her published papers on the topic and prepared her book, which was subsequently published (Dua 1999). This is among the rarest of gestures by a teacher for a student. Once, when we inquired about his work on Dua's manuscript, he said, 'Veena Dua's work has some interesting observations, and I thought it is important that these are known to other scholars. It was a joy to work for her book.' Shah wrote the foreword to the book.

Shah's students and colleagues seek his counsel in their personal sphere as well. In 2000, he offered Lancy Lobo his house in Baroda for him to use as his research centre, Centre for Culture and Development. Several of his students in distress found shelter in his home, whether in Delhi or Baroda.

Shah is a hard taskmaster and pursues his work with single-minded devotion. Once, while a few students were helping him proofread his book, *The Household Dimension of the Family in India*, he worked until after six in the evening. Aneeta Minocha drew his attention to the fact that Mohini Anjum's husband was waiting for her and that she had got married the previous day. To this Shah responded that once that bit of work was done they could leave for the day. This was a surprising reaction from him. Two days later, he invited Mohini and her husband home for lunch, and they enjoyed the Gujarati delicacies prepared by Mrs Shah, who is known for making and lovingly serving the food. He does not make any show of concern but has his own ways to express it; he is there when his advice is most needed.

A man of outstanding integrity, his upright spirit is like his elegant simplicity. Just as he never allowed his eye problem to become a handicap in his work, he did not allow his academic position to come in the way of administrative work in Delhi University and the Department of Sociology. He devoted himself wholeheartedly to any assignment he took up. His students recall fondly his dedication to teaching and learning. He insisted on clarity of data and on finding and communicating the logic on any issue, whether he was lecturing to Master's students, or tutoring a group of students, or discussing research with students and colleagues. Those whom Shah taught at the Master's level found it an exhilarating experience. A few of the authors in this volume were among the first few batches that Shah had taught when he joined Delhi University. He taught the course on kinship, which most students had initially detested for its complicated charts and terminology. But, despite its intricacies, Shah's lectures made kinship an interesting course. The examples he gave from African societies are vividly imprinted and continue to remain fresh in their minds even after four decades. His tutorial students were fortunate to have him as their tutor. The discussions during the tutorial meetings were thorough and insightful, and they taught his students what to look for and how to interpret sociological writings. They also learnt how to write with precision.

The students who had Shah as their MPhil or PhD supervisor, attribute their sociological nurturance to him. Three remarkable characteristics emerge from the research students' experiences with him: his style of selection of a topic for doctoral work, his untiring reading and comments on several drafts of a thesis, and his explaining of the theoretical and methodological goal of doing a doctoral thesis. His style of selection of a PhD topic is a pedagogic tool in enabling participation. He not only helped Anjum select her doctoral topic, but also impressed upon her the importance of women's voluntary associations in India's urban life. He insisted and eventually pushed her to go to the field. Gradually she realised that it is the field more than anything else which teaches a student what data to collect and how.

In his initial meetings with a student wishing to work for a PhD, Shah would gauge the student's interest. He would inquire about his/her family background and about any interesting experiences and observations in society. In the process of these meetings a PhD topic would emerge. That topic would be set for preliminary exploration in the field and the library. Invariably, the topic turned out to generate enough research interest in the student and become the research topic for the doctoral degree. Coming from a family of medical doctors, Minocha, after the initial prolonged and relaxed conversations with Shah, selected a hospital in Delhi for her PhD—those days it was a new area in sociological research. Minocha's thesis was recommended for publication by the University of California Press; it somehow got delayed and was published much later elsewhere. She found it a rewarding experience to arrive at a PhD topic through long and relaxed conversations, and she followed this practice with her own research students. Even if he did not take lecture classes for MPhil students, he would make himself available to them for advice. He was warmed to learn that Lobo was interested in working in Gujarat and that Patel had collected household data in a village in Rajasthan. Shah encouraged Patel to use her field data to write her MPhil dissertation contrary to the preferred policy of the Department. In the meanwhile, Patel had published a paper on fertility and status of women (Patel 1982), which had been selected for the Library of Congress in the USA. The topic for her doctoral study was in a way drawn from this publication. It had been accepted for publication by an international journal, but the communication to this effect got lost in the post owing to her change of residence. By the time the second letter informing Patel of the date of publication came, the paper had been accepted by an Indian journal. She resolved this confusion by following Shah's sagacious advice to stick to the Indian journal and honestly write to the other journal regarding the status of the paper. Patel lost the opportunity of publishing her first academic article in an international journal, but there have been no regrets. She cherishes the truthfulness and ethical stance, learnt from Shah, which is highly valuable in academic life.

Shah advised Lobo to visit, initially, several villages in Mehsana district in north Gujarat and told him, 'Keep your eyes and ears open and get the first-hand feel of Gujarat'. It was a demanding work, and Lobo wrote a report about the villages in each *taluka*. He developed an understanding of the people and the field and could see what was in store for him. Shah read and made numerous corrections in Lobo's report. They discussed the conflict between Patidars and Thakors in the area. While there was enough work on the Patidars, there was little on the Thakors who wanted to be known as Kshatriyas. There was work on the vertical dimension of caste, but its horizontal dimension begged a thesis. This became the topic for Lobo's study. After realising that covering too many villages in the district would not give a clear picture about Thakors, he decided to undertake an intensive study of one village.

It would be worth recalling that Shah was convinced of the value of fieldwork and writing about it early on before deciding the topic of one's study. He once mentioned, 'My fieldwork background played an important role in my teaching. I was an assistant to Professor Srinivas during his fieldwork in Rampura for two months in May—June 1952, when I was a BA student. Then, I did fieldwork on my own in the Panchmahal district in Gujarat in two trips for a total period of about six months during the last year of my BA and the first year of MA. And then, I did fieldwork as well as archival work for three years after MA. The archival work led me to read a great deal of early ethnographies. This long period of field and archival work helped me understand sociological theory with reference to facts, which was reflected in my teaching.' His observation on his own research experience guided Shah in being a research supervisor. He said, 'I became a supervisor of PhD students in 1964. By this time the phase of village, caste and tribe studies was almost over. Srinivas had himself begun to implement in Baroda the idea of opening up studies of other aspects of society through application of the fieldwork method. For example, N. R. Sheth studied a factory and R. D. Parikh the Gujarati newspapers. This was a two dimensional strategy. One, since many aspects of Indian society had never been studied, it would be desirable to open up the study of the complex reality of a particular aspect by first studying a small part of it through fieldwork. And two, fieldwork was the best way to train a beginner to cultivate sociological sensitivity'.

Shah said, 'Srinivas and several other teachers, including myself, in Delhi carried forward this strategy. Although every student came to me with a proposal to study an aspect of society of his/her choice, I always advised him/her to conduct fieldwork to study it. Thus, for example, among my early students, Aneeta Minocha studied a hospital, Veena Dua two Arya Samaj communities, and Mohini Anjum women social workers. Even in the case of Vishwanath who planned to study mainly archives, I advised him to spend some time in the field to get a feel of the people and their society and culture. I believe that due to this strategy every one of my students has made at least some contribution to development of the study of his/her chosen field.'

Shah is a pragmatic guide. His suggestions to many of his doctoral students have been the same, as Lobo recalls, 'One can always produce one's master piece after the PhD. What you need to master now is the methodology, how to collect and handle data at the PhD level'. He also states, 'In social science research you do not make earth-shaking inventions and discoveries. If your doctoral research can point out a small idea, view or practice in society, you have made a contribution to development of the existing body of knowledge.' His idea of step-by-step advance can be seen in a Gujarati *bhajan*— *Premal Jyoti*—that he is fond of. It is included in Mahatma Gandhi's collection of bhajans called *Ashram Bhajanavali* (1947). Actually, it is an English prayer titled, 'Lead, Kindly Light', written by Cardinal Newman, which Gandhiji got translated by an eminent Gujarati poet, Narasimharao Divetia. Shah says, 'One stanza specially appeals to me, and I quote it in English.

> Keep Thou my feet, I do not ask to see
> The distant scene; one step enough for me.

In sociological research, as in any field of research, one should be happy if one makes even one step forward.'

He read the penultimate draft of Anjum's thesis within two months of his eye operation, while she had taken unusually long to write it. He carried her draft to Japan and Australia soon after the surgery. All his research students learned to write and evolved as researchers under his able and patient but unrelenting guidance. His comments and questions sharpened students' sociological imagination, while restraining them from getting carried away by jargon and received ideas. He was interested in making his students into scholars.

Shah had published as many as ten papers before he received his PhD in 1964. He recalls, 'Srinivas had read and commented on their drafts closely, and it was a great learning experience for me. However, as regards writing my PhD dissertation, he, as also I. P. Desai who replaced him as my supervisor, left me entirely to myself. Srinivas did not even see the draft, and Desai just flipped through it. Both asked me not to bother too much about theory, and Desai told me, "Go where your data takes you." Srinivas's and Desai's behaviour toward me as their doctoral student left a deep mark on my mind, and guided me in my behaviour toward my doctoral students. Like them, I also always gave high priority to looking after my doctoral students' work.'

Shah continues his commitment to academic work even at the age of seventy-eight. He continues to reflect and write on the topics he has specialised in: family, caste, kinship, village, religion, higher education, and so on. He has published a revised version of his PhD thesis, *Exploring India's Rural Past*, after his retirement. His edited book, *The Grassroots of Democracy* (Shah 2007) has a remarkable history. It is a collection of nineteen papers by sixteen authors who worked on a departmental project on the general elections of 1967 and the mid-term polls of 1971. All of them were research students and/or teachers in the Department of Sociology. Shah had all the draft reports preserved safely for nearly four decades. Thirteen of the papers had been published in different journals, and six had remained unpublished. Even though a considerable time had passed, he did not give up, and finally succeeded in publishing all the essays in a volume in 2007.

III

This volume is divided into four parts. Part I deals with some issues in gender relations, touching upon the family in various ways. Shah is often described as 'the family man' because of his contributions to the study of family. His book on the family pointed out the importance of treating every member of the household—male as well as female—as being equally important. We therefore decided to keep the essays on gender in Part I.

Mohini Anjum's portrayal of Muslim women in old Delhi moves out of the conventional representation of women and enters into their real life. Her women are bold and daring. Her paper, as any true ethnography should do, gives us a peep into the life of women who stand out and refuse to match the stereotypes describing Muslim women. She also provides a glimpse of how Muslim wedding rituals are symbolic of an egalitarian spirit with respect to gender relations.

Data on Muslim women in Bangladesh in Tulsi Patel's essay does not give as optimistic a picture. Her paper discusses the interplay between women's agency and patriarchal structure. It is based on secondary data—a collection of cases of heart-rending experiences of poor Muslim women in villages—chiefly through the credit programme for self-employment of the well-known NGO, Grameen Bank. Patel explores what happens at the grassroots when local efforts seem to make a positive difference to people's life. She analyses these women's trials and tribulations. Based on the group collateral scheme for credit, small groups of women stand guarantee for one other, but there was another struggle they had to encounter for being the wrong gender. The paper deals with issues of poverty, religion and gender hierarchy engulfing these women and with the struggle they have for survival in circumventing the very structures that bound them into dependence, oppression and exploitation. For women, life is harsh right from childhood. Deprived of play and school, they have to help in household chores from the beginning, and most of them are also married off before the age of sixteen, some as early as seven years. Married life is no less painful. They have to work all the time, and are beaten up regularly by lazy, drunken husbands without any reason. But life without a husband, when a woman is divorced, abandoned, separated, or widowed, is worse, as she faces the cruelty of the entire society instead of only the husband's.

Women resent their condition and feel like revolting, but never disrupt the household even though they suffer in it. When everything fails, they may blame their fate for their plight. This offers some consolation. The Grameen Bank tries to help poor women through microcredit, making them economically self-sufficient. The conservative elements in the society, however, oppose it. Yet something is better than nothing. Through careful analysis of rich case studies, Patel presents the harsh dilemmas these women face and the obstacles they encounter while trying to escape from them.

Boserup (1974) said that with the entry of women into the labour force outside home, patterns of division of labour will take different and varied forms. Women continue to do double shifts and are valued primarily for their reproductive and caring roles. Like Boserup's general statement, the Grameen Bank's women were willing to do double shifts, but it was an ordeal for them to get out of home and enter the labour market. Patel analyses the context of the agency of these poor women who withstood familial and community opposition to generate income in their efforts to fight starvation. To overthrow *purdah* and get over starvation has been an achievement not only for women themselves but also for their families. While the clamps of the patriarchal structure of Bangladeshi society are strong, women's agential capacity to bring about a little change has been enhanced through the microcredit programmes of the bank. The pressure to repay the bank's loans has created peculiar adversities for women. Families encourage them to get the Grameen Bank loan but soon take away the cash, thus causing women to lose their money. They are thus deprived of investing the money and consequently of repaying the loan.

Vishwanath's paper on female infanticide during the colonial period in India is an example of how history and anthropology inform each other. It would not be out of place to provide a section of the letter Vishwanath wrote in 2003 to Tulsi Patel when she contacted him to present a paper at a seminar she was organising on the political economy of emotions with regard to missing girls in India: 'In the mid 1960s, Professor A. M. Shah told me that there is considerable data in the historical records on female infanticide, and I could, with a background in History, tap that source. I accepted his suggestion and worked on the subject; but I did not foresee then that the practice would continue and turn into female foeticide. Much less did I think that it would become so widespread'. With female foeticide assuming the proportions it has, the institution of female infanticide becomes all the more relevant to understand the present through its past. With the women's property bill having been passed in India's parliament in December 2005, the issue of property and female infanticide gets further complicated when approached historically. The impact of British policies in this regard makes Vishwanath's paper all the more apposite.

The archives on female infanticide during colonial rule provide information on the castes practising it. Vishwanath points out that for some of the castes resorting to this practice, the records provide data on sex ratios at different levels of the hypergamous hierarchy. They show that female infanticide was a mechanism for maintaining status and dominance among castes such as Rajputs, Kanbis, Lewa Patidars, Jats, Ahirs, Gujars, and Khutris [sic] in parts of north and west India.

For the Rajput princes and *talukdars* in peninsular Gujarat, Rajasthan, and east U.P., the British complicated matters by freezing political boundaries. Most high-status rural Rajputs did not take advantage of the avenues for social mobility opened by colonial rule, since they were conscious of their Kshatriya status. Consequently, the land they owned was the only economic resource for them. Those Rajputs who preserved female children, faced the loss of the whole or part of their ancestral land because hypergamous marriages involved substantial dowry payment to the groom's side. A further complication introduced by British rule for the Rajputs and for some other castes practising female infanticide was the stricter mode of revenue collection in areas under direct colonial rule. The Rajputs' land came up for auction sales for arrears of revenue. Threatened with erosion of their socio-economic status, the Rajputs resorted to extensive female infanticide during the nineteenth century (Cohn 1987). Despite these complications, it would be simplistic to argue that female infanticide was a colonial creation. An elaborate status hierarchy existed among the Rajputs, Patidars and Jats before colonial rule.

Part II includes essays dealing with religion, including an essay on religious communalism. Alphonsus D'Souza's paper focuses on the model of organising community life with the notion of an ideal society. He brings up the interesting concept of 'our own priests'. In Catholic doctrine, the common priesthood of the faithful provides to every Catholic direct access to God. The provision of priests meant to minister, that is, to be of service to the faithful, is different from, say, the expectation of Hindu priests primarily to inspire, to lead the faithful, and to pontificate. The essay describes the hierarchy of priests and the process of becoming one. The role conflict between preaching the word of God against social evils and social criticism is situated in the context of the local church as well as the Vatican. The paper is based on a study of 1,069 laity in Mangalore. These respondents convey that the priests should engage in social activism, enter into politics, and manage and teach in educational institutions, and thus demonstrate the prophetic aspect of their priesthood. The laity wishes that 'our own priests' share their joys and sorrows. Incidentally, all the priests are from Mangalore, born and bred, and even trained for priesthood, in the same city. D'Souza brings to us the local flavour of the relationship between priests and laity obtaining in this city.

The differences of perception lead to tensions between bishops, priests, and other church authorities. D'Souza describes how the cultic, prophetic, and administrative duties along with activist and political ones for the men of God have gradually come to be accepted. He attributes this to the processes of secularisation and modernisation influencing the Catholic church since the second Vatican Council of 1962–65.

Ragini Shah (henceforth Ragini) describes the nuanced practices of this-worldly Hinduism. Through a case study of Muni Seva Ashram, which runs a chain of social welfare activities pertaining to education and health in a backward part of rural Gujarat, she provides an example of dedicated humanitarian work by Anuben Thakker, a *sadhwi* (female ascetic) inspired by her guru Shri Munidas Maharaj and by the teachings of the great spiritual leader Swami Vivekanand. She is neither an ordinary social worker wanting to help the poor and needy, nor is she a trained professional social worker. She is basically a religious worker steeped in the teachings of Hindu classics such as Bhagwad Gita, and of the spiritual thinkers who inspired her to undertake social work with dedication and determination for the poor people in a backward area.

Anuben began her work in 1978 on a modest scale with a creche for children of poor labourers who could not look after their children when they went to work. By the time she died in 2001, in about twenty-three years of her career she had achieved a lot. In this backward and poor part of Vadodara district, notorious for high levels of criminal activity, she set up more than a dozen institutions, from a nursery school to a high school, from an ordinary health centre to a highly specialised cancer hospital, and an ideal home for cows looked after by animal husbandry specialists. All this was achieved through charity collected in good faith. Government grants were minimal.

Of course, similar work is done by many social workers but from a secular perspective unlike Anuben who was inspired by religious teachings. This gave Ragini reason to engage with the theories of Max Weber who studied world religions in a comparative perspective. For Weber, Hinduism was an other-worldly religion whose followers believed not in this world and its concerns but more in the other world, which was an obstacle to material well-being and economic development. By presenting her case study, Ragini challenges Weber's simplistic and misleading notion that Hinduism does not care for life in this world. She has put forward a persuasive argument based on a case study rich with ethnographic details.

The essay by Lancy Lobo and Biswaroop Das, based on media reports, deals with the ghastly communal riots in Gujarat following the notorious Godhra carnage. Since the last two decades, Gujarat has experienced, more than other states, the rise of Hindutva and communalist forces. Much of the recent developments in the state can be traced back to the 1990s, particularly to the ascendancy of the BJP as a political party in the state. The Godhra carnage and its aftermath are only manifestations of complex political and religious processes. They also highlight the complexity of religiosity and the role of ideologies of different religious communities in politics. The authors attempt to map the changing patterns of communal riots in the state. The Godhra carnage has brought extremely sharp reactions from within and outside the country. The majority religious community is itself divided, holding different and often contradictory views, emanating from different ethical standpoints.

The vernacular press in Gujarat has been largely supporting Hindutva and provocation of hatred towards the minorities. Therefore, Lobo and Das have chosen two vernacular newspapers, one representing a majority and the other a minority community, in deriving data for their paper. The volatility of communal provocations is thus expressed in the essay. It is helpful to know the stance of the newspapers beforehand. The reach of the fourth estate, the mass media, is an important force to reckon with in modern society and polity. Putting face-to-face two representations derived from two different community vantage points, Lobo and Das analyse the discourse of representation in critical times in the life of the Indian state and the plurality of its religious communities.

Part III includes essays pertaining to the sociology of industrial cooperatives, development, migration and medical ethics. Scarlett Epstein's essay is distilled from her long-standing and widespread research experience on issues of development and social change. Education, information and communication through various mechanisms have been attempted for over half a century as a means of developing people, usually from the less developed countries of the world. Epstein highlights one of the potential resources left untapped in this educational and developmental process. Her paper points to the chord linking the child with parents one generation removed, that is, grandparents. Unlike most of the focus on old people at the present time as a problem category, Epstein looks at them rather positively. She links the grandparent with what may be called third age education and gives it a gendered dimension. Her third age education is not for the old grandmother herself. Rather, she brings out the enormous potential grandmothers may have in being mediators for developmental messages. In the spirit of a development expert, she opens up an opportunity for turning what is seen as a problem into an asset, especially in the rapidly changing times when one generation's knowledge is not seen as valuable for the next. She argues why grandmothers in different parts of the world are a resource as yet untapped for the purpose of action-oriented social change. Based on her own fieldwork in south India and drawing from nineteen field studies of her doctoral students in Asia and Africa, Epstein is able to cull out and identify the possibility of having grandmothers—women outlive men and spend more time with children at home—as mediators of social change. This is in striking contrast to some of the family planning surveys that put the blame on grandmothers for higher fertility among all those people who, according to development experts, need to curtail fertility. Grandmothers' embodied views may be a lesson or two for development workers themselves. An active involvement of grandmothers with development messages can be a force to reckon with.

Epstein infuses a new meaning into the temporality of female life, especially in Asian and African societies, where the chances of grandchildren spending time with grandmothers are higher than in the West. She thus proposes what is more than a merely fortuitous resource for a few families. She, rather, makes a convincing case for the entire category of grandmothers as holding a key to social change.

B. S. Baviskar and D. W. Attwood show how cooperatives have helped to promote industrialisation of rural areas in some regions of India. They first provide an overview of Indian cooperatives in general and of agro-industrial cooperatives in particular, and then try to account for the different degrees of success of agro-industrial cooperatives. They outline some patterns of success and failure as well as some of the common erroneous explanations of these patterns. They analyse the real factors contributing to the varying degrees of success of these cooperatives. They argue that three major factors play a significant role. First, the political economy of a region, including its landowning structure and caste system, which creates relatively favourable or unfavourable ground for the cooperatives to flourish. Second, the nature of the commodity and the level of investment needed for processing it influence the behaviour of producer members in terms of their loyalty and participation. Third, because cooperatives are a state and not a federal responsibility, the policy of a given state government to allow autonomy and freedom or to interfere in the working of cooperatives strongly determines their chances of success or failure.

Baviskar and Attwood conclude that industrialisation of rural areas offers the potential to reduce poverty and stimulate economic growth. It is also likely to check migration of people to urban areas, providing much needed employment and income to rural people. Moreover, it enables them to acquire new technical and organisational skills. Rural industrialisation begins with agro-based industries, since they provide the crucial advantage of access to raw materials. Once the foundation is laid, other industries are likely to follow in course of time as a result of availability of infrastructure and skilled human resources. Since the cooperatives thus have an important role to play in industrialisation of rural areas, the authors suggest the need to understand the nature and process of cooperation to realise their full potential.

P. J. Patel and Mario Rutten's essay is a fascinating account of the Patidar diaspora in England (mainly central London) and its relationship with the land of its origin in central Gujarat (mainly Kheda and Anand districts). There are about 30,000 Patidars in London. Of them 72.7 per cent were driven out of the east African countries of Uganda, Kenya and Tanzania in the 1960s. Having British passports, they preferred to settle down in England rather than return to India. Besides, 27.3 per cent of the Patidars migrated to London directly from Gujarat to seek better opportunities.

Patel and Rutten tell us in detail the history of Patidar migration to east Africa at the end of the nineteenth century. Patidars are a landowning, middle-ranking dominant caste of central Gujarat. They are enterprising and status conscious, and value self-reliance rather than subordinate service to others. In Patidar hierarchy, status is measured on the basis of marriage 'circles' (endogamous units called *gols* in Gujarati). They try to achieve higher status by marrying their daughters into Patidar families of higher gols rather than in their own. For this purpose they offer huge dowries to the bridegroom and his family and celebrate wedding ceremonies lavishly. Central Gujarat had fertile land and adequate irrigation facilities. But, economic opportunities were restricted owing to fragmentation of land among sons in every generation. They felt constrained and frustrated. Luckily for them the right opportunity came from east Africa, where the British colonial rulers were engaged in introducing modern administration and infrastructure facilities for a modern economy, such as railways. The Patidars volunteered to migrate and take up challenging jobs. They were so absorbed in the new enterprises that the local railways were called 'Patel Railways'. They also helped other members of their family and kin to join them in east Africa to take up trading, business, and allied activities. This made them prosperous.

Migrating to another continent did not discourage the Patidars from maintaining close relations with their villages and caste fellows. With the newly acquired wealth they acquired land, built impressive houses in their native villages, and arranged marriages for their daughters and sisters with eligible boys in the higher gols by offering attractive dowries and spending lavishly on weddings.

On their expulsion from Africa in the late 1960s, the Patidars settled in central London and the neighbouring towns. With limited education they could not join the middle-class professions, but they succeeded in capturing small corner shops, post offices and newspaper stalls, and made good money with their hard work and frugal style of life, which was inclined toward saving rather than spending.

The authors highlight the dilemmas faced by the Patidars in the second and third generations. The younger generation is better educated and has entered the professions, small shops being no longer very attractive. Some of them have migrated to Canada and USA for better business opportunities in trading and the motel business.

The Patidars in England make special efforts to maintain their culture, build Hindu temples, and perform rituals and prayers. They also run a large number of coaching classes to teach Gujarati to the younger generation. They make continuous attempts to retain and strengthen relations with the village and the kin groups in Gujarat with a view to continue the traditional pattern of marriage relations and to celebrate religious events, although these efforts create tensions in their relations.

Aneeta Minocha's paper explores the socio-cultural context of informed consent in medical practice through the micro-interactive accounts of relation between doctors and patients in India. The doctrine of informed consent rests on the premise that every individual controls his body and has a right to decide what can and shall be done to it. The doctrine requires the patient to give permission to the physician to carry out specific diagnostic and treatment procedures on him as a part of his medical treatment. The informed consent given by the patient has to be a truly informed one, and it is the physician's legal obligation to inform his patient about the latter's disease, its prognosis, and the various possible lines of treatment. He must inform the patient about the different therapeutic alternatives and the risks, outcomes, and side effects involved in each of them. He must also tell the patient about the consequences of his decision of not undergoing any treatment.

The doctrine of informed consent has challenged the traditional paternalistic model of patient-physician relationship in which the physician took all the important decisions on the patient's medical treatment, and the patient acquiesced, subordinating his own ideas and opinions. The new doctrine, by laying stress on the patient's active participation in medical decision-making and on his power vis-a-vis the physician, reverses this model. In this doctrine the patient is viewed as an independent, autonomous, and rational person with his own values and beliefs influencing him in making his decisions. It endows the patient with certain rights vis-à-vis the physician.

The precept and practice of the informed consent doctrine continues to be a hotly debated issue. Scholars have raised several issues concerning suitability and applicability of the doctrine in the context of different cultural values and norms prevailing in societies in general and in relation to illness behaviour and roles in particular. Doubts are being expressed about the applicability of the doctrine to the illiterate and the uneducated in Indian society who have limited exposure to modern medicine. The patient role is still treated here as one of dependence on others, with the family playing an important supportive role in his treatment. The concepts of individual's autonomy and freedom of choice in the medical domain still remain extrinsic to the Indian thought process.

Minocha's essay examines this doctrine and delineates the socio-cultural and other constraints that tend to influence its translation into the patient-physician relationship in the Indian context. She also raises the issue of informed consent flowing from the possible situations one could encounter in such an interaction. She provides various possibilities and probabilities of how informed consent could go awry despite the best of intentions. And, absence of informed consent is another difficult issue. Informed consent of the individual is a culturally variable phenomenon. In many societies, the social body is more prominent than the individual body. Consent of a woman or man comes not just from the individual alone but from the family, kin, or even others concerned. Minocha's case study of a father refusing the amputation of his daughter's leg despite the doctor's advice is illustrative of the complex connections between an individual and a social body with its cultural and politico-economic trappings.

Three essays in Part IV by André Béteille, Rajni Palriwala and Shanti George deal with approaches and developments in the disciplines of sociology and social anthropology. Béteille's essay takes up the old kinship puzzle for tracing the basic kinship ties in what is called the 'elementary unit of kinship' or the 'atom of kinship'. He attempts to negotiate, through this puzzle, two different approaches to kinship studies. These two approaches are also the two levels on which a kinship system manifests itself and is accordingly understood and analysed. Levi-Strauss introduced the separation of these two levels of kinship, calling them 'systeme des appellations' and the 'systeme des attitudes'. On the first, the analysis of kinship terminology takes place. The second is the normative level which deals with the analysis of the institutional acts and forms of behaviour between kin. These include all the kinship practices empirically observed, such as gift giving, joking and avoidance relations, inheritance, and prescriptive and proscriptive marriages. It is important to state that these two levels of kinship are separated only for analytical purposes. It is in this context that the title of Béteille's essay, 'Empirical Meaning and Imputed Meaning in the Study of Kinship' may be seen. The first level is the categorical level and the second is the normative and empirical level. Thus, a kinship system is to be seen as a combination of the two levels. The relationships in this unit or atom comprise a woman, her brother, her husband, and her son, in other words, the relationships between spouses, between parents and children, and between siblings. Given this atom or unit, how does one analyse a given kinship system?

Béteille juxtaposes the symbolic frame of structuralism with the social structure of kinship in unravelling these basic relationships in his attempt to negotiate between the two approaches to kinship studies. They may be brought together to see if the two levels or subsystems of kinship are structured in an analogous way or not. He argues for incorporation of personal experiences in the analysis of kinship, taking into account studies by Radcliffe-Brown, Fortes, and others. He suggests that the empirical observation and the axiom should be brought together. He mentions Schneider at one place to clarify his stress on separation between person and relative. Kinship studies have moved on, and there is more scope in the analysis of kinship for incorporation based on recent empirical observations. The essay indicates Béteille's preference for the attitudinal and normative approach to the study of kinship.

Rajni Palriwala's paper recounts her experiences as a teacher in dealing, especially, with gender studies in social sciences. The interrelationship between academic and activist concerns has become closer for over half a century. This is especially true in the case of feminism. Though the feminist movement is over a century old now, an informed feminist scholarship in university curricula, in social anthropology in particular, developed since the 1960s. With the publication of three edited volumes by Reiter (1975), Rosaldo and Lamphere (1974), and McCormack and Strathern (1980), women's studies gained ground in academic circles. This development changed information, knowledge and perception about the world. The other half of the world that was muted and hidden from history was exposed in academic research and teaching. The information of male anthropologists and their male students who learnt about women's lives by speaking with men was no longer the same when women anthropologists spoke to women in the field. For example, the study by Annette B. Weiner (1976) of the Trobriand Islanders, made famous by Malinowski's (1922) study, found women very much present and actively participating in social, ritual and economic life. New vistas opened up with the entry of women's studies in the university system, more or less, all over the world. The spread of gender studies, called in some university departments as women's studies, has been a worldwide phenomenon.

Palriwala analyses a number of issues she encountered in the process of framing courses on gender studies at the Department of Sociology, University of Delhi, where she teaches. The course under consideration is named 'Gender and Society'. Parliwala discusses the practice of framing the syllabus for the course, the various considerations that it involved at the academic as well as pedagogical levels, and the logistic considerations at the students and the faculty level. The academic justifications of the converts and of those not favourably inclined to the course are issues that the thinking academics in educational institutions might often encounter, points out Palriwala.

Shanti George's paper embodies her reflections on her earlier field research, especially on her commonly followed method of collecting data from adults. She wonders why she did not consider children and their views during her fieldwork in different parts of the world. Like most anthropologists who can bring up their lived experiences in the field, George tries to recall some of her experiences with children. Tulsi Patel is in resonance with George, as she found children absorbing experiences like sponges. In her own work (Patel 2006) a few powerful instances are reported on how children know exactly what adults in a situation would be expected to do and expect them to do.

George in her usual gentle manner makes an assertion for providing ethnographic space to children. Her essay is a fresh reflective piece in this regard. She is not making a point about childhood levity and the ensuing interest in child psychology to understand the child's problems. She is arguing rather about talking to the child as an ethnographic participant, besides knowing the child's world. There is a revival of interest in childhood and children as an independent category in its own right in the twenty-first century. And it is a sign of how temporal contexts focus on different chronological categories of age structure in human life. George's concern is beyond the above. She asks for knowing the children's world through their version.

The volume ends with an epilogue in Shah's honour by his lifelong friend and colleague, N. R. Sheth. They studied sociology together from the undergraduate level onward as students of Professor M. N. Srinivas at the M. S. University of Baroda. They had also shared a flat with two other fellow students. This relationship of over five decades has enabled them to know each other intimately. Sheth describes the major stages in Shah's growth as a man and as a scholar involved in teaching and research. Right from his childhood, Shah was a follower of Gandhian ideology and way of living. He tried to practise Gandhian teachings in his day-to-day life. He was the main organiser of the student group's collective life. The qualities of simplicity, honesty, integrity and straightforwardness always guided his behaviour. This essay looks at Shah's work in the contemporary context, focusing on some of the areas of Shah's interest in sociology and social anthropology that have flowered and matured over time. Sheth also highlights his lasting contributions to the efficient functioning of professional and academic institutions with which he was associated in various capacities.

References

Ashram Bhajanvali. 1947. Ahmedabad: Navjivan Prakashan.

Boserup, E. 1974. *Women's Role in Economic Development*. New York: St Martin's Press.

Cohn, Bernard. 1987. *An Anthropologist among the Historians and Other Essays.* Delhi: Oxford University Press.

De Beauviour, S. 1949. *The Second Sex.* Harmondsworth: Penguin.

Dua, Veena. 1999. *Arya Samaj in Punjab Politics.* Delhi: Picus.

Dumont, Louis. 1961. The Role of Tradition in Indian Society. *Economic Development and Cultural Change* 9(2): 210–12.

Frost, Marcia J. 2002. A Gem of Economic and Social History. A review of A. M. Shah's, *Exploring India's Rural Past. Economic and Political Weekly* 37(22): 2137–38.

Kessinger, Tom G. 1976. Historical Demography of India: Results and Possibilities. *Peasant Studies* 5(3): 2–8.

Malinowski, B. 1922. *Argonauts of the Western Pacific.* New York: E. P. Dutton.

McCormack, C., and M. Strathern, eds. 1980. *Nature, Culture and Gender.* Cambridge: Cambridge University Press.

Omran, A. R. 1971. The Epidemiological Transition: A Theory of the Epidemiology of Population Change. *The Millbank Memorial Fund Quarterly* 49(1): 599–638.

Patel, Tulsi. 1982. Domestic Group, Status of Woman and Fertility. *Social Action* 32(4): 363–79.

———. 2006. *Fertility Behaviour: Population and Society in a Rajasthan Village.* 2nd ed. Delhi: Oxford University Press.

Reiter, R. R., ed. 1975. *Toward an Anthropology of Women.* New York: Monthly Review Press.

Rosaldo, M. Z., and L. Lamphere, eds. 1974. *Woman, Culture and Society.* Stanford: Stanford University Press.

Shah, A. M. 1955. A Dispersed Hamlet in the Panchmahals. *Economic Weekly* 3(4–5): 109–16.

———. 1973. *The Household Dimension of the Family in India: A Field Study in a Gujarat Village and a Review of Other Studies.* Delhi: Orient Longman. Berkeley: University of California Press, 1974.

———. 2002. *Exploring India's Rural Past: A Gujarat Village in the Early Nineteenth Century.* Delhi: Oxford University Press.

———. 2006. Sects and Hindu Social Structure. *Contributions to Indian Sociology* (NS), 40(3): 209–48.

———., ed. 2007. *The Grassroots of Democracy: Field Studies of Indian Elections.* Delhi: Permanent Black.

———., and I. P. Desai. 1988. *Division and Hierarchy: An Overview of Caste in Gujarat.* Delhi: Hindustan Publishing Corporation.

———., and R. G. Shroff. 1958. The Vahivancha Barots of Gujarat: A Caste of Genealogists and Mythographers. *Journal of American Folklore* 7(281): 246–76.

Reprinted in Milton Singer, ed. 1959. *Traditional India: Structure and Change.* Philadelphia: American Folklore Society, pp. 40–70.

Shah, A. M. 1973. Foreword to *The Household Dimension of the Family in India: A Field Study in a Gujarat Village and a Review of Other Studies* by M. N. Srinivas. Delhi: Orient Longman.Berkeley: University of California Press, 1974, pp. vii–xi.

————., I. P. Desai. 1988. Foreword to *Division and Hierarchy: An Overview of Caste in Gujarat* by M. N. Srinivas. Delhi: Hindustan Publishing Corporation, pp. ix–xiv.

Srinivas, M. N., and A. M. Shah. 1960. The Myth of Self-sufficiency of the Indian Village. *Economic and Political Weekly,* 10 September, 1375–78.

————. 1968. Hinduism. In *International Encyclopedia of the Social Sciences*, ed., David L. Sills, 358–66. Vol. 6. New York: Macmillan and Free Press.

Weiner, A. B. 1976. *Women of Value and Men of Renown: New Perspectives in Trobriand Exchange.* Austin: University of Texas Press.

Part I
Gender Issues

1

Assertive Voices
The Other Side of *Burqa*

Mohini Anjum

This paper is based on observations of and personal interactions with Muslim women in the walled city of Delhi; they are spread out over a period of about a quarter of a century. Being a Hindu woman married into a Muslim family and living in the community in the predominantly Muslim-inhabited Jama Masjid area, I was in an advantageous position, for I was both an 'insider' and an 'outsider'. My research interest in the lives of Muslim women was rarely seen with suspicion; it was often brushed aside as an innocent attempt to adapt to the culture. In a way, I was a member of the community, but, this was not the only reason for my interest in the lives of Muslim women in Delhi. When I first entered the community as a young bride, a little over three decades ago, many of my notions and stereotypes about Muslim women, as being docile and submissive, suffered a rude shock. I soon realised how little non-Muslims know about the community and how inadequate their knowledge is about Muslim women.

Studies, for example, by Jeffery (1979) and Lateef (1990), have portrayed Muslim women as being subservient, oppressed, and subjugated because of various indicators of low status associated with them. Imtiaz Ahmad (in a seminar hosted by the Sarojini Naidu Centre for Women Studies in Jamia Millia Islamia, New Delhi, 2000) has referred to them as a 'double' or even a 'triple minority'. According to most scholars, Muslim women have low status because they are women, because they belong to a minority community, and, above all, because of purdah. More recently, Zoya Hasan and Ritu Menon's study (2004), 'Unequal Citizens', reiterates the low position of Muslim women across the country. My interface with Muslim women brought out the other side of the picture presented by the above-mentioned scholars. Within the broad framework of a patriarchal society, in spite of purdah and burqa, in spite of Muslim women's unequal position regarding divorce and inheritance rights, and in spite of the sanction that allowed Muslim men to take up to four wives, Muslim women, in general, emerged as assertive individuals, who are able to create space for themselves and make their voices heard in an otherwise perceptibly 'closed' society. My interactions with and observations of Muslim women in different life-cycle rituals brought out the important roles involving decision-making played by them. My observation revealed that Muslim women in general were assertive in their day-to-day lives. And, with each new situation or challenge, they emerged as strong, assertive individuals. What is their source of strength and power? To understand this, I looked at the life histories of five Muslim women and also observed closely the life-cycle rituals, which seemed to be vehicles or mechanisms geared towards gender equality. In the first part of the paper, I would like to present case studies of five Muslim women in the walled city of Delhi. What they shared in common was the burqa; they belonged to middle-class and upper-middle-class families, and all of them were housewives except for the first, that is, Amda Begum, and they were in the 60–70-year age group. The names of the five women mentioned below are fictitious. In the second part of the paper, I present a description of the life-cycle rituals, which assign to Muslim women important roles and which, thereby, strengthen their position in Muslim society.

Amda Begum belonged to one of the well-to-do families of Delhi. Her father was the principal of a college where he taught Urdu to the British. Amda Begum had never been out of her home alone except clad in a burqa and carried in a *doli* (palanquin) as a young girl. She was married to an engineer at a very young age and became a widow at the age of twenty-six. She had five children—one son and four daughters. She had studied up to middle level (that is, eighth standard) in an English-medium school, before she got married. After the death of her husband, when she was only 26 years old, she once again resumed studies, completed her tenth standard education, did *Adeeb Fazil* (Urdu examination equivalent to BA degree) and engaged a *pandit* (Brahmin scholar) to learn Sanskrit at home. She received basic education in a teachers-training course and secured a job for herself as a primary school teacher; later she became the headmistress of the school.

During partition (1947), when a large number of her relatives, including her mother, migrated to Pakistan, Amda Begum stayed back with her young children, perhaps, because of her inability to generate resources to migrate to Pakistan. Without much support from either her in-laws or parents, she struggled hard to maintain herself and her young children and educated them enough for them to be able to find jobs for themselves. Today, all her children are well educated and not only her son but all her daughters have good jobs. Amda Begum not only pursued her job with great devotion and dedication and won several national awards for excellence in teaching but also taught children in the neighbourhood to recite the Quran. Parents in the neighbourhood considered it a privilege to send their children as *shagirds* (students/disciples) to Amda Begum and fondly referred to her as *ustanji* or *ustaniji* (respected lady teacher). They knew that Amda Begum would not only teach their children how to recite the Quran but would also socialise them and train them to be responsible and confident human beings. For her remarkable strength and courage, Amda Begum was respected by one and all and almost became an icon in the area. People, young and old, men and women, sought her advice in situations of conflict and dispute, especially those pertaining to their families.

All her daughters, like Amda Begum, are very confident, assertive women, who can, without any doubt, be referred to as empowered women. She often said, 'I have taught my daughters to fight their way, I am sure no one can exploit them, oppress them or be unjust to them.' Amda Begum proved her point by supporting one of her daughters in her decision to break her engagement with her fiancé, who was being unfair to her, and to marry someone else. Although Amda Begum herself wore burqa all her life, she encouraged and helped her young daughters to discard it. And this was achieved in spite of strong opposition from close relatives and neighbours, and that too soon after the partition of India when burqa and purdah were being strengthened owing to the insecurities that surrounded Muslims and Muslim women in particular. Also, being reduced to the status of a minority overnight, Muslims were trying to reassert their identity, and the burqa assumed symbolic importance, which it continues to be even today. It was in this social milieu that Amda Begum insisted that her daughters give up the burqa. And, her reasons were that if her daughters had to take up jobs (which she was sure they would) and be successful in life, the burqa would be a hindrance. Times had changed and she could foresee that the demands of a competitive society would necessitate the movement of women outside the *mohalla* (neighbourhood); then burqa would be a hindrance. As far as she was concerned, even though she had a job, it was within the walled city, and for women of her generation, it provided security as well as respectability. So, she continued to wear burqa all her life but freed her daughters from it. Also, she felt that if her daughters were to give it up of their own accord, the people of her mohalla would be critical, but if she was to approve of it, the neighbours would not be as critical. This proves the point that Amda Begum was a very progressive woman, but she was also equally a religious woman, for she read the Quran four to five times a day, never missed her *namaz* (prayer five times a day, as prescribed by Islam) or *roza* (fasting during the month of Ramzan), and gave *zakat* (giving two and a half per cent of one's income as charity to the poor, preferably during the month of Ramzan) not only during the month of Ramzan (the most auspicious month for the Muslims, the month of fasting, offering prayers and giving charity to the poor) but round the year, especially on Fridays. Besides, she also sent food to destitute women in the neighbourhood, every Thursday.

Amda Begum can best be described as a very religious and yet a very forward-looking, modern Muslim woman and certainly an assertive woman. From whatever I could gather from Amda Begum, her mother was also a very strong-willed woman. Till the time she was alive, Amda Begum's mother was the decision-maker for her own family as well as the family of her children. Her house was a hub of activity for ceremonies, fasting, and feasting. But, after Amda begum's mother moved to Pakistan in 1947, Amda Begum, who had lost her husband by then, took charge of herself and her five children—in fact six children—for she informally adopted another girl from the neighbourhood. This also proves the point that she was a great supporter of gender equality—she adopted a girl and not a boy, in spite of having four daughters of her own and only one son. Until the end of her life, Amda Begum's house was the centre of activity for her son's family as well as the families of all her daughters. Major decisions relating to all these families were taken in consultation with Amda Begum or on her advice. All the daughters of Amda Begum idolised their mother and followed in her footsteps. Their own lives were modelled after their mother; they were able to discard burqa, stay in hostels, study up to masters level, and take up jobs at a time when it was not easy for Muslim women to do so. Perhaps they had acquired this confidence from their mother, who symbolised strength and power.

Farhat Begum was the daughter of a well-to-do man in the hotel business. She was the only daughter, loved and cared for by her three brothers and a father, for she had lost her mother at a very young age. She was married to a handsome young man (a close relative) considered to be one of the most eligible bachelors around. Apart from being very good-looking, he spoke English very fluently and rode a motorbike—this was quite a rare phenomenon those days. Farhat Begum had four children, two sons and two daughters. She took the major decisions regarding the education of her children, their employment, and their marriages. Her husband had little say in the matter and accepted a peripheral position in the family. Farhat Begum was a housewife; she had almost total control over the family resources, including the income of her husband. In times of financial crisis, her brothers always came to her rescue. They even made her husband a shareholder in their hotel business. Her husband was often seen requesting his wife for small change (coins) to buy cigarettes or *pan* (betel nut), which was handed over to him only after irksome arguments, because his wife considered these as extravagances. He died of a heart attack. After his death, Farhat Begum, who was in her mid-fifties, took over the role as head of the family. She was already partly performing this role, during her husband's lifetime.

Farhat Begum also had a large number of shagirds, who came to learn the Quran from her and help her in all her household chores and run errands for her. Her daughters and sons are now married and both daughters and daughters-in-law are school teachers. When the grandchildren were still young, the daughters would leave their children with her and the daughters-in-law with their own mothers. Perhaps the reason for this is that mothers are closer to their daughters than to their daughters-in-law and prefer to look after their daughter's children as compared with their son's children. Also daughters have greater faith in and are more comfortable with their mother's style of socialisation, and most decisions pertaining to their families were taken by Farhat Begum or in consultation with her. Farhat Begum's house, like Amda Begum's house, was the focus around which the daughters' and sons' families revolved. This situation of the mother being the focus of the family (family of procreation), even after the sons and daughters are married, portrayed an interesting blend of patrilineal and matrilineal kinship; it exhibited some features of matrilineal kinship found in some parts of the northeast and Lakshadeep, not in terms of descent and property, as discussed by Dube (1969), but in terms of care of the young and socialisation of the grandchildren. And, this was a little intriguing because of the general nature of patrilineal and patriarchal kinship associated with the Muslim society of north India.

Like Farhat Begum, both her daughters grew up to be assertive women, but the two daughters-in-law of Farhat Begum were often described as subservient and obedient and were admired for it. Their mother-in-law (Farhat Begum) had willingly taken up the responsibility of looking after her grandchildren—daughter's children—but refused to look after the children of her sons. So these grandchildren (paternal) had to be taken care of by their mother's mother. And, this arrangement was seen as convenient by most women. It gave the daughters an opportunity to meet their own mothers at least once if not twice a day when they went to drop and pick up their children on their way to and way back from the school. The strong bond between the mother and daughter reveals a significant dimension of the patrilineal Muslim kinship system operating in the walled city of Delhi.

Mumtaz Begum was born into a well-to-do family, which migrated to Pakistan. But just before partition, she was married to a lecturer in Delhi university. She was educated in an English-medium school in Delhi. She always harboured the dream of one day joining her parental family in Pakistan, especially because it became very affluent after the migration. But, because of her husband's job and the property which he inherited from his father, her husband decided to stay back in India. And thus, Mumtaz Begum's dream to migrate to Pakistan was shattered. She resented his decision and never forgave her husband all her life. Once, when she went to Pakistan with her two children, one son and one daughter and stayed there for three years, she never wanted to return to India and requested her husband to join her; he did not relent, and she had to return because of pressure from relatives. After that, relations between the husband and wife were never amicable. They lived under the same roof, but in separate rooms, hardly ever interacting with each other except when she needed some money and he needed some food. Her son and daughter were always with her, supportive and comforting her. Her husband was almost marginalised by the family. His role was merely to provide money and that was all. Towards the end of his life, he almost became a nervous wreck, and died of a brain haemorrhage.

Qudsia Begum belonged to a large lower middle-class family engaged in petty business. She had very little education. She was married at the age of about eleven or twelve to a man about twenty to twenty-five years of age and hardly any education, who was engaged in *satta bazar* (forward trading or betting). She gave birth to twenty children, of whom twelve survived. People in the neighbourhood often doubted whether all these children were of one father, for many stories were circulating in the neighbourhood about Qudsia Begum's illicit relations.

In spite of her large family, Qudsia Begum was always well dressed and her burqa was designed more to reveal her attractive body (even after repeated births) than to hide it. She always spoke in a loud voice while her husband almost whispered. She was in full command of the family and even neighbours were scared of her quarrelsome nature, for she could easily switch over to abusive language. As her sons grew up (she had nine sons and three daughters), she became more dominating for they provided not only financial support but were also always accessible to her. They were considered to be the musclemen of the area, dreaded by all. But at home they were 'mama's boys'. Qudsia Begum always wore the burqa and was one of the most mobile women in the neighbourhood, and behind that burqa was to be heard one of the loudest voices that even men were scared of. Interestingly, Qudsia Begum only sent her daughters to school, not her sons who just wandered in the streets of the mohalla; whatever little education they obtained was through informal interactions in the neighbourhood mosque, from their ustani (teacher who taught them to read the Quran), the peer group, and films.

Noor Jahan Begum was a very beautiful woman and belonged to an upper middle-class family. She was married to a government officer at a young age. She lost her husband soon after marriage. As the story goes, he committed suicide because the couple could never get along with each other and also because he could not meet her demands, especially financial demands. Noor Jahan Begum, who did not have any children, spent the rest of her life in the home of her brother, who had three daughters and who also became a widower at a young age. Noor Jahan Begum became the lady of the house taking all decisions pertaining to property, education and marriages of her brother's daughters. Noor Jahan Begum wore a burqa all her life, a sparkling white burqa, which made her distinct from most other women who wore black burqas. She was generally the first visitor/ guest to arrive in almost all gatherings, get-togethers, functions and ceremonies within the kin group. What struck me as a characteristic feature of Noor Jahan Begum was that at every function where food was served, after her brother, her nieces, and she had eaten, she would insist on food, to suffice for a day or two, being packed for her to carry home, and nobody would dare oppose it. Stories about her love for good food and good living circulated amongst close relatives. She lived in style all her life unmindful of her brother's economic resource fluctuations, often compelling him to live beyond his means. All her life, Noor Jahan Begum craved to migrate to Pakistan, but could not go in her younger days because of the responsibilities of looking after her three nieces, especially after the death of her brother. But towards the end of her life, when all the nieces were married and one of them migrated to Pakistan along with her husband and grown-up children, Noor Jahan Begum, who was by then in her seventies also accompanied her niece to Pakistan, where she died a few years later.

The above case studies have been cited as examples representing a vast majority of Muslim women in the walled city of Delhi. For reasons beyond examination, all the five women described above outlived their husbands by 20 to 50 years. It would be an exaggeration to say that all Muslim women are assertive; but, by and large, and as compared with women of other communities, especially Hindus, Muslim women struck me as more assertive, and at times even aggressive, especially as grandmothers, mothers, mothers-in-law and as daughters. As the case studies reveal, none of these women lived with their mothers-in-law, either because their parents-in-law had passed away or migrated to Pakistan. Almost all of them were in the 50–70 age group by which time they had acquired a position of power. But, it is equally clear that daughters-in-law are expected to be subservient and obedient; the double standards for daughters and daughters-in-law are more than obvious; thus, married daughters enjoyed a more privileged position in their mother's house than in their mothers-in-laws' house.

Some Muslim men in the community often expressed the view that Hindu women make better wives because they (Hindu women) are more submissive than Muslim women. In an attempt to understand the cause of this assertiveness, I realised the importance of some of the institutionalised mechanisms built into the structure of Muslim society and sanctioned by Islamic ideology in empowering Muslim women within a patriarchal system. It was, therefore, important to examine some of the life-cycle and other institutionalised mechanisms that contribute to empowering Muslim women in the walled city of Delhi. What follows is a description of these rituals and mechanisms which, I believe, play an important role in the lives of Muslim women and help to elevate their position within the family as well as strengthen their position vis-à-vis men. In most of the life-cycle rituals like birth of a child, *aqiqa* (initiation), *bismillah* (initiation into the learning of the Quran), *mangni* (engagement), *nikah* (marriage) and all the negotiations and preparations for the marriage as well as the decisions regarding the bride's trousseau and the rituals to be performed, women play important roles as mothers, wives and close relatives.

LIFE-CYCLE RITUALS

Birth of a Female Child

Muslims do not see the birth of a daughter as a 'curse' as many Hindus do. They are disappointed if there are only daughters and no sons, but a woman is not deserted because she cannot 'produce' sons. Well, there is the possibility of having a second wife; but I did not come across a single case of bigamy within the kinship network to which I belonged as also within the immediate neighbourhood. One or two cases of bigamous marriages were reported about some distant relatives in the past, but the reasons for bigamy were other than giving birth to only daughters. Of the case studies cited above, we can see that Amda Begum had four daughters and one son and adopted another daughter and Noor Jahan Begum had three nieces. The case studies clearly revealed that having daughters did not affect the status of Muslim women adversely.

Aqiqah

Muslims are expected to perform aqiqah for the well-being of the child, for both male and female child. Apart from shaving of the hair, a male goat (preferably two male goats) are sacrificed for a male child and one goat for a female child. It is also a way of thanking God for blessing them with a child. The meat of the goat is distributed amongst poor relatives and neighbours, and the rest is cooked for a feast in which close relatives are invited who bless the child and give him/her gifts in cash or kind. Ideally, the mother and father of the child should not eat this meat but they often do. Aqiqah is performed any time after the birth of a child, preferably within seven days of birth or at least within one year but sometimes be performed as late as the marriage of the girl or boy. When aqiqah is performed within one year of the child's birth, it is often accompanied by the name-giving ceremony of the child. The name or at least the first letter of the name is generally selected from the Quran. However, when aqiqah is performed just before marriage, it is not accompanied by shaving of hair. What needs to be emphasised is the fact that Muslims consider the birth of a son as well as daughter as a 'blessing' of God and aqiqah is performed for both. There is, however, a difference; two goats are sacrificed for a male child and one for a female child.

Bismillah

Bismillah literally means to begin with the name of Allah; commonly also it refers to initiation into the learning of the Quran. As a ceremony it is performed for both a male and a female child between the ages of five to six years when he/she is entrusted to the custody of an ustani (female teacher), who is well versed in the recitation of the Quran. She is often also a highly respected woman in the community known for being a disciplinarian with an Islamic world view, exemplified by her own lifestyle. The ceremony is generally a simple one and is marked by garlanding of the ustani and shagird (student) and the learning of the first verse of the first *sipara* (chapter) of the Quran, (there are thirty siparas in the Quran). The children learn the Quran from the ustani and in return help the ustani in all her household chores, from cooking, to cleaning, to washing clothes, running errands to relatives and friends in the neighbourhood, shopping for groceries and vegetables in the local market, and a whole lot of other things. The ustani plays an important role in the socialisation of these children for they generally spend four to five hours a day at their ustani's house. Some children—girls and boys—at a very young age are also sent to the mosque to learn to read the Quran, but girls are withdrawn from the mosque much before they attain puberty. Teaching the recitation of the Quran is rated as amongst the highest *sawab* (religious merit) that one can achieve. Since majority of the children go to the ustani for this, she is elevated to the status of a religious teacher and, often, the relationship between the shagird and his/her ustani is a lifelong relationship, where the ustani enjoys a special position whenever there is feasting or fasting in the life of a shagird. For example, the ustani will be the first to be sent a plate of *iftari* (snack with which to 'open a fast') during the month of Ramzan (month of fasting for the Muslims), *sawaiyan* or vermicelli on Eid-ul-Fitr, festival to mark the end of Ramzan, or share of goat meat on Bakr-Eid or Eid-ul-Zuha (festival which coincides with Haj—pilgrimage to Mecca—which is celebrated by sacrificing a goat). At the time of aqiqah, birthday, or marriage of the shagird, the ustani is often the chief guest and is presented with sweets and a dress in accordance with the socio-economic status of the family of the shagird In case the ustani is unable to attend the function, her share of food, sweets and clothes will be sent to her. Bismillah emphasises two things—first, that it is equally important for both boys and girls to learn to recite the Quran, and second, that the ustani is a female teacher who enjoys a very elevated status in Muslim society. This tradition of ustani is often passed on from one generation to the other. For example, Amda Begum had taught three generations of women—grandmothers (maternal), mothers and daughters. Parents, who cannot, for some reason, send their daughters to a particular ustani, as the next best option, send their daughters to a shagird of the ustani or the daughter of the ustani, who has now become an ustani. The plausible explanation seems to be that young boys are soon withdrawn or weaned away from the ustani after a year or so, because they start attending school, or they are sent as apprentices to learn some skill, which helps them to earn a few rupees, or because they just lose interest, or cannot be forced to go to the ustani's house. Girls generally continue to be associated with the ustani for a longer period, and even when they start going to school, some girls continue to learn the Quran at the ustani's house. Sometimes, they also carry their school bags there so that they can complete their homework with the help of the ustani, if she has received some formal education, or on their own, or with the help of other shagirds. Sometimes this relationship continues till their marriage is fixed, and, in exceptional cases, may extend beyond marriage. Generally, therefore, girls' association with the ustani and the learning of the Quran is much longer than that of boys, and they become more 'qualified' to teach the Quran than men. However, not all women enjoy the position of an ustani. In addition to her skill of teaching the Quran she must have a good reputation and respectability in the community, and her house must be a 'safe place' to send young daughters. The ustani enjoys a 'special' position in the Muslim community and this position is not shared with men. Also the process of socialisation that takes place in the ustani's house helps young girls to learn to respect their ustani, who is a woman and, in a way, also learn to earn respect for themselves. The ustani almost becomes a role model whose characteristics also include assertiveness and the ability to order people around. Of the five case studies described above, four were ustanis; only Qudsia Begum was not an ustani; she was neither an educated woman nor was her house considered to be a safe place.

Marriage and Marriage Related Rituals/Ceremonies

Muslim marriages provide a lot of room for women to assert themselves. The moment marriage begins to be discussed, women in the family come to acquire a special position. The first event in the marriage rituals is the *paigham* (proposal), which always comes from the bridegroom's family to the bride's family, thus elevating the status of the bride. It is generally the women in the bridegroom's family, who bring the paigham. Earlier, and to some extent even today, the proposal was sent twice or thrice—to prove that the bridegroom's family is serious about the proposal. And, therefore, the first time a proposal is received, it is generally rejected or not taken seriously, especially if there is a great divide between the economic status of the bride and bridegroom. Once the bride's family is convinced of the seriousness of the proposal—they try to ascertain the opinion of the bride, and it is generally the mother who discusses the matter with her daughter. In case the daughter is positively inclined, word would be sent to the bridegroom's family to send his *ruqaah* (bio-data). The ruqaah is closely examined by the relatives of the bride, and they also try to verify the data from close relatives or friends of the bridegroom. The mother of the bride to be plays a very important role in deciding whether the proposal is 'suitable' or not and whether the socio-economic status of the groom to be matches the status of their family. Detailed discussions between the husband and the wife take place before the final decision is taken. What is important is that the wife plays a very significant role in accepting or rejecting a proposal for her daughter, and a lot of importance is attached to the opinion of the daughter. Note how Amda Begum supported one of her daughters to break an engagement and get married to someone else.

Exchange of Gifts before Marriage

Mehr (Promised bride-price)

Once the proposal is taken seriously and accepted, negotiations for fixing the mehr begin—the bride's family always wanting it to be higher than the bridegroom's. Generally it is fixed in between the two positions for an amount acceptable to both the families. Comparatively, the amount of mehr is less if the bride and bridegroom are cousins—parallel or cross, or are closely related. The mehr, in case of strangers is likely to be higher, the assumption being that there is greater security and stability in marrying close relatives; also, being too fussy about higher mehr when the two parties involved are close relatives would be tantamount to casting aspersions on the bridegroom's family. Mehr is seen as providing security to the bride and stability to the marriage and is, therefore, a source of strength to the Muslim woman. Although mehr is given to the woman only in case of divorce, or after the death of her husband, ideally, the Muslim woman can at any time demand from her husband half of the mehr fixed at the time of nikah (marriage). Mehr is an essential part of nikah.

Mangni or Engagement

Once the mehr is fixed, then begins a series of exchange of gifts starting with mangni, where apart from the exchange of rings between the bride and bridegroom, a large number of other gifts are exchanged between the two families. The gifts for the bride almost invariably outnumber those for the bridegroom, which include clothes, jewellery, flowers and sweets. Here again, it is the mother of the groom who decides what is to be given to the bride and when it should be given. Not only does the mangni emphasise the importance of the bride, it is, in a sense, also meant to reassure the bride's family that the bride is going to be welcomed in the bridegroom's family. Also, in almost all the rituals and exchange of gifts beginning from mangni to marriage, women play an important role; men have been assigned organisational roles, such as making arrangements for guests, booking of banquet halls, and arranging a *Qazi* (priest) to perform the marriage. Most of the purchasing of gifts for the bride and bridegroom is done by the women, except for wristwatches, shoes and the wedding dress for the bridegroom, which are purchased by the men.

Mangni is followed by a series of gifts, especially for the bride from her mother-in-law, given on various occasions, whether it is Eid-ul-Fitr or Eid-ul-Zuha (also called Bakr-Eid—when a goat is sacrificed and the meat distributed amongst relatives, neighbours and the poor) or whether it is the bride's birthday. Each occasion is marked by gifts for the bride. Although gifts are sent also to the bridegroom; there is a basic difference—gifts are sent first to the bride and only then are *paltawa* or return gifts sent to the bridegroom. This custom emphasises that the initiative in giving gifts is always taken by the bridegroom's family. Traditionally, sometimes, gifts were taken in a procession. What gifts should be sent, from where they should be purchased, who should purchase these, and who should deliver these gifts are matters decided by the women in the family. More often than not, women also do most of the shopping related to marriages, and even otherwise shopping is considered to be the prerogative of women, especially when it involves buying jewellery and clothes.

Maiyon (Pre-nuptial ceremony)/Mehndi (Henna)

Maiyon and mehndi take place two to four days before the wedding, when the bridegroom's family sends the *bari* or marriage gifts for the bride. These gifts consist of jewellery, clothes, footwear, the wedding dress, make-up kit, dry fruits, fresh fruits, and sweets. Traditionally, all these items were spread out with decorations on *thalis* (big round plates) and carried on the head by young boys or hired labourers in a procession. The procession is becoming less and less popular except when both the families are living very close by and within the walled city. After these gifts are received by the bride's family, they are displayed for all relatives on their side to see. These gifts are, in a way, also a display of the socio-economic status of the bridegroom's family. The bride is dressed up in a yellow dress and seated in the middle of the gathering; and gifts are showered on her first by the bridegroom's female relatives and then by her own female relatives. The most expensive gifts (jewellery) will be given to the bride by the groom's mother, followed by his sister, aunts, sisters-in-law, and cousins in order of the closeness of kinship ties. After her in-laws have given her the gifts, it is the turn of her own close relatives to give her the wedding gifts (mostly cash). This is followed by mehndi and a grand feast.

On this occasion, all the close relatives of the bride, especially the female relatives most of whom also wearing shades of yellow, collect at her place and apply *bhutna/uptan* (a kind of traditional face-pack) made from herbs to make the bride look more beautiful on the marriage day. All women, according to their seniority (according to age and social status) apply a little bit of bhutna on the bride's face. This marks the beginning of the marriage rituals after which the bride is isolated from the other members of the family and is not allowed to go out of the four walls of the house. What gifts (cash or kind) are to be given to the bride are generally decided by the women and are given on the occasion of maiyon/ mehndi by close women relatives of the bride. Close women relatives of the bridegroom are also invited to this ceremony. As close relatives of the bridegroom, these women play an equally significant role in this ceremony. Each one of them, according to their seniority as grandmother, mother, aunts, sisters and cousins give gifts to the bride, which are brought for the occasion by the mother of the bridegroom. The mother and grandmother, sisters, brother's wives, *phuphis* (father's sisters), *tayis*, wives of *tayas* (father's elder brothers), *chachis,* wives of *chachas* (father's younger brothers) in order of seniority give jewellery, and all the younger female relatives decorate the bride with *gajras* (flower strings). After the first round, when the bridegroom's female relatives have performed their part of the ritual, there is generally a feast where all the relatives of the bridegroom have dinner, after which they leave. Then, it is the turn of the bride's close female relatives to have dinner and give gifts (in cash or kind) to the bride. This is followed by a ceremony where close female relatives of the bride apply bhutana and feed her with sweets brought by the bridegroom's family as a symbolic gesture as well as with *pindi* (big round sweet balls) prepared by her close female relatives or by a professional (*halwai*) which are later distributed amongst all the female relatives of the bride.

Maiyon is followed by mehndi which is first applied on the hands of the bride, and then all the other female relatives and friends of the bride take turns in applying it on their hands. Nowadays, henna specialists are brought in and paid for the job.

Sanchak (Gifts for the bridegroom)

One day before the wedding, the bride's family sends the paltawa (return gifts), in this case called sanchak, to the bridegroom's family; these include not only the wedding dress for the bridegroom but also gifts for his close relatives as also the dowry for the bride. This is also displayed for the benefit of close relatives and friends in the groom's house and is followed by a feast in the bridegroom's family. Here again details of the gifts to be sent to the bridegroom are decided by the women, especially the mother of the bride; which relative should give which gift to the bridegroom is also decided by the mother of the bride, for example, the most expensive gift, such as, a gold ring, gold buttons, wristwatch will be given by the brother of the bride. Parents of the bride do not accompany the sanchak.

Nikah (Marriage)

The wedding takes place at a site chosen by the bride's family, but the qazi (priest) who is called to solemnise the wedding is brought by the bridegroom's family and the fee for the nikah is also paid to him by the bridegroom's family. The nikah is performed in the presence of two witnesses, who sign the *nikah nama* (marriage certificate) but not before they have obtained the consent of the bride, who is informed of the amount of mehr fixed for her marriage—mehr is an essential part of the nikah nama. Generally close relatives of the bride are invited to act as witnesses and are called *vakils* (advocates). The bride is expected to repeat '*qabool hai*' (I accept) three times before the qazi proceeds to the bridegroom for his consent; and after obtaining it, pronounces the nikah once the witnesses have signed the nikah nama. This is followed by distribution of small packets of dry fruits to all the guests. These packets are specially prepared for the occasion by the bridegroom's family. This is followed by the marriage feast, which is hosted by the bride's family. It is important to emphasise that nikah cannot take place without the consent of the bride.

And, it is only after she has consented that the consent of the bridegroom is obtained.

Walima (Feast hosted by the bridegroom's family the day after the wedding)

The feast one day after the wedding is called walima and is hosted by the bridegroom's family. The bride's close relatives are special guests on this day, just as the bridegroom's close relatives are special guests on the previous day, that is, the wedding day. Friends and close relatives give gifts in cash or kind, both on the wedding day and on the day the walima is held. This is followed by a series of feasts called *chouthis* and *chalas,* feasts arranged for the newly wedded couple. Chouthi (fourth day) feast is arranged by the parents of the bridegroom. This is followed by chalas arranged by the relatives of the bride, for example, chalas arranged by married brothers and sisters of the bride would be followed by chalas arranged by uncles, aunts and so on.

Gradually, as the period of feasting comes to an end, the bride and bridegroom's visits to the bride's family become frequent—this is expected to help the bride adjust better into her conjugal family. These frequent visits play a very important role in the lives of the newly wedded couple. They provide a lot of support and strength to the young bride and bring her husband close to the family of his wife. The relationship with the wife's family becomes stronger as the woman has children and as the children start to grow up. If she is a working woman, the likelihood is that she will leave her young children with her mother and pick them up on her way back, especially if she is living in the same locality. And there is a strong possibility of this, because of the preference for parallel and cross-cousin marriages (that is, children of brothers and sisters marrying), who generally live within the walled city. This has been clearly illustrated in the case of Farhat Begum cited earlier; her daughters and daughters-in-law left their children with their mothers. Thus a mother, daughter, and grandchild bond becomes stronger and provides greater security and strength to the woman—also greater stability to the marriage; more so if the husband and wife are cross- or parallel cousins before marriage.

OTHER PRACTICES

Cross-cousin and Parallel Cousin Marriages

Cross-cousin and parallel cousin marriages are preferential forms of marriage among the Muslims in the walled city of Delhi. When the parallel cousins are children of two brothers, there is a strong possibility that they also live in the same joint family, have grown up together and have been socialised together. Sometimes, even as children, if a boy and girl show a little 'extra' interest in each other, other cousins and even elders often encourage and start visualising a marital bond between the cousins. They tease them, 'there goes your little bride or little bridegroom'. Where such marriages materialise, the couple not only get an initial warm welcome in each other's family but also lot of moral support from parents-in-law who are close relatives. In case of differences between the young couple, the parents and parents-in-law play a very important role in helping the couple overcome differences, and thus they enhance the stability of the marriage. Cross- and parallel cousin marriages, therefore, become a great source of strength to the woman, especially soon after marriage, as she has the support of her parents-in-law and other relatives who know her right from childhood. This helps her to assert her position in the husband's family and in the society for she is not at the mercy of strangers but in the company of close relatives. Also, the usual mother-in-law and daughter-in-law conflict is reduced considerably, especially if the mother-in-law is a *khala* (mother's sister) or phuphi (father's sister). This also reinforces the position of a newly wedded bride and the process of adapting to the conjugal family becomes smoother. The youngest daughter (adopted) of Amda Begum was married to her parallel cousin, that is, mother's sister's son and has carried forward the tradition of being the decision-maker of her family. One of Farhat Begum's sons was married to his mother's brother's daughter (cross-cousin) and this is often referred to as an ideal marriage.

Jahez (Dowry)

Jahez (dowry) is an essential part of the Muslim marriage, but to demand it or even expect it as a right is considered to be an unpardonable offence. No discussion on dowry ever takes place. If the bride's family gets even an inkling of the bridegroom's or his family's expectations of dowry before marriage, it is possible that the mangni will be broken and the marriage be called off. To emphasise the point, I should like to cite the example of a girl who got married to a man, who, in a weak moment, disclosed to her that he had married her because he was interested in the dowry she would bring so that he could marry off his sister with that dowry; the marriage was dissolved within a month and the girl returned to her parent's house with all her dowry intact. When the bride and bridegroom are parallel or cross-cousins, the question of demanding or even expecting a dowry is out of the question. Dowry deaths were unheard of among Muslims in this part of Delhi and such deaths among Hindus shocked the Muslim sentiments. Interestingly, there is no word for dowry in Urdu; the word jahez in all probability is a derivative of the Hindi word *dahej*.

Burqa

The cloak with a veil, which covers a woman from head to ankle and which is traditionally meant to protect the woman from the lustful gaze of men (strangers), has come to acquire a new significance in modern times. Burqa, often has a liberating effect on a woman (Anjum 1992). It was observed that under burqa, women felt less restricted to go out to the market or elsewhere. The anonymity provided to them by the burqa, allowed them to go out as many times a day as they wanted. Also, there was no need to 'dress up properly' before going out, for the *burqa* hid even their shabby clothes. Further, under burqa the bargaining power of the woman in the market increased, for she could shout at the shopkeeper, even abuse him, for trying to cheat her and get away without fear of being recognised (for details see, Anjum 1992). Some of these veiled women often shared their experiences in the market and admitted that minus the burqa they would never have had the courage to go out to the market so often, at night, at odd hours, and/or shout at the shopkeeper who was trying to cheat them. They seemed to 'enjoy' the anonymity provided to them by the burqa. Whether in the marketplace or in the bus, men are scared of eve-teasing burqa-clad woman, first, because it is difficult to find out whether the woman under the burqa is old or young, beautiful or ugly, stranger or relative, and second, because she is more likely to retaliate, hit them or shout at them, and get away without being recognised. This is the general impression that men, young and old, Muslim and non-Muslim, carry about veiled women. Many of the Muslim women I interacted with often discussed amongst themselves how the burqa had helped them to meet challenges (generally caused by eve-teasers) in the streets, in the market place, or in the bus. For example, one of them said, 'A young fellow was teasing me in the bus today—I told him, go and say all this to your mother or your sister. The fellow, not expecting such a sharp reaction, was shocked and disappeared into the crowd'. Another one shared her experiences thus, 'you know, one of my brother's friends was teasing me in the market, I shouted at him and said "you should be ashamed of yourself—I am old enough to be your mother".' And she laughed because she was only 19 or 20 years old, and there was no way the boy could guess her age because of the burqa. She seemed to enjoy this anonymity and use it to her advantage. Qudsia Begum, whose case study I have already described above, was once teased by a young boy in the bus; she was in her forties then. She hit the young boy so hard that his mouth started bleeding.

Many of these women, including women whose case studies have been described above, expressed the different ways in which the burqa provided strength to them. One of them said once, 'Thanks to the burqa, I once slapped a man who was trying to molest me in a crowded bus. I could never have had the strength to do so, had I not worn the burqa.' The burqa seemed to provide some sort of shield, security to these women and, under cover of anonymity, also, in a sense, the strength and courage to fight, hit back, make room for themselves in an otherwise 'hostile' environment. There is some awe and 'respect' attached to a burqa-clad woman, and this also helps her to assert her identity as a woman and as a Muslim woman. The question then arises: why then did Amda Begum encourage her daughters to give up burqa? This is because within the neighbourhood and the walled city, burqa provides a cover for them. But, if they have to go out to work, every day, then it becomes a hindrance because burqa is generally seen as a symbol of low socio-economic and educational status by the wider society. Amda Begum was aware of it and decided to free her daughters from it.

Dastarkhwan

Dastarkhwan is a rectangular piece of cloth on which food and plates are placed, and family members sit around it and have their meals. Generally, the cloth used to make a dastarkhwan is yellow in colour and, verses from the Quran are written on it in red, which convey that whatever we eat is given to us by God, so let us share it with others, and thank God for it. This traditional dastarkhwan is generally fished out during festivals. Normally, when the family sits together for their daily meals, an ordinary rectangular piece of cloth or soft plastic sheet may be spread out as a dastarkhwan. The dastarkhwan in the true spirit of Islam is a great equaliser; everybody in the family, relatives, guests—rich and poor—eat from a common dastarkhwan, for, there is a lot of emphasis in Islam on sharing of food, eating together, even eating out of a common bowl, for it is expected to strengthen ties within the community and enhance harmony.

Dastarkhwan provides certain special powers to a woman, especially the lady of the house, for she generally occupies a position at the head of the dastarkhwan, and although, in principle, food is shared equally by all, in effect, its distribution is based on the discretion of the lady of the house. Also, unlike most north-Indian Hindu homes, where the lady of the house serves the other members of the family hot *chapatis* and is usually the last to eat, in Muslim homes, food, even chapatis, are readied beforehand, and there is emphasis on 'eating together' from a common dastarkhwan. Often husband and wife sit together and eat from a common plate. The length of the dastarkhwan can be increased or decreased by attaching another piece of cloth or plastic or folding it depending on the number of people eating the meal. At the dastarkhwan, the lady of the house is the 'master', and she does not discriminate between her sons and daughters in the distribution of food, and this is important.

Talaq (Divorce)

Talaq is easy among Muslims and triple talaq, although prohibited by Islam, is often practised in which case the husband pronounces the word talaq thrice at one go and ends the marital bond. But there are checks and balances like mehr and cross-cousin marriages, which counterbalance the fear of talaq among Muslim women. Also, the possibility of widow remarriage and divorcee remarriage seem to provide some remote sense of security to Muslim women. Or, is it the fear of a triple talaq that gives women the strength to control their lives and the lives of others around them in the family in such a manner that men become dependent on women and are fearful of them? This is a question worth examining. Commonly shared jokes among Muslim men as, 'all gentlemen are afraid of their wives, the only way to a successful marriage is total surrender to your wife', seem to convey the above mentioned message.

Widowhood

Widows do not enjoy an elevated status among Muslims, but they are not cast away and not considered as inauspicious as among the Hindus. All the five women, whose case studies have been cited above, became widows and yet played important roles in the social life of the community. In fact, they emerged as 'stronger' women, after they lost their husbands. When faced with challenges, they found ways of coping with them and emerged as more empowered women. The fact that Islam has encouraged marriage of widows, and there is sawab (religious merit) attached to marrying widows keeps the possibility of widow remarriage open, and there were at least four cases of widow remarriages that I witnessed in close circles. There were also marriage proposals for widows with three, four, and even five children, which were not accepted by the widows. But, the possibility of a remarriage is always there, and this is a source of great strength to Muslim women.

The Urdu Language

Apart from some of the institutions described above, which are instrumental in providing some space to women where they can exercise their rights and take important decisions, especially in life-cycle rituals, Urdu has also contributed to the empowerment of Muslim women. With its emphasis on respect, as in 'Aap Janab' (thou)—you (with respect)—unlike the Punjabi language, where the wife addresses her husband as 'Tusi' (thou), but the husband addresses his wife as 'Tu'—you—in which the element of 'respect' is missing, many Muslim men address their wives as begum (queen), or begum sahiba (queen with respect). There appears to be respect shown to the opposite sex in the Urdu language, and this mode of expression is often referred to as 'aap janab culture', which is sometimes extended to the children as well.

CONCLUSION

The above description provides some insights into the lives of Muslim women in Delhi and shows how within the broad framework of a patriarchal society, Muslim women are able to create space for themselves and assert their positions. The case studies citied above and the description of some of the life-cycle rituals as well as other institutional practices bring out the different ways in which Muslim women express and assert themselves. This paper is an attempt to rediscover the Muslim women in the walled city of Delhi. It is an attempt to rethink some of the notions regarding the subjugation of Muslim women in Indian society. It has tried to highlight through the five case studies, life-cycle rituals and some other practices, such as aqiqah, bismillah, burqa, dastarkhwan, Urdu language, customs related to marriage, preference for cross-cousin and parallel cousin marriages, sawab on marrying a widow, and taboos related to dowry. These have enabled Muslim women to assert themselves. This study brings out the important role played by Muslim women in the domestic domain, where they have an important voice, are assigned responsibilities, and exercise their judgement in decision-making.

We can say, on the basis of this study, that Muslim women, far from being passive, subjugated, etc., are assertive, even authoritarian, independent, vocal, and articulate. We have seen how they as mothers pass on these personality traits to their daughters and as ustanis to female shagirds. The proof of the above is to be seen in the case studies which show how Muslim women, when called upon by circumstances, play active responsible roles, for example, when widowed, when left destitute, and even otherwise, as wives, mothers, and mothers-in-law, they tended to be assertive. In addition to these practices are emerging newer practices like modern education, employment, exposure to media and role of women's activist groups, which are conducive to making Muslim women even more empowered.

References

Anjum, Mohini. 1992. Behind Burqa. In *Muslim Women in India*, ed. Mohini Anjum. New Delhi: Radiant Publishers.

Dube, Leela. 1969. *Matriliny and Islam: Religion and Society in the Laccadives*. Delhi: National Publishing House.

———. 1992. Women in a Matrilineal Muslim Community. In Anjum, *Muslim Women in India*.

Hasan, Zoya, and Ritu Menon. 2004. *Unequal Citizens*. New Delhi: Oxford University Press.

Jeffery, Patricia. 1979. *Frogs in a Well*. London: Zed Press.

Lateef, Shahida. 1990. *Muslim Women in India*. New Delhi: Kali for Women.

2

Heart Beating with Fear and Eyes Filled with Rosy Dreams
Experiences of Poor Muslim Women in Rural Bangladesh

Tulsi Patel

INTRODUCTION

Gender-based inequalities in households are a harsh reality. Women are given inadequate recognition and low valuation for their work within the household. This is closely related to the lower status accorded to them. Though women have always worked in and outside the household, this has come to be somewhat accepted only since Boserup's (1970) famous work on the role of women in economic development and the 1975 World Conference, which opened the UN decade for women. Studies by Afshar (1985) on third world women, Krishnaraj (1988) on Indian Women, Young (1989) on third world women, Begum (1990) on Bangladeshi women, and the series on women and household in Asia by Singh and Kelles-Viitanen (1987), Agarwal (1988), Dube and Palriwala (1990), and Krishnaraj and Chanana (1989) have thrown a great deal of light on women's work and status. Young (1989) refers to the androcentric blindness of not registering that women have been

An earlier version of this ssay was presented at the seminar, 'Muslim Women in India' at Jamia Millia Islamia in December, 1986. The author is thankful to Professor Mohini Anjum, Mohd. Talib, Rosalind Boyd, and Punam Zutshi for their comments.

working outside the household. Kak (1984), like Agarwal (1989), points out the conceptual and data bias related to rural women's work participation in India and the third world respectively.

In all societies, the work of men and women is valued differently. Men's work has greater value, even if they make dolls in one society, and women's work is less valued though they do the same in another society. Survival in the third world largely depends on women's work, though it is undervalued and invisibilised. Women are viewed as dependants whose earnings, if at all, are supplementary to those of the 'bread winners'. The spheres of male and female functioning by definition are regarded not only as separate but also unequal. From narratives of adult women who had taken Grameen Bank loans, information about men (fathers, husbands, sons, community leaders and priests) and women other than themselves (daughters, sisters, mothers, co-wives and mothers-in-law) figures throughout women's life stories. Being women and performing women's roles show gender-based disparities in the organisation of social life.

In the context of gender-based inequalities prevalent in Bangladesh, this paper attempts to delineate the situation of poor rural Bangladeshi Muslim households, especially through the perspective of women. The data for this paper is based on secondary sources, that is, a collection of sixteen case studies of extremely poor Muslim women of Tangail district in Bangladesh. This volume, edited by the director of the Grameen Bank, Muhammad Yunus (1984) is titled, *Jorimon of Beltoil Village and Others: In Search of a Future.*[1] The struggle that equipped the poorest of the women to break out of the hard shell of purdah with the help of Grameen Bank loans is the focus of attention here. It may be noted that customary stringencies are somewhat lax among the lowest strata in most societies. In this light, the paper takes the case studies, as they are narrated in the book, on the assumption that perhaps women's struggle to work independently of their male protectors amounts to notionally giving up of purdah. We shall see,

---

[1] A note on citation is needed here. Page numbers cited without being accompanied by author's reference, are meant to identify the cases from Yunus' (1984) collection of case studies, which constitute the subject matter of this paper. Often, the quotes are used to portray the misogynist and rigid patriarchal structures.

below the dichotomy between the domestic/familial space and the space outside, which purdah symbolises for Muslim women. It is not for the men in the family that they observe purdah, but for the men outside the family.

The case studies were collected in the wake of initial attempts by the Grameen Bank's project of giving loans to landless poor women. These case studies provide rich and in-depth ethnographic material and biographical accounts of the women. What makes the volume valuable is the care taken by the editor and the translators to preserve the bare appeal of the biographical experiences as narrated by the informants. Each case study unfolds to reveal a detailed life story, exactly as seen, lived, felt, and judged by the women, who went through all that happened to them. The first-hand account from the narrator's point of view—of her life's past, present and future, and her plans and hopes—constitute a rich database. In addition, the investigators in each case study provide an almost live picture of the minimal effects/belongings in the house—(huts/shed), dress, food items, utensils, etc., and details of other activities occurring before their eyes. The women belong to that stratum of society where life is full of sorrow, suffering, pain, agony, scarcity, hunger and starvation.

Although, the present scenario in rural Bangladesh may not be the same as depicted in these case studies, it is important and worthwhile to register and analyse the numerous struggles, failures and successes of these landless rural Bangladeshi women who did not give up hope despite the most challenging and life-extinguishing conditions they faced on a more or less regular basis for a prolonged period of time. The opinions, attitudes, plight and actual encounters of the landless women in Tangail district are analysed here in the light of issues, such as gender, household, family and work that women face as members of their society. Discussing and acknowledging the travails and traumas faced jointly by these women and the Grameen Bank, this study should provide an understanding of the issues of gender relations, women's work and banking (microcredit).

The state of abject poverty can be judged by the descriptions of their houses (sheds or hut). A house usually means a hut which may also have a roof. In the case of a few fortunate ones, the house has all the four walls. Women dream of a culture where their children would get some food to eat and their faces would look radiant. It is a great achievement if the family can get rice thrice a day. Some vegetables growing wild can be taken from other people's fields and firewood for cooking may be foraged. Occasionally, a small fish may be brought in by children. The _fitra_ (alms) distributed to poor Muslims on Eid festival (celebrated at the end of the holy month of Ramzan) brings hope for some good food and also clothing to cover their nakedness.

HOUSEHOLD AND SECLUSION

Managing the home and looking after the household members is the woman's responsibility. And, she must do all this work within the four walls of the house. Thus, by observing purdah, she maintains the family honour and the honour of the male group she belongs to (Mandelbaum 1988). Jeffrey (1979) highlights the notions of _sharm_ (shame) and _izzat_ (honour) that keep Muslim women in India secluded like frogs in a well. Purdah is strict among Muslims in South Asia. Reviewing the comparison highlighted by Jacobson and Papanek, Vatuk (1982) states that Muslims value and use these practices to safeguard their women from men outside the family and kinship and to keep them in their own feminine world. Sharma (1980) discusses the dichotomy between purdah and public space. It is this characteristic of purdah among the Muslims that keeps even the poor Muslim women out of the public space and, as a corollary, within the domestic/feminine (protected) space. This dichotomy perpetuates the gendered division of labour, and the invisibility and lower recognition of women's work. Papanek and Minault (1982) and Mandelbaum (1988) argue the above view effectively with regard to South Asia. The world remains divided by sexes. The wider world belongs to the man and the woman's place is in the home. In most societies, women belonging to the lower rungs of the social and economic order have often had to go out of the house to work. But, how does the strict observance of purdah in Muslim societies deal with the hunger pangs that force the poorest women, often with frequently absent husbands and grown-up sons, to fend for themselves and their families? How and why is a woman forced to step out of purdah, and what does it entail both within and outside the household?

Regulation of female sexuality is as important as the economic and social aspects. Hindu girls are socialised into suppressing their sexuality (Dube 1988). Meillassoux (1981) and Saadawi (1980) have deliberated on these complexly intertwined issues. Purdah in Bangladesh deprives women of mobility and access to essential services, even if survival for poor women depends only on moving out of the house. Young (1989) describes how women are bound in a fine and virtually inescapable mesh of prescriptions and practices, which restrict their sexuality and place severe limitations on their spatial mobility. The effect of poverty, seclusion and unemployment on the poor household generates certain tensions, conflicts and violence. How do women take all these? Even written and unwritten laws and interpretations of the Quran are tied up with local traditions and used against women in Bangladesh (Sobhan 1992).

The rural, landless Bangladeshi women are caught in a double bind between poverty and gender prejudice. Mehtab (1989) argues how these factors are detrimental to women owing to their dependence on the male-dominated power structures in the families and households. The feminist rethinking on the family by Michelle and McIntosh (1982) shows the family to be a seat of oppression for women. Like for most radical feminists, for Jain and Banerjee (1985), the household is tyrannical, a central part of society's power structure. It sustains patriarchal power in the public world and is itself a source of women's oppression. The radical feminists think that it is far from being a natural arrangement or individual choice based on mutual love. It is an institution which they view as a seat of exploitation of women's labour and violent expression of male sexual power. The economic and non-economic dimensions are so enmeshed that it is not easy to separate one from the other. What poor, hunger-driven women can do, especially outside the house, in what, where, and when they can work, what do they receive in return and what they do with it are not simply economic matters.

The principle of class or the economic condition of the household and community are crucial in retaining women in purdah (Patel 1987, 1994). The position of women in households belonging to different classes and religious communities is rarely uniform, though lower classes try to emulate the ideals of the upper classes. People withdraw women from paid work outside the household not merely because there has been upward economic mobility but also to mark their social mobility and enhance their status, though this occurs only in very specific conditions of social and economic organisation. Women of such households then engage in status-enhancing activities within the households (see Papanek, among others, 1989). Irrespective of whether the institution of purdah is rigidly observed by a community or not, status is lowered once out of purdah or when working for wages as against those remaining indoors and being provided by their menfolk. Gulati's (1981) poorest of the poor wage workers in south India and Sen and Sen's (1985) analysis of NSS results show that if economic need forces women to go out for work and wages, it is not status raising.

Feminist literature is replete with the view that the sexual division of labour—a male personality is different and superior to a female personality—is subject to historical processes (de Beauvoir 1960). Chodorow (1978) brings out, psycho-analytically, the processes that reproduce genders and argues that child-rearing practices have political dimensions. A set of standardised prescriptions for proper behaviour for both men and women is accepted as the norm. These are internalised from childhood and become part of one's personality. Dube (1988) and Chanana (1988) convincingly argue that gender is socially constructed. Aziz (1989) also elaborates on the differential socialisation of boys and girls from birth to adolescence in rural Bangladesh. He elaborates the manner of seclusion, avoidance, distanciation, responsibility allocation, etc., which creates a gendered society. Patel (1994) discusses how young girls in Rajasthan get to imbibe the idea that they have to behave like other senior women in the community. For Millett (1985), the family's main importance was as an agent of socialisation. It is the primary institution through which young children learn the values and expectations of their society. It is within the family that boys and girls first encounter patriarchal power and the sexual division of labour, and it is through the examples and admonitions of their parents that they are first taught the roles, temperament and status appropriate to their sex. Such lessons are reinforced by peer groups, schools and the media. The cult of domesticity emerges at a very early age. The myths, notions of honour and shame, and the cosmology associated with these impel women to their given situation. They thus acquire a world view which governs and nurtures their ways of feeling and seeing the world. When senior women and women from better-off households set examples of 'good feminine' behaviour, others attempt to follow them, thereby perpetuating patriarchal values.

The purpose here is to understand the thought and behaviour of the poor landless Bangladeshi women in their social setting, to analyse how they struggle to fulfil the social, cultural and reproductive roles expected of them by tradition and society and to understand the cosmology they derive from mythology, religion, rituals, institutions, etc. What are the problems and dilemmas encountered by women in their enactment of normative femininity? How do women belonging to the bottom rung of society resolve the conflicting demands of an ideal wife-mother, on the one hand, and of the breadwinner in the face of severe economic compulsion, on the other? Pressures of poverty make it difficult for women to observe traditional practices, thereby preventing them from being the ideal of femininity. How do they manage to combine the two contradictory roles into complementary ones? How are the compromises made? How do they encounter the outer world in the face of strong sex-role stereotypes, while stepping into the man's domain by taking up economically productive ventures? Do they conclude that their fate is preordained, given by God, and simply resolve it by accepting what comes their way (or what their husbands and others inflict on them) or do they struggle, experience anger and resentment at how things have shaped up for them and in knowing that they could have been handled otherwise? What future do they cherish or contemplate for their daughters as future women of the same society?

THE CASE STUDIES

For the purpose of the present analysis, the sixteen case studies are divided into three sections to cover the various phases of a woman's life: early childhood, child bride and married life, and life as deserted/separated/widowed or divorced.

Life in Early Childhood

As a child Sakhina had spent most of her time in the fields tending cows and goats and gathering firewood. The only brother, who was also the youngest, did not do any work. After the death of her father things changed. Besides her own household work, Sakhina's mother started husking paddy in other people's houses. Sakhina started to accompany her mother to work.

(p. 62)

Shumari learnt to help her mother in the household chores from early childhood. She used to sweep the floor, wash the dishes, and fetch water from the well. In addition, she used to help with cooking. She also tended the kitchen garden, helped to clear the weeds, and kept an alert eye for the cows, goats, ducks, chickens that spoilt the plants. Furthermore, she looked after the cowshed and made fuel cakes from cow dung and dried them.

(pp. 161–62)

At the age when rich children go to school, Koituri had to earn her own bread by doing odd jobs in neighbours' houses.

(p. 240)

As Bachaton's husband was disabled, her two daughters, Amena and Maleka not only helped her in her work, the two carried loads of paddy and chilli from the market to the house and also carried these loads to retail in market. Bachaton's two daughters were like two strong men supporting their disabled father.

(p. 51)

Tara bewa's daughter Royeka felt bad for her mother and helped her to husk, spread, and dry paddy. Her whole body would be wet from perspiration and smeared with sand while she made *muri*. Her mother felt proud of Royeka's capabilities and commented that she had been working like this from early morning. It was past mid-day and she was still working alone without taking any bread.

(p. 269)

Collecting cow dung, twigs, firewood, and wild-growing vegetables, like spinach and *Kochu* (a starchy tuber), is usually done by small girls. Daughters are not only trained in domestic chores, they are also taught to become responsible towards the whole family early in their childhood. The young daughters are well equipped to perform their duties and take up the tasks expected of a woman in the household. Chodorow (1978), Dube (1988), and Chanana (1988) provide a comparative picture of gender socialisation.

Life as Child Bride and Married Woman

As soon as a daughter is around ten, the mother's biggest worry is to marry her off. She hopes to find a decent husband for her and contemplates a happy married life for her. She dreams a life without sorrow, beating and suffering for her, although deep inside there is a strong premonition that things will go awry. The fear of the dream failing looms large. The only desire of the desperate parents is to marry off their daughter to anyone. Parents are keen to marry their daughters at a tender age. The marriage age ranges (of the sixteen women under study) between seven to sixteen years, though most of them were married at about eleven years of age

> Three of Shumari's elder sisters were married off even before Shumari was born. The only sister's wedding that Shumari saw was that of her immediate elder sister Noori. Shumari was then 10 years old. As soon as Noori was married off, Rajjan Khan the father started making plans for getting a good groom for her.
>
> (p. 162–63)

The groom always has an edge over the bride irrespective of parents' economic position, capabilities of the prospective spouses, and even physical appearance. The asymmetrical relationship between bride givers and bride receivers adds to a woman's powerlessness in the conjugal household (Vatuk 1975; Madan 1975). Yet, it is only through marriage that a girl gets security in the household and protection of her sexuality. She fears the wider world less if she is married. The woman also gets status through marriage (Patel 1994). The honour-virginity syndrome around marriage makes it the most desirable rite of passage for an adolescent girl and more so for her parents on whom lies the burden of protecting her virginity (Patel 2004)

> The dark complexioned Halima was married at the age of 13 to Alauddin who was slightly deranged and people called him Mad Ala.
>
> (p. 149)

Poverty, sorrow, pain and suffering had made Alekha's mother extremely weak. When Alekha reached 15 her parents' worry was her marriage. Dowry had to be given even though it was a terrible hardship for the poor family. The few proposals that came always demanded one thing or the other. One such proposal came up. Without probing anything, Alekha's father hurriedly arranged to give a dowry of Taka 1100 by selling (some) cultivable land for Taka 500 and added to it his own savings plus some money he borrowed from a relative.

(p. 133–36)

Despite doing all the household work, Asia could not satisfy her husband's family because her father had not spent much on her marriage.

(p. 273)

Same was the problem with Mafia's parents who took great care to keep their son-in-law happy.

(p. 180)

Khalil Mian being the only son became rather spoilt under his father's fond indulgence. He squandered both his father's and his own hard-earned money. When Hatim Mian realised this he arranged a marriage for his son, who did not change.

(p. 96)

Jorimon the ten-year-old little girl came to her new home with heart beating in fear and eyes filled with rosy dreams. But within a few days, all her dreams faded into thin air, 'I never had any wish fulfilled at my father's home. Neither did I have any better luck at my husband's,' says Jorimon.

(p. 180)

Asia Begum's is a story of pain, suffering, humiliation and broken dreams. A happy family life was not a great expectation but Asia had to go through three marriages in search of the receding mirage. She ended up in a morass of dejection and self pity.

(p. 271)

The prospect of marriage is an alluring prospect for all concerned. Patriarchal values enjoin upon parents to marry off their daughters; protecting a daughter's sexuality after puberty involves greater risks to the natal family honour. Virginity and chastity are values held in high regard, especially critical for a girl's marriage prospects. The status of both the households is enhanced—of the natal household by marrying off the daughters and of the conjugal one by secluding the household's married women. For a groom, the prospect of dowry is an added attraction. Also, for the girl facing poverty and voicelessness, marriage is a mirage. Marriage appears the best model for economic and social honour. It remains the only career for the poorest purdah-observing women. Boserup (1975) blames the absence of economic opportunities for keeping women within the house and for the perpetuation of traditional values.

Choudhary (1985) comments on the poor Bangladeshi women, who suffer the most not only owing to pressing problems of poverty but also patriarchy. They are well aware that being humble and submissive would maintain their own and their family's status. In the face of hunger, household drudgery and humiliation are preferable. They submit to outrage and victimisation. They are flogged and accept this mortification. They are inculcated with the idea that they must pardon, and absolve the man who inflicts the outrage. Women idealise this. They receive recognition and praise for being feminine thus (docile, humble, non-complaining, self-effacing, etc.). This maintains the status quo and upholds an orthodoxy. This is one striking example of the family as an oppressive institution, especially for women.

Home-making and housekeeping are central to the numerous roles expected of an ideal married woman. Her merit lies in her ability to run the house efficiently. The task is extremely challenging for the poorest of women who rarely have a house made of four walls and a roof, let alone other items required for even mere survival. Though the private sphere is non-supportive, women are expected to be regulated by its norms

> Asia's father would turn wild if his meal was not waiting for him after he had taken his bath, irrespective of the fact whether there were any provisions for a meal in the house. He would let out his fury by slapping, beating up and kicking the offender. Asia's mother bore the brunt of his torture. She gave birth to seven children without ever being spared of his beating.
>
> (p. 272)

Bachaton was labeled 'jinxed' when the horses died due to an epidemic.

(p. 35)

Not cooking well and on time are enough reasons for beating a wife (Patel 2004). The training at their natal homes instils in girls the conviction that only by keeping their husbands and their kinsmen happy can they establish themselves in their conjugal homes. If anything goes wrong or against the expectation, the blame is put on the newly wedded bride

> For eight years after her marriage. Sakhina did not have any children. People called her barren and infertile. Afaz Ali himself thought so and did not spare any opportunity to make remarks about this. But eight years later, she silenced all her critics by giving birth to a child, a daughter. Sakhina's face lit up with joy and satisfaction.
>
> (p. 65)

> Abdul married seven times, Rabeya's mother was his last wife, the only one to have produced children. She gave birth to three daughters and a son before becoming a widow.
>
> (p. 223)

> After Asia was divorced by Hamid, her father arranged her marriage with Buzrat Ali who had married thrice earlier. His first wife died after giving birth to a son, the second wife was very lazy and was also not good looking. She did nothing but eat, sleep and socialise in the neighborhood. Buzrat Ali divorced her on these grounds. He also divorced his third wife because she was a shrew and quarrelsome woman. She was also accused of hating Mansur Ali, Buzrat's son by his first wife. Asia was his fourth wife. After a year of her marriage, Asia gave birth to a daughter. The birth of a female child did not much please him. Later Asia gave birth to a second daughter, who soon died. The birth of two daughters did not go well with Buzrat Ali. His love and affection for Asia began to cool. Asia once again gave birth to a daughter. He did not hide his disgust and anger. He became alternately angry and indifferent. He often beat up Asia. A mean villager counseled Buzrat to divorce Asia. 'She will never give you a son. . . . Who will then give you food or look after you if you are ill?' Buzrat constantly tortured Asia and divorced her one day.
>
> (pp. 274–76)

The reproductive role of women is a major obligation. It is absolutely normal to expect the wife to produce children for her husband. There is a fear of being turned out or having to put up with the husband's second wife if she cannot bear children within a few years of marriage (McCarthy 1994; Patel 1994). The value of a son is more than that of a daughter. The woman certainly improves her status by bearing a son for her husband. She is insecure about her future in the conjugal home if she has no son. Asia's case is clearly an illustration

Mamtaz and her husband were the only members of their small family. She had always wished to build a nice happy family. All her life Mamtaz had been free from the duties and responsibilities at her parents' home. But now she herself took up the burden of building her own home and family. Sheikh Ali was not much concerned about his family, he had no thoughts about the future. Mamtaz used to argue with him every day and tried to make him face the reality. And he gradually improved.

(p. 215)

Rabeya lived with her in-laws for three years after marriage. Kuddus did not do any work and used to loaf around, his father had tried to reform the boy but Kuddus did not care for his father. Finally, Kuddus was separated from the family. But this did not change his habits. He still preferred not to work. He did not stay home much. So Rabeya had to starve. She stayed on, although it meant enduring hunger and pain. Sometimes she confronted her husband when he came home; 'Where do you go every day? Who would give me food if you leave me like this?' Kuddus would reply, 'If you don't like it, you are free to go'.

(p. 225)

Though wives are expected to have the influence to reform deviant men, they are unable to exert any pressure, even if men fail to follow household norms. Even the larger community's pressure on truant men is near absent compared with the close vigilance kept on women.

Life as Separated, Abandoned, Widowed, or Divorced Women

Most of the women enter marriage with high hopes and yet live pathetic lives under the constant threat of being thrown out of the house. The stigma of divorce dishonours and devalues them. Divorce is the worst form of insult inflicted on a woman. It robs her of her prestige (the good fortune of being married) and degrades her into being a lesser human being. Most of the younger women have been harassed for dowry though not the older women, as dowry, was not as institutionalised as recently. Perhaps dowry is gaining ground among the very poor in Bangladesh in their attempt to emulate the rich. This is similar to lower-caste Indians practising dowry in order to enhance their status, reflects Srinivas (1984). Besides seeing dowry as an honourable practice, it is also believed to provide against dire poverty and hunger. The poor have become serious victims of the dowry system. Once their parents had exhausted all resources and even incurred debts to pay dowry, those women did not have the heart to return to their natal homes upon being divorced

Asia could not satisfy her husband's family despite all her efforts. The main reason was that the wedding ceremony was not as colourful as they expected and Asia's father did not give dowry to Hamid, Asia's husband. His stepmother was after her right from the day she stepped into their house. All her complaints were listed to Hamid. She gave him several examples of others who gained by marriage. Hamid started disliking his in-laws. He was displeased with them. He divorced Asia in a year after marriage. Hamid kept all her ornaments. Asia came back to her father's house with nothing except the sari she was wearing. She was a burden in the year of drought.

(pp. 243–44)

Rabeya's eyes glistened with tears revealing her fear of being deserted by her husband. With deep regret Rabeya remarked that if she had a son she could lead the rest of the life with him. There was no meaning in a life without a son and a fear of her husband leaving her to her own self.

(pp. 237–38)

Rabeya's fears of divorce in the face of sonlessness came true. She was divorced by Buzrat Ali. Women have also been divorced because their husbands did not find them appealing or took fancy for some other woman.

Jorimon's husband was a terribly ill-tempered man. In her words, 'He is a Khan in name as well as in deed'. He used to beat her up on the slightest pretext and threatened to divorce her all the time. At times Rustom's beating left her entire body bruised

and bleeding. Yet she suffered every thing in silence for the sake
of children and household honour.

Fuljan had serious problems of housing after she was divorced
even though she had no problems in earning for herself and her
son from her tailoring skill. She shifted from house to house and
to other villages before she could find a quiet place to earn a
living.

(p. 103)

Rabyea's mother was evicted from their homestead and had
to beg on streets after she became a widow.

(p. 224)

Alekha's parents tried hard to get her married again. But it
was extremely difficult to find a husband for a divorced girl.
Although one or two proposals did come, a lot of problems of
dowry arose and everything fizzled out.

(p. 138)

Asia was prepared to put up with a life of humiliation only
if it meant a secure home. But Kudrat Ali moved decisively to
put Asia away for good. He divorced her and sent her to her
brother's home, while his daughter was nine and son only two
years old.

(p. 278)

Divorce and desertion generate the most dreadful fear in women's
minds. Removing the 'married' label and wearing the label of 'divorce'
spells doom in a number of ways. In addition to the economic
problems, the divorcee is thrown into the world without any social
status or physical and other security. She belongs to no one (and by
implication, to everyone who can abuse her). She is thrown from the
frying pan to the fire. Cruelty from one man or one household is an
easier alternative than from any man in the society. Her remarriage is
far more difficult than that of an unmarried girl. She is a burden on
her already hard-pressed parents and she has nowhere else to go. She is
doomed. In the absence of any property and income, she is an absolute
burden on her natal kin on whom lies the onus of protecting (including
routine monitoring of) her sexuality at least until she is remarried.

The cruelty of social institutions such as divorce and remarriage
for women is the apex that drove Alekha to take her own life to save
her father from selling everything he had to arrange her remarriage

after her divorce. The world is no less cruel to a widow. She has to face the challenges and burdens of life all by herself, and it is worse if she has very small children. Women thus believe that it is better to accept the torture of the husband than to suffer the wrath of the whole society.

A virtuous woman accepts as proper whatever her husband has to offer her: love, beating, kicking, abuse and threat. She should not cause any displeasure to him or else she will have to bear the brunt. She realises that her security (physical protection from sexual abuse by any and everyone in the absence of the husband because a woman without a husband is regarded as fair game) is only assured in being someone's wife, and however she may be treated by him remains unimportant. Women's lives are deeply embedded in the household and the family. The senior women, including mothers, are adept at convincing the younger complaining women of the value of the conjugal household on the basis of their experiences and wisdom. They can effectively argue that sticking to one's marriage and conjugal household is the only possibility for a woman. Any other option is dangerous and problem ridden. For the sake of household honour, her own self-interest included therein, the woman continues to accept her miserable state and perpetuates patriarchy in the process

> Afaz Ali seized the wooden lampstand and cursing loudly fell upon Sakhina beating her ruthlessly. There was not an inch of her body that did not bear the brunt of his wrath. In outrage he put all his weight on her chest and began strangling her. Sakhina lost consciousness and lay in a bloody mess all that night. Her head was wounded and she was seriously hurt. The next three days she lay helplessly in bed. But Afaz Ali did not even once inquire about her or bring her any medication. Sakhina's brother later took her home and her mother learnt everything that had happened. Sakhina cried and begged, 'Mother please don't send me back to that house, I don't want to go there'. Her mother however, tried to convince her that a woman gets married only once, and has to face up all the pain and sorrow. Sakhina understood that her mother's door was no longer open for her. She understood that there was no way but to accept what fate had in store for her.
>
> (p. 64)

Shumari's husband Ramjan had married a second wife and did not bother about Shumari. Her father accepted her misfortune and believed that she was not fated to have any happiness. He pleaded with Ramjan to give a place to Shumari in his house after he was dead along with a part of his land. But Shumari was forced to continue to stay with her brother. It was only when Ramjan and his second wife were suffering from sorrow and hardship while Shumari was doing well by raising cows that Ramjan wanted to bring Shumari to live with him. Despite all her suffering, humiliation and insult inflicted by Ramjan, she agreed to join him and his second wife with a hope to help them out of their suffering.

(p. 168)

Women's sacrifice and abnegation are for the welfare of their husband's and/or conjugal household's as also the honour of their natal family. Dube (1988) aptly attributes the role of socialisation to the effective moulding of women to conform to the mandate of their culture. Observing cultural norms adds value to her, and makes her virtuous. As young daughters, the women have observed it all happening to their mothers and other female relatives.

RESILIENCE AND RESIGNATION

Most women suffered in silence at their husband's or in-law's cruelty. But suffering in silence is not always equal to absolute submission. The feelings and ideas that come to their minds during their non-protest or meek silence are significant indications of deep pain and displeasure against the oppressor (McCarthy 1994, and a few studies of this genre for forms of women's resistance). Suffering silently through starvation is also a strategy in the absence of any alternative. With the support of Grameen Bank loans these women have made attempts at least to fight their hunger. The role of microcredit for women in extreme poverty holds a promise, though not an easy one

Bachaton's condition worsened after her husband was struck down with paralysis. She begged for *marh* (residual water drained after rice is boiled, usually drained away, after rice is cooked) from her neighbours for the children. She could not

bear to see the famished look of their starving faces. She felt as
if her heart would break. Their cries for food drove her mad.
Utterly desperate, her frustration and resentment at her own
helplessness caused her to beat them severely at times. And
then, when she was alone she cried out to the heavens, beat her
breast and wept bitterly.

(p. 40)

Sakhina had an argument with her husband who had
misinformed her that he owned property, while he owned none.
Words led to more angry words. Sakhina called him a cheat and
wicked. She was struck immediately in the head and ruthlessly
beaten. Helpless to move she suffered silently in bed.

(p. 64)

Fuljan was unhappy about her husband's interest in Bela. One
night, they fought over this issue angrily. He beat her up. Fuljan
was dejected and did not speak to him for days.

(p. 101)

Fuljan was very sad and dejected with her marital life, her
undesirability at her brother's house and later at her aunt's
house. She was unhappy with the hurdles her aunt's family
created for her despite her self-sufficiency as she earned her
living by stitching garments with the help of Grameen Bank
loan.

(p. 105)

Shumari was not pleased with Ramjan marrying Shano. She
continued to live in her father's house in disapproval in the midst
of pain, anguish, and suffering. When the badly-off Ramjan
came to take her back she showed her anger, 'I can't go to your
house just because you wish me to. When I was starving, when I
was wearing torn rags, when Sobur was dying from disease and
neglect no one came forward to help me. But now you are here'.
[Shumari raised cows with a Grameen Bank loan].

(p. 175)

The subterranean tussle in women's minds is palpable. Starving
Bachaton beats her children when they pester her for food, which she
cannot provide, but later cries her heart out and weeps bitterly at her
helplessness and failure to provide for her children. The clash is visible
in women's attempts to get their deviant husbands to take interest
in household matters. Yet they are always careful not to disrupt the

household apple cart. Though the women cherish a better life, they do not have the heart to overthrow the patriarchal household

> Halima did not assign any problem to fate instantly. It was after her struggle with childbirth, loss of children, rearing them up and the long-drawn struggle to maintain her life that she invoked fate.
>
> (pp. 147–58)

> Divorce of Koituri, snatching away and abandoning both her sons on the roadside to be picked away, drove Koituri crazy. She wept uncontrollably for deprived motherhood and commented that others could not feel her pain, a mother's pain at the loss of her children. It was much later that she came to accept all this misfortune as god-given.
>
> (pp. 239–52)

> Mafia's first child, a boy, died soon after birth. Her mother-in-law blamed Mafia for this and stepped up her ill treatment. She was starved and thus could not carry a child. The foetus was either dead or died soon after birth. Mafia got a serious injury from her husband's beatings that left a deep scar. But she did not want to leave him. She tried her best to pull along for a few years before she finally left him. It was at this point that she invoked fate.
>
> (pp. 179–92)

> As mentioned earlier, Asia's only dream was a happy married life for which she was married and divorced thrice. She blamed her fate in the end but had expected a better fate for her daughter, Hazera. Hazera was overworked at her in-law's place. They did not care for her when she fell ill. Asia brought her medication on learning about Hazera's suffering. Her husband spent his days in illness and her mother-in-law disliked and troubled her. Hazera was soon divorced and lived with her mother. Hazera was Asia's greatest worry. She could not imagine that her daughter's fate would be identical to hers.
>
> (p. 282)

Dreams about an ideal married life with a husband who is responsible, that is, one who earns and cares for the wife and children come from numerous sources. Not all the poor women have had absent/truant/non-earning fathers—they are also exposed to family life in better-off homes where hunger is clearly not a fait accompli for women and children. These middle-class homes are examples of ideal homes to the poor in Bangladesh. While the women believe in fate, they do not see their state of affairs as fait accompli. Their experiences show that they try in various ways to alter their life conditions. Only after having been through a process of trying to help make difference to their miseries, they accept their conditions as a part of their fate. Almost all the women have earnestly endeavoured to improve their circumstances and conditions. It is only after continuous failure to overcome suffering at the hands of in-laws, beatings, threats and divorce by husbands that these women attributed everything to their fate. They resisted and tolerated cruelty with the hope of a better and honourable future in the community. But fate became a scapegoat only when all efforts of altering their marital and family life proved ineffective.

Belief in fate seems to have rescued them and offered some consolation. Thus they never disbelieved in the critical institutions of marriage, family, and the practices of dowry and divorce, which existed as bastions of patriarchy in the larger society.

SURFACING FROM SECLUSION

Women's potential to withstand suffering and to struggle for a better deal, as much as strength and power permit them, are the source of hope in their lives. It is hope that keeps them alive amidst an open Pandora's Box. They ultimately come to surrender to pressures of patriarchy and accept as fate all male tutelage in the familial domain. As already mentioned, in the familial domain, they rarely accept defeat in the beginning, despite being enmeshed in a culture of female subordination. Their resistance has been much greater in the extra-familial domain, which is an 'all male' domain.

The economic pressure of being landless, uneducated, casual wage earners is easy to understand—more so, given the frequency of droughts and floods that ruins the crops and the few possibilities of work opportunities. Even when work is available, the wages are so low that it is not possible for a man to support his family. This does not mean that the man does not experience hunger. Of course, men suffer form hunger as well. But the hunger of women and children is relatively grave, especially because like a good wife/mother, women feed adult men and children in that order before they themselves eat. This is a trend reported for South Asian women in general, which made Amartya Sen (1991) reconsider the economic understanding of working out, on a per capita basis, the distribution of resources in the household. Households are cooperative conflicting units and distribute their resources in accordance with the norms and ideals of the society. The poor in Bangladesh suffer from hunger, but poor women suffer more than men. There is hardly a family that did not experience hunger and starvation for days at a stretch. Some of them have never had a hearty meal all their lives, and mothers cherish a family of well-fed children. The suffering caused by poverty and hunger is not easy to put up with. It reaches beyond the capacity of mothers to bear all this.

Women found themselves at crossroads in the face of such a mind-boggling situation; it was mental turmoil for them. They could improve the situation and save their children from hunger if they earned something in cash or kind. But scarcity of work apart, they were faced with a strange dilemma. The values and norms confining the woman to the household prevailed strongly, on the one hand, and the emaciated faces of starving and naked children constantly chilled the mother's spine, on the other. But the woman's place was only in the home. Even religion and scriptures are used to strengthen the separation of domains on sex lines. Jahan (1982) reports that women suffer from numerous gender-based inequalities in the distribution of resources: there is little employment and, furthermore, permission from a husband is needed, though rarely given, to be employed if at all there happens to be work available, and finally, they have no education. Even educated women in Bangladesh suffer from discriminatory traditional laws and participate only to a small extent in politics despite reservations for them. She assigns the poor representation of Bangladeshi women in politics primarily to the institution of purdah

After her husband's death, Sakhina's enormous pain and helplessness, however, did not confine her to the house for too long. The more she thought she would not leave the house, the more her empty stomach and the cries of her starving children compelled her to venture out. Only five days after her husband's death, Sakhina had to forget her prestige and was at her neighbour's door soliciting help. In her words, when Shahinoor, her son, starts to bring up blood (that is, vomiting blood), 'all my strength and outrage disappear. I wish I had died earlier. There is no one on this earth who will look after this fatherless child. If he does not live, how can I keep myself alive?' Sakhina's family faced abject poverty and starvation. In utter helplessness she had to throw aside shame and delicacy and go about begging.

(pp. 65–69)

Many others also had to beg or borrow in worst times.

(pp. 43–44)

Jamuna had never asked for anything to anyone, and had never gone to work at other's homes. She had a strong sense of self-respect. The women who worked in other's houses were clear in their minds that they had no self-respect or dignity as they stepped out to work. When hard days came, Jamuna sold her ornaments. Her husband was the only earning member. If he earned anything they ate, otherwise they went hungry. On top of this, other adversities like natural calamities, floods, storms and the war of independence struck them one after the other. Their miserable life became more and more unbearable.

(p. 198)

The only path to survival was to work in well-off neighbours' homes. During the harvesting season there was much to do in the farmers' houses, like cleaning, parboiling and husking paddy. But the decision to step outside the house to support the family or add to the man's earning meant doing away with decency. The norm, more heightened among the Muslim community in Bangladesh, that a decent woman remains indoors, as a means to maintain the social structure, although women come to accept it as an end. Attitudes and beliefs reflect an ideal world. They show that women dream of having things and relationships as per their will, doing tasks suitable to graceful and happily married women, and everyone being like one of them

Like many others, Bachaton's family sold land to save themselves from starvation. Her days were spent in semi- or complete starvation. The food she and her family ate would not be called

food at all. When things became unbearable, she stretched out
her hands to her brothers but even that had a limit. So, she
pitifully requested her neighbours to lend her money. However,
she never had to pay any interest on the loans. She used to
sell whatever chickens or goats she reared (through Grameen
Bank loan) to repay the money. Bachaton recalled how angry
she was when she was absolutely helpless and wanted to earn a
living. She commented that the children went practically naked.
'. . . I myself had no clothes. I had only a torn rag of a sari which
I wore month after month. I was so ashamed, I avoided going
out in front of people'.

(pp. 43–44)

To uphold the social values and live a life of dignity, the women
thought of working outside only in utter desperation. Their hunger
drove them to seek work outside, that is, mostly in other people's
homes. They struggled their utmost to save face until they were
virtually overpowered by starvation. Family property was also sold to
save women from working outside. The pressures making woman's
economic contribution to the household imperative are also listed
by Hossain (1987). The war of 1971 followed closely by famines and
inflationary policies led to landlessness, immiserisation, and greater
woman-headed households in Bangladesh

When Sagir Ali was ill and confined to bed, all responsibilities
fell on Bachaton. Her children were too small to earn a living.
But so many mouths would not listen to reason alone. When
starvation and suffering reached such a stage that they could
not bear it any longer, Bachaton decided that she had to stand on
her own feet. She could not be tied down to the prohibitions of
society any more. And at night under the cover of darkness, she
started cultivating their land. During this time the village elders
became very busy in reminding her of the norms of society and
the duties of a respectable woman, but she turned a deaf ear
to them. At night she worked on her own land and during the
day she husked paddy and worked in other people's houses in
return for whatever little she got for the family.

(p. 40–41)

Within a month of her marriage, Sakhina was compelled to look
for work in neighbouring houses. She was not afraid of working
outside. It was worse to suffer and worry inside the house.

(p. 63)

> Wazeed Ali's protracted illness drove Tara helpless and the
> relatives became reluctant to offer further help. So Tara went to
> work at neighbours' houses without letting anyone know.
>
> (p. 258)

In Bangladesh, women's moving outside the house and attaining greater autonomy by taking up male tasks violate both the sexual and economic control on them. It is pertinent to note that the pressure on women to stop coming out of their houses was not the same for all jobs that women did outside the household. The objection was covert and mild when women took up jobs as helping hands in other people's houses and farms. Poor women in India work alongside their men in construction and farming activities, where separate tasks are taken up by men and women. But women of those communities that customarily practise purdah do not take up such tasks outside the household. The restriction in Bangladesh is of the latter category rather than the former. The cases of Bachaton, Jorimon, Moyfal, Sakhina, Koituri, and others reveal that they did not face major obstacles from their families or society's elders when they looked for the odd chores in neighbouring households. Their working in neighbours' houses did not much violate the male control over economic resources and sexuality of women. Entry into upper class/landed households exposes poor women to the formers' lifestyle, mannerisms, norms and values, and it is thus tolerated at times. However, the distance between the role of family structures and ideology of the upper class and that of the landless poor continues to remain intact through the above arrangement, wherein the poor women seek waged work in upper-class homes (Abbot and Sapsford 1987).

We shall see below that the communication of disapproval was quite strong whenever women took up major roles outside the household. There was displeasure when women took up jobs which were customarily the exclusive tasks of men, such as cultivating and ploughing land, as done by Bachaton, or petty trading done by Sakhina and Halima, who peddled wares and other goods, or paddy-husking business by Moyfal and Jorimon with the intervention of the Grameen Bank. People created all sorts of fears in the minds of the villagers because women were overthrowing purdah. They called it a death trap and an instrument of killing poor people. They did not object when Bachaton was carrying head loads of firewood to sell. But when she began her independent husking trade, they protested vehemently. The rich cultivators, the village elders, the headmen, the *moolahs* [*sic*], all opposed the bank loan scheme that found favour with women. They spread malicious and absurd rumors and created a feeling of fear among women

> The *moolahs* passed all kinds of religious verdicts aimed at restraining the women.
>
> (p. 54)
>
> Some people frightened Moyfal. They warned her that if she could not repay the money properly, her house and land would be confiscated, and she would be tied up and thrown into prison, and so on.
>
> (p. 126)
>
> When Alekha told her father about the bank loan, Kabil Mondal stubbornly opposed the idea. He told her sternly that it was impossible for her to use the money profitably and pay back the weekly installments regularly especially since Alekha was a woman. It is not possible for a woman to run a business.
>
> (p. 144)
>
> Shumari was deterred on the same ground.
>
> (p. 173)
>
> Mamtaz was barraged with the sentiments of neighbours and kinsmen against bank loans taken by women. 'The women who visit the bank and hold meetings have no self respect'. The money lenders were furious and didn't care what they said about the bank and these women.
>
> (p. 219)
>
> A few village elders did not like Rabeya's visits to the bank. They took her to task. 'Shameless woman, you are not satisfied with your own shamelessness. You have to turn the head of a few other decent girls too. If you dare to set foot at the bank once more, we will drive you off from the village.' Rabeya was starving that day. She had nothing to lose and did not fear any more the guardians (influential persons who think and act like protectors of traditional ways of the community) of society. She told them, 'When I starve with my family do you care to give me

a morsel to eat. I have not taken anything for the whole day but you don't seem to care. When I go to the bank you think I have done a crime against you'.

(p. 233)

Jorimon recalls her past when she went from village to village with a heavy load of firewood on her head. People used to ignore us all the time. No one ever looked at us with grace or favour. But today with an independent paddy husking trade (that materialized through Grameen Bank) Jorimon does not have to put up with any affronts or insults.

(p. 28)

Both direct and indirect forms of disapproval of women's economic independence are revealed as women gather courage and cross the cordons of traditional values and boundaries. Men seem to be the most ruthless and critical when women take over in the 'outer' spheres. This seems to threaten male domination and patriarchal values exercised against women. Males seem to fear their dispensability, when women tend to show signs of self-sufficiency or independence. It is in this context that one may understand the objections of elders of the society to women's efforts towards economic independence. A woman's access to money and subsistence is obtained through domestic service and mediated by the man, concludes Meher (1981). The household, the so-called private sphere, has ramifications beyond the household. Self-employment creates autonomy and horizontal power relationships. I would not go so far as to agree fully with this view, but one has to acknowledge that self-employment has enabled Bachaton and other women to at least fight against chronic hunger and poverty. However, people in Bangladesh, especially the men and religious leaders, felt threatened by women's self-employment and made every attempt to retain power by dissuading women from becoming economically independent. When their women venture into the erstwhile male domain, of petty trading in the market for instance, their masculine honour is at stake. It is not bank loans and the idea of working with interest on loans per se, but by hurting their 'ego' by moving to the public domain that was a more serious offence committed by women. Among the poor, this immediately comes to symbolise an effeminate husband who cannot feed his family, especially when women of the house have to move out for employment.

Severe reactions from men were observed when women were stepping out of their houses, especially when they sought bank loans for gainful employment. Rabeya's retaliation to village elders has already been mentioned (p. 233). McCarthy (1994) found similar retaliations when womanly virtues were extolled without bothering about women's survival. Anger and resentment, be it overt or covert, is a response to the oppression of women when it becomes unbearable for them. They are resentful but suffer in silence only as much as they can tolerate. They speak out when the seams of their toleration give way. Some totally withdraw from the scene as Alekha did.

CONCLUSION

In the higher and middle strata where property is inherited by males across generations, women, who are traditionally secluded, are more submissive and tolerant. Status of women in the poorer, non-propertied sections of the society is assumed to be better, and these women appear to be somewhat less tolerant of male dominance, especially in the sphere of seclusion, argues Patel (1987). Experiences of torture and tolerance levels of women across classes are variable. Lack of property and frequent male unemployment clubbed with a lack of sense of household responsibility typical of men who are from non-property, unemployed sections of society, force women to move out of seclusion in order to support the family. This is revealed by many Jorimons of this study. But we must hasten to note that men still retain control over them. Though the women have sought gainful employment, they are not out of the surveillance range of the males and elders in their family. We have also seen that most of the women do not live in joint households. Shah (1998) has reiterated the fact that poor and low-caste households in India tend to separate and form nuclear households earlier than others. The ideal of egalitarian conjugal ties in a nuclear family assumes the emancipation of the individual from the domination of family elders and the kin group. Also, the nuclear family's so-called egalitarian norms are considered to be the strongest instrument for the emancipation of women from male tutelage. But this study does not support such a view. It does not hold good for the poor where most families are nuclear as against joint families. These women are hardly more emancipated than those in joint families. The tyranny of the household seems to be all-pervasive for women and poverty further compounds adversity in the poorest households. The household is an ambivalent mix of domination, nurturance, conflict, supportiveness, security, and esteem. To understand the predicament of women, it is necessary to see the various interlinkages between the individual household and the wider structures and processes of the society. Women's position in the household is subject to the influence of the position of that household in the social hierarchy. Women from upper-class households can afford to remain in purdah and thereby enhance the household status, but seclusion and its associated restrictions are in no way a panacea for the hungry and poor women of the non-propertied and unemployed sections of society.

In the process of a constant spirit of pardoning, most women tend to accept male tutelage as their fate. Non-fulfilment of Fuljan's wishes, constant threats to Bachaton who was branded as jinxed, sorrow as the constant companion of Sakhina who commented that God had created and sent her to this world only to suffer and why should he then allow her to have a glimpse of happiness, are a few cases in point. The non-appealing Alekha and Fuljan gradually came to accept their plight as their misfortune. Alekha hardly ever complained to her own parents about the beatings she was receiving for she knew she had to stay in her husband's home no matter what happened. She was aware that the tyranny of the household, however atrocious, was lesser than that in the larger society outside. She decided to opt for the lesser evil.

The present paper analysed the invocation of the structural principles governing women's oppression—gender relations, marriage, household, purdah, and class in the background of conjugal obligations in a Muslim community. The women in the present study are poorer than their husbands; they are the 'second sex'. They are not indispensable and can be subjected to frequent divorces and remarriages. Belonging to the Muslim community, the women's obligation to observe purdah is more stringent than among non-Muslim women of similar economic background. This further strengthens a larger cosmology for male domination and female suppression. It would be relevant to point out that one of the sixteen women studied here is a Hindu and her plight was not very different compared with other Muslim women.

Were Engels and the socialist feminists being over-optimistic in professing that emancipation would follow from women's full-fledged entry into social production? The fact, however, remains that these self-employed women have been able to break out of their misery and frequent starvation with the help of the Grameen Bank's efforts. The struggle for cracking the gender, poverty and community shell has been an extremely uphill and tedious task. The crossover to the public sphere from the private one in some cases (for example, venturing into independent petty trade) has violated the community norm of the private-public dichotomy, and the hurdles and backlash that women faced in making the crossover clearly shows that it is not easy to overthrow the private-public dichotomy. Those who worked in other people's houses did not invite as severe a condemnation as did those who set up independent petty ventures. Women moved to the public domain to ameliorate their economic miseries but clearly preferred to remain under the protective umbrella of the household for social status, thus reinforcing gender roles, patriarchy, and their space in the private sphere. Many socialist feminist theorists would like to argue that women's ability to earn an income paves the way for female emancipation, but this study shows that it only changes the character of women's subordination, as several contributors in Afshar (1985) conclude. It acknowledges that earning an income enables women to negotiate with patriarchy, once there is some food in their stomach. But the women of Beltoil seem to fight starvation as an end rather than as a means to an end. Nevertheless, they have managed to create some space for themselves, however negligible it might seem to be, in the process. The women under this study continue to negotiate with the wider community from the prevailing patriarchal structural and ideological contexts, as Gulati's (1981) poverty profiles of non-purdah-observing women in south India reveal.

Kelkar (1992), Agarwal (1994), and Agarwal and Panda (2003) advocate property and resource ownership for women as a means to curb violence against them. Economic independence is one important dimension in analysing women's oppression and violence inflicted on them. While they live in households, belong to families and communities, the economic and household domains are imbricated. These need to be seen together to understand women's lives in their everyday existential context. Unequal power relations exist even if they are not based on economic dependence. Has women's command over resources, mediated through the Grameen Bank, helped them to challenge the onslaught of oppression of the household and the community? What effect does income generation have on women's autonomy and status? We cannot turn to radical feminists like Delphy (1980), who see women's oppression in the domestic mode of production as an economic feature shared by them, which thus makes them into a class. Socialist feminists like Barrett and McIntosh (1979) disagree with this view because it ignores changes in women's lives over time and between classes. They rightly recognise that the shared experiences of gender are often fractured by class and other social divisions. Thus, post-modern feminism (Butler 1990) de-essentialises biology (sex) from gender and lays stress on agency, performance in the dialectics of interaction.

We have seen that without overthrowing the patriarchal authority, women have not remained sheer passive, starving victims of authoritative males in the household and the community. The cases make it amply clear that the poor women are not identical to one another, nor do their conditions remain the same throughout their lives. And, in their attempts to overcome their starvation they have often managed to overcome starvation in the household. This is supported by studies in Asia and Latin America as well. Trivelli's (2004) study of poor women in Peru shows that poor women respond more to satisfying household needs than individual goals of personal development and empowerment. She advocates the feminisation of anti-poverty programmes. One of the principles of Grameen Bank credit is based on the assumption, and also the experience of a quarter century, that lending to women brings greater benefits to the family than lending to men. If the mother is the borrower, the children are immediate beneficiaries, reports Yunus (2004).

The case studies reveal that the Grameen Bank loan has enabled the women to exercise some amount of autonomy, however negligible it may be, in the sphere of income generation. They have stood their ground despite odds from their husbands, community and religious leaders to ease the pangs of starvation. But none of the cases reveal any autonomy exercised by women in the familial domain. The condition and position of women clearly shows that earning an income by itself does not bring them greater autonomy within and even outside the household. In other words, mere economic independence may be a necessary condition but is not a sufficient one in a society which oppresses women with its customs, traditions and rituals so very interlinked and supported by women's self-perceptions and notions of 'fate', honour, and *lajja* (shame). For the sake of honour derived from marriage, for the protection of sexuality, women respect and desire to be in the family and have children, especially sons. This saves them from stigma and gross dishonour. The women have preferred to venture into economic arenas which least expose them to sexual vulnerability. Women need both economic independence and social and sexual protection, thus posing a serious challenge to socialist, radical, and Marxist feminist positions.

The institution of the family is critiqued by feminists for being the bastion of gender discrimination and disparity (for more on this Young, et al. 1981, and Sen for the household as a cooperative conflicting unit 1991). The cases in this paper have shown how the resilience of the family is unchallenged. The family's hold on the income-generating women has, if anything, become more stringent. We must also be clear in our analysis that none of the women wished to be left alone. Each one desired and dreamed to have a family, that is, be with one's husband and children. They have fought against the pressures of patriarchy as long as they were starving. Once their hunger was quelled they wished to be under the protection of a husband and to live respectfully as family women. Microcredit-led developmental initiatives get culturally adapted and naturalised to suit the prevalent gender disparity. Even after a century of feminist struggle, the gender question and gender disparity continues to be linked with the question of the family. Unlike what feminists like

Shulamith Firestone (1970), had imagined, the family is still the most cherished institution for the women as this study shows.

Though their lives do not tend to be identical with one another, their poverty and the struggle to come out of purdah, just for keeping body and soul together, but without overthrowing the interlinked instituitions of patriarchy, are similar. In fact, the organisation of instituitions such as the family and marriage to meet human material needs are as important as their economic systems (Ferguson 1989). The changing unchangeableness of the family (Patel 2004) socially reproduces itself and therefore insists that it is not reducible to economic change. Even if the husbands could not provide them food and shelter and were often callous in their attitudes towards household obligations, all the cases in this study, more often than not, show a pattern: all the women hope and dream of a future for their daughters to be happily married to men with stable incomes where they will not be forced to break out of purdah and work outside for mere survival.

References

Abbot, P., and R. Sapsford. 1987. *Women and Social Class*. London: Tavistock.

Afshar, H., ed. 1985. *Women, Work and Ideology in the Third World*. London: Tavistock.

Agarwal, B. 1989. Work-Participation of Rural Women in the Third World: Some Data and Conceptual Biases. In *Serving Two Masters*, ed. K. Young, 1–25. Allahabad: Allied Publishers.

————., ed. 1988. *Structures of Patriarchy*. New Delhi: Kali for Women.

————., and P. Panda. 2003. Home and the World: Revisiting Violence. *Indian Express*, 7 August, p. 9.

Aziz, K. M. A. 1989. Gender Creation from Birth to Adolescence in Rural Bangladesh. In *Gender and the Household Domain*, ed. M. Krishnaraj and K. Chanana. New Delhi: Sage Publications.

Barrett, M., and M. Barrett. 1979. Christine Delphy: Towards a Materialist Feminism? *Feminist Review* 1, 95–106.

Beauvoir, S de. 1960. *The Second Sex*. Harmondsworth: Penguin.

Begum, H. 1990. *Women in the Developing World: Thoughts and Ideals*. New Delhi: Sterling.

Boserup, E. 1970. *Women's Role in Economic Development*. London: George Allen and Unwin.

————. 1975. Women in the Labour Market. In *Indian Women*, ed. D. Jain. Delhi: Publication Division, Govt. of India.

Butler, J. 1990. *Gender Trouble: Feminism and the Subversion of Identity*. London: Routledge.

Chanana, K. 1988. *Socialization, Education and Women: Exploration in Gender Identity*. Delhi: Orient Longman.

Chodorow, N. 1978. *The Reproduction of Mothering*. Berkeley: University of California Press.

Choudhary, A. K. M. A. 1985. Maternal Nutrition in Rural Bangladesh. In *Women and Poverty: The Tyranny of the Household*, ed. D. Jain and N. Banerjee. New Delhi: Vikas Publishers.

Delphy, C. 1980. A Materialist Feminism Is Possible. In *Feminist Review* 4, 79–105.

Dube, L. 1988. Socialization of Hindu Girls in Patrilineal India. In *Socialization, Education and Women: Exploration in Gender Identity*, ed. K. Chanana, 166–92. Delhi: Orient Longman.

————. 1989. Preface to *Gender and the Household Domain*, ed. M. Krishnaraj and K. Chanana. New Delhi: Sage Publications.

————., and R. Palriwala, eds. 1990. *Structures and Strategies*. New Delhi: Sage.

Ferguson, A. 1989. *Blood at the Root*. London: Pandora Press.

Figes, E. 1970. *Patriarchal Attitudes*. London: Virago.

Firestone, S. 1970. *The Dialectic of Sex: The Case for Feminist Revolution*. New York: William Morrow.

Gulati, L. 1981. *Profiles in Female Poverty*. Delhi: Hindustan.

Hossain, H. 1987. Capitalist Penetration into Handicrafts Manufactures: An Historical Review of Women's Work for the Market in Bangladesh. In *Invisible Hands*, ed. A. M. Singh and A. Kelles-Viitanen. New Delhi: Sage Publications.

Jahan, R. 1982. Purdah and Participation: Women and Politics of Bangladesh. In *Separate Worlds: Studies of Purdah in South Asia*, ed. H. Papanek and G. Minault, 262–82. Delhi: Chanakya.

Jain, D., and N. Banerjee, eds. 1985. *Women and Poverty: The Tyranny of the Household*. New Delhi: Vikas Publishers.

Jeffery, P. 1979. *Frogs in the Well*. Delhi: Vikas Publishers.

Kak, S. 1994. Rural Women and Labour Force Participation. *Social Scientist* 22(3–4): 35–59.

Kelkar, G. 1992. Gender, Development and Human Rights for Women. In *Gender, Development and Human Rights*, ed. L. Madsen. Canada: Mutual Press.

Krishnaraj, M. 1988. *Women and Development*. Pune: Shubhada Saraswati Prakashan.

————., and K. Chanana, eds. 1989. *Gender and the Household Domain*. New Delhi: Sage Publications.

Madan, T. N. 1975. Structural Implication of Marriage in North India. *Contributions to Indian Sociology* 9(2): 217–43.

Mandelbaum, D. G. 1988. *Women's Seclusion and Men's Honour*. London: University of Arizona Press.

McCarthy, F. E. 1994. Development from Within: Forms of Resistance to Development Processes among Rural Bangladeshi Women. In *Gender and Political Economy*, ed. A. Clark. Oxford: Oxford University Press.

Meher, V. 1981. Work, Consumption and Authority Within the Household: A Moroccan Case. In *Of Marriage and the Market*, ed. K. Young, C. Wolkovitz, and R. McCullagh. London: Routledge and Kegan Paul.

Mehtab, M. 1989. Health, Education and Nutrition of Rural Women in Bangladesh: The Household Interface. In *Gender and the Household Domain*, ed. M. Krishnaraj and K. Chanana. New Delhi: Sage Publications.

Meillassoux, C. 1981. *Maidens, Meals and Money*. Cambridge: Cambridge University Press.

Michelle, B., and M. McIntosh, eds. 1982. *The Anti Social Family*. London: Verso.

Millett, K. 1985. *Sexual Politics*. London: Virago.

Papanek, H. 1989. Family Status-production Work. In *Gender and the Household Domain*, ed. M. Krishnaraj and K. Chanana. New Delhi: Sage Publications.

————., and G. Minault, eds. 1982. *Separate Worlds: Studies of Purdah in South Asia*. Delhi: Chanakya.

Patel, T. 1987. Women's Work and Their Status. *Social Action* 37(2): 126–49.

————. 1994. *Fertility Behaviour: Population and Society in a Rajasthan Village*. Delhi: Oxford University Press.

————. 2004. *The Everyday Violence Women Experience: A Study in Bundelkhand*. Report for Oxfam, Lucknow.

Saadawi, Nawal El. 1980. *The Hidden Face of Eve: Women in the Arab World*. London: Zed.

Scott, James. 1990. *Weapons of the Weak: Everday Forms of Peasant Resistance*. New Delhi: Oxford University Press.

Sen, Amartya. 1991. Gender and Co-operative Conflicts. In *Persistent Inequalities*, ed. I. Tinker. New York: Oxford University Press.

Sen, G., and C. Sen. 1985. Women's Domestic Work and Economic Activity: Results from NSS. *Economic and Political Weekly* 20: WS-49–56.

Shah, A. M. 1998. *The Family in India: Critical Essays*. Delhi: Orient Longman.

Sharma, U. 1980. *Women, Work and Property in North-West India.* London: Tavistock.

Singh, A. M., and A. Kelles-Viitanen, eds. 1987. *Invisible Hands.* New Delhi: Sage Publications.

Sobhan, S. 1992. Women Living under Muslim Law. In *Gender, Development and Human Rights*, ed. L. Madsen. Canada: Mutual Press.

Srinivas, M. N. 1984. *Some Reflections on Dowry.* Delhi: Oxford University Press.

Standing, H. 1985. Women's Employment and the Household: Some Findings from Calcutta. *Economic and Political Weekly* 20: WS-23–38.

Stolcke, V. 1981. Women's Labours: The Naturalisation of Social Inequality and Women's Subordination. In *Of Marriage and the Market*, ed. K. Young, C. Wolkwitz, and R. McCullagh. London: Routledge and Kegan Paul.

Trivelli, C. 2004. Women, Poverty and the Survival of the Household. In *Promises of Empowerment: Women in Asia and Latin Maerica*, ed. P. H. Smith, J. L. Troputner, and C. Hunefeldt, 149–66. Lanham, Boulder: Rowman & Littlefield.

Vatuk, S. 1975. Gifts and Affines in North India. *Contributions to Indian Sociology* 9(2): 155–96.

⸻. 1982. *Purdah* Revisited: A Comparison of Hindu and Muslim Interpretations of the Cultural Meaning of *Purdah* in South Asia. In *Separate Worlds: Studies of Purdah in South Asia*, ed. H. Papanek and G. Minault. Delhi: Chanakya.

Young, K., ed. 1989. *Serving Two Masters.* Allahabad: Allied Publishers.

Yunus, M., ed. 1984. *Jorimon of Beltoil Village and Others.* Dhaka: Grameen Bank.

⸻. 2004. Grameen Bank Microcredit and Millennium Development Goals. *Economic and Political Weekly* 39(36): 4077–80.

3

Towards a Conceptual Understanding of Female Infanticide in Modern India

L. S. Vishwanath

INTRODUCTION

In this chapter, an attempt is made to analyse how some scholars have conceptualised female infanticide and female neglect, mainly with reference to modern India. The conceptual frameworks discussed include: evolutionary theory, structural analysis, the mode of production model, and the demographic perspective. The demographic perspective discussed in the last section of this paper is not strictly speaking a conceptual scheme. But I have included it because it is one of the ways in which female infanticide is sought to be understood by a scholar. Evolutionary theory does not discuss female infanticide and other social institutions with specific reference

This essay was first presented at the Indian History Congress, 53rd Session, Modern India Section, held at Aligarh Muslim University in December 1994. Subsequently, it was extensively revised for a Festschrift in honour of A. M. Shah edited for publication by B. S. Baviskar and Tulsi Patel. On behalf of the students, colleagues and friends of A. M. Shah who have contributed to this volume, I place on record my deep debt of gratitude to Baviskar and Tulsi Patel for taking up the onerous responsibility of editing the Festschrift inspite of their other commitments.

to modern India. Though John F. McLennan used examples from primitive and non-primitive communities in different parts of colonial India to support his evolutionary framework, his theory, as he conceived it, had universal validity applicable to all primitive societies. Structural analysis and the demographic perspective relate to the colonial period of India's history; the mode of production model deals with the post-independence period and is based on the 1961 census data and ethnographic studies of rural India. Since most of these conceptual theories discuss female infanticide and female neglect in relation to the colonial or the postcolonial period in terms of their time frame, the use of the term 'Modern India' in the title of this chapter is probably justified.

After the passing of the Female Infanticide Act in 1870, census officials were reporting that to escape detection from the police and also the provisions of the Act, the castes which had been practising female infanticide were resorting to deliberate neglect of their female children (census 1911). Even before the passing of the Female Infanticide Act, a British official, who investigated female infanticide in the Benares region of the North Western Provinces in 1855–56, reported that some Rajput parents were deliberately neglecting (Moore 1868: 44) their female children. Besides actual infanticide, there was also deliberate neglect which took the form of refusal of parents to feed the female child. As if the extreme form of discrimination against females involving their killing or neglect was not enough, a worse practice involving sex determination tests even before the birth of the child has come into vogue over the last thirty years or so.

EVOLUTIONARY THEORY

It was the evolutionary anthropologist, John F. McLennan, who not only made female infanticide an important part of his evolutionary theory, he also argued that exogamy (a term which he coined and gave to social anthropology) originated as a result of female infanticide (McLennan 1970: 58). A Scottish lawyer by background, McLennan tried to show the interconnections of social institutions on the basis of what he perceived to be rigorous logic. In *Primitive Marriage*, published in 1864, he argued that most primitive communities practised female infanticide because of harsh conditions of existence. Since female infanticide resulted in a shortage of females, the primitive tribe resorted to polyandry and also capture of females from other primitive tribes. Moreover, as primitive tribes were forced to capture and marry women from other primitive communities, it gave rise to the institution of exogamy (McLennan 1970).

McLennan's 'logical' construct made him argue that endemic hostility among primitive peoples resulted in blood feuds, which in turn contributed to the suppression of female infanticide, as the tribe tried to protect its female (and male) children from other hostile tribes. McLennan further took the position that in the beginning, all primitive communities were promiscuous; subsequently, promiscuity gave way to homogeneous communities based on matriarchy and matrilineal kinship. This development was ascribed by McLennan to his idea that the ties of the mother with her child were 'likely to be recognised before and be more certain than that with the father'. A still later stage in social evolution was agnation based on male kinship. However, with agnation, female infanticide reappeared, because the 'beneficial action of the blood feud', which protected the females, ceased to operate among the homogeneous agnatic kindred (McLennan 1970: 12).

What is interesting about McLennan's evolutionary theory and the series of assumptions he made about the universal prevalence of female infanticide in all primitive societies—along with associated institutions such as blood feud, polyandry, marriage by capture, matriliny followed by patriliny and so on—is that though his focus was on primitive societies, he freely chose examples from both ancient and modern India to support his arguments. Thus, for example, to show that polyandry was at one time universal, he cited the instance of polyandry in the Mahabharata where Draupadi is married to the five Pandava brothers. Nayar polyandry—described as 'crude', because the husbands of the Nayar women were unrelated—and Tibetan polyandry—described as 'less crude', because the husbands of the women were related—were also chosen to support the same argument; these cases of polyandry existed till the late eighteenth and nineteenth centuries. The existence of polyandry in the colonial or modern period was, of course, not a problem for McLennan; for him they were 'survivals' of a past universal practice.

Among other sources, McLennan used James Tod's work, *Annals and Antiquities of Rajasthan* (1971), to show that the Rajputs had at one time matrilineal kinship. Tod's work is basically a compilation of Rajput history, ballads and legends in which he discusses, among other things, the various puranic myths in connection with the origin of the Rajputs. Some of these myths suggest that Rajput society was at one time martilineal. Though Tod's account also deals with the probable origin of the Rajputs from Sakas or Scythians who came to India from outside and were absorbed into Hinduism, McLennan ignores it and cites Tod's work to show that the ancient Rajputs were polyandrous and that they recognised kinship through females as well.

Moreover, Tod refers to Rajput female infanticide and clearly states that it was related to Rajput pride, hypergamy (he does not use the term 'hypergamy' but is clearly referring to it), and their inability to marry their daughters below their rank. Yet McLennan, who surely consulted Tod, ignores it and maintains that exogamy originated from female infanticide.[1]

As is to be expected, McLennan's ideas came in for considerable criticism. Herbert Spencer pointed out that if all primitive tribes practised female infanticide, they would all be equally short of women. He further pointed out that the higher death rate of men among primitive tribes would balance out female infanticide and that there would therefore be no shortage of women. Lowie pointed out that female infanticide and polyandry were not widely prevalent (Evans-Pritchard 1965: 14–15). Morgan severely criticised McLennan for confusing descent groups such as clan with the tribe. McLennan was also wrong in assuming that marriage and family were later developments in the history of primitive communities (Evans-Pritchard 1981: 67).

There were, no doubt, serious flaws in McLennan's theory; but as Evans-Pritchard (1981: 61–68) has pointed out, McLennan should be judged on the basis of his contribution to anthropological thought. McLennan was among the earliest thinkers to emphasise the interrelatedness of institutions. Though Radcliffe-Brown rejected evolutionary theories, calling them 'conjectural history' (Radcliffe-Brown 1952: 49–50), the stress of the earlier thinkers on interconnections between social institutions (however wrong these interconnections may seem to us today) and seeing them as part of society had much influence in social anthropology. Moreover, McLennan made extensive use of the comparative method and gave to social anthropology classificatory concepts of importance. These inluded: exogamy, matriliny, totemism and marriage by capture (Evans-Pritchard 1981: 66).

Furthermore, McLennan's ideas should be viewed from the background of the interest theories of social evolution generated during his time. If structural functionalism had its heyday under Radcliffe-Brown in England, so did the theories of social evolution in nineteenth-century England. McLennan entered into debates with the prominent intellectuals of his day. He rejected the thesis put forward by Morgan in *The Systems of Consanguinity and Affinity* (1871) as a 'wild dream—not to say nightmare'. He also rejected Maine's argument put forward in *Ancient Law* (1861) that the partriarchal family was the earliest form of the family. In fact, it is suggested that McLennan wrote *Primitive Marriage* (1864) to counter Maine, who was rated a legal luminary of his day. Maine held important academic positions at Cambridge and drafted the Indian Succession Act as a member of the Third Indian Law Commission. Later, in his *Early History of Institutions* (1874) Maine modified his views and was less categorical about the patriarchal family being the earliest form of family organisation (Maine 1861: 142).

The relationship posited by McLennan between female infanticide and exogamy and his argument that the former was the cause of the latter was criticised by Herbert Risley, who was the Census Commisioner in 1901 and wrote detailed ethnographic accounts about Indian society. Risley pointed out that instead of female infanticide forcing men in a primitive tribe to capture women from other tribes and thereby leading to exogamous marriages, exogamy itself may well lead to female infanticide. In other words, Risley turned McLennan's theory the other way round and argued that instead of female infanticide leading to exogamy it was vice versa among primitive communities. Risley wrote

> For if men were restrained by inexorable usage from marrying the girl in the sept or local group of blood kindred, the temptation to kill the bouches inutiles would probably be very strong. Not

only would girls be useless to the men of the tribe as wives, but the more of them there were, the more would the tribe be preyed upon by neighbours in quest of wives.

(Risley 1969: 172)

In support of his arguments, Risley cited information given to Colonel McCulloch, the Political Agent in Manipur in 1859, regarding female infanticide among the Naga tribes. McCulloch was told on making enquiries that all female children were killed 'to save themselves from the annoyance of being harried by wife hunting parties from a stronger clan' (Risely 1969).

Risley also refers to Major MacPherson's account of the Khonds of Orissa and points out that the Khonds, like the Nagas, practised female infanticide owing to the fear that they may be harrassed by wife-hunting parties.

Interestingly, in the case of the Naga tribes, Risley and McLennan refer to the same source to reach opposite conclusions. Risley, as noted, cited Colonel McCulloch to say that the exogamous rule contributed to female infanticide among Naga tribes; McLennan also refers to Colonel William McCulloch's article titled, 'An Account of the Valley of Mannipore and of the Hill Tribes' (1859). However, after citing McCulloch's finding that he (McCulloch) could not find a 'single female child in the village of Phweelongmai, McLennan goes on to argue that female infanticide seriously disturbed the 'balance of the sexes and forced primitive men to prey upon one another for wives'.

Major McPherson's account of the Khonds of Orissa is cited by McLennan to show that marriage by capture was probably once prevalent among them. McLennan refers to female infanticide among the Khonds but he says: 'among Khonds, female infanticide was found to be an institution of religion' (McLennan 1970: 68).

STRUCTURAL ANALYSIS

I selected female infanticide as the subject for my research when I joined the Department of Sociology, Delhi University, as a research student under the guidance of A. M. Shah in 1966. Since I came to sociology with a background in history, I decided that my primary sources of information would be historical data. Moreover, as considerable unpublished and published archival data on female infanticide were available for the Gujarat region during the nineteenth century, I decided to focus on that region. The archives, also, had printed records on female infanticide in north India during the nineteenth century. These records were less detailed than those for Gujarat, but they were certainly useful for trying to obtain a comparative perspective on the subject of my research.

From the outset, it became clear to me that I would have to relate the historical data on female infanticide to the social structure of the castes who practised it. As I look back, this was perhaps inevitable. Research students like me who did not have a background in sociology, had to attend lectures on social structure. Radcliffe-Brown's *Structure and Function in Primitive Society* (1952) and Evans-Pritchard's *The Nuer* (1940) were compulsory reading. Srinivas' book on Coorg society (1952) was also recommended reading. An essay which Srinivas asked me to read was Evans-Pritchard's Marret Lecture on 'Social Anthropology: Past and Present' (1950).

I have discussed in detail female infanticide and social structure in colonial west and north India in my doctoral thesis and in publications (Vishwanath 1973, 1976, 2000). In this section, I shall give a brief resumé of the information in the records on female infanticide in colonial west and north India, and how I tried to analyse the data in terms of the history of the two regions and the social structure of the castes who practised it.

It was abundantly clear from the information in the records that in colonial Gujarat and north India, female infanticide was practised by hypergamous castes, who were also locally dominant. In Gujarat, the two castes which, according to the records, resorted to female infanticide during the nineteenth century were: the Rajputs of the peninsular region and the Lewa Patidars and Kanbis of central Gujarat in the mainland region. The peninsular region comprised Kutch and Saurashtra known as Kathiawad during the nineteenth century. The mainland region extended from north to south Gujarat. It was more fertile and more densely populated than peninsular Gujarat or the highland region. In north India, the castes resortng to female infanticide during the nineteenth century included: Rajputs, Jats, Ahirs, Gujars and Khutris. All these castes had within them an elaborate status hierarchy; the lower-status groups within these castes aspired to give their daughters in marriage to the higher ups and they had to pay for their ambition in the form of a large dowry. Some of the castes who practised female infanticide, such as, Rajputs, Jats, and Ahirs, had chiefs and princes at the higher levels of the status hierarchy.

Soon after their discovery of female infanticide, British officials were reporting that the practice was related to Rajput pride and the desire of the Rajput lineage to maintain its status by avoiding payment of large dowries. Therefore the landowning Rajput lineages did not want to marry their girls below their rank, as this was considered 'dishonourable'. Their getting a groom from a Rajput lineage of higher status, as per the hypergamous norm, not only involved payment of a huge dowry, it could also lead to financial ruin through sale or mortgage of the landed estate. The latter eventuality would lead to a drop in socio-economic status, and hence, to avoid it, they killed or deliberately neglected their female children.

Among the Jadeja Rajputs of Kathiawad and Kutch, the British found extensive prevalence of female infanticide. Alexander Walker, the British Resident at Baroda who was asked by Jonathan Duncan, Governor of Bombay (1795–1811), to investigate the practice, reported to him in March 1808 that female infanticide was not only extensively prevalent among the Jadejas, it was related to their high position in the Rajput hierarchy and dowry avoidance. Walker reported

> They (the Jadejas) pleaded their aversion to relinquish a custom which they conceived to attach renown to their caste [sic] and to distinguish it above all other Rajpoots in this quarter at least ... strangers to parental emotions and affections, the great cause for destroying their children is avarice, and that they may not be exposed to the cares and expense attending their establishment in life.
>
> (*Selections from the Records of the Bombay Government* [*SRBG*] 1808: 327)

Walker's report regarding the relationship of female infanticide to the high position of the Jadeja Rajputs in the Rajput hierarchy was confirmed by reports of other officials—for example, Blane, the Political Agent in Kathiawad, reported to the Bombay Government on 31 July 1828

> The chief motive with Jharejas to commission of infanticide is pride which leads them to consider the other tribes of Rajpoots unworthy of receiving their daughters in marriage, and as no Rajpoot can marry a female of his own tribe(clan), they prefer putting them to death to the prospect of the dishonour which is likely to result from their living in a single state.
>
> (*SRBG* 1808: 434)

As regards the number of Jadeja females destroyed, Walker estimated in March 1808 that the total number of Jadeja households in Kathiawad and Kutch was 1,25,000, and the number of Jadeja females annually destroyed was about 20,000 (*SRBG* 1808: 333–34). The subsequent reports of British officials on Jadeja female infanticide were quite alarming. On 20 June 1817, Ballantine, the Assistant Resident at Baroda, submitted to the higher authorities a complete register of female children in Jadeja Rajput households in various taluks of Kathiawad. The register showed that in many taluks inhabited by Jadeja Rajputs, there was only one female child among Jadejas and in some taluks not even one. Ballantine reported that though Drappa taluk contained more than 400 Jadeja Rajput households, 'there was not a single female child in any of them'. The register did not give the total number of Jadejas in Kathiawad, but it showed that in the whole peninsula, there were only 63 female children in Jadeja Rajput households (*SRBG* 1808: 389). In 1834, John Pollard Willoughby, the then Political Agent in Kathiawad, took a census of the Jadeja population to determine the extent of female infanticide. He found that there were 102 Jadeja males and twenty females of the age of one year and below. Overall, the census revealed that the Jadejas had 1,422 males under 20 years of age and 603 females alive of all ages (*SRBG* 1808: 445).

Piecing together information from a number of sources, I found that the Jadejas did indeed occupy the topmost position in the Gujarati Rajput hierarchy from about the thirteenth century AD till independence. The Sultans of Delhi, who conquered mainland Gujarat in the later half of the thirteenth century, did not disturb the Rajput chiefs of peninsular Gujarat. The Marathas, under the Gaikwads and the British, after they started ruling in Gujarat (1803), did the same. The fertile mainland area was the coveted region for Muslim, Maratha and British invaders. The Rajput chiefs in central Guajrat lost three-fourths portion of their estates to the Muslim rulers in the thirteenth century and were relegated to a lower position vis-à-vis the Rajput chiefs of the peninsular region (Shah 2002: 18–20). After the political boundaries were frozen by the Muslim rulers and later by the British, the Rajput chiefs in peninsular Gujarat, such as Jadejas, Jhallas, Gohils, Jethwas, Parmars, etc., were left in control of their respective estates. The Jadejas, however, controlled the largest chunk of territory in the peninsula (9,931 square kilometres) consisting of estates of varying size under the *Jam* of Nawanagar, the head of the Jadeja clan, and a number of Jadeja chiefs who were talukdars. The Jam on his own controlled 3,791 square kilometres. This was much more than the estates of other non-Jadeja Rajput chiefs (*Bombay Gazetteer,* VIII 1884). Moreover, the other prominent non-Jadeja Rajput clans acknowledged the Jadejas to be the highest by giving their daughters in marriage to them. There is ample evidence of this in the records (*SRBG* 1808: 526–27). Owing to their pride and their warrior-ruler ideology, the Rajputs avoided avenues of mobility, such as trade and commerce, which became available during Muslim and, later, colonial rule. Conquest of new territory was ruled out for the Rajput chiefs after the Muslim, Maratha and British rulers each in turn established their paramountcy in Gujarat. All this gave the Rajput status hierarchy its characteristc rigidity. Besides British officials, modern social anthropologists have also commented on Rajput pride (see Hitchcock 1959; Steed 1955).

Overall, I was able to argue that the extensive female infanticide among the Jadejas was related to Rajput social structure and, in particular, to the top position of the Jadeja clan in the Rajput social hierarchy in Gujarat. Walker's remark in his report of March 1808 that 'even poor Jadejas were reluctant to taint their blood with an improper alliance' shows that the avoidance of marrying girls below their rank applied both to the propertied and the poor levels of the hierarchy within the Jadeja clan.

It seemed at first puzzling why the archival records referred only to female infanticide among the Jadejas and not to the prevalence of the practice among the Jhallas, Gohils, Parmars and Waghelas. These Rajput clans also owned landed estates, and in a frozen hierarchical system, they too would have practised female infanticide to 'protect' their social status through dowry avoidance. There was, however, an important difference in the position of the Jadejas and the non-Jadeja Rajput clans. Since they were the topmost clan in the Gujarati-Rajput hierarchy, the Jadejas' options for selecting eligible grooms were closed within Gujarat region. The non-Jadeja princely and talukdari lineages had an option in that they could marry the girls they preserved to the Jadejas or the Rajput lineage structurally above them. The records indicate that the structure of marriage preferences among the royal Rajput lineages of Kathiawad in descending order of rank was as follows:

Jadejas
Jethwas
Jhallas
Gohils
Waghelas

Besides having the option of marrying their girls hypergamously,[2] two other factors would have contributed to better chances for the girl child's survival among the non-Jadeja Rajput princes, talukdars, and the owners of smaller estates in Gujarat. These were: the almost constant revenue demands of the British rulers, because Kathiawad was under indirect British rule, and less expensive cross-cousin marriages (Ghurye 1963; Karve 1965). Unlike the landowning Rajput lineages in the North Western Provinces (NWP), the Rajput lineages in Kathiawad and Kutch were not subjected to the varying revenue demands of the British government; nor did their lands come up for auction sales for failure to pay land revenue.

After the commencement of British rule in Kathiawad (c.1800), there were 193 estates, large and small, most of them owned by Rajput chiefs. Walker was asked to settle the revenues to be paid to the government with the chiefs in the province. He reached a settlement with the chiefs. In 1808, Walker estimated the entire revenues of Kathiawad at Rs 51,95,550 of which Rs 9,97,880 was paid as tribute. In 1880, the total revenue of Kathiawad was estimated at Rs 1,65,50,310 while the tribute amounted to Rs 10,77,570. This means that over a period of seventy-two years, the tribute paid by the chiefs had remained almost constant while the revenues had more than trebled (*Bombay Gazetteer* 1884).

Besides the almost constant tribute, what contributed to the comfortable financial position of the Rajput chiefs in the peninsula was that they derived income from a number of sources. The bulk of it was derived from land. The chief took a fixed share of the crop, supplemented by cash levies. The total amount of levies averaged from one-third to one-half of the crop. States with seaboard derived revenue from export and import duties. The maritime states also had a monopoly on salt trade. All the states in Kathiawad which managed their own financial resources (these included the estates of thirteen major chiefs with a total area of 14,810 square miles) also had the monopoly of salt and opium and were entitled to keep two-thirds of the value of all smuggled opium within their territories. The other taxes levied by the princely and talukdari states included: house tax, tax on artisans and shopkeepers, grazing fees called *masvari* levied on herdsmen, special taxes levied on spirit shops, and a tax on fishermen for each boat. The last was a source of income in the maritime states.

Before the British introduced the court system, fines levied for civil and criminal offences were also a source of income. The *Bombay Gazetteer* (1884) makes specific reference to the fact that the revenue accounts of the major states in Kathiawad, except those under the temporary management of the British, were 'never submitted to the Agency', that is, the British Political Agent at Rajkot and his assistants. The *Gazetteer* further observes that 'there is always a large uncertain quantity never brought to book in state accounts but credited to the private income of the chief or to members of his family'.

Thus, on the one hand, the tribute paid by the chiefs to government remained almost unchanged till 1880; it is very likely that the same position continued well beyond that date. On the other hand, the chiefs enjoyed financial autonomy from the British and also augmented their states' as well as private income in various ways.

This, and the existence of the less expensive cross-cousin marriage could have meant that the non-Jadeja Rajput chiefs brought up as many daughters as they could afford to marry. The 'silence' of the historical records on female infanticide among the non-Jadeja Rajputs was related to the fact that the British turned a blind eye towards the practice unless it was too blatant to be ignored. In the case of the Lewa Patidars, some British officials firmly denied that female infanticide existed in the caste on the ground that the police had not received any reports of the practice.

The Lewa Patidars of twelve villages known as Baragam located in the Charotar area of central Gujarat constituted the top stratum in the caste. The British discovered female infanticide among the Lewa Kanbis and Patidars in 1847, some forty-seven years after they found its prevalence among the Jadeja Rajputs in 1800. Since female infants were done away with secretly, the practice generally did not come to light. Moreover, unlike the Jadejas, the top strata among the Kanbis and the Patidars did not resort to wholescale or blatant female infanticide. Again, unlike the Gujarati Rajput hierarchy, which was rigid and got frozen after the Muslim and later British conquest of Gujarat, the Lewa Patidar-Kanbi hierarchy was open and flexible. The Lewas were a peasant caste and had a commercial 'ethos'. They took advantage of the avenues for upward mobility thrown up by trade and commerce during Muslim and colonial rule. Hence new status groups emerged among the Kanbis which laid claim to Patidar status. Though the old aristocratic Patidar tried to exclude the newly rich Kanbis, the latter managed to get included in the ranks of the Patidar when the Patidars needed or were tempted by the huge dowry offered by the ambitious Kanbis (Pocock 1957; Vishwanath 1973: 396; 1996: 194).

The emergence of the 'new Patidars' meant that though the elite Patidars faced the problem of locating eligible grooms within a restricted circle of Patidars with appropriate status and had to pay a huge dowry if they succeeded in finding an eligible groom, they were in a better position compared with the Jadejas whose options were closed within Gujarat region.

The settlement reports and the census revealed that in British-administered Kaira district, the Lewa Kanbis had a disproportion of females throughout the nineteenth century (Clark 1983: 9). The average sex ratio per hundred males ranged from 74 females in 1826 to 80 females in 1901. Though separate sex ratios for the elite Patidars of Charotar are not available till Cooke's census of 1872, Webb, Collector of Kaira, conducted a census in January 1849 and found that in seven taluks, the Lewa Kanbis had 71,470 males to 51,703 females—that is, they had 73 females per hundred males. Webb commented in his report that 'principally the practice (female infanticide) is said to prevail among the richer portion of the community called Potidars' (Wilson 1855). Ashburner, the Collector of Kaira, commented in his report of June 1857 that though overall there was disproportion of females among Lewa Kanbis, generally, it was considerable in the elite Lewa Patidar villages of Charotar (MSS 1857). Cooke's census of the child population among Lewa Kanbis of Kaira district under British jurisdiction revealed that in 1872, the proportion of girls to boys below twelve years of age was 74 girls to 100 boys. The census also showed that thirteen elite Lewa Patidar villages of Charotar had only 39 to 53 girls to 100 boys under twelve years (*SRBG,* Cooke 1875). Ashburner, the Revenue Commissioner, who forwarded Cooke's report to the Bombay government, observed that Cooke's statistics 'showed great disproportion (of females) in the Lewa caste as a whole, and the disproportion was greatest in the Kulia (elite) villages of Charotar' (MSS 1873). Finally, the decennial census enumerations showed that the elite Patidar villges in Charotar had considerable disproportion of females both in the British-administered part of Kaira district and in the part under the control of the Gaikwad of Baroda. The 1891 census enumeration revealed that seven elite Patidar villages under the Gaikwad had, on an average, only 707 females per 1000 males (census 1901: 267). The 1911 census showed that the same seven villages had only 679 females per 1,000 males. The 1911 census for the Bombay Presidency showed that six elite Patidar villages in British Kaira had on an average only 706 females per 1,000 males (census, 1911: 118).

Several British officials noted in their respective reports that the Lewa Kanbi-Patidar social hierarchy extended in ascending order of rank from Surat and Broach in south Gujarat to Charotar in Central Gujarat and that the 'most honourable' Patidar villages were located in Charotar. For reasons of space, it is not possible to go into all the factors which gave the Lewa Patidars a pre-eminent position within their caste. However, I will mention two important ones. First, since the pre-British Maratha period, the landholding Lewa Patidar lineages in Charotar, which constituted a coparcenary, paid fixed revenues to government regardless of the improvements made on the land. This was known as the Patidari or Narwadari tenure. The Patidars commanded great prestige owing to this priviledged tenure. The British continued the Patidari tenure unless the coparcenary broke down (*Bombay Gazetteer* 1879: 106, 109). Second, during Maratha rule, the Patidar lineages took up revenue farming—that is, there was a system of revenue contracts which enabled the elite Patidars to make enormous profits. The British put an end to the revenue contract system from 1812 onwards (Shah 2002: 43–44). The records mention Patidars telling British settlement officers that though the profit-making from revenue contracts had ended, 'the marriage of daughters continues to be expensive' (MSS 1848: 192–95). It is difficult to say how far the British complicated matters for the Patidars as far as payment of dowry and female infanticide are concerned. I could not find figures on Kanbi or Patidar sex ratios for the pre-British Maratha period.

Overall, I argue that female infanticide among the Lewa Patidars and Kanbis was related to their social structure, and that the extensive female infanticide among the elite Patidars was related to their high structural position in the caste. Besides dowry avoidance, the Patidars, in particular, were faced with the problem of having to choose grooms from a restricted circle of elite villages. A historical factor of significance was that in Central Gujarat, Rajput dominance was replaced by Patidar dominance following the decline of Rajput power in the area in the thirteenth century. As Pocock has mentioned, in the past, the Patidars tended to imitate the Rajput style of life (Pocock 1957).

In the past, and even today, there are four upper castes in Gujarat. They are: Rajput, Lewa Patidar-Kanbi, Anavil Brahmin and Bania. All four had within them a differentiated status hierarchy. Of these, the first two practised female infanticide. The Anavils and the Banias did not do so. The Anavil Brahmins are an interesting case. They had a differentiated status hierarchy consisting of the aristocratic Pedivala Desais at the top rung of the ladder. The elite Desais were tax collectors and rulers of villages during colonial rule. Below them were the lower-level Bhathelas, who claimed Desai status and sought hypergamous alliances for their daughters among the elite Desai families. The Bhathelas, who made money through trade and commerce, were prepared to pay huge dowries to the Desais (Veen 1972: 24). Though the elite Desais, like the elite Patidars, faced the problem of locating eligible grooms within a restricted circle of elite families, neither they nor the lower-status Bhathelas practised female infanticide. Being a Brahmin caste, they probably thought it a sin to kill female children.

Since towns were the centres of trade and commerce, most elite Banias lived in the towns of Gujarat. They had a weak hypergamous hierarchy with the less well-to-do Banias trying to marry their daughters to the elite. But large dowries were not given among the Banias (Shah 1982). And the Banias did not practice female infanticide. The point is that elite, propertied status and a high structural position in the hierarchy within the caste or hypergamy by itself did not lead to female infanticide.

For north India also, the evidence in the records suggests that generally those who occupied a higher structural position among the Rajputs, Khutris and Jats practised female infanticide more extensively than did those of lower status in these castes. For some areas in the north, the information on female infanticide and its extent is qualitative; though statistics is available for other areas, it is not detailed for analytical purposes. For example, Wilkinson, who was the British Political Agent in several princely states of Rajasthan in the 1830s, states in his report that the royal Rajput lineages in Udaipur, Jaipur, Bundi, and Kotah resorted to 'extensive female infanticide' (1844: 282). But quantitative data is lacking. For the Punjab, acquired by the British in c.1848, some statistics are available for only Bedi Khutris of Jullunder district. The records say that the Bedi Khutris occupied a high position among Sikh Khutris, as they claimed to be descendants of Guru Nanak, the founder of the Sikh faith. They also owned considerable land. Major Lake informed the Punjab Board of Administration in 1851 thus

It is an undoubted fact that there are a thousand families of Bedees who, for the last four hundred years, have destroyed all their female offspring; humanity demands that special measures be taken for the suppression of this barbarous and unnatural custom.

(Brown 1857: 45)

But, similar information for Bunjai Khutris, who gave their daughters in marriage to the Bedi Khutris with huge dowries is not available. The measures taken by the British to suppress female infanticide, which included a proclamation issued under the orders of Lord Dalhousie, the then Governor General, stating that the castes which resorted to female infanticide in the Punjab will lose their landed estates if they persisted in it, produced dramatic results. Figures collected by Maddocks, Deputy Commissioner of Jullunder district, showed that by 1854–55, the Bedi Khutris had 145 boys to 88 girls alive. Though the records say that the royal house of Kangra, who belonged to the Katoch clan of Rajputs, practised extensive female infanticide, even brief statistics are not available (Kangra was then part of Punjab). The position is the same for the Jats in the Punjab (Brown 1857).

Fortunately for the north, detailed statistics on female infanticide among Rajputs in the Benares region of North Western Provinces is available as a result of a special investigation conducted by a British official, W. R. Moore, in the winter of 1855–56. Briefly, the statistics on sex ratios for children below six years collected by Moore, after he visited hundreds of Rajput-dominated villages, revealed that nearly a dozen Rajput clans practised extensive female infanticide. The ratio of boys to girls for children below six years in many of the clans was 80 per cent boys and only 20 per cent girls. Many Rajput villages visited by Moore had no Rajput female children. And in many Rajput villages, the marriage of a Rajput girl was 'a rare occurrence' (Moore 1868: 122).

The important point to note in regard to the statistics provided by Moore is that not all the Rajput clans who resorted to extensive female infanticide in the mid-nineteenth century in the Benares region occupied the top structural position in the Rajput hierarchy in the region. Thus the Suryavamshi Rajputs of Amroha Pargana in Gorakhpur district controlled 78 villages and enjoyed a high position in the Rajput hypergamous hierarchy in the region. They had, in

1855–56, 721 boys to 129 girls below six years, the proportion being 82 per cent boys to 18 per cent girls. The Rajkumar Rajputs of Ungli Pargana in Jaunpur district controlled 40 villages and married their daughters hypergamously to the Suryavamshis. The Rajkumars had, according to Moore's statistics, 283 boys to 80 girls below six years, the proportion being 72 per cent boys to 28 per cent girls. The Raghuvamshi Rajputs, who resided in the same pargana and district as the Rajkumars and controlled 50 villages, gave their daughters in marriage to the Rajkumars. The Raghuvamshis had 775 boys to 162 girls below six years in the proportion 79 per cent boys to 21 per cent girls (Moore 1868).

These data did not fit with the information for the Rajput clans of peninsular Gujarat where, as I noted, the records are silent about the prevalence of female infanticide among the non-Jadeja Rajput clans, leading me to surmise that given their more comfortable financial position and less expensive cross-cousin marriage, they probably resorted to less extensive female infanticide than did the top-ranking Jadejas. The Rajput clans of Benares region and elsewhere in the NWP had to face the heavy revenue demands of the British since the NWP was under the direct rule of the colonial rulers. Their lands came up for auction sale unless the revenue fixed at the time of Duncan's settlement (1795) was paid. In a fixed and frozen hierarchical system, the Rajput lineages in the Benares region found it difficult to pay the revenue exactions of the British.

As Cohn has noted, during the nineteenth century, the Rajputs in the Benares region lost about 40 per cent of their lands mostly to urban commercial interests owing to their inability to meet the heavy revenue demands of the colonial state. They, however, retained their dominant position in most parganas of the region by resorting to a variety of stratagems, which included preventing the bidding of their estates, not cooperating with auction purchaser, engaging in a running battle with him, and so on. One of the strategies used by the Rajputs of the region to prevent further erosion of their dominance was dowry avoidance through female infanticide (Cohn 1987: 183). This then seemed to explain the extensive female infanticide at different levels of the Rajput hypergamous hierarchy in the Benares region of the NWP.

The historical data I collected also indicated that in western India (Gujarat) as well as north India, the hypergamous castes had a shortage of marriageable females at the lower levels of the hypergamous hierarchy owing to the upward movement of women. At the top levels of the hierarchy, there was polygyny. In Gujarat, the lower status Kolis, who were numerous and worked as agricultural labourers, provided wives to the lower-status Rajputs and Kanbis who needed wives.The records refer to 'traffic in Koli girls' owing to a shortage of marriageable women among Rajputs and Kanbis (MSS 1849). The lower-status Kanbis also resorted to exchange marriages (described in the records as *Satoo* and *Trekaroo* unions) to solve the problem of shortage of marriageable women within their caste (MSS 1857).

In north India, British officials reported that there were established brokers who procured women from non-Rajput castes for Rajputs who needed wives.To procure women for marriage, the lower-status Rajputs had to pay bride-price and a brokerage fee (*Selection from the Records of Government [SRG]* 1868: 14–15). The Jats resorted to *Mol Lana* (marriage by paying bride-price) and *Bhaga Lana* (marriage by elopement) to solve the problem of shortage of marriageable women (Pradhan,1974). As regards polygyny, most ruling families in Kathiawad and north India were polygynous (*SRBG* 1837: 534). For the Patidars, British officials noted that the lower-status Kanbis were prepared to marry their daughters to the Patidars even if the latter already had several wives (MSS 1857).

Shah encouraged me to look at my data from the viewpoint of their interconnections—that is, female infanticide, hypergamy, status hierarchy, the shortage of women, which drove the lower-level Kanbis, Rajputs and Jats to break the endogamous rule and procure women from outside their caste; polygyny at the higher-status levels were all interconnected. This way of perceiving the data did seem to have an advantage over historians' writings on female infanticide, which were mainly descriptive and highlighted British efforts to suppress female infanticide (see Panigrahi 1972; Das 1957, 1959). I also remember Shah suggesting that while looking at the interconnections, I should not push the 'systemic framework' too far. In Britain, Radcliffe-Brown tried to promote the scientific study of society by suggesting that the methods of enquiry applicable in the natural sciences could also be applied to social anthropology, therefore the researcher should study society in a systemic framework. A whole generation of British social anthropologists and some Indian sociologists who were trained under Radcliffe-Brown followed his approach in some of their writings. However, by the mid-seventies, when I was doing my doctoral research, the enthusiasm for regarding sociology/social anthropology as one of the natural sciences with similar methods of enquiry had waned.

Tʜᴇ Mᴏᴅᴇ ᴏғ Pʀᴏᴅᴜᴄᴛɪᴏɴ Mᴏᴅᴇʟ

An important study which uses the mode of production framework to explain female infanticide, female neglect, and sex ratios in north and south India is by Barbara D. Miller in her work titled, *The Endangered Sex*. The study is based mainly on census data (1961 census) and ethnographic studies by anthropologists of rural India. The author notes fairly early in her work that though she is not oriented towards classical Marxism, she does 'lean on some of its broad ideas' (Miller 1984: 26). I shall first present Miller's framework and later comment on it in some detail.

The major thrust of Miller's hypothesis is that generally in north India, especially north-west, females are unwanted because of the predominant wheat cultivation, which requires male labour to work the plough. This had adverse implications for female survival in the north. By contrast in south India, the females had better chances of survival from childhood to adulthood as they were required for agricultural operations connected with cultivation of paddy such as weeding, transplantation, harvesting, etc. Thus, Miller argues that the population dynamics as reflected in juvenile sex ratios (JSR) in north and south India had a lot to do with female labour participation (FLP) and the mode of agricultural production in the two regions. Into this dichotomous perception of juvenile sex ratios in north and south India, she introduces two important parameters: ownership of property or the means of production, which in rural India is obviously land, and marriage costs. These parameters are then viewed in relation to FLP.

An explanation of what is meant by high, medium and low JSR is in order before further discussion of Miller's hypothesis. A high JSR connotes a low proportion of females in the juvenile population; a medium JSR means more or less balanced sex ratios, and a low JSR means a higher proportion of females in the juvenile population.

Drawing inferences from her data, Miller concludes that among northern propertied castes the JSRs are high, the FLP is low, and marriage costs in the form of dowry and other payments by the bride's side are high. The northern unpropertied castes have high FLP and low marriage costs. The JSR among the northern unpropertied is however medium. It is the southern propertied groups which present some problems for Miller's model. While her dichotomous model would require a high FLP, low marriage costs followed by low JSRs, what she actually finds is that while JSRs are indeed low, there is a mixed pattern in regard to FLP and marriage costs. She notes that the FLP as well as marriage costs are low, medium, or high among southern propertied groups. Some parts of Kerala have high FLP; others have low FLP. The Nangudi Vellala are described as 'a very intriguing case'. Among them, except for the cost of the marriage feast which was shared by both the bride's and the groom's side, all other wedding expenses, including dowry, was borne by the family of the bride. The Okkaliga peasants of Rampura do not allow their women to work in the fields and 'give dowry like gifts' at the time of a daughter's marriage; other south Indian propertied castes not only allow their women to work in the fields, but there is reciprocity from the groom's side in sharing of marriage costs. The southern unpropertied have high FLP, low marriage costs, and low to medium JSRs. Miller presents the following model

Category	Female labour participation	Marriage costs	Juvenile sex ratio
Northern propertied	Low	High	High
Southern propertied	Low-Medium-High	Low-Medium-High	Low
Northern unpropertied	High	Low	Medium
Southern unpropertied	High	Low	Low, Medium

Miller says that in terms of culture, north India is Brahminical and south India is Dravidian or Agamic. However, northern Brahminism 'most solidly established among the upper social strata of northern India' is in the 'process of spreading' to the south. This explains why increasingly females are being removed from active participation in agricultural production and also the greater emphasis on 'dowry over reciprocity or bridewealth' (Miller 159).

Miller's framework is important and deserves serious attention from scholars. However, in the past or even today, south India was never free from female infanticide as Miller's dichotomous model seems to suggest. Rivers, in his study, refers to female infanticide among the Todas and associates it with polyandry. Edgar Thurston's *Ethnographic Notes on Southern India* (1989: 503–4) refers to female infanticide among the Kallars even in the nineteenth century. Moreover, enquiries in the mid-1980s in Usilampatti taluk (Madurai district), where the Kallar constitute 80 per cent of the population, showed that out of 600 Kallar female babies born in government hospitals, as many as 570 'vanished with their mothers'. According to hospital sources, nearly 80 per cent of the 'vanishing babies were killed'. Often old women known to the family were entrusted with the job of killing the female infant. Generally, the first child, even if female, was not killed. Parents were afraid that they might be left without any offspring if they killed the first child. Subsequently, born females were killed (*India Today* 15 June 1986). Significantly, Krishnaswamy states that in addition to the dowry problem, female infanticide among the Kallars should be understood in terms of their cultural traits and past history. The Kallars were warriors in the Chola army and were known for their 'ferocity' and 'turbulent nature' (Krishnaswamy 1984: 297–302).

Furthermore, Miller has co-authored a paper (1992) which discusses female infanticide among the Gounders of North Arcot, Amdedkar district. The study was carried out for four years beginning in September 1986. In a study of population of 13,000, there were 773 recorded births involving 759 live births, of which 378 were male and 381 female. Among the live births, 56 infants died in a period of two and a half years (1 April 1987 to 30 September 1989); of the 56 infant deaths, 23 were male and 33 female. Out of the 33 female infant deaths, 19 were 'confirmed infanticides'. As many as 17 of the 19 confirmed cases of female infanticide were among the Gounders. The milk of a plant locally known as 'Erukkanbal' served as poison for killing the infants. Significantly, out of the twelve villages selected for study, female infanticide took place in the six villages where the Gounders were predominant. The other six villages are described as non-infanticide villages by the authors of the study.

The study also reveals that in the six villages where all cases of female infanticide occurred, the incidence of consanguineous marriage was much higher compared with the other six villages which did not have female infanticide. Uncle-niece marriages accounted for 6 per cent of all marriages in the non-infanticide villages, while such marriages accounted for 11.2 per cent in the six villages which practised female infanticide. Regarding the economic position of the Gounders, the study states

> They are the upper social stratum in their villages. In fact Gounders own a significant portion of the land in North and South Arcot districts. To assert that relatively speaking the Gounders are well off does not mean that they do not feel economic pressures when it comes to raising daughters.
>
> (George et al. 1992: 1153–55)

The study notes that female infanticide has been practised in the area for the past several generations and possibly the practice has 'antecedents far back in time'. The authors of the study also stress that a historical reconstruction is necessary before firm conclusions can be arrived at.

These cases of female infanticide in rural Tamil Nadu suggest that south India was not free from the practice and a north-south dichotomy needs to be modified. According to another study based on Primary Health Centres statistics in Tamil Nadu, female infanticide is rampant in the districts of Madurai, Salem and Dharmapuri (Chunkath and Athreya 1997). It seems to me that the subjugation of women by dominant castes in rural south India, their cultural traits, level of sanskritisation, and how these communities maintained their dominance—all these require investigation for the past and present.

A major problem with Miller's framework is the division of castes in north and south India into 'propertied' and 'unpropertied'. The fact that in the north (and west) the 'propertied' castes had within them an elaborate gradation based on a variety of criteria does not receive adequate attention from her. Very briefly, she notes that for purposes of analysis, she has divided the rural population into two broad classes: the propertied and the unpropertied and this 'introduces a certain amount of error, for such a translation tends to idealize a caste as a homogeneous class in relation to property, something which no caste ever is' (Miller 1984).

Both in Gujarat and north India, castes which practised female infanticide had at the higher levels of the status hierarchy groups, which owned considerable property and were generally sanskritised; they paid dowry for their daughters and received dowry for their sons, and for status reasons did not allow their women to work in the fields. At the lower levels of the hierarchy among castes such as Rajput, Lewa Patidar-Kanbi, Ahir and Gujar, there was, in most cases, payment of bride-price owing to a shortage of marriageable girls. As Pocock's data indicates, the lower-status Kanbi women certainly worked in the fields. Whether the poor Rajput, Ahir, Gujar and Jat women worked in the fields depended on pressing economic need. If economic need was not pressing, the plebian levels in these castes may try to get included with their propertied castemen and not send their women to the fields for 'status' reasons. Out of the twenty-six cases based on ethnographic studies cited by Miller for the north, there are four cases where the participation of women in agricultural operations is high even among those designated as 'propertied.' by Miller. In two of these cases of high FLP for the north (Bunkipur and Sujarupa in Udaipur district), Rajput women worked in the fields. These two cases in a caste known to practise female infanticide brings into sharp focus the problems presented by Miller's analysis. One cannot imagine that the Rajputs of high status, such as, the former princes and talukdars, would send their women to the fields for work connected with agricultural operations. However, poor Rajput households had to send their women to the fields if there was pressing economic need. Needless to say, the poor included the propertied owning some land, say two to five acres.

The categorisation which forms part of Miller's mode of production framework of the north as Brahminical and the south as Dravidian or Agamic, with Brahminical culture spreading to the south is also problematic. In Gujarat, for example, which belongs basically to the north Indian cultural area, the Rajputs in the peninsular region had cross-cousin marriages. The high-status Lewa Patidars were sanskritised. They did not eat meat, and frowned upon practices, such as widow remarriage, payment of bride-price and exchange marriages. However, their fellow castemen of low status, namely, the Lewa Kanbis, consumed meat and, as noted above, resorted to payment of bride-price, widow remarriage, and exchange marriages to solve the problem of shortage of females at that level of the social hierarchy. These practices, considered low by the sanskritised Patidar, were sought to be given up by the Kanbis when the latter acquired some wealth and tried to get included within the ranks of the Patidar. Again, as noted above, the lower-status Rajputs in Gujarat and in north India and the Jats in the north paid bride-price to procure women for marriage while those of higher status in these castes paid dowry.

Overall, among most of the castes, which practised female infanticide in north and west India, there was a sanskritised level, which was usually propertied and constituted the upper strata. These castes also had a 'propertied' (owning small amounts of land) or landless lower strata, who had customs, which were disapproved or frowned upon by the sanskritised upper sections. Besides different levels of sanskritisation within the same caste, which certainly had implications for FLP and marriage payments, I have emphasised the 'ethos' and specificity of castes which practised female infanticide in rural north and west India (Vishwanath 2000). It is true that Miller's framework, based on census data and ethnographic studies, is for the post-independence period, while my work, based on historical data, is for the colonial period. However, we should consider the fact that both before and after independence, the castes known to practise female infanticide, such as, Lewa Patidars and Kanbis, Rajputs, Jats, Ahirs and Gujars had an elaborate status hierarchy with both high status and plebian ends. Therefore, categorisation, such as, 'propertied' and 'unpropertied' castes, is bound to be misleading. Miller's model, drawing inspiration from classical Marxism, is a two-class one in terms of the haves and the have-nots.

Moreover, right till the time caste formed part of census enumeration (1931), the decennial census repeatedly refers to castes, such as, Rajput, Jat, Patidar, Ahir, Gujar, as having a low proportion of females and as having 'a tradition' of female infanticide. The scope of the 1941 census was limited owing to the war. Even though caste enumeration stopped after independence, Miller's analyses of the 1961 census shows that certain regions in the north, especially the north-west, had high sex ratios. Hence, as Miller argues, there was a continuity since colonial times in the north-west as far as female infanticide and neglect is concerned (Miller 1984: 49–67).

Finally, Miller notes from the 1961 census that though the sex ratios in Kerala are 'very feminine' and that among landless labourers the female workers outnumber males in many districts, yet the FLP in districts in Kerala is low. This she finds is 'especially puzzling'. She further notes that Kerala 'should not be in the predominantly northern category of low FLP'. Male unemployment in Kerala which is 'the highest for any state in India' also receives comment. While male labour participation (MLP) in parts of India is above 80 per cent, it is below 80 per cent in all districts in Kerala except Cannanore and Palghat. The MLP in Alleppey is a low 70 per cent.

An important reason for the high male and female unemployment of farm labourers in the Kuttanad region and some other areas in Kerala was the militancy of the communist-led unions of agricultural workers. Unwilling to meet the ever growing demands of the militant unions, the employer farmers gave up the labour-intensive paddy cultivation and switched to the less labour-intensive garden cultivation. Miller, of course, does not comment on the unionisation of agricultural workers and its impact on FLP/MLP and pattern of cultivation in Kerala. However, I have drawn attention to it because it underlines the complex factors which govern farm employment.[3]

The Demographic Perspective

This perspective attempts to correlate female infanticide with caste, class and fertility. It is put forward by Alice Clark (1983). The castes chosen for study are the Lewa Patidar-Kanbis and the Kolis of rural central Gujarat during the nineteenth century. Clark bases her analysis on nineteenth-century records, settlement reports and census data. Though the area and castes selected are specific, the study has wider implications as I will show.

Clark discusses socio-economic differentials with reference to demographic trends among the Lewa Patidar-Kanbis and Kolis in three Lewa-Patidar-dominated taluks: Nadiad, Anand and Borsad. She notes that between the 1820s and 1890s the population of Lewa Patidar-Kanbis declined from 31 per cent of the population to 22 per cent. By contrast, during the same period, the population of Kolis grew from 22 to 34 per cent. Figures for Petlad taluk in Charotar are cited to show that the Kolis had many more children per 100 adult women than 'either the Kanbis or the population average'. Clark points out that the Lewa Patidar-Kanbis, who were enterprising farmers 'efficiently managed' their resources by limiting their female children through female infanticide and neglect. The 'efficient management' of resources meant dowry avoidance by killing female children. On the other hand, the lower-status Kolis, most of whom were poor and worked as agricultural labourers in the fields of the Patidar, did not try to control or restrict the number of their female children through female infanticide and/or neglect.

These tendencies of the Lewa Patidars and Kolis respectively, Clark argues, got reflected in the size of the population in each group towards the close of the nineteenth century. She further argues that the British helped the Patidar in efficient management of their resources by 'deliberately feigning blindness' towards female infanticide and neglect of female children. She states

> While they (the British) did not fully understand the economic logic of hypergamy (evident by their anxiety about it) they favoured its maintenance nevertheless as it played a part in efficiently managing the agrarian system by assisting Patidar family groups in consolidating their hold on the land. Thus partly unwittingly and partly by feigning blindness, British administration ultimately supported the continuation of female infanticide and female child neglect.
>
> (Clark 1983: 18)

A problem with most studies which correlate socio-economic differentials and fertility is that they are not consistent in the use of the criteria for defining caste, class, or fertility. It is frequently generalised that while the propertied tend to restrict their children, the unpropertied are more fertile. Since Clark's study is specific in terms of its time frame, castes, and area chosen, it certainly has its advantages. Even though there were Kanbis who did not own land under the priviledged Patidari tenure in the Patidar-dominated villages and were either landowners or tenants of the Patidar (there were also poor Kanbis), these differentials would not vitiate the conclusions because what Clark is looking at are broad demographic trends in three Charotar taluks where most Patidars owned land under the Patidari tenure. Moreover, as noted, Clark's analysis and her overall framework have implications beyond rural central Gujarat, as Patidars were not the only caste trying to maintain their dominance through female infanticide and female child neglect. Thus, the Jadejas in peninsular Gujarat and the Rajput clans in north India were also avoiding expensive daughters' weddings involving dowry and trying to maintain their dominance in their respective regions and their position in the Rajput hierarchy through female infanticide. The same is true of some other castes such as Bedi Khutris, Jats, Ahirs, Gujars, etc.

There are mainly two problems with Clark's framework. The first is her stress on the economic logic of female infanticide among the Patidars, who, she says, 'efficiently managed' their resources through female infanticide, and this was reflected in the population trends between the Patidars and the Kolis. Second, she asserts that the British assisted the Patidars in the management of their agrarian resources by 'feigning blindness towards female infanticide'.

As I have indicated, female infanticide and deliberate neglect of juvenile females should be viewed in relation to the structural position in the status hierarchy of the hypergamous group, its ethos, maintenance of dominance (or resources as Clark says), history, and culture. In fact there is near unanimity in the view that culture plays an important part in the killing and neglect of and discrimination against female children. For example, Rajput pride in their history and culture, which made their hierarchy rigid and which certainly had implications for female infanticide, was assimilated in a variety of ways. These included: tales of heroism and bravery, such as the heroic deeds on the battlefield of Maharana Pratap or Prithvi Raj Chauhan, the heroes in the epics (the Ramayana and Mahabharata), and the geneological records maintained by their *barot* (Shah and Shroff 1959).

Historical factors were no less important. The Jadejas' top position among Gujarati Rajputs got frozen owing to the freezing of the political boundaries. But for this, there was at least the possibility of 'promotion' or 'demotion' in the hierarchy of competing Rajput clans in a fluid situation. In the case of Lewa Patidars, the recognition by the Marathas (Gaikwads) and then the British of the privileged Patidari tenure with its fixed revenues gave them (in addition to the other historical factors noted earlier) an elite position in their caste. Moreover, if the Muslim rulers had not curtailed the power and estates of the Rajputs in central Gujarat in the thirteenth century, the conditions for the emergence of Lewa Patidar dominance might not have existed.

I agree with Clark that management and control of resources was important. But it would be wrong to look at female infanticide and female neglect only from this angle. The control of resources, mainly land, through female infanticide enabled the Patidars, Rajputs, Jats, Khutris and Ahirs to maintain their dominance ('leadership position' as Clark rightly says) in their respective areas in west and north India. Though the basis of this dominance was mainly economic, its cultural content was no less important. The dominant Kshatriya groups tended to mediate their culture to the other castes in the area. Some British officials in the North Western Provinces commented that a few castes were trying to imitate the dominant castes by practising female infanticide (*SRG* 1879: 127–28).

Regarding Clark's perception that the British encouraged the Patidar to efficiently manage their resources by 'feigning blindness' towards continuation of female infanticide/neglect, the records I consulted suggest that only a section of the British establishment played blind, and it seems to me that this kind of game was possible because of the social structure of the Lewa Patidar-Kanbis. As I noted, for the Gujarat region, while the topmost rung of the hypergamous hierarchy among Rajputs practised very extensive, almost wholesale, female infanticide, the elite Patidar did not do so. This was due to their relatively open hierarchy and the emergence of the new Patidars. Moreover, in their interviews with British officials, the Jadejas were generally open about admitting the prevalence of female infanticide and even justified it as a Rajput 'custom'. The Patidars by contrast kept female infanticide under wraps till the British discovered it in 1848.

The less extensive female infanticide and the tendency of the Patidars to keep the practice a secret, enabled some British officials to assert that the Patidars did not practise female infanticide. Another section of the British establishment was equally assertive in stating that the practice existed in the caste. From 1848 to 1872 and possibly beyond that date, there was a debate among British officials on whether or not the Lewa Patidars practised female infanticide. Some British officials took the position that since no reports were made to the police regarding female infanticide, the practice probably did not exist (MSS 1856: 45). At least one British official (H. R. Cooke) was of the view that since female infanticide cannot exist without detection in the British-administered districts, the practice did not prevail (*RBG*, Cooke 1875). Officials who firmly believed that the practice existed pointed to their interviews with the local people and also to the statistics showing a low proportion of female children among the Patidars. For example, in 1872, Ashburner, the then Revenue Commissioner ridiculed the view of his colleagues in the establishment that female infanticide did not exist because no reports were made to the police. He said that it was naive to expect parents who murdered their female child to report it to the police. He also pointed out that the neighbours and others in the village would obviously not want to incur the enmity of the dominant caste by reporting them to the police (MSS 1873: 151). British officials who denied the existence of female infanticide among the Lewa Patidars-Kanbis, achieved a decisive victory in 1872. For in that year, the Bombay governemnt decided to put the Female Infanticide Act in abeyance and not apply the operative rules of the Act to the Lewa Patidar-Kanbis (see Vishwanath 2000: 113).

CONCLUSION

The first two conceptual frameworks discussed in this paper have much in common with the development of British social anthropology. There is, however, an important difference in that while British social anthropology moved from evolutionary theories for the study of society based mainly on secondary sources to empirical studies of social structure based on fieldwork, I have used archival data to attempt a structural analysis of the castes which practised female infanticide in west and north India during the nineteenth century. Perhaps because of the influence of British social anthropology in India and also the background and training of the scholars who founded departments of sociology in India, the development of the discipline in some universities in India was not very different from that in Britain. Thus evolutionary perceptions of society and caste in India gave way to structural studies based on empirical fieldwork.

The concept of structure was implicit or explicit in regard to the other conceptual frameworks as well, namely evolutionary theory, the mode of production model, and the demographic perspective. Thus, when McLennan wrote about female infanticide in primitive societies, he was implicitly referring to their structure as reflected in rules relating to descent, inheritance, marriage, etc. The mode of production model and the demographic perspective are more explicitly structural in that the analysis centres round ownership of the means of production in rural India, access to it, and participation in farm employment. If all four conceptual approaches are implicitly or explicitly structural in terms of their analytical frame, then where does the difference lie? It seems to me that the difference lies in the way in which each researcher tries to understand female infanticide. Conceptual frameworks after all have their use in terms of helping in a better understanding of the subject being studied.

If structural analysis is discussed in greater detail it is because having worked on female infanticide for a number of years, I had detailed information on it. Though I have offered a critique of some other conceptual frameworks, I should like to state that in terms of their analytical frame, they are extremely useful. Diehard Marxists or structuralists (with the ascendancy of post-structuralism, the structuralists seem to be a vanishing species) may assert the superiority of one framework over the other but such claims are bound to take us away from the scientific approach.

Endnotes

1 By the time *Primitive Marriage* appeared (1864), considerable literature relating to female infanticide in India in the form of *Selections from the Records of Government* had already been published. For example, a volume of selections from the records of the Bombay government dealing briefly with the institutional ramifications of female infanticide and with the suppression of the practice in considerable detail titled: *Measures for the Suppression of Female Infanticide in the Province of Kattywar* was published in 1856. A few monographs by administrators and missionaries were also published before 1864. For example, John Wilson's account of the *History of the Suppression of Infanticide in Western India* was published in 1855. Charles Raikes, who tried to suppress female infanticide in the then North Western Provinces recorded his experiences in his work *Notes on the North Western Provinces* published in 1852. However, McLennan does not refer to these anywhere in his *Primitive Marriage.*

2 James Erskine, the Political Agent in Kathiawad, in his report to the Bombay Government dated 30 June 1837 provides information on the marriage preferences of the royal Rajput lineages in Kathiawad. The report shows that a neat one-to-one relationship between the size of the estate and the position in the hypergamous hierarchy did not apply to some of the royal Rajput lineages. For example, the estate of the Rana of Porbandar on coastal Kathiawad was less than quarter the size of the estate of the Maharaja of Bhavnagar; yet the Rana's lineage occupied the number two position after the Jadeja royal lineages in the Rajput hypergamous hierarchy in Gujarat.

3 The data shows that owing to the demands of the farm labour unions, the employer farmers found a solution by giving up the labour-intensive paddy cultivation and taking up coconut cultivation. The proportion of the area under rice to total cropped area for all Kerala declined from 33.16 per cent in 1960–61 to 29.84 per cent in 1970–71. During the same decade, the area under coconut increased in proportionate terms from 21.32 per cent in 1960–61 to 24.52 per cent in 1970–71 for all Kerala. See in this connection, Jeemol Unni, 'Changes in the Cropping Pattern in Kerala', *Economic and Political Weekly* 18, no. 39, September 1983.

References

Manuscript Sources (cited as MSS)

At the Bombay Secretariat Record Office.

General Department. 1873. Vol. 28.

Judicial Department. 1849. Vol. 15, no. 237.

Political Department. 1848. Vol. 4, 2014 and 2181.

Political Department. 1857. Vol. 119.

Reports

Bombay Gazetteer VIII, 1884.

Census of India, Reports. 1901, 1911, 1921 (Appendix VI). Punjab and United.

Moore, W. R. 1868. *Papers on the Subject of Mr W. R. Moore's Investigation and Report Regarding Female Infanticide in the Benares Division.* Calcutta: A. Dozey, Home Secretariat Press.

Provinces Census Reports, 1911, 1921.

Other Works

Brown, John Cave. 1857. *Indian Infanticide: Its Origin, Progress and Suppression.* London: W. H. Allen.

Chunkath, Sheela Rani and V. B. Athreya. 1997. Female Infanticide in Tamil Nadu. *Economic and Political Weekly* 32(17).

Clark, Alice. 1983. Limitations on Female Life Chances in Rural Central Gujarat. *The Indian Economic and Social History Review* 20(1).

Cohn, B. S. 1987. Structural Change in Indian Rural Society, 1596–1885. In *An Anthropologist among the Historians and Other Essays.* Delhi: Oxford University Press.

Das, M. N. 1957. Movement to Suppress the Custom of Female Infanticide in Punjab and Kashmir. *Man in India* 36(4).

————. 1959. *Studies in Economic and Social Development of Modern India, 1848–1856.* Calcutta: Firma K. L. Mukhopadhyay.

Evans-Pritchard, E. E. 1940. *The Nuer.* Oxford: Clarendon Press.

————. 1951. *Social Anthropology.* London: Cohen & West.

————. 1965. *The Position of Women in Primitive Societies and Other Essays in Social Anthropology.* New York: The Free Press.

————. 1981. *A History of Anthropological Thought.* London: Faber and Faber.

Female Infanticide in Western and Central India. 1844. *Calcutta Review* 1(2): 282.

George, Sabu, Rajaratnam Abel, and B. D. Miller. 1992. Female Infanticide in Rural South India. *Economic and Political Weekly* 28(22).

Ghurye, G. S. 1963. *Anthropo-Sociological Papers.* Bombay: Popular Prakashan.

126 L. S. VISHWANATH

Hitchcock, John T. 1959. The Idea of the Martial Rajput. In *Traditional India: Structure and Change*, ed. Milton Singer. Philadelphia: American Folklore Society.

Karve, Irawati. 1965. *Kinship Organisation in India*. Bombay: Asia Publishing House.

Krishnaswamy, S. 1984. A Note on Female Infanticide: An Anthropological Inquiry. *The Indian Journal of Social Work* 45(3): 297–302.

Maine, Henry Sumner. 1861. *Ancient Law*. London: John Murray, p. 142.

————. 1874. Lectures on the 'Early History of Institutions', deliverd at London.

McLennan, John F. 1970. *Primitive Marriage*. Reprint. Chicago: University of Chicago Press.

Miller, Barbara D. 1984. *The Endangered Sex: Neglect of Female Children in Rural North India*. Ithaca: Cornell University Press.

Naik, T. B. 1956. *The Bhils*. Delhi: Bhartiya Adimjati Sevak Sangh.

Panigrahi, Lalita.1972. *British Social Policy and Female Infanticide in India*. Delhi: Munshiram Manoharlal.

Pradhan, M. C. 1974. *Political System of the Jats of Northern India*.Delhi: Oxford University Press.

Pocock, D. F. 1957. Inclusion and Exclusion: A Process in the Caste System of Gujarat. *South Western Journal of Anthropology* 13(1).

————. 1971. *Kanbi and Patidar: A Study of the Patidar Community of Gujarat*. London: Oxford University Press.

Radcliffe-Brown, A. R. 1952. *Structure and Function in Primitive Society*. London: Cohen & West.

Raikes, Charles. 1852. *Notes on the North-Western Provinces of India*. London: G. Barclley.

Risley, Herbert. 1969. *The People of India*. 2nd ed. Delhi: Oriental Books Reprint Corporation.

Rivers, W. H. R. 1986. *The Todas*. Reprint. Jaipur: Rawat Publications.

Selections from the Records of the Bombay Government (*SRBG*). 1856. Measures Adopted for the Suppression of Female Infanticide in the Province of Kattywar. Bombay: Education Society's Press.

————. 1873. Repression of Female Infanticide in the Bombay Presidency by H. R. Cooke. No. 47 (New Series). Bombay: Govt. Central Press.

Selections from the Records of Government (*SRG*). 1879. Female Infanticide. Vol. V (I & II). Allahabad: North West Province and Oudh Govt. Press.

Shah, A. M. 2002. *Exploring India's Rural Past: A Gujarat Village in the Early Nineteenth Century*. Delhi: Oxford University Press.

————. 1982. Division and Hierarchy: An Overview of Caste in Gujarat. *Contributions to Indian Sociology* (N.S.) 16(1).

————., and R. G. Shroff. 1959. The Vahivancha Barots of Gujarat: A Caste of Genealogists and Mythographers. In *Traditional India: Structure and Change*, ed. Milton Singer. Philadelphia: American Folklore Society.

Srinivas, M. N. 1952. *Religion and Society among the Coorgs of South India.* Oxford: Clarendon Press.

————. 1966. *Social Change in Modern India.* Berkeley: University of California Press.

Steed, Gitel P. 1955. Notes on an Approach to a Study of Personality Formation in a Hindu Village in Gujarat. In *Village India*, ed. Mckim Marriott. Chicago: University of Chicago Press.

Thurston, Edgar. 1989. *Ethnographic Notes on Southern India.* Reprint. New Delhi: Asian Educational Services.

Tod, James. 1971. *Annals and Antiquities of Rajasthan.* Reprint. New Delhi: K. N. N. Publishers.

Veen, Klass W. Van der. 1972. *I Give Thee My Daughter.* Assen: Gorcum.

Vishwanath, L. S. 1973. Female Infanticide and the Lewa Kanbis of Gujarat in the Nineteenth Century. *The Indian Economic and Social History Review* 10(4).

————. 1976. Changes in Kinship and Society in Two Selected Areas in India: A Study Based on Female Infanticide Records During the Nineteenth Century. Unpublished PhD dissertation, Department of Sociology. University of Delhi.

————. 1986. Role of Peasant Organizations and Voluntary Agencies in Rural Development. In *The Process and Effects of Modernization in Indian Rural Communities,* ed. S. S. Thekkamalai. Tanjore: Tamil University Press.

————. 1996. Female Infanticide and the Position of Women in India. In *Social Structure and Change,* ed. A. M. Shah, B. S. Baviskar, and E. A. Ramaswamy. Vol. 2. Delhi: Sage Publications.

————. 1998. Efforts of the Colonial State to Suppress Female Infanticide: Use of Sacred Texts, Generation of Knowledge. *Economic and Political Weekly* 33(19), May 9–15.

————. 2000. *Female Infanticide and Social Structure: A Socio-Historical Study in Western and Northern India.* Delhi: Hindustan Publishing Corporation.

Wilson, John. 1855. *History of Suppression of Infanticide in Western India.* London: Smith Taylor and Company.

Part II
Sociology of Religion
Belief, Perceptions and Practices

Part II

Sociology of Religion

Belief, Perceptions and Practices

4

Popular Perceptions of the Role of Catholic Priests

Alphonsus D'Souza

INTRODUCTION

Christians in India belong to several churches, denominations and sects. From the sociological perspective, it is possible to make a clear distinction between them. (Eshleman 1987: 404–7; D'Souza 1993: 15–16). A church is an institutionalised organisation of people who share common beliefs and practices, with stable membership and a formal structure with trained religious and other officials. It is called an ecclesia if it represents the state religion and includes all or most members of society. A church is called a denomination if it is not officially linked to the state. A sect is a relatively small group that has broken away from a parent church, often with a call to reform. It is obvious that in India there is no Christian church associated with the state. Hence, from the sociological point of view, there are only Christian 'denominations', not 'churches' in India. However, in this essay we shall adopt the term 'church', as it is in common usage among the Christians in India to refer to their institutionalised organisations. According to Barrett (1982: 377–79), in 1982, Indian Christians belonged to more than 150 denominations and sects, among which the Catholic Church was the largest, as it accounted for 46.43 per cent of the Indian Christians.

The Catholic Church is made up of the Christians who accept the Pope as their supreme religious head (McBrien 1981: 567).

There are two dimensions in the organisation of the Catholic Church. The first is the territorial organisation, and the second is the hierarchical organisation. The supreme head of the Catholic Church is the Pope. He has religious authority over all the Catholics in the world. The worldwide Catholic Church is divided into territorial units called dioceses. A diocese is headed by a bishop, who is appointed by the Pope and has religious authority over the Catholics living within his diocese. A diocese is further divided into territorial units called parishes.

A parish is headed by the parish priest, who is appointed by the bishop. The hierarchical organisation of the Catholic Church is based on the classification of the members of the church into two categories, namely, the clergy or the priests on the one hand, and the laity or the ordinary believers on the other.

The nature and role of a Catholic priest is fairly well recognised by tradition and is defined by Canon Law, as the law of the Church is called (*Code of Canon Law* 1983). But there are differences of opinion regarding the precise substance of the role of a Catholic priest and variations in actual performance of the priest's role. This essay deals with the perceptions of the laity regarding the nature of the role of the Catholic priest on the basis of empirical data obtained in the course of a larger study of the religious life of Catholics in the diocese of Mangalore. The larger study, carried out in 1993, covered a wide range of questions and the report was finalised in 1994 (D'Souza 1994). The present essay has a limited scope as it examines in greater detail only a few questions relating to the role of the Catholic priests among the Catholics of Mangalore. The first part of the essay looks at the role of the priest as recognised by tradition and defined by Canon Law, and the second part examines the perceptions of that role by the people.

NATURE AND ROLE OF PRIESTHOOD IN THE CATHOLIC CHURCH

Catholic theologians generally assert that the nature of the priesthood in the Catholic Church cannot be explained in terms of any model taken from the history of religions because of the special features of Catholic priesthood (Palmer 1967). One such feature is its doctrinal basis or basis in the Catholic belief system (*Catechism of the Catholic Church* 1994: 296–97). The official Catholic doctrine is that every Catholic, male or female, has a priestly character because he or she has a direct access to God and therefore does not need an intermediary in his/her approach to God. In Catholic doctrine this is known as the *common priesthood* of the faithful. But Catholic doctrine also asserts that in addition to the common priesthood, there is an *official priesthood* exercised by those who have received the Sacred Orders, that is, those who are ordained or commissioned to function as official priests. Official priesthood is known as *ministerial priesthood* because it is *meant to* minister to, that is, be of service to the faithful who already possess the common priesthood. Only those who are ordained to function as official priests constitute the clergy, while the other Catholic faithful are collectively called the laity. In this essay we shall deal only with *official* or *ministerial* priesthood, and use the word *priesthood* to refer to it, and the word *priest* to those who exercise it.

Catholic doctrine states that priesthood is hierarchical because it has three levels, namely, the episcopate, presbyterate, and the diaconate (Catechism 1994: 297). Consequently there are three ranks among the clergy: (i) bishops, (ii) presbyters, and (iii) deacons. According to Catholic doctrine, a bishop has the fullness of priesthood, while presbyters and deacons depend on the bishop for the exercise of their priestly functions. In this essay, in keeping with popular usage, the terms *priest* and *priesthood* stand for presbyter and presbyterate respectively. It means that the roles of deacons and bishops are not directly covered by the discussion that follows. In the hierarchical structure of the priesthood, the bishop occupies the most important position. As already noted, the bishop is appointed by the Pope, the supreme religious head of the Catholic Church, and placed by the Pope as the head of a diocese. It is the bishop who ordains or commissions the priests.

Priesthood in the Catholic Church is neither hereditary nor a privilege reserved to a chosen few families. It is not even a profession or occupation that a person takes up in order to earn his livelihood. In fact, it is a basic Catholic belief that a person becomes a priest because of a vocation or divine call. Catholic doctrine accepts the possibility that a vocation to the priesthood may be occasionally made known to the individual concerned in a special and dramatic way. But ordinarily a vocation to the priesthood is manifested in the inclinations of the individual, which come from temperament, family background, education and other circumstances of life.

Though an individual becomes a priest in response to personal vocation, he must fulfil certain conditions and requirements. Only a male can become a priest. He must also have normal physical and mental health. He must have a good reputation and moral probity. Also, he must be accepted by a bishop as a candidate for the priesthood and undergo a period of training that lasts, according to Canon Law, at least six years. While a candidate undergoes training, his vocation is 'tested' in the sense that his suitability for the priesthood is continuously assessed. One cannot survive the long and rigorous training without a genuine vocation. Hence the bishop, on the basis of information provided to him by those in charge of the training, may conclude that a particular candidate has no vocation to the priesthood and may ask him to give up his plans for the priesthood. It is also possible that the candidate himself realises that he has no genuine vocation and discontinues his training for the priesthood.

When a candidate has successfully completed his training, he is ordained a priest by the bishop of his diocese. It is essential that a Catholic priest belongs to a particular diocese or an equivalent organisation, because no priest can perform his priestly functions without receiving a commission from a bishop. An important requirement for ordination to the priesthood in the Catholic Church in most parts of the world is the vow of celibacy made by a candidate.

As already noted, official priesthood exists only in the service of the common priesthood. This implies that priesthood necessarily has a social dimension. It is a Catholic belief that an individual receives the divine call or vocation to the priesthood for the sake of the community and that his priestly life and activity must be in the service of the community. Consequently, the role that a priest is called upon to play is necessarily social. Further, this role is played within the context of the parish or the territorial unit of a diocese over which he is placed by the bishop and in service of the community of the Catholics who live within the parish.

According to Catholic doctrine, a priest has a triple role, namely that of a sanctifier, teacher and ruler, representing respectively the cultic or ritualistic, preaching, and administrative aspects of priesthood (*Catechism* 1994: 296–97). It is beyond the scope of this essay to examine the manner in which the acceptance of the triple role of the Catholic priest evolved over the centuries. What is of direct concern here is the substance and practice of this triple role as understood at present.

It is easy to understand the cultic or ritualistic or sanctifying aspect of the priestly role, because it is directly related to rituals of all types and worship in all its forms. In the case of a Catholic priest, his cultic role includes the performance of a great variety of religious rituals. Catholicism has a set of elaborately institutionalised rituals called the Sacraments. There are seven Sacraments, out of which two are of major significance as they can be performed only by a priest. These are the Eucharist and Penance. The Eucharist is an elaborate ritual and a Catholic is expected to participate in it at least on Sundays. In popular parlance it is called the Mass, and the priest's role in it is described as 'saying Mass'. It is usual for a priest to 'say Mass' every day. Penance is the ritual in which a Catholic confesses his sins to a priest. In popular language it is called 'Confession', and the priest's role is to 'hear Confessions'. The cultic function of a Catholic priest includes the performance of many other rituals. But we need not examine them here.

The function of a Catholic priest as ruler or administrator is derived from the position he holds in the hierarchical structure of the church. As already noted, a priest is usually placed at the head of a parish. According to present understanding, a priest is required to administer the properties and other financial assets of the parish entrusted to his care, usually under the direction of the bishop and in accordance with the provisions of Canon Law. In practical terms, the administrative function also includes the day-to-day management of schools and colleges wherever they exist. But more importantly, the priest is the leader of the parish community, the organiser of its activity, and ultimately the focal point of its unity. As a ruler or administrator, a priest is invested not merely with a human authority based on knowledge and experience but also with a religious or spiritual authority coming from his ordination to the priesthood. His vow of celibacy and the absence of a family depending on him add to his dignity as an administrator, because he is seen as a person without family interests. Therefore, even as an administrator of material goods and property, a priest has a special spiritual or religious character.

The prophetic aspect of the role of a Catholic priest is a complex one. In the Catholic tradition, a prophet is basically one who 'speaks on behalf of God' (McBrien 1981: 1254). He claims to bear a message from God and to speak on behalf of God. As the envoy or messenger of God, he performs various functions at different levels. At the most basic level, he professes to communicate to the people or preach the word of God that he has received to elucidate it to the people in the fashion of a teacher and guide. At another level, his very lifestyle assumes a witness-value in the sense that he is expected to practise what he preaches, or rather, preaches in deed as well as in word. At a different level, a prophet is also a religious and social critic, and his preaching becomes social criticism, especially against all forms of social evils, including social injustice. At a still different level, a prophet is also a social activist in the sense that he leads or initiates or at least supports activities against various types of social evils. Thus the prophetic role of a priest can be understood as encompassing social criticism and social activism and such things as preaching against social evils.

The teaching or preaching dimension of the prophetic aspect of the Catholic priest's role has been greatly institutionalised. In fact, at the time of priestly ordination, he is commissioned by the bishop to preach the word of God. But the dimension of prophetic function as a social critic cannot be easily institutionalised. Therefore, it can be a source of role conflicts among the priests and also tensions between the priests and the bishops or other church authorities. Sometimes these tensions have resulted in the passing of strictures by the church authorities on the priests, and at times even a prohibition from performing cultic functions, on the so called 'activist priests' in some parts of the world, particularly in the Latin American countries where social criticism first found articulation in the so-called Liberation Theology and its praxis. In particular, active participation in politics by priests has attracted sanctions from the church authorities, and the priests who contested and won elective offices, as an expression of their political rights and commitment to social activism, have been asked either to give up their offices or to leave the priesthood. The reason advanced in such cases is that activities of this type do not really belong to the priestly role. Priests are forbidden to participate in active politics because politics is said to be a purely secular activity that is outside the domain of priestly functions.

Though a distinction between the cultic, prophetic and administrative aspects of priesthood can definitely serve heuristic purposes, the three aspects do not exhaust the totality of the multiple roles of a Catholic priest. In addition to activities that may be clearly identified as belonging to one of the three aspects, there are several others that combine two or even all the three aspects. But we do not need to examine them in detail here.

It is important to remember that till about 1960 the popular perception of the priestly role was largely confined to his cultic or ritualistic and administrative functions, because social criticism, social activism and active participation in politics were considered alien to the life of a priest. This relatively narrow view finds expression even today when people say that the priests should be 'men of God' and holy and that they should confine themselves to strictly ritualistic and religious functions. But such a view has been gradually changing. Processes of secularisation and modernisation have initiated a change to include social criticism and social activism within the ambit of the priestly role. Within the Catholic church itself, fresh thinking on the nature and role of priests began in the 1960s, especially after the Second Vatican Council, a meeting of all the Catholic bishops that took place between 1962 and 1965. Thus, a general change in the understanding of the priestly role has taken place all over the world during the last four decades among the Catholic clergy as well as the laity.

POPULAR PERCEPTIONS OF THE ROLE OF PRIESTS

On account of the multifaceted and multilayered nature of the role of a Catholic priest, it is not easy to conduct an empirical study on what a priest may do as an actualisation of his role. It is impossible to operationalise all the facets of the priestly role in order to find out the peoples' perceptions on the entire range of activities that a priest may undertake in fulfilment of his vocation and ordination. A practical approach in this situation would be to select those activities that are actually undertaken by a Catholic priest in a definite area. The present study has adopted this approach and sought the opinion of the laity on three clusters of activities that are actually taken up by the priests in the Diocese of Mangalore.

As noted earlier, the question on activities proper to or that may be taken up by a Catholic priest was included in a longer questionnaire seeking information on the quality of religious life in the Diocese of Mangalore. This questionnaire was administered by trained interviewers to a sample of 1,069 lay persons selected by means of stratified random sampling technique from a population of about 250,000. The sample included 658 (61.55 per cent) males and 411 (38.45 per cent) females belonging to fourteen different parishes that were earlier identified as representative of the diocese as a whole on the basis of historical origins, cultural characteristics, and geographical distribution. Only 88 persons or 8.23 per cent of the sample were illiterate, others being literate, and many well educated. As many as 438 (40.97 per cent), 310 males and 128 females, held some office or other within the parish organisation. Thus, the sample was made up of people who were generally knowledgeable about church matters and familiar with the priests.

The question, which was addressed to this sample on the role of the priest, asked them to indicate the minimum level of the activities or functions proper to a priest, that is, activities and functions that were in conformity with his role in the church. The exact wording of the question was as follows:

'In your opinion, which of the following functions are proper to the priests?

    saying Mass
    hearing Confessions
    preaching
    teaching in schools or colleges
    organising welfare programmes

managing schools or colleges
taking up causes of social injustice
taking part in politics
any other'

It was explained to the respondents that this question sought their opinion regarding the minimum level of activities that a priest could take up. In other words, the respondents were told that if they gave a positive answer only to 'saying Mass' they would not think of a priest doing anything else. Similarly, if they gave a positive answer to 'preaching', they would automatically accept 'saying Mass' and 'hearing Confessions' as activities that were in conformity to the role of a Catholic priest

The answers of the 1,069 respondents are given in summary form in Table 4.1. A detailed classification of the respondents according to different age groups, along with their responses is given in Table 4.2. It is important to note that though the tables present statistics in terms of numbers and percentages, this information must be taken as indicative of trends rather than well-defined categories. This is because of the difficulty of operationalising all the facets of the role of a priest. Further, as already explained, an activity considered proper to a priest includes all the other activities that are above it, so that preaching includes hearing Confessions and saying Mass, and taking part in politics includes all the activities that are listed above it.

All the respondents are agreed that saying Mass, hearing Confessions, and preaching are activities proper to priests. These are clearly cultic or ritualistic in nature. Even routine preaching is a cultic activity, because it is a normal part of saying Mass and of the celebration of rituals. However, today, Catholic priests and laity alike generally accept that a priest should go beyond purely cultic functions and involve himself at least in pastoral care. Perhaps the questionnaire was not nuanced enough to bring out this aspect. Nevertheless, it is surprising to find that 110 (10.29 per cent) of the respondents, more or less evenly spread over different age groups, would restrict the priests to the performance of these purely cultic or ritualistic functions. This restrictive view is an indication that there is a significant segment of the people whose thinking may be termed traditional and even conservative, and they would not like a priest to involve himself in any activity that is not deemed specifically religious or ritualistic. Probably this segment is also critical of those priests who deal with social issues and problems in their routine preaching. To put it slightly differently, this segment wants the priest to be a 'man of God, who confines himself to purely religious activities.

Table 4.1. Respondents' expectations from Catholic priests

Activity	Respondents accepting it as proper to Catholic priests	
	Number (%)	Cumulative Total (%)
Saying Mass	—	—
Hearing Confessions	—	—
Preaching	110 (10.30)	110 (10.30)
Teaching in schools and colleges	20 (1.87)	130 (12.17)
Organising welfare programmes	35 (3.27)	165 (15.44)
Managing schools and colleges	121 (11.32)	286 (26.76)
Taking up causes of justice	497 (46.49)	783 (73.25)
Taking part in politics	173 (16.18)	956 (89.43)
Other activities	113 (10.57)	1069 (100.00)
Total	1069 (100.00)	3449 (100.00)

Table 4.2. Classification of respondents into age groups

Activity	Age groups of respondents			
	18–25 years Number (%)	26–35 years Number (%)	36–55 years Number (%)	Above 55 yrs Number (%)
Saying Mass	—	—	—	—
Hearing Confessions	—	—	—	—
Preaching	15 (9.38)	20 (8.74)	46 (10.17)	29 (12.72)
Teaching in schools and colleges	2 (1.25)	2 (0.87)	12 (2.65)	4 (1.75)
Organising welfare programmes	6 (3.75)	15 (6.55)	10 (2.21)	4 (1.75)
Managing schools or colleges	24 (15.00)	24 (10.48)	56 (12.39)	17 (7.45)
Taking up causes of justice	67 (41.88)	102 (44.54)	222 (49.12)	106 (46.49)
Taking part in politics	29 (18.12)	38 (16.59)	54 (11.95)	52 (22.81)
Other activities	17 (10.52)	28 (12.23)	52 (11.50)	16 (7.02)
Total	160 (100.00)	229 (100.00)	452 (100.00)	228 (100.00)

The Diocese of Mangalore, with 144 primary schools, 61 high schools and 10 colleges, as also a large number of other educational institutions, is deeply committed to the cause of general education. There is at least a primary school in most of the parishes, and many priests are teachers in schools and colleges, dealing with such secular subjects like mathematics, chemistry and history. This is in keeping with a fairly widespread practice in the Catholic Church all over the world, with priests engaged in teaching secular subjects at all levels, including research. In this context, it is surprising that only 20 (1.87 per cent) of the respondents consider teaching as a proper activity of the priests. There may be various reasons for this. In Mangalore, some lay persons feel that priests should not teach secular subjects and that priest-teachers take away employment opportunities from the laity. Besides, some of the priests themselves, even when they are qualified to do so, do not wish to take up teaching in schools and colleges. There are also a few cases of priests who have opted out of teaching in order to fully dedicate themselves to pastoral care and to organise other activities that they consider relevant to the needs of the times.

Though only a few consider teaching in educational institutions as an activity that may be taken up by priests, there is a sizeable number of respondents (121 or 11.32 per cent), more or less evenly spread over different age groups, that considers the management of schools and colleges as a work that priests may take up. This may be because they feel that parish schools managed by the priests are in adequately efficient hands, or because they consider this activity as an expression of the administrative aspect of the priest's role. In spite of some complaints of mismanagement and favouritism, the laity in the diocese generally consider the priests as impartial and capable administrators. Lay persons would, by and large, like the clergy to continue to manage the educational institutions rather than hand over their management completely to the laity. Similar support is found also in the case of organising welfare programmes and other social services like running orphanages by the priests. It is possible that such support is given because priests are generally considered as service-minded and dedicated men who have sacrificed family life through the vow of celibacy for the sake of others. It may be worth noting here that in the discharge of their administrative functions, priests are perceived as possessing spiritual authority by virtue of their ordination.

From the information given in Table 4.1 and Table 4.2, it can be seen that as many as 497 or 46.49 per cent of the respondents, spread more or less evenly among different age groups, say that taking up causes of justice is a part of the priest's role. This question needs some clarification. The respondents were told that the term 'causes of justice' included a variety of things. It included not only matters dealing with social justice as such, but also questions of public morality, honesty, probity, and integrity and all types of social evils. The respondents were then asked whether a priest could involve himself in activities that sought to remedy such social evils, and thus go beyond mere preaching against them. In other words, the respondents were asked whether a priest could be a 'social activist' and not merely a 'preacher against evils' and a 'social critic'.

There was a special reason for including this question in the interview schedule. There were some instances in the Diocese of Mangalore when priests provided ideological and organisational leadership to the laity in fighting for justice for individuals or groups wronged by church authorities. There were also instances when priests joined and even organised protests meetings against government policies negatively affecting Christians in India. Further, there were instances when some priests actively helped people of all creeds to fight for their legitimate rights as in the case of securing rights to land under the land reform laws. All these instances were fairly well known to the respondents because there was a good amount of discussion on such activities by the Catholic priests. Hence the question was included to find out what the respondents thought about social activists among the Catholic priests. The fact that as many as 497 or 46.49 per cent of the respondents consider that taking up causes of justice is an activity that priests may undertake as an expression of their ordination and commitment indicates that a vast number of the laity support the social activists among the priests.

The question that immediately arises at this juncture is: why do so many respondents hold this view? The answer to this question is given by several respondents who say in so many words: 'They are our priests. They are our own. They must share our joys and sorrows. They must share our life'. This answer needs some elaboration. At present all the Catholic priests of Mangalore are natives of the place; they were born and brought up there. In former times there were some missionaries from outside. But at present there are no outsiders. Besides, most of the present priests did their studies at their native village and had their priestly training in Mangalore. Even as priests they maintain close relationships with their parental families, siblings, and former neighbours and friends. Therefore the priests truly belong to the people. It is but natural that they should be expected to share the joys and sorrows of the people.

There is another reason why the respondents support the priests who take up causes of justice. Though the priests are natives and 'belong to the people', priests are also seen as individuals with no personal interests. This is because they have dedicated themselves to the service of the people through their vocation and priestly ordination. In particular, priests are seen as individuals without personal interests because of their celibacy. This dimension of a priest's life is of critical importance because of which people readily trust them, something that would not do in the case of secular leaders.

Canon Law forbids priests from seeking elective political office, and in the Diocese of Mangalore so far no priest has contested election at the national or state level, probably not even for the local bodies. Besides, priests have generally refrained from active propaganda in favour of any particular political party or individual contesting elections, even though candidates have sought the blessing of priests and met the people outside the churches when they gather for worship on Sunday. At the same time, priests have sought to enlighten the laity on their duties as citizens to cast their votes in favour of a suitable candidate. In this context, the 173 or 10.57 per cent of the respondents who say that priests may take part in politics, evidently wish that the priests continue to perform this function of providing leadership and promoting awareness about political affairs, so that the laity can properly perform their political duties as citizens.

CONCLUSION

On the basis of the discussion presented above, it is possible to conclude that the vast majority of the laity in the Diocese of Mangalore would like the priests to do much more than perform purely cultic or ritualistic functions. The laity would like the priests to be much more than persons who are separated from the laity because of their priestly ordination. The laity, in fact, would like the priests to be persons who are also actively involved in the life and welfare of the people, providing leadership in other areas, even in taking up causes of justice. The laity would like the priests to be with them, to be relevant to their life, to share in their joys and sorrows. In brief, the laity would like the priests to perform all the activities that are in keeping with their role as priests. This would require the priests to be 'men of God' and 'men for others' at the same time. As men of God, priests must be detached from all types of narrow and particular loyalties, and as men for others they must be involved in all the spheres of life of the community.

The emergence of such a broad perception of the role of the Catholic priests is due to various factors. In the first place, as already noted, there has been considerable new thinking among priests within the Catholic church in the context of modernisation or updating, especially after the Second Vatican Council. Today the priests themselves generally see their role as embracing a variety of activities, including social criticism and activism. In India, priests have, for a long time, actually undertaken works like education and welfare programmes and have asserted that such activities are a concrete expression of their priesthood, thus giving a theological basis and justification for their broadened role. In recent times, Catholic priests in India have also been actively involved in protesting against unjust practices within the church as also against government policies that negatively affect the weaker sections and minorities, particularly the Christians. In doing so, the priests lay claim to giving a concrete demonstration of the prophetic aspect of their priesthood. This essay on the popular perception of the priestly role shows that such an understanding of the role of the Catholic priests is accepted by a great majority of the laity.

References

Barret, David B., ed. 1982. *World Christian Encyclopaedia*. Nairobi: Oxford University Press.

Catechism of the Catholic Church. 1994. New Delhi: Theological Publications in India.

Code of Canon Law. 1983. Bangalore: Theological Publications in India.

D'Souza, Alphonsus B. 1993. Popular Christianity. Unpublished PhD thesis. University of Delhi.

————. 1994. An Evaluation of Evangelisation in the Diocese of Mangalore. Unpublished Report. Mangalore: Bishop's House.

Eshleman, Ross and others. 1987. *Sociology*. Boston: Scott Foreman & Co.

McBrien, Richard P. 1981. *Catholicism*. New York: Harper Collins.

5

Religious Cover for Political Power
Narratives from People and the Vernacular Press on the 2002 Riots in Gujarat

Lancy Lobo and Biswaroop Das

THE BACKGROUND

Conflicts and riots among Hindus and Muslims in India are not a new phenomenon. They have, however, been less frequent and not as intense in terms of scale and nature of violence as witnessed in some of the recent riots. The Gujarat 2002 riot is one among a series of riots that has perhaps been the most violent compared to riots occurred so far in the state as well as in the country.[1]

Riots in India during the post-independence period have gradually acquired a character qualitatively different from those occurring during the British period. These have no more remained assertions to gain economic and political space by subjugating different minority groups at the local and/or regional level. Instead, they now draw their contents from a new form of political discourse that grew first in a latent and subsequently in an explicit form through a sustained introduction of a

This article is based on a study titled, *Geography of Gujarat Riots 2002: Causatives and Spatial Spread Patterns of Related Factors,* that was completed in April 2004 at the Centre for Culture and Development, Vadodara, India.

'communal' and divisive ideology. Institutionalised through supportive structures, its components spread wider and, to a large extent, became a pan-Indian phenomenon. Intermediated with the ideology of *Hindutva* (Hinduness), such a form of communalism has encroached upon spaces which could not be guarded well by forces claiming to oppose such formations. Compulsions of participating within the framework of a democratic party representing a wide range of caste- and class-based sectarian interests made several political parties respond to changes through accommodations, alliances and adjustments. To what extent have other political parties in the country been 'secular' within the vote-based political arithmetic of gaining, regaining, retaining and reaffirming power is difficult to ascertain. It can be said, however, that the contents of political discourse and their articulation in different forms by parties like the Congress have been quite different as far as the degree of including the tenets of a 'religio-political' discourse is concerned. Evidently, such a discourse formed an explicit part of articulation on the part of the 'Hindu nationalist' BJP (Bharatiya Janata Party) and its political as well as 'non-political' allies and associates.

Gradual integration of the notion of a unified India—propagated through a sub-text of 'Hindu nationalism'—emerged as an important component of the BJP's project of nation-building. And within this context, the state of Gujarat emerged as one of the forerunners where the BJP witnessed a substantial rise in the political arena. This is evident from its having gained progressively increasing number of seats in successive elections since 1989, except for its recent downfall in the 2004 parliamentary election. At the state level, however, the party continues to rule after strengthening its position substantially in the 1990 assembly elections by winning 68 of the 143 seats contested and subsequently gaining an overwhelming majority in the 2002 assembly elections.

THE CONTEXT

Forming a large part of western India, Gujarat is one of the most industrially prosperous states of the Indian union. With 82 per cent of its Gross State Domestic Product coming from secondary and tertiary sectors and a much higher average annual rate of growth compared with other states, it has improved its economic position substantially, especially during the last two decades. In spite of a high rate of growth, growing industrial investments and facilitating economic environment for a sustained growth of the manufacturing sector, the state has been witness to a number of large-scale riots and unrest between Hindus and Muslims.[2] It must be noted that the state has for long been a riot-prone region, though such occurrences became frequent after 1950, reaching a peak during the 1960s with the 1969 riots as the first of such major outbreaks. Subsequently, the initial half of the 1980s witnessed some bouts of intense and widespread riots, especially during 1985, though casualties and loss were less intense when compared with that of 1969.

Quoting Shah (1970), Sengupta and others (Sengupta et al. 2003) write that the riots of 1969 had occurred with the 1965 Indo-Pak war in the background and a host of other events and factors including that of the then chief minister's plane being shot down by a Pakistani war plane during the war; shifting Muslim votes from the Congress to the Swatantra Party; RSS rally calling for a Hindu rashtra as a reaction to certain demands put forth by a section among Muslims; Jan Sangh leader, Balraj Madhok's flaunting the Muslim protests against an attack on a mosque in the Middle East; protests by sections of Muslims and Hindus on incidents of insulting the Quran and the Ramayana by a Hindu and a Muslim officer, respectively; and the Jana Sangh leader's calling for the formation of the Hindu Dharma Raksha Samiti. As against this, the riots of the 1980s can be placed in the background of latent as well as manifest social unrests, the Navnirman agitation of 1974, and the anti-reservation stir of 1980 against the inclusion of socially and economically backward classes within the realm of benefits of such reservations (Sengupta et al. 2003).

The 2002 riots in Gujarat that preceded the assembly elections not only witnessed unprecedented violence, arson and loot, in terms of its nature as well as intensity, but also resulted in the exclusion of Muslims in most parts of the state in a definitive way. These riots occurred when the form of political discourse(s) had already witnessed a notable change, and the BJP had emerged as the dominant power in the state, while also ruling at the centre. The background over the decade of the 1990s was also punctuated by the L. K. Advani led *Rathyatra* (chariot tour) from Somnath (in Gujarat) and the December 1992 demolition of the Babri Masjid (Babri mosque) followed by communal riots in Gujarat and elsewhere; efforts, debates, actions and reactions on the building of the Ram Mandir (temple for Lord Rama) at Ayodhya, politicisation of the *Ramjanmabhoomi* (birthplace of Lord Rama) issue, and its consolidation through shilapujan (worship of stones) and "knitting" of bricks from across different parts of the country.[3]

Notwithstanding the above context and background, the focus of this paper is to (i) briefly narrate how these riots were generally portrayed by two widely circulated newspapers, namely, *Gujarat Today (GT)* and *Gujarat Samachar (GS)* during as well as in the immediate aftermath of the related incidents across the state, and (ii) record the explanation and speculation as expressed by a cross-section of individuals on the causes, intensity, effects, as well as implications of these riots in the near future. A total of twenty individuals were interviewed, which included teachers from different universities in the state and social activists belonging to organisations working for the development of the marginalised sections, especially on rights-based issues, legal aid, etc., in the cities of Baroda, Surat, Anand and Ahmedabad.

POINTERS FROM THE NEWSPAPERS

Spontaneity or Revenge and the Role of the State

In broad terms, the following pointers emerge from the contents of *Gujarat Today* (i) whatever might have been the reasons for triggering the Godhra incident, which involved untold misery and massacre of people in the two compartments of the Sabarmati Express, the event was appropriated by the 'Hindu nationalists' to legitimise their sustained revenge against the Muslims all over Gujarat. The violent revenge remained unabated for a long period; (ii) the acts of revenge got further legitimacy and strength when the chief minister of the state justified them as a legitimate reaction; (iii) the feeling of revenge being pronounced within the already fragile base of social relations between the two communities, revenge could easily make enough space for itself almost to the extent of being hyped; (iv) hardly any attempt was made to unearth the immediate cause that triggered the torching of the two compartments in the Sabarmati Express; (v) a possibly spontaneous reaction that was transformed into revenge was followed by systematic identification of Muslims and attacks on their localities across many rural and urban settlements, especially that of select pockets in central Gujarat by Hindu mobs; (vi) the Dalits and Adivasis were encouraged and used in the execution of riots in few parts of the state; (vii) the state lent tacit support to the ongoing happenings, for it supported the *bandh* call, by the Vishwa Hindu Parishad (VHP) in Gujarat and continued to remain soft on the rioters in several parts. Appendix 5.1 to 5.5 illustrate the spontaneity and revenge theory of these riots as seen in *Gujarat Samachar* and *Gujarat Today*.

As against *Gujarat Today*, the tone and contents of the news and editorials in *Gujarat Samachar* were not as critical of the state and of the situation, though it did focus on adverse comments made by the National Human Rights Commission on the functioning of the state. It featured reports critical of the VHP and Bajrang Dal and highlighted the concerns of the BJP MLAs with regard to the deteriorating law and order situation and their emphasis on keeping a strict vigil especially on *madrasas*. It also stated that, ironically, when every religion aims at forbidding competition, conflict, and revenge, man has been hunting man in these riots in the name of religion. That the pseudo-secularists were in support of and biased in favour of minorities is another point that some reports in the *GS* highlighted. Significantly, in some of its narrations, Pakistan, Kashmir, and terrorism were referred to as counters to such groups.

Role of Politicians in the Riots

Both the papers took positions rather opposed to one another while commenting on the political parties and the political leaders during the period of the riots. The *GT* not only linked the killings with the vested interests of select groups, but also emphasised that it was the duty of a democratically elected government to deliver proper governance and not allow emergence of forces leading to loss of innocent lives. It equated 'Ramrajya' with good governance. While celebrating the central elements of justice and love as parts of such a concept, it was critical of the politicians' apparently indulging in unfair deeds. The essence of its position as well as the contents of its coverage was critical about the visit of the then prime minister, A. B. Vajpayee, to Ahmedabad on 4 April 2002 and his refraining from holding the Modi government responsible for what had happened in Gujarat. Appendix 5.6–5.8 give evidence of the role of politicians in the riots as seen in *Gujarat Samachar* and *Gujarat Today*.

Going along the line of argument that terrorism was implied in the whole incident and that it was difficult to thwart the revenge, the *GS* highlighted the apparently 'neutral' narrative of the tragedy as visualised by the prime minister. At the same time, it drew attention to atrocities perpetrated by Muslims in Godhra from a long time, accusing Muslims in Pakistan of complicity with terrorists in Gujarat, especially by quoting people at high places such as the state home minister (*GS* 5 March). It also expressed an anti-Congress stance by blaming them for their 'soft' and 'pseudo' line in favour of the minorities (*GS* 27 March).

Role of Police and Media in the Riots

That it was possible for the police to control the riots and related events in a more effective way if it had been sufficiently alert was the essence of writings in the *GT*. Projecting the lack of willingness on the part of the police to take a tough stand, it quoted Mumbai based super-cop Julio Rebeiro: 'with appropriate body language five policemen can control a crowd of 5000 people' (*GT* 21 March). On 10th April, Abdul Latif, columnist, wrote in the *GT* that while it was the duty of police to protect the interests of citizens, it appears that the police got involved with rioters, tacitly helping them to loot and kill. The *GS*, however, in some of its reporting, was concerned about why the police was shying away from conducting the needed combing operations in the Muslim localities (*GS* 1 April).

The *GS* commented on the role of the media, emphasising how certain television channels and newspapers were carrying items that were two to three days old in a manner as if they had occurred afresh with the view of inciting people (*GS* 2 March). The *GS* also wrote about how some of the English newspapers and TV channels were carrying reports equally selective and biased. While being soft to the minorities, such groups in the media were failing to give voice to the sentiments of the majority: this was the essence of such pointers emerging from reports appearing in the *GS*.

Impact of Riots

In contrast with the above, the *GT* focused on the impact of Gujarat riots on the state and the country. Its reports included (i) views on how a sustained communal divide had for long been responsible for eroding and destroying our heritage; (ii) that criminalisation of the polity had got further legitimised by communal conflicts and skirmishes; (iii) how the bandh ended up in more violence resulting in social and economic losses; and (iv) the extent of damage the riots had placed on the image of Gujarat in the country and on the image of India the world over. Pointing out that the social structure of the country was facing severe erosion with widening faultlines, the *GT* also emphasised the aspects related to the country being weakened by these happenings, especially because the minorities had now lost trust in the Constitution and the state. In addition, the paper also emphasised that the image of the country in the international community was fast emerging as a negative one and that it was essential to reverse and halt this process. Appendix 5.9 to 5.13 illustrates the impact of riots as seen in *Gujarat Samachar* and *Gujarat Today*.

The *GT* also covered narrations focused on such questions as: how has the Hindu religion and society called itself generous and non-violent when it could torture and burn its widows, cut open the bellies of pregnant women, and see women die from the fear of being raped. Recalling the Sikh massacre of 1984 by quoting Rajkishor, a columnist, it suggested, on 16th April, that the Hindus had now become violent. The point was further emphasised through other statements, including that of Joseph Macwan in the issue dated 24 April, where he asks what kind of a religion was this where saints were supporting systematic massacre of innocent Muslim women and children? Congress had its KHAM (Kshatriya, Harijan, Adivasi and Muslim) theory to come to power, but the BJP has used religion to destroy it and succeed to power (Macwan, *GT* 24 April). Explicit as well as implicit appeals to secular Hindus to come forward and contest the happenings were also apparent in the tone and slant in some of the *GT's* narrations.

A Few General Observations

In addition, the *GT* has drawn the contours that indicate the changing modes of political discourse and the occurrence of the Gujarat riots as being mainly an associated event. It suggests a rising 'Hindu nationalism' that has moved ahead by appropriating a wide range of philosophical and ideological position(s) emphasised and advanced by Vivekananda, Gandhi, Sardar and Ambedkar. Further, there are pointers indicating that the seemingly opposed position of Gandhi and Sardar had been celebrated resulting from its 'hard nationalistic' views by the Sangh Parivar. The paper also tends to highlight the processes leading to propaganda against the Muslims that has the potential of making them more vulnerable, and it indicates that the phenomenon has resulted in the nurturing of fascist tendencies in the state. Quoting M. J. Akbar (7 April) and Ramsuman (14 April) it says that even the top leadership in the Sangh Parivar did not criticise the riots and that the Sangh Parivar wants the prime minister to carry a *trishul* (trident) in his pocket to assert his Hindu identity as Modi does in Gujarat.

What appears from the above is that through the narratives carried by the two newspapers, viz., *Gujarat Today* and *Gujarat Samachar*, they get placed in opposition to one another. Pitched from different vantage points they seem to echo the essence of expressions albeit in a different manner. The 'we' and 'they' remain implied in much of their coverage. The *GT* points at the tendency of Hindu nationalist and allied groups to appropriate conflicts and skirmishes in order to create legitimacy of a majority vs minority—a Hindu vs Muslim politics. The *GS* points to the tendency of minorities having potentials of emerging as anti-nationals at the pan Indian, and aggressive at regional levels.

Perceptions of Lead Individuals on the Riots and Associated Factors

A few knowledgeable persons from scholars, people working in NGOs, social activists and leading citizens of both communities were interviewed on the causes, intensity, spread, impact, and implications of riots for the future.

Why Gujarat is More Riot Prone?

According to many, a change in political discourse with potentials to create communally divisive politics has been a prime factor for the culmination of events into such riots. Responses suggest that (i) in spite of the state being developed in terms of economic parameters, it has always been 'traditional', holding strongly to the identities associated with religiosity, rituals, castes, sects, and a wide range of other similar denominations; (ii) while assertion of an identity or efforts of negotiating a space in the changing social milieu had facilitated the emergence and sustenance of many such groups, projection of an apparent cohesion among them under a broad umbrella of 'Hindutva' had been easy, especially in the absence of any other radical or progressive social and/or political form; (iii) the caste system and corresponding divisions in the Gujarat society have been more rigid and continue to remain so, paving the way to a political discourse that can, unlike in many other states, be mediated by religious tenets having potentials of linking with a variety of religio-political platforms. These factors were able to create an environment where the Sangh Parivar could sustain and reinforce a social divide between the Hindus and Muslims within a decade. The focus, however, remains more on central Gujarat where institutionalisation of the above-mentioned factors and processes has not only been intense but also celebrated through constant delivery of religious discourses, moral teachings, construction of temples and an emphasis on worshipping some of the gods and goddesses.

The second set of factors identified by most of these respondents relates to the rise of the BJP as a political power in the state and, along with it, the growth of activities of the RSS, VHP and Bajrang Dal. With the erosion of the Congress in the state, the combined power of the BJP and the Sangh Parivar, according to them, was able to penetrate the social base of the OBCs as well as the upcoming urban middle classes through different forms and modalities. A section among them emphasised the manner in which the Patidars had prospered since independence and the way in which they were able to use their political and economic strength, which they expressed through different means. The central tendency of such a set of opinions indicates that the Patidars, who have been dominant in terms of money and political power, have often been a part of religious organisations, which together have led towards creating a political base for themselves. That this group has been able to appropriate much of the larger social sphere in their favour facilitated, albeit, by reinvented sanctions and financial supports coming in mainly from the NRIs abroad. This marked tendency is substantiated by a response: 'The Patidars have lately used specific religious structures and sects as platforms to strengthen the socio-political base for themselves, supported by remittances as well as donations meant ostensibly for developmental activities but essentially laced with religious undertones. And the process has led to a kind of insulation among them that has potentials of nurturing opposed positions and may have emerged as factors facilitating the disturbed situations in parts of Gujarat.'

The third set of factors points toward the role of Hindutva forces, especially that of the Sangh Parivar, towards sustaining a communally divisive environment that has, according to many, helped the riots to last for a long time. Differentiating the 1992 riots from the recent ones, these responses tend to place the immediate causes of the former on the inability of the state to respond to the rising aspirations of the middle classes and the related 'reservations' issue, while the latter, according to them, has been affected by a constant rise of communalisation of society across different levels. While emerging as important pointers, the following expressions by some of our lead respondents sum up the above mentioned views

> Undoubtedly, the State of Gujarat has not only emerged as a more riot-prone region in the country, but also more riots have actually taken place in this State. The violent riots of 1992 were

mainly caused due to the competing factors linked with the 'Reservation' issue that subsequently turned communal.

The recent riots however have been propelled by the concerted activities and propagation of specific ideology by the Sangh Parivar. Much of the damage caused in the State in these riots has been due to the emergence and growth of these and similar forces.

The overwhelming religiosity expressed often in an outwardly manner is a prominent component that characterizes a large part of the Gujarat society and it is this element that has been appropriated and used by these forces where the idea of Ramjanmabhoomi, shila poojan programmes and different yatras have influenced the common people.

And processes like this have led towards increasing the social distance among Hindus and Muslims that resulted in sustaining the 2002 riots for an unprecedented long duration.

Many expressed that such processes have led to a near complete segregation of Hindus and Muslims and strengthened the feeling of 'living only with one's own group'. According to one of the respondents, 'Pakistan' had now become a metaphor for isolated living by Muslims in Ahmedabad; this denotes a deviation from so-called mainstream norms. Such spatial polarisation has not only got strengthened in the urban areas but also in many villages, where Muslim households had fled out of fear during the riots.

The fourth set of factors points, as the causes of increasing communal riots in the state, to its urban growth rate and the patterns of investment in its 'golden' and 'silver' corridors since the early nineties. Such a growth pattern, according to some, has on the one hand attracted a sizable number of migrants from other regions in the country, and on the other, has raised aspirations of the middle classes. The changing social fabric of these cities has seemingly transformed the 'political demography' in select urban areas, which tend to act as prime nodes of competing interests and which have the potential of sustaining communal and other similar unrests. Some respondents also related the length of the 2002 riots with the closure of textile mills that had retrenched lakhs of workers who could not get alternative employment and/or re-establish their social positions; thereby they became easy targets for being recruited as riot-mongers or looters.

Differences between the Riots of 1992 and 2002

We present here a few narratives substantiating some of the related observations. About a quarter of our respondents placed the issue in a time perspective and linked the riots of 2002 with the rise of the BJP, irrespective of their varying intensity. According to them, since the last decade and a half, the BJP had been actively pursuing the task of strengthening its base in the country as a whole. Initially the party established close contacts with the upper castes, and having created this base, succeeded in getting elected in some states, while also acquiring power at the centre with help from smaller parties. During this process, they were helped by Hindu fundamentalist organisations. In Gujarat, by organising programmes against reservations as well as the OBCs, they initiated a new form of politics. With the Ayodhya issue at its peak in 1992, the party became very important in Gujarat, but during the post-earthquake period it did not perform well and began to lose ground. Having lost in the panchayat elections, there was a dire need for it to stage a come-back in the assembly elections, and the 2002 riots facilitated their springing back to power. Hence, the BJP might have had an interest in sustaining the riots in order to be able to harness a substantial amount of political capital.

While linking the causes of the long duration of the 2002 riots to the political interests and aspirations of the BJP, respondents highlighted that it was the most violent riot in the state in terms of lives and property lost. To some of them, Hindus had become more violent in 2002, and the VHP more than any other organisation had worked towards the creation of such an environment. What happened after 28 February 2002 could have happened on any other day, for the essential reason for this riot was a concerted effort to gain political mileage. Some respondents went on to say that the complaints launched all over the state had a similar pattern and that this is a clear pointer that political interests were being mediated and articulated through a definite set of machinations. Two of the respondents coming down heavily on the VHP, stated that the

> Game plan of VHP was not only dangerous, but also in the long run had the potentials of emerging as harmful to the country

and the society at large . . . . They are bent upon dividing the society on the basis of religion for selfish political gains.

Having participated in the riots, sections among the Hindus think that they are brave and that what has been carried out is worthwhile. . . . But the real aim of such tasks was to safeguard the Hindu vote bank and this is what the BJP succeeded in doing.

A point that found repeated reference in our discussions with most of the respondents had to do with what they labelled as state support to the 2002 riots, something which, according to them, was absent in the 1992 riots. Some of them stated pointedly that the riot-mongers in 1992 were not helped by the government; while in 2002 it was a party to the riots to a large extent. Specifically, it misused the police. Failure of the government to protect people's lives and property has been highlighted by many. They also emphasised that the very act of violence was qualitatively different in the 2002 riots in comparison with that of the 1992 riots. As an extension of this argument, some observers clubbed together the BJP and the VHP, as the bandh called by them was supported and facilitated by both of them. This, to the observers, was a clear pointer to their having been in sympathy with each other and being the facilitating agencies in the riots.

That these riots were systematic and planned was another point identified by many. How else, according to them, would the events have been the same from day to day and directed specifically against the Muslims? Specific comments were also made on the speeches and the character of the language used by the VHP General Secretary, Pravin Togadia, meant to incite the Hindus against the Muslims. According to one of the respondents, '. . . in 1992 they sowed the seeds and in 2002 harvested a bumper crop'. In the words of another respondent

The riots in 1992 were not so violent, but those of 2002 were extremely brutal and rather well spread over the space. Crossing the boundaries of select cities, it went down to the villages. Pre-planned, the methods used in this riot were frightening. Gas cylinders were used for explosions and petrol to fuel the fire further. When, in some areas, Muslims approached the police stations, there were officers saying that they were instructed not to register and/or entertain complaints coming from them. And these indicate that the *Hindutvawadi* organizations, the BJP, and the bureaucracy were at least in tacit support of these riots.

As victim and witness of attacks, another respondent stated

We had not moved out of here, for we are a big number at this location. Even after a year we haven't been able to forget the way our daughter died in the police firing. We had to plead and then pressurize the police to register our complaint. With no government help coming at all, we remained alive only with the support provided by our own community during the entire period that was full of fear, anxiety and tension. Two among us died and five seriously injured with the fight here between the police and the Muslims. We were fired at without any provocation. The PSI (Police Sub-Inspector) here is himself a member of the Bajrang Dal. Being a *Bhaiya*,[4] he was helping the Bhaiyas and instigating them against us. The Muslims here complained to Gill about his behaviour and he got him transferred. But soon after Gill's departure, he was posted back here. . . . And the 2002 riots were much larger in scale compared to those of the 1992 riots, for ideas associated with Hindutva and Hindu power had been propagated well. There was no one to hear us and the Congress party had become ineffective. Participants in the riots were earlier targeting the government properties but now the Muslims and their belongings had become their prime targets. Most of them have repeatedly been told that Muslims are anti-social and must be taught a lesson.

Another point, though only raised by some, had to do with what they termed as growing economic rivalry between the two communities, especially in the city of Ahmedabad. According to them, the post-1992 period witnessed the flight of a section of Muslim entrepreneurs towards its western suburbs where a section among them invested heavily in putting up restaurants, fast-food joints, other eateries, shops and shopping complexes. Many of these were easy targets because of the vulnerability of their locations, something which was not as easy to target earlier during 1992.

Major differences between the two riots as observed and collated from the narratives and interviews can be put in the following capsule form.

Major differences between the 1992 and 2002 riots as revealed by the interviews

1992	2002
• Short-lived	• Long-drawn
• Placed in the context of the reservation issue	• Sustained anti-Muslim and pro-Hindutva propaganda
• Demolition of the Babri Masjid	• Mobilisation towards Hindu unification
• Less lives lost	• More lives lost
• Extent of property damage low	• Extent of property damage very high
• Less brutal and not as violent	• Highly brutal, dreadful, and very violent
• No state support	• State support evident
• Spontaneous to some extent	• Systematic and well planned
• Less widespread (mainly in urban areas)	• Very widespread (inclusive of many rural areas).

Reasons for Intense Spread of Riots and Participation of Dalits

Villages, indeed, had remained generally untouched by riots or, at best, had experienced only sporadic skirmishes and conflicts. But, the 2002 riots engulfed parts of rural areas in certain regions in the state. A majority of the respondents related the reason for this unusual and intense spread of riots in villages to a sustained anti-Muslim propaganda by the BJP, VHP and RSS combine and to the activities carried out by a variety of religious and quasi-religious organisations. In tribal areas where traditionally the Congress had a stronghold, Muslims were projected as being opposed to Hindus and, by extension, Indian society. In many such villages, the Muslim shopkeepers-cum-moneylenders were projected as exploiters. This helped the Sangh Parviar in weakening the hold of the Congress in certain tribal pockets. Another related propaganda of this type could have become successful mainly in the tribal settlements located in the plains and valleys, because a large section among them was exposed for a long time to Hindu cultural practices and rituals—especially, during recent decades, through the institutionalisation of a wide range of sects, including Ramanandi and Kabirpanthi, and the entry of many Hindu gods and goddesses through a variety of modes. The villages on the hills and slopes had, however, remained farther from such influences, for they had not been included as much in the process of being part of the 'mainstream' and the market economy as had been the tribal groups living in the plains and more fertile valleys. In specific pockets, like the district of Dangs, such forces were, however, able to create antagonism between Hindus and Christians, something that had facilitated the assertion of Hindutva elements across select pockets within a short time.

Parts of central Gujarat, where we conducted most of our fieldwork, has been labelled as a region that had a strong institutionalisation of certain factors that led to the articulation of Hindutva. The Patidars, economically and socially the most powerful group in the region, have reasserted their hegemony through their association with organisations such as the VHP, and they have included the other lower-caste and poorer groups within the 'Hindutva umbrella' in a manner that was more discrete and fluid. That directly or indirectly the lower-caste groups were incited by the Patidars to loot the Muslims while remaining backstage was a pointer identified by a few of our respondents. According to one of them

> Through new branches of different Hindu organizations, the related ideology has reached the villages where even the last person has not remained untouched by such a process. At many places, teachers at the village schools have been involved and in such activities the Patidars have been the most active—a majority of whom are anti-Muslim and members of the VHP or RSS.

Emphasising the same point, another respondent said

> Patidars have facilitated and helped sustaining these riots especially by using the caste groups who have no choice but to depend on them economically across major pockets in Central Gujarat . . . . They appear to be accepting them as Hindus—and a part of their own fold through various programmes like offering trishul deekshas and distributing trishuls, but in heart of hearts want to keep them at their present levels—downtrodden and dependent on them economically . . . . They do not want them to share political power that could help them gain in terms of social and economic advantages, but the dalits get attracted to such programmes as they have been subordinate and subservient to the Patidars since long and have continued to remain poor as well as under-employed. And with tacit support and cover provided by Patidars, the riots had come to some dalits as an opportunity to derive quick gains through robbery and loot without having done much work.

Participation of the Dalits in the riots, especially in cities was also highlighted by some of our respondents. What emerges from their narratives is that, although the Dalits have been living closer to the Muslims for a long time, during these riots, a section among them was compelled to come out and strike, because of the perception that while Muslims could attack and kill them, they would not be saved by any other group or agency. Because of the closure of textile mills that had rendered more than one lakh Dalits jobless and that had intensified their level of poverty, the next generation, in the absence of any appropriate employment, was easily influenced by the religio-political discourses of the BJP and its allies. Many of them who could take up only illegal and/or other 'underground' jobs were vulnerable enough to be used during the riots. The generation born after 1980–81 knows little about the discrimination faced by their parents and grandparents at the hands of upper-caste Hindus. Sections of such a big contingent of youth, fed on sustained Hindutva propaganda and political expressions could be used easily for reacting to the chain of events unfolding during the riots.

Affirming the role of Dalits in riots in certain villages in certain parts of central Gujarat and in specific urban pockets, four of our respondents linked such a behaviour of the Dalits with the rise in number of what they identified as 'outposts' of the VHP, RSS and Bajrang Dal groups in the villages, towns, as well as cities and their propagation of anti-minority and pro-Hindu biases on a sustained basis. Such propagation, according to them, involved dialogues and discourses that highlighted aspects of Hindu religion, its amorphous nature, and 'all inclusive' characteristics as well as an Indian nationalism and culture rooted essentially on such discrete tenets. Through these routes, they project the minorities as being in opposition to such 'culture' and thereby in conflict with larger national interests.

Other Causes of the 2002 Riots

Two other causes identified by a number of our lead respondents pertain to what they have labelled as the Modi-factor and NRI support. While highlighting the former, their narratives centre on the following. The former Chief Minister, Keshubhai Patel, was not able to deal well with tasks associated with provision of adequate relief to earthquake victims and also to respond effectively to issues linked with the Narmada Dam. This resulted in a fall in his popularity and eventual ouster, with Modi riding in the saddle. Essentially a front-runner and an organisational activist of Hindutva politics, Modi was able to soon create an impression on a large section of people that he meant business and was alone capable of creating the needed space for the Hindus. Shankarsinh Vaghela of the Congress was no match to him. Modi, through a reorganisation of the state bureaucracy and the much hyped *gaurav yatra*, was able to rejuvenate a discourse that led to a clear social division between Hindus and Muslims. Thus, the factors for conflict had already crystallised before the Godhra incident, and, therefore, the riots took a violent and brutal form immediately after the incident.

Emphasising the role of Gujarati NRI support, the respondents generally opined that a large proportion of these NRIs endorse the activities of the Sangh Parivar, whose organisations receive huge donations for helping the needy. A substantial part of such money, however, is used for exhibiting and articulating religiosity that tends to emerge as divisive and competitive at the same time, through *kathas*, *pravachans*, and other religious programmes. Most of these NRIs residing in UK and USA belong to upper-caste groups and are members of numerous branches of allied Hindu religious and political organisations. A section apparently transfers money from abroad illegally through *hawala* of which no account can be traced easily. This money is used for a variety of similar programmes. This has led to a visible increase in the rate of popular participation in the state in religious discourses, visits to shrines and pilgrimages. That all these processes have facilitated creation of a consciousness across a large number of caste groups, giving rise to an expression of contest and conflict vis-á-vis the Muslims, has been the essence of these responses.

Social Distance between the Two Communities

It was stated by all our respondents that the 2002 riots in Gujarat have created deep scars on the relations between the two communities, and most of these scars are difficult to heal. A majority of them emphasised that these riots have resulted in a near complete segregation of the two communities and that even villages in many parts of the state have not remained untouched by this phenomenon. While some of them reflected on the short- and long-term implications of such clear communal divisions, others pointed at the very vulnerability of the situation itself, such that it could be engineered by vested interests for quick political and allied gains. The environment of mistrust between the two groups that generally envelopes the state now, has made it impossible for both the communities to work together in such areas as forming cooperative housing societies, or for Muslims to be tenants to Hindu houseowners and vice versa, or in dealing with enterprises and other business activities. Even the forms and modalities of transactions associated with the delivery and receipt of services at different levels have got communalised. Expressions of boycotting and marginalising Muslim traders, petty shopkeepers and vendors have begun to be articulated in practice, albeit in sectors where it is possible. According to one of the respondents

> Depending on the situation as it comes by, the perceived mistrust or trust between the two communities creates anxiety or freedom from it on a day-to-day basis while buying vegetables or fruits, hiring an autorickshaw or even getting a cycle or a scooter repaired, for the general belief that has set in, makes a Muslim service provider likely to cheat his Hindu clients and vice versa. Obviously, hence, both the communities now try to depend on their own people to the extent possible rather than others. And this creates an extreme situation where one does not mind being cheated or overcharged by people belonging to his/her own community.

In the same context, some other respondents highlighted that marginalisation of Muslims by the Hindutva political forces had been on the rise since the early 1990s, and that with the 2002 riots the project of bracketing the community was complete. They have been socially subordinated, economically impaired and culturally pushed out. The net result is manifest in 'ghettoisation' that carries the potential of creating an environment where the minorities can negotiate with their lives without having any anxiety about the majority community.

On the question of whether or not the existing gulf between the two communities could ever be bridged, a majority refrained from responding. A section, however, emphasised that the possibility of the two communities coming together was continuously being weakened owing to the reinforcement of the process of hardening of the 'we' and 'they' syndrome. Based on how things were being projected, viewed, perceived, and internalised, the majority in both the communities were opting for segregation rather than intermixing, and separation rather than assimilation. According to one of the respondents

> The gap now created between the two communities is difficult to close. It may remain for long and perhaps widen further, for the present leaders are not interested in bridging it. They keep inciting people and do not allow them to come together again. The entire Muslim community has been blamed and is so projected for what happened in Godhra that they are constantly under tension and fear. In connivance with allied forces Hindutvavadis are trying to destroy the Muslims economically by boycotting them in business and trade. Social relations between the two groups have deteriorated further. The gap is now so wide and deep that it may not ever get filled, and if it does it may take decades for the same.

Future of Hindutva in India

The Hindutva lifeline was viewed by the respondents in two sets: (i) an intense but short span of no more than five years, and (ii) its overwhelming presence and sustained growth. Responses and narratives related to the former point out that (i) the rise of Hindutva factors could gain much strength only in select states in the country, especially in areas where alternative structures were either weak or had been eroded owing to a variety of internal as well as external factors; (ii) centred around systematic efforts by upper and middle castes to gain and claim newer spaces in the socio-political arena, the concept was used by such forces to strengthen the communally divisive politics for quick political gains, albeit through a reassertion of hegemony over the lower-caste groups and the minorities; (iii) the concept, essentially aimed at gaining political power, has been abridged, edited, and propagated and is, thus, very much a rhetoric. It was successful in the state of Gujarat, for with the growth of a void in the political arena, the religious and political discourses were able to reshape the socio-cultural life. To sustain a formation which itself is an aggregate of discrete instruments, the respondents were of the view that, pitched from a different vantage point, Hindutva and the related polity will have to face disarray owing to the contradictions that would naturally emerge in such forced ensembles that are neither assimilative nor cohesive. In continuation, some of the respondents also emphasised that the BJP will be compelled to change its modalities, for the absence of claims and counter-claims, contests, and compromises posed and articulated by conflicting interests within its own fold will aid its dissipation.

Narratives related to suggestions of a sustained growth of Hindutva and its associated political discourse remain centred around (i) divisive caste-based society and conflict-ridden politics. Since such a politics has already been shaped in a framework laced with the essentials of opposition between the Hindus and Muslims, the modalities of such instruments will further grow, especially in the context of a vote-based democratic framework; (ii) the likely erosion of regional parties that had grown through the projection of sectarian interests and that are not linked with any pan-national feeling, as that of Hindutva or Hindu nationalism, will make way for Hindutva to enter further, facilitated by the institutional structures of the BJP and its allies; (iii) the possibility that across cities, towns and villages of the Indian union, there exists a wide range of channels, structures and modes, which can be used on a continuous basis to propagate and articulate the religiosity of Hindutva, and the same can be used to harness electoral gains at appropriate times by groups that are working towards legitimisation of a 'Hinduized Indian nationalism'; and (iv) the impact when Hindutva can be placed at the level of such emotions and then mediated through a politics that promises to further it through statements having mass appeal.

CONCLUSION

The narratives appearing in the two newspapers we have examined are placed differently. While *Gujarat Samachar* seemingly remains critical of the 'pseudo-secularists' and appears to suggest that the Godhra incident and subsequent riots are related to the overall atmosphere of terror and terrorism, *Gujarat Today* highlighted the role of criminalisation of politics and the modalities through which communal divisions were legitimised, which led to systematic attacks on the entire Muslim community after the episode. In addition, it also focused on the rising Hindu nationalism and its potential for creating the politics of majority vs minority that could further marginalise the Muslims in the state.

Responses and narratives drawn from the interviews point to the state of Gujarat being more riot prone than other states owing to a variety of factors that among others include the social environment where Hindutva forces could sustain corresponding propagation and harness political gain. Seemingly, aided by a conducive social environment and a religio-political discourse, the BJP and its allies were able to use Hindutva as a political mobiliser and capture power in the state. Such rise of BJP had also been facilitated by the erosion of Congress support in select pockets.

With the overwhelming victory of the BJP in the 2002 assembly elections, the communally divisive politics got a further boost. This was also complemented by the nature of the 2002 riots. Unlike the earlier riots, it took a big leap forward in strengthening the already existing divisions among the Hindus and Muslims. The process this time also engulfed the rural areas in a definite as well as intense manner. Whatever lies in future for the BJP and Hindutva or for the political parties in opposition or in alliance with them, given the scenario, it seems that the communally divisive politics may continue to grow, albeit in a latent mode with potentials of it being appropriated by vested interests in times to come.

Endnotes

[1] The torching of bogey S-6 of the Ahmedabad-bound train, Sabarmati Express, at Godhra on 27 February 2002 in which 58 passengers, including 26 women and 12 children were burnt to death, was shocking. The burned corpses of the ill-fated passengers became a justification for armed squads for BJP with its 'brother' organisations—RSS, VHP, Bajrang Dal—to launch a pogrom against the Muslims of Gujarat.

Around two thousand Muslims were killed in the post-Godhra riots that continued for months. Eyewitnesses and victims, survivors and observers, put the crowds who terrorised them at less than two thousand; most often, even in remote villages, they were closer to 10,000–15,000-strong mobs, armed with deadly agricultural implements. Key men carried guns and rifles. A few in the crowd even carried mobile phones to enable coordination of the attacks. Dead bodies no longer resembled human beings: they were reduced—whenever they had not been burned to ashes—to a grotesque and pathetic sight. Rape was used as an instrument for the subjugation and humiliation of a community. Pregnant women's bellies were slit open with swords and foetuses flung in the fire. A chilling and hitherto absent technique was the deliberate destruction of evidence—barring a few cases, women who were gang raped were thereafter hacked and burned (see 'Genocide Gujarat 2002' in *Communalism Combat*, March–April 2002).

Contrary to popular belief, the intensity and main spread of the 2002 riots in Gujarat have been concentrated in areas within its central and northern zones, leaving peninsular Saurashtra, Kutch, and the south Gujarat regions largely devoid of direct clashes and riots between the two communities. This becomes evident from the maps showing the spatial distribution of a large number of related events (data on which were collated by us from reports of two vernacular newspapers, viz., *Gujarat Today* and *Gujarat Samachar* over a period starting 1 March 2002 to the end of April 2002), carefully aggregated, analysed and plotted under the heads of: (i) triggering events; (ii) clashes; (iii) rumours; (iv) damages; (v) other effects; (vi) interventions by agencies towards rescue and relief; (vii) state action, and (viii) extent of the spread of riot. What emerges from these maps is that the cities of Ahmedabad and Vadodara, including their outskirts and talukas of Anand and Chhotaudepur in the central Gujarat and Kadi in northern Gujarat, can be grouped under very highly affected areas. This is followed by talukas of Borsad, Sojitra, Jetpur, Naswadi, Kawant, Halol and Nadiad in central Gujarat: Bayad in the northern and parts of Bhavnagar in the Saurashtra region coming under highly affected category. Moderately affected areas had been in the talukas of Padra, Dabhoi, Khambhat, Petlad, Thasra, Godhra, Limkheda, Mehmedabad, Daskroi and Viramgam in the central zone; Mehsana, Prantij, Vijapur, Meghraj, Modasa, Himmatnagar, Idar, Vadali and Vijaynagar, in the northern zone, and Jhagadia in the southern zone. Excluding the cities of Ahmedabad and Vadodara and, at a much lower scale, Surat and Rajkot, riots, clashes and damages were mainly witnessed in 35 of the 211 talukas or 16 per cent of such blocks in the state. However, of the talukas in the central zone, as much as 31 per cent (19 of the 62 talukas) and those in the northern zone as much as 24 per cent (10 of the 42 talukas), witnessed higher intensity of these riots. For more details and especially maps showing spatial spread of the variables mentioned (see Lobo and Das 2004).

2   Available data (Joshi, Srinivasan, and Bajaj 2003) indicate that the proportion of Hindus to the total population in Gujarat has remained steady at a little

below 91 per cent since 1951. In 1991, their share was 90.83 per cent followed by 8.73 per cent of Muslims and 0.44 per cent of Christians. Christians form a significant proportion of population only in one district of Gujarat, Dangs—where its proportion has gone up from 1.33 per cent in 1981 to 5.43 per cent in 1991. Surat adjoining the Dangs, has a Christian presence of 0.94 per cent and Kheda near Ahmedabad has 1.48 per cent. In Ahmedabad (including Gandhinagar), Vadodara and Bharuch their proportion is between 0.5 and 1 per cent. In all other districts of Gujarat, their presence is negligibly small.

Distributed in the entire state, Muslims nearly form 5 per cent or more of the population in all districts, except in the Dangs. Their presence is smaller in the north-eastern districts but rises in the southern Gujarat districts, most of which have a Muslim population of around 10 per cent. Among these, Bharuch has an exceptionally high Muslim presence at 16.60 per cent.

In the south-west, within its Saurashtra sub-region, Muslim presence is higher in the western districts of Jamnagar, Junagadh and Rajkot and relatively lower in the eastern districts of Surendranagar, Bhavnagar and Amreli. In Jamnagar their share is 13 per cent followed by Junagadh and Rajkot, where they form somewhat less than 10 per cent of the population. In Surendranagar, Bhavnagar and Amreli their presence is around 6 per cent.

The district of Kachchh in the north-west has the highest proportion of Muslims in the state. In 1991, they constituted 19.64 per cent of its population.

Since 1951, the proportion of Muslims in most districts of Saurashtra and Kachchh sub-regions has remained unchanged, or has declined, while it has shown a slight rise in most districts of the Gujarat sub-region, thus keeping the proportion of Muslims in the state as a whole more or less unchanged.

Corresponding to the all-India trends and figures, a larger proportion of Muslims in Gujarat remains located in its urban areas. In 1991, 58 per cent of Muslims as compared with 32 per cent of Hindus were living in cities and towns of the state. The highest proportion of Muslims at 40 per cent is in Godhra of Panchmahals district, though their proportion in the district as a whole is only 4.6 per cent. Bhuj in Kachchh with Muslim presence of 24 per cent, Patan in Saurashtra with 27 per cent, and Bharuch in south Gujarat with 28 per cent are other towns with high Muslim presence. Jamnagar and Junagadh in Saurashtra and Surat in south Gujarat also have relatively high Muslim shares of 20, 18 and 14 per cent respectively. Of the other major cities in the state, the share of Muslim populations is 12.50 per cent in Ahmedabad, 10.28 per cent in Baroda and 7.55 per cent in Rajkot.

³ The 1990s gradually witnessed a definite slant in the character of riots, for it was during this period that an otherwise diverse and amorphous basis of Hinduism began to be projected as a monistic and unified system aimed at giving a new religio-political meaning to Hindutva. Manipulating this in the

form of a new religio-cultural nationalism that continued to define the we (the Hindus) vs they (the Muslims and in some cases the Christians) emerged as a major instrument for the BJP and its associates to harness support of the 'majority' community at various levels in the social and political arena.

4   A generic way of identifying a person belonging to the states of Uttar Pradesh or Bihar.

Appendix

5.1   Hindu nationalists have succeeded in projecting and legitimizing the post-Godhra riots as revenge by Hindus against Muslims held responsible for burning two compartments of the Sabarmati Express at Godhra on 28 February 2002. The feeling of revenge was so hyped that the few relief camps run for Muslims were threatened to be terminated so that Muslims die of hunger. Isn't it worse than Hitler's gas chamber? (*GT* 10 March)

5.2   No chief minister ever in the past called such madness a reaction and while trying to justify, it gave a free hand to the rioters for 48 hours. Why should the entire community suffer because of the mistake of a few (quote from a former member of Parliament). (*GT* 6 April)

5.3   Referring to Kuldip Nayyar the *GT* wrote on 6th April that the police were not seriously dealing with the rioters, in fact they were protecting them.

5.4   Yashwant Mehta wrote in the *GT* on 23rd of March that after the attack on the twin towers, America did not allow people to take law into their own hands. Could this not have been done in Gujarat?

5.5   The so-called secularists advise the Hindus about tolerance but do not say anything about the atrocities committed in Jammu and Kashmir on Hindu Pandits. . . . They say nothing about the complicity of Pakistan with Muslims of Kashmir and their training camps and the arms. No wonder when the Gujarati Hindu majority expressed their anger these secularists were shedding tears. (*GS* 28 April)

5.6   Politicians misusing their power for selfish motives are not followers of Ram but represent Ravanas as they have multiple sets of faces which keep changing in accordance with their changing self interests. . . . Narendra Modi has not fulfilled his constitutional obligations and the PM has only shed crocodile tears. . . . They should realize that the country is more important than the party. (A. Munshi, *GT* 27 April)

5.7   The PM refrained from holding Modi responsible for what had happened in Gujarat and chose to keep quiet on the lethargy of the Modi Government during and after the riots. . . . This is not a good sign for democracy. Dipankar Gupta and Romila Thapar. (*GT* 5 April)

5.8 What happened in Gujarat is also a kind of terrorism and who was going to stop it. Prime Minister Vajpayee who visited sites at Ahmedabad after a month of the Godhra incident expressed his shock at the tragedy and reasserted on the rights of a citizen for all Indians as per the tenets of the Indian Constitution. He said that he had not come to count the number of corpses. (*GS* 5 March)

5.9 The minorities have lost trust in the Constitution and State. . . . Hindu Communalism has disregarded the courts, the Parliament and the Constitution. (Asgar Ali Engineer, *GT* 3 April)

5.10 By dividing the State along communal lines Modi has succeeded to return into power. . . . If the existing atmosphere of hatred is not halted, it will divide the nation into two. (S. Naqvi, *GT* 2 April)

5.11 While committing crimes with impunity, the criminals and those located at the wrong sides seem to be winning and gaining and their success is dangerous for the country. (Abdul Latif, *GT* 10 April)

5.12 Shubha Mudgal was referred to as saying that those who destroy our heritage are enemies of the country. (*GT* 14 April)

5.13 Hindus must have the courage to say that something wrong has entrenched into their religion and that they are ashamed of it . . . . Brahmins dominated the society for the first thousand years before Christ. . . . Gandhi sacrificed his life to bring Hindus and Muslims together, but the present Hindutvawadis have taken his conception of Ramrajya and his ideology beyond repair and redemption. (*GT* 20 April)

References

Joshi, A. P., M. D. Srinivas, and J. K. Bajaj. 2003. *Religions Demography of India.* Chennai: Centre for Policy Studies, pp. 66–97.

Lobo, Lancy. and Biswaroop Das. 2004. *Geography of Gujarat Riots, 2002: Causatives and Spatial Spread Patterns of Related Factors.* Vadodara: Centre for Culture and Development (mimeo).

Sengupta, Chandan, Anil Kumar, and Katy Gandevia. 2003. *Communal Riots in Gujarat, 2002: A Study of Contextual Factors.* Mumbai: Tata Institute of Social Sciences.

Shah, Ghanshyam. 1970. Communal Riots in Gujarat. *Economic and Political Weekly* 5(3–5): annual number.

6

This-Worldly Hinduism
A Case Study

Ragini P. Shah

INTRODUCTION

Social scientists often draw attention to a common feature of all human societies, namely, the distinction between sacred and profane. Certain things, places, acts, books, or even words are considered sacred and therefore awe-inspiring. They are believed to be holy and hence treated respectfully. On the other hand, certain things are viewed as mundane, this-worldly and not given any special treatment. They are evaluated in terms of their utility and without any special reverence or emotion. The realm of sacred is the realm of religion.

Religion is a social institution. It consists of a set of beliefs, ideas, values, norms and rituals concerning supernatural beings (gods, goddesses and demons) and places (heaven and hell) commonly shared by a group of people. Although religion is a universal phenomenon, it varies in its content. Therefore we have a number of religions having diverse doctrines, practices, beliefs, rituals and

I presented this paper in October 2000 at Gujarat Sociological Conference held at Mumbai when Anuben was alive. I had long discussions with her twice during the process of data collection in which she strongly expressed her dislike for publicity of her work. I regret her absence when this paper is being published. I am thankful to Professor A. M. Shah for his comments on an earlier draft of this paper.

organisations. In each religion there are special places of worship (temples, mosques, churches, gurudwaras, synagogues, agiaris, etc.) and there are specialised roles to deal with the supernatural (such as priests, rabbis, imams, etc.).

Prior to the study of religion by social scientists, some thinkers believed that religion was a kind of irrational thinking, which was a remnant of human beings' primitive and pre-scientific past. However, Durkheim was one of the first sociologists to view religion in the social context. According to him, religion is an integrated system of beliefs and practices related to the sacred, and it unifies all those who share these beliefs and practices into a single moral community (1947: 47). He said that the social group reinforces its identity by performing religious rituals from time to time.

However, Karl Marx differed from Durkheim and perceived religion as the 'opium' of the masses, which keeps them quiet despite injustice caused by class inequalities (1962: 42). According to Marxists, religion is a major source of 'false consciousness'. Therefore, the communist countries (example, former Soviet Union and China) systematically made efforts to suppress religion, though they have not been successful in this regard.

Malinowski (1955) tried to specify the psychological functions of religion by emphasising the fact that religion is an escape from the stress of powerlessness experienced by man on occasions such as death.

On the other hand, Max Weber pointed out that religion provides meaning to social life. According to him, religion is not separable from this-worldly life. He stresses the fact that religion is a way of life, which influences the ways of acting of different people following different religious doctrines. In his celebrated works on Protestantism, Hinduism and Buddhism, he empirically examined the relationship between the beliefs and practices of these religions and their functional or dysfunctional consequences for the development of the modern rational economic system called capitalism (1951, 1955, and 1958). Following Weber's analysis of Hinduism, many scholars are tempted to believe that Hinduism is an other-worldly religion and, therefore, it diverts its follower's attention from this world and from secular activities.

However, if we closely examine some doctrines of Hinduism, we find that Hinduism also emphasises this-worldly activities.

For instance, the Vedas, one of the major sources of Hindu religion, are full of *karma*-oriented philosophy. Even in the Bhagvad Gita, one of the major religious texts of the Hindus for centuries, has clearly elaborated the philosophy of karma. Yet, the critics argue that this philosophy has remained only in books and that the Hindu religion has never played a major role in uplifting human kind from these worldly miseries in the same way as Christianity has done through its missionary activities, most notably in the fields of education and health. Even now, some of the best schools and hospitals in India have been set up and run by Christian missionaries. There are, of course, some missionary institutions like Ramakrishna Mission in Hinduism, but they are dismissed as exceptions and considered to be imitations of Christian missions and having very limited influence.

Therefore, the question arises: is it true that Hindu religion is merely concerned with the other world and therefore largely ignores this-worldly or secular activities? To examine this question I have undertaken a series of case studies. One of them was the study of a Hindu temple, Santram Mandir, in a town in Gujarat (Shah 1998). The present study is the second in this series.

Muni Seva Ashram: A History

Muni Seva Ashram is situated on the outskirts of village Goraj on the banks of river Dev in Vaghodia taluka of Vadodara district in Gujarat state. It is roughly 30 kilometres away from Vadodara city. There is a regular bus service between Vadodara and Goraj everyday and many other buses ply via Goraj.

The ashram was founded on 10 May 1978 by Anuben Thakker and named after her guru, Shri Munidas Maharaj. She was not only the founder of the ashram but continued to be its guide, inspirer, trustee, and president until her death on 18 November 2001. She belonged to Sanand village near Viramgam in Ahmedabad district in north Gujarat. Since childhood she and her family were devotees of a saint named Muni Maharaj in Sanand. He observed silence *(maun)* for twelve years and therefore he was named Muni Maharaj.

Anuben often discussed various topics with her guru. She was very much influenced by the writings of Swami Vivekanand and emulated him in her life and activities. After a number of discussions with Muni Maharaj, she decided to do social work in a rural area. Keeping this in mind, she went to Vedchhi in Surat district and underwent training for three years in the Montessori method of child education under two staunch Gandhians—Jugatram and Annapurnaben. While in Vedchhi, she came in contact with other well-known Gandhians, such as Ravishankar Maharaj and Babalbhai Mehta. Thus, she was influenced by Gandhi's philosophy as well. She went back to her home village Sanand and started Rushi Bal Mandir, a children's school, there. However, she did not feel satisfied with this activity and wanted to do something more for the needy and the poor.

One day Anuben asked for the blessings of Muni Maharaj to establish a mission for orphans, where she could be their surrogate mother. He said that this was possible only by establishing an ashram and suggested four places to begin her work. She visited all the four places suggested by him and selected Goraj, a place known for extreme poverty and criminal activities, to start her mission. Muni Maharaj blessed her with a coconut and wished her success in her mission. As soon as she arrived at Goraj, the Sarpanch (head of the village council) extended whatever little help she wanted. However, he warned her about the dangers of living alone in this desolate place on the bank of a river. Only 10 kilometers away from Goraj there is a village named Desar in Panchmahal district, which is known as the robbers' village. Members of an Adivasi tribe named Nayaka lived in this village; their main occupation was robbery and theft and were said to have indulged in crimes like killing people by wringing their necks. The place Anuben selected for starting her mission and for building a hut for her to live was a place for the Nayakas to distribute their plunder. However, with full trust in the blessings of Muni Maharaj she decided to live here and make it her *karmabhumi* (place of work). With the support of some followers of Muni Maharaj in the surrounding villages, she began to live on the bank and ravines of the river in 1978. A tribal woman from Goraj village, named Dollyben, decided to be with her, as it was dangerous for an outsider woman to live alone in that place.

During the day, Anuben used to visit the surrounding villages to find out the conditions of village life. As a Montessori-trained teacher, she was attracted by children first. On her first such visit, she observed that there was extreme poverty and found children being left alone in homes while their parents went to work. She convinced some parents to send their children with her and promised their safe return in the evening. Extreme poverty and attraction of free food forced the parents to permit Anuben to take their children when they were away for work. To begin with, she collected five children from three villages, brought them to Goraj, gave them baths and proper clothes to wear, provided them with snacks, and returned them safe to their parents in the evening.

Anuben continued to survey the surrounding villages. One day she saw a three-year-old child taking care of an infant. She felt the need for a cradle house and started one even without the facility of a building. Gradually she began to receive help from people. A person from the nearby village of Vaghodia gifted her with a cow to provide milk to the children. Later a person from Bombay constructed two small rooms for the cradle house.

One day, while surveying the village, Anuben came across a child sleeping alone with heavy fever and infection. She took him to a nearby hospital, and arranged for necessary treatment, owing to which the child survived. Thus, she realised the need for medical check-ups, treatment and health care. She contacted some junior doctors at SSG Hospital in Vadodara and convinced them to give their service once a week at Goraj. Dr Kapadia, an internee at the SSG Hospital, agreed to go to Goraj once a week and give free treatment. The news soon spread and a large number of people began to come to the ashram for treatment on Sundays. This initial open-air, free dispensary under a tree started in 1981 and has grown today into a 92-bed hospital called Arogya Mandir. A courageous project of constructing a cancer hospital at the cost of Rs 30 crore was Anuben's dream. She launched that project in 1999 and realised it largely during her lifetime; after her death in 2001, Dr Vikrambhai has taken up the challenge to complete the remaining work.

Anuben wanted to serve the most poor and needy and therefore chose this backward area to begin her work. She surveyed villages to find out their needs and realised that the people of this area needed education, medical service, health care and, most important, moral development, that is, overall personality development. With these goals in mind, she established Muni Seva Ashram and began her activities with a cradle house and a Montessori training school and later continued to add more activities. She served different sections of the society, namely, children, mentally retarded adults, old people, orphans, and patients, with a continuous emphasis on development of moral values. All buildings in the ashram are decorated with teachings from the Gita and excerpts from the writings of Swami Vivekanand.

Activites

At present, the ashram is involved in various activities. I have studied them on the basis of interviews of active members of the ashram and secondary sources of information such as brochures, magazines and newspaper reports. I now describe the different activities one after another.

Cradle-House-cum-Kindergarten

The ashram is situated in a rural area and is surrounded by villages. The main source of livelihood for the villagers is agricultural labour and other labour outside the village. To assist the parents, a cradle house was set up for infants and a kindergarten for children in the age group of three to five years. Every morning a van from the ashram goes to the villages to collect the children and bring them to the cradle-house-cum-kindergarten. The cradle house, situated on the ground floor of the building, is where the infants are looked after, and the kindergarten, situated on the first floor of the building, is where the older children are looked after(who are in the age group of three to five years). It has a common kitchen. The children eat only after a prayer. The children in the kindergarten learn the basic skills of reading and writing; they listen to stories and they play. The environment is very homely, peaceful, warm and inspiring. In the evening the van carries the children back to their homes. A Montessori-trained teacher is in charge of the cradle house. This facility is extended to sixteen villages in the surrounding region so that the children do not have to travel long distances.

Each cradle house accommodates thirty children. No fees are charged from any one. The kindergarten has a well-furnished library to enable children to read books containing stories, songs, pictures, poems, etc. A continuous interaction between parents, teachers, and Anuben facilitated the overall development of the child. Anuben cared for the personality development of every child.

The teachers' skills are updated from time to time. They organise talks, seminars and workshops on the current trends of child development at regular intervals. Training camps for parents are also organised to impart to them the knowledge and significance of child development and to teach them how to bring up the child and take care of his/her health.

Thus the cradle-house-cum-kindergarten looks after the overall development of children, facilitates poor parents' working without any worry, and educates the parents to perform their role satisfactorily.

Sharda Mandir

This is a residential primary school for the children of the backward class communities living in nearby villages. (The Backward Class Commission appointed by the Government of Gujarat known as Baxi Panch classified these communities as backward.) It is a co-educational school with all facilities, such as, a building with science and sports equipments, and a hostel building with a well-equipped kitchen and a dining hall. The emphasis is given on character-building and education, but the children are also trained to work in agriculture. This facilitates them to earn their livelihood after completion of their studies. Thus Sharda Mandir distinguishes itself by imparting technical education in agriculture, which is useful and necessary for them, and which therefore makes the education more meaningful.

Vivekanand Uttar Buniyadi School (High School)

This is situated at a distance of four kilometres from the ashram at a village called Vankuva. It imparts education from the seventh to the tenth standard. It is a residential and co-educational school with all facilities. Nearly two-hundred students study here. Throughout the day, they are engaged in various activities, such as, cleaning of the school and hostel building and its surrounding area, training in agricultural skills, such as, tree planting and vegetable gardening, and study. They are also trained to look after cattle. Study tours and workshops for vocational training are organised from time to time.

A child who joins the cradle-house-cum-Montessori school, studies in the primary school and then in the high school. Thus, a child lives in the ashram and is trained by the ashram up to high school education. These three educational activities are restricted to the children of Vaghodia taluka alone. The education is completely free.

Parivar Mandir—an orphanage

This is a home for orphans, but Anuben considered them as members of her family. She called the orphanage 'my family'. The Parivar welcomes infants and children disowned and abandoned by their parents. Love, warmth and homely environment are the characteristics of the Parivar Mandir. The children attend schools run by the ashram. There are eighty orphan children living in Parivar Mandir. The ashram allows their adoption.

Bhagini Mandir—a home for mentally retarded women

The Bhagini Mandir is a home for mentally retarded young girls and adult women. A wealthy father requested Anuben to start a home for mentally retarded women and donated a huge amount to construct the home. He was worried about his mentally retarded daughter. Anuben realised the need for such a home and accepted the donation. Mentally retarded people require special care. They are unable to adjust with others in the family. Often they are subject to neglect and even contempt. They are very sensitive. Even a small incident is enough to hurt their feelings. In many cases there is no one to look after them, because many families do not desire to keep them in the house. There are one hundred such women living here in peace and happiness. Some of them are taught the skills of reading and writing, some are trained to make *papad* and *papadi*, and some are taught tailoring, embroidery and drawing, depending upon their interest and their capacity to learn. Anuben permits the retarded women to stay free of cost if their families are poor and cannot afford to pay. Initially this facility was provided free of cost to all the inmates, but later it was decided to levy a charge, as the number of inmates increased and as some of them came from the economically better-off families, to provide better facilities, including a weekly medical check up. All inmates have to pay a fixed amount fixed by the ashram towards their maintenance.

Vanaprastha Mandir—a home for senior citizens

Generally people above the age of sixty years stay here. There are 80 to 100 inmates. Excellent facilities are provided. They are free to spend time in the manner in which they want to. Some are engaged in religious activities, some in reading, and some in the ashram's kitchen. Senior citizens have to pay a fixed amount fixed by the ashram for food, accommodation, and all other facilities provided to them. Anuben permits very poor senior citizens who have no family member to support him/her to stay free of cost. The inmates do not have to work; the ashram manages everything. They get morning tea, milk, lunch, evening tea and dinner. There are separate rooms with attached bathroom (each room accommodates two people) with furnished bed, a chair, cupboard, etc. The ashram arranges for the cleaning of rooms and washing of clothes.

Gau Mandir—a home for cows

The ashram has a total of 140 cows in this mandir. It provides milk, curd, buttermilk and ghee to the entire ashram complex. It also facilitates the training of students in animal husbandry. Cows regularly are medically examined. The mandir has properly designed cow sheds to keep them in a neat and clean environment. The majority of the cows are donated and some are purchased.

Assistance to the Handicapped

The ashram gives tricycles to the handicapped children as well as adults to enable them to study or to earn their livelihood and thus to become self-reliant. A total of sixty-nine tricycles have been distributed so far.

Other Departments of the Ashram

Four other departments of the ashram include the handloom section, the flour mill, the consumer store, and the bakery. Young weavers are recruited and trained at the ashram to weave carpets, towels, etc. These products are then sold in the consumer store. This store provides the daily necessities to the people of surrounding villages. The flour mill is used by the ashram complex as well as by the villagers. The excess ghee and butter are used in the bakery to prepare many varieties of biscuits, bread, etc.

Arogya Mandir—a hospital

A small open-air dispensary was started in 1981 as an OPD; it was held once a week on Sunday mornings, under the shade of a tree. It has now developed into a well-equipped hospital with ninty-two beds. Along with treatment and prevention of diseases, health-care activities are also emphasised. Two ambulances and a well-equipped modern laboratory are available at a nominal charge. Specialists in various disciplines of medicine and surgery, such as ear, nose and throat, gynaecology, dermatology, heart, chest, and lungs, paediatrics, neurology, gastroenterology, nephrology, orthopaedics, psychiatry, and plastic surgery are available once a week. The hospital serves the people of all nearby villages. A nominal fee of Rs 2 to 10 per day is charged from patients coming to the OPD. The indoor patients have to pay Rs 50 per day for treatment, medicines, food, room and food for one attendant. Concessions in fees are given to needy patients. Sometimes fees are completely waived.

Cancer Hospital

There is a specialised hospital, where the number of patients is steadily increasing. At present only surgical and chemotherapy treatment is available. The majority of patients, however, require radiotherapy, for which they have to go to Ahmedabad or Bombay. The ashram, therefore, has taken up the project of constructing a fully equipped cancer hospital at the cost of Rs 30 crore. It is a gigantic and difficult project. Its objective is to diagnose early stages of cancer, treat them for immediate cure, and provide complete facility for the treatment of various stages of cancer. The ashram plans to complete the project in two to three years.

THE ASHRAM ORGANISATION

Muni Seva Ashram is a registered trust. It publishes a newsletter called *Goraj*, which gives information about various activities as well as various schemes of donations for the diverse activities of the ashram. A person can become a well-wisher of the ashram, or can pay for the expenditure of one child in the orphanage, or of one student studying in school, or of a retarded girl. The donor for any activity gets the benefit of relief from income tax under Section 80G of the Income Tax Act, but a donor to the cancer hospital gets a 100 per cent special relief from income tax. The ashram receives grants from the state government for schools and the hospital, but otherwise it raises necessary funds by way of charity. However, the main source is donations from well-wishers and from those others who believe in service to mankind. The ashram has also organised religious programmes to collect funds on its premises. The well- known saint, Moraribapu, gave two to three programmes abroad during which funds were collected exclusively for the ashram. Anuben said that donations come partly because of the charisma of the founder. She called it *guru krupa*. She strongly believed that her activities spoke for themselves. 'People saw the activities and donated to the Ashram. I need not explain. My activities explained and attracted the donors,' she used to say.

The Arogya Mandir and the Cancer Hospital can be viewed as formal organisations but they function in a semi-formal manner. The lack of administrative hierarchy and bureaucratic procedures seem to contribute to efficiency and facilitate quick decision-making. There is a committee of technical specialists and professionals, who discuss and decide all technical matters related to the cancer hospital, but even these decisions had to be finally approved by Anuben. Other activities are also carried out in a semi-formal manner, that is, all financial matters are recorded but there are no written norms for the inmates. Norms are communicated orally and can be changed.

All those who work for various activities of the ashram are paid by the ashram, but there is no hierarchical structure. All are expected to be oriented to the philosophy of service (*seva*). There is no fixed scheme of promotions. Thus, the final decision in all matters rested with the founder, Anuben. The development of the cancer hospital reflects the highest level of motivation and efficiency on the part of the ashram. A committee of doctors, chaired by Anuben, took decisions about the cancer hospital. It also reflects the inability of the state government to fulfil this requirement of people living in rural areas. The ashram is committed and responsive to the needs of the people in the surrounding region. Thus, it is oriented to the welfare of the people and provides services for them.

CONCLUDING REMARKS

The description of Muni Seva Ashram presented above clearly shows a relationship between religious-philosophical ideas and society. From the point of view of the critiques of the Hindu religion, it is assumed that Hinduism is concerned with the other-worldly goal of *moksha* (release from the cycle of birth and death; salvation) and therefore its religious philosophies are criticised as being traditional, less humanitarian, and less service oriented. Anuben herself was a *sadhvi* (religious acsetic) but she had undertaken so many this-worldly humanitarian activities. She undertook all activities to serve people, to solve some social problems of society, and reduce human sufferings. Her activities pertain to the day-to-day life of people, and thus she emphasised on this-worldly activities to reduce human sufferings. This is a this-worldly aspect of Hinduism. She did not emphasise worship of god alone, she saw god in every human being. Apart from the teachings of the Gita, the views of religious reformers such as Swami Vivekanand, Ramkrishna Paramhansa, Mahatma Gandhi and Vinoba Bhave influenced her. According to her, religion does not mean only intellectual discussions and debates on principles of religion. Religion means to live for the Supreme Being and to identify oneself with Him. Religion means self-revelation. She said, 'I do not want kingdom, heaven or salvation. I wish to heal the suffering of the poor and the needy.' She wanted to be the 'mother' of all children around her. She did not want to restrict love and affection to a few. She saw god in children every moment. Thus, with a broad concept of motherhood, she had undertaken these activities to serve various sections of the society, that is, children, adults, the old and the sick, but she cared most for the poorest of the poor and the needy. She adopted Gandhiji's philosophy in the true spirit: 'There is no better way of living than the service of the sick. Most of the religion is included in it.' This shows that the social service activities undertaken by Muni Seva Ashram are concerned more with this-worldly activities, and therefore it undertakes several social service programmes. The social service activities of Muni Seva Ashram suggest that the Hindu religion and the Indian philosophers have been concerned with the sufferings of human beings. Anuben was influenced by the teachings of Gita and the philosophies of Indian philosophers, and therefore undertook many social service activities.

Muni Seva Ashram can be seen as an NGO making important contributions in the field of education and health in society. Usually, NGOs are viewed as secular in character and part of what is often called civil society (a secular concept). However, here is an NGO inspired by a religious outlook and yet contributing to civil society.

References

Baviskar, B. S. 2001. NGOs and Civil Society in India. *Sociological Bulletin* 50(1), March.

Durkheim, E. 1947. *The Division of Labour in Society.* New York: The Free Press.

Malinowski, B. 1955. *Magic, Science, and Religion and Other Essays.* New York: Doubledey.

Marx, Karl. 1964 (1844). Contribution to the Critique of Hegel's Philosophy of Right. In *On Religion* by Karl Marx and Fredrich Engels. New York: Schochem.

Shah, Ragini P. 1998. Religion and Society—Case Study of a Hindu Temple. *Journal of the Maharaja Sayajirao University of Baroda* (Social Science Number) 45(2).

Weber, M. 1951. *The Religion of China.* Glencoe, Illinois: The Free Press.

————. 1955. *The Protestant Ethic and the Spirit of Capitalism.* New York: Charles Scribner's Sons.

————. 1958. *The Religion of India.* Glencoe, Illinois: The Free Press.

Part III
Development and Modernisation

7

Grandmothers Hold the Key to Social Change

T. Scarlett Epstein

INTRODUCTION

In this chapter I focus on African and Asian rural societies and investigate why their traditional cultural behaviour patterns have been rather slow in adopting the many socially desirable behavioural changes that developers have been advocating throughout the past fifty years.

The results of my own research in south India (Epstein 1962, 1973, 1998) and the micro-societal studies of my nineteen African and Asian doctoral students,[1] who participated in the two 'Action-Oriented Cross-cultural Studies' I directed, clearly indicate that children of no more than four years of age already know the behavioural norms and patterns associated with their own traditional culture and follow them. Our research also showed that unlike Western culture, where youth is hero-worshipped and senior citizens try their best to hide their age, because the aged are not shown much respect, in African and Asian rural societies senior citizens are respected because of their age and family members value their experience and expect grandparents to teach and advise the younger generation. Moreover, the widespread existence in these societies of gender-specific roles designates to the grandmother the responsibility of advising their daughters or daughters-in-law during their pregnancy and to care for their grandchildren, particularly during their early childhood.

This has meant that over many generations, grandmothers have been responsible for childcare arrangements and in doing so have socialised their grandchildren. There exists thus an effective communication channel between alternative generations to which grandmothers provide the key point of entry. Unfortunately, the majority of developers have so far concentrated solely on passing their social change messages to those who are still within their working ages and have ignored trying to convince grandmothers of the desirability of changing the content of the socialisation package they pass onto their grandchildren.

In this paper I argue that grandmothers hold the key to sustainable socially desirable changes and that the neglect of involving them in these change efforts has been detrimental to development processes. I stress that the involvement of grandmothers in introducing socially desirable attitudinal and behavioural changes constitutes a necessary precondition of effecting sustainable improvements in the quality of life of African and Asian villagers.

BACKGROUND

Each society has its own traditional cultural pattern, which includes not only attitudes, values, behavioural norms and practices but also an inventory of solutions. In order to survive, collectivities have over the generations had to develop a system of solutions to deal with the problems arising out of their natural and social environment. For example, since high infant mortality threatened group survival, most 'cultural inventories of solutions' include magical measures to ensure the continuity of the collectivity, such as, guidelines on what barren women should do so that they may bear children, or how to protect the health of a newborn child. For most African and Asian rural societies, the threat to their continuity from having too many surviving children is a rather new phenomenon. Therefore, understandably, the traditional 'cultural inventories of solutions' have not yet been adapted to include guidelines on how to deal with this problem.

Hardly any attempts have so far been made to inform grandmothers of the fact that the recent drastic decline in maternal and infant mortality rates had brought about a rapid population increase; basing their socialisation messages on their own experience and on what their own grandmothers had told them, they keep telling their grandchildren, 'When you grow up you must have many children, because many will die.'[2] The emphasis on high fertility has thus continued to remain part of the mindset of succeeding generations. This helps to explain why it has taken so long for these societies to consider the existence of rapidly growing populations a threat and why they were so slow in adopting family planning and making it part of their cultural inventory of solutions.

Formal education is widely regarded as panacea for bringing about social changes. Alas, it usually takes two or three generations before the impact of education takes effect. But what is even more important and often overlooked is the fact that by the time children begin attending school, they are already fully socialised. Socialisation takes place during early childhood, when cultural norms are inculcated in the succeeding generation. Often we are unaware of why we behave the way we do. We may try to rationalise our behaviour but many of the values we hold and the norms we follow as adults are predetermined by what we are taught as infants. This is just as true of health and fertility behaviour as it is for moral and social norms as well as general behaviour patterns. Like computers we are all pre-programmed by the time we grow up. Though the content of different traditional cultures does change, it does so though hardly ever radically or quickly. On the rare occasions when sudden or quick social changes do occur, they rarely become part of the socialisation package that is handed down by grandmothers to their grandchildren, and these changes are therefore usually not sustained over succeeding generations.

CULTURE AND DEVELOPMENT

Only very few developers understand the cultures of their target societies; most consider the different ongoing cultural practices as old-fashioned and obstacles to change. They expect third world societies to adopt new behavioural patterns as if no traditional cultural norms and channels of communication had existed. For example, numerous innovations which medical experts are convinced would improve levels of health in developing societies have failed to be adopted by target societies. A common fallacy, particularly among 'scientific' health professionals, may be described by altering the biblical parable of the 'old and new wine'. The vessels in this instance are the clients of health action, and one cannot exchange them for new ones. Medical health workers, who wish to pour the new wine of scientific ideas into these vessels, often forget that they are not empty. Popular health culture is the wine that fills them, and ignoring this often results in spilling the new wine on the ground. Thus one may refer to the fallacy of the empty vessels.

Most agencies concerned with the different aspects of rural development are ill at ease when it comes to dealing with cultural factors. Social sciences are still widely regarded as soft sciences. Therefore, these agencies concentrate on hiring technical expertise related to the field of their intervention. For instance, a nutritional project will hire nutritionists and food engineers all of whom are considered hard scientists. A social scientist, who would ensure that due emphasis is given to the cultural background into which the project has to fit, is seldom hired. Yet, before a technical expert can be expected to effect desirable changes in behavioural patterns and therefore cultural practices, it is essential that they understand the relevant aspects of the existing cultural pattern and its rationale. Moreover, they also need to be aware of the existing communication channels through which messages have traditionally been passed onto succeeding generations in what used to be often illiterate oral societies. This would enable them to use these very same channels now to initiate changes that will achieve socially desirable objectives. Unfortunately, this is rarely the case, which indicates that the success rate of many development projects could be considerably increased if every project team included at least one social scientist with experience in developmental problems. The case of Meena, a young Indonesian village woman, clearly illustrates how the lack of understanding the cultural background of a target society can adversely affect project sustainability

Meena became pregnant when she lived with her husband and his widowed mother. By that time Donor Agencies had decided to try and raise the nutritional status of Indonesian pregnant women and their infants by establishing *Taman Gizi* (Nutritional Training Centres) where pregnant women and young mothers of infants were offered advice of how to improve nutritional levels. Amongst other things this advice stressed the nutritional values of bananas for pregnant women. This seemed a sound advice as there was an abundance of locally grown bananas that were either subsistence crops or could be bought at low prices. From a nutritional and economic point of view this advice was obviously well thought-out, however, it failed to take into account the traditional dietary food taboos and the important role senior women occupy in rural Indonesian households. After returning from a *Taman Gizi* training session Meena began to eat bananas. When her mother-in-law saw what she was doing she got agitated and immediately tried to stop her, telling her 'You must know that we consider bananas as hot food and that in our society hot food is taboo for pregnant women'. Yet Meena, who was committed to accepting what she believed were 'modern' practices continued to eat bananas. This greatly upset her mother-in-law and she told Meena: 'Mark my words, you will be punished for breaking this dietary taboo; when this happens you will then regret that you did not listen to me and continued to consume bananas, a tabooed food for pregnant women'. Still Meena took no notice of all these warnings. Subsequently she gave birth to a healthy baby boy and everything seemed fine. However, when the child was seven months old he got very sick and almost died. This caused Meena great distress. Yet her mother-in-law showed no pity for her and told her repeatedly: 'I warned you that something like this would happen when you insisted to eat bananas during your pregnancy, but you refused to listen to me. Now you are paying the price for having broken our society's accepted food taboos. I only hope that this will have taught you a lesson'. It certainly taught Meena a lesson. When a couple of years later she became pregnant again she faithfully followed her society's food taboos and did not eat food items that were categorised as hot food and were, therefore, taboo for pregnant women. Although this did adversely affect her own nutritional status, she was not prepared to take any more risks. Meena's mother-in-law acknowledged her submissiveness gleefully. Meena's second child was born somewhat underweighted but grew up without any serious health problems. This re-affirmed not only her mother-in-law's but also Meena's own conviction of the importance of observing customary dietary food taboos.[3]

This case clearly indicates that the Nutritional Training Centres would have been well-advised to have a rural sociologist or social anthropologist in their team, who could have alerted them to the importance of not only of traditional food taboos but also of the crucial role senior women occupy in perpetuating traditional customary norms as long as nobody convinces them that these norms have now become redundant.

A systematic study of the influences of grandmothers exert on successive generations conducted in Sudan[4] pointed out that they were involved in shaping every aspect of the lives of the younger generations. They laid down the rules by which pregnant women had to abide as well as how they should deliver their babies and then breastfeed them. It is also the grandmother who perpetuates the emphasis on son preference and the practice of female genital mutilation for their little granddaughters. Moreover, she also prepares her grandchildren for the gender-specific lifestyle they have to pursue when they grow up and teaches them their culture's traditional rituals connected with the life-cycle phases. Figure 7.1 sets out clearly how grandmothers perpetuate traditional cultural practices by inculcating them into their grandchildren. According to modern scientific testing, many of these practices are beneficial, as, for instance, breastfeeding, whereas others such as female genital mutilation (FGM) are extremely harmful to the health of young girls. FGM is a deeply rooted traditional practice. It is also a form of violence against girls and women that has serious physical, health and psycho-sexual health consequences. Yet it is mainly senior women who insist on perpetuating this deplorable practice.

All this shows the strategic position grandmothers occupy in African and Asian rural societies, which makes it difficult to understand why developers still overlook the fact that senior women constitute a ready point of entry for trying to ensure sustainable, socially desirable changes.

Negative Stereotyping of Grandmothers

The reluctance of developers to involve grandmothers in development processes seems to spring from negative stereotyping of senior women.

There are several aspects to this negative stereotyping:
1. Grandmothers are believed to be 'old-fashioned' and therefore, their ideas and practices are at best inappropriate and at worst harmful.
2. High illiteracy rates among grandmothers are associated with low levels of intelligence and that prevents them from understanding the advantages that changing behaviour patterns may have to offer.

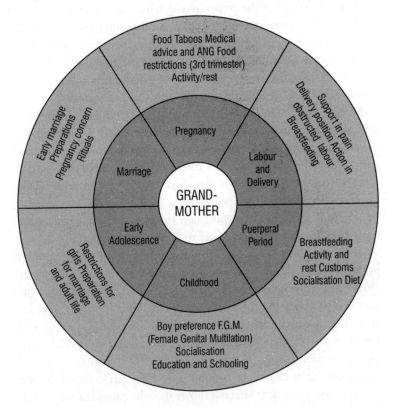

Figure 7.1 Grandmothers' influences on maternal and child health (Sudan case study)

3. Grandmothers are thought to be too old and set in their ways to be able to grasp new ideas.
4. Modern high-tech is providing new and highly efficient channels of communication even in remote rural areas, so much so that

the days when grandmothers were influential communicators to succeeding generations are a thing of the past.

5. It is generally considered that grandmothers do not have many more years to live and, therefore, trying to involve them in developmental processes would not only be difficult but also result in wasted efforts.[5]

An examination of the extent to which the negative stereotyping of grandmothers reflects the factual situation that still persists in African and Asian rural societies clearly indicates that hardly any relationship exists between them; in the few areas where the negative points have some truth they are largely the result of grandmothers having been ignored far too long by modern developers and educators.

Meena's mother-in-law is one of many, many senior women whose attitudes clearly indicate that nobody had ever tried to tell them that bananas are highly nutritious and, therefore, should form an important part of every pregnant woman's diet. Intelligence tests conducted in different cultures have shown that there is only very little correlation between literacy and intelligence levels. Moreover, illiteracy does not prevent individuals from learning new things or accepting new tasks, it only takes longer to communicate to them what they entail.

The way grandparents have responded to the HIV/AIDS epidemic proves beyond doubt that they are capable of responding to new challenges. Throughout the third world, older people not only offer care and support for their sick sons and daughters, but also look after their grandchildren after the parents have died, in spite of the fact that the grandparental generation is excluded from HIV/AIDS education campaigns. 'According to UNAIDS estimates about 11 million children have been orphaned by HIV/AIDS in sub-Saharan Africa alone. New data analysis shows that the extended family takes care of nine out of ten of these orphans. In most cases responsibility for care falls on grandparents, usually the grandmother'(HelpAge International 2004). In Ethiopia, 68 per cent of adults who died from HIV/AIDS-related illness left orphans in the care of their older parents. A WHO study in Zimbabwe found that 74 per cent of these carers were grandmothers.[6] In Tanzania, a key reason why only 1,000 of 146,000 children orphaned by HIV/AIDS attend secondary school is because their grandmothers cannot afford to send them. The large numbers of young children and adolescents living in households headed by their grandmothers throw into relief the important role grandmothers can play in influencing their behaviour, beliefs, values and attitudes as well as in helping them attain life skills.

Although the spread of HIV/AIDS has certainly reaffirmed the grandmothers' role as carers and socialisers of their grandchildren, and there are also many micro-societal studies available that clearly indicate that little has changed in the strategic role grandmothers play in caring and educating their small grandchildren, thereby helping to shape the lives of future generations, hardly any attempt has so far been made to involve grandmothers in HIV/AIDS-awareness promotion activities. AIDS awareness work tends to be totally youth orientated, using language that is not relevant to older persons. Not only does this put grandmothers at risk, but it also makes it hard for them to give the right messages to the grandchildren in their care.[7] 'Older people must be targeted with information on HIV and AIDS and the consequences of orphanhood in order to be part of the global effort to halt and reverse the spread of HIV/AIDS' (HelpAge International 2004: 6).

Residence Pattern and the Composition of Rural Households

Many rural households used to be made up of three generations where grandmother and/or grandfather lived with one or more of their children and grandchildren. In societies with patrilineal kinship and where the young married couple settle in the husband's place of residence the young bride becomes a member of her husband's household and comes under the influence of her mother-in-law.

Much of the rural sector senior women's knowledge was and still is derived from their own personal experience and what they themselves were told by their own grandmothers. In most places, it is still the grandmother who passes onto future generations what she considers as her culture's traditional norms and behavioural practices.

The often severe social constraints that are still placed on women in or facing their reproductive years are usually relaxed for older women. There is generally a marked contrast between the timid or prudish behaviour of young women and the more outspoken language and ways of older women. Among the Taita of Kenya, for example, it is taboo for parents to speak with their children about sex, and grandmothers are charged with the task of passing on the sexual dos and donts to young girls. Senior Taita women lead girls who have reached maturity into seclusion for a period of one to three months. They teach these girls to be proud of their femininity, to bear many children, and to be hard-working and supportive of their families. The senior women instruct their wards telling them, 'Sexual intercourse between husband and wife has a functional objective: it is to prove the man's potency and the woman's fecundity. Therefore, you must bear many children to prove yourself'.[8] These senior Taita women, like so many other grandmothers among rural societies, are obviously still oblivious of the problems caused by excessive rates of population increase. Nobody had ever even tried to explain to them the quite considerable impact that rapidly declining maternal and infant mortality rates have been having on societies.

The allocation to grandmothers of an integral part in development processes is not only necessary, because of their role as communicator, but also due to advances in medicine are reflected in drastic changes in the global demographic structure. By the year 2050, we can expect that people over sxity will outnumber people under fourteen years of age. The global demographic structure is becoming increasingly more heavily weighted in favour of the senior generations.

ONGOING DEMOGRAPHIC CHANGES

We now live at a time of unprecedented rapid global ageing. Whereas until not so long ago growing old was associated only with developed countries, advances in medicine have resulted in a considerable extension of the expectation of life worldwide. This is reflected in the fact that already most of the world's older people live in developing countries. In the year 2000, there were 374 million people over 60 in developing countries; they composed 62 percent of the world's older people. It is estimated that by 2030 their numbers will have increased to over a billion and they will constitute three-quarters of the world's older people. Ageing has thus become one of the defining global issues that will shape the future of the world's societies.[9]

Recognising the importance of this changing global demographic structure, United Nation member states adopted a 'Plan of Action on Ageing' at a meeting held in Vienna 1982. However, the enlightened content of this plan has so far hardly made any impact on policies pursued by governments, NGOs, or donor agencies. Hardly any developing country governments have so far paid any attention to the role the elderly play in society or what their needs are. Unfortunately, there are no figures available that indicate the proportion of the total number of households in any country that include either grandparents or a widowed grandmother. But, many intensive rural micro-studies report that the majority of households have at least one senior member, who is usually the grandmother. Yet, only very few international and national agencies concerned with development recognise the impact of the growing numbers of grandmothers, the increasing extension of their life expectancy, and the crucial impact their socialising role has on societies and their development.

Increasing Female Work Participation

More and more young rural mothers of small children are now seeking formal employment. However, supply of labour by far exceeds its demand. This often puts women at a disadvantage in their competition with men for the scarce jobs that may be available. In South Asia overall only 40 women per 100 men are reported to be in formal employment and this figure must be much smaller for rural areas. Poverty forces rural women to pursue income-earning activities; they simply cannot afford not to work. They have to take whatever work is available and the majority of them end up working in the informal sector, such as agriculture or the service industries. Seventy per cent of South Asian rural women work in agriculture but only less than 10 per cent own the land on which they work (ILO 2004).

As the volume of male rural-urban migrants grows, increasing numbers of rural households are becoming female-headed. Demands on these women's time are becoming even more intense than they had ever been before. To relieve the pressure on them they need someone to look after their small children. This reinforces their dependence on help from either their own mothers or their mothers-in-law. Though the number of extended three-generation families has been declining even in the rural sectors of developing countries, the link between children and their grandmothers has remained as strong as ever. When grandmothers become widows, they themselves and their sons' or daughters' families are usually pleased to live under one roof. This arrangement enables the young mothers to pursue income-generating activities. It proves beneficial not only to both these parties, but it also benefits the grandchildren, who are assured of the loving care and attention of an older relative.

If one or both grandparents do not live with their children, they frequently live close by. This facilitates a close relationship between grannies and their grandchildren. Batchana Bayass, a fourteen-year-old Togo girl whose grandmother lives near her own home related

> My grandmother taught me how to wash dishes, make fire, cook a sauce and other meals. She lectured me on hard work and insisted that I should show respect to my own parents and elder brothers and sisters. Every noon I go to her house, which is near my own home and she fixes lunch for me. After eating, she always encourages me to do my school homework. She stopped people from beating me. She warned me against stealing and instructed me to take care when playing with my friends. She also taught me the names of different plants. When I work by her side on our farm she teaches me how to sow millet, sorghum, corn and peanuts. Moreover, she also taught me how to take care of my younger siblings when my mother is busy grinding corn.[10]

Socialisation

Every small child needs to be prepared to play her/his part as a member of the society into which s/he has been born. Children are generally expected to follow in their forefathers' cultural footsteps and it is generally the grandmothers' task to socialise their grandchildren. Children have to be taught not only their vernacular, but also the whole set of their ancestors' behavioural norms and practices.

Most traditional societies emphasised cultural continuity, which included hereditary succession to political offices. For example, when the son of the *patel,* village headman in the south Indian village I studied in the mid-1950s, was no more than three years old, he was already called 'little headman'. His grandmother made him realise that his future role in the village demanded behaviour from him that distinguished him from all his village peers. The small son of a central African tribal chief was similarly groomed for the leading position he was expected to occupy in his society after the death of his father.

In all societies, children when they are little have to be instructed on what will be expected of them when they will be grown-up. The Indian caste system institutionalised cultural continuity; right from birth, the future lifestyle of the child would already be predetermined: for instance, everybody would expect that the son of a carpenter would grow up to follow his father's profession, marry a girl from his caste, and get his wife to join him in living with his parents and brothers' families.

Grandmothers who socialise successive generations act thus as a storehouse of the traditional knowledge and practices of their societies. In oral cultures, which predominated in most rural societies before literacy training became a widespread phenomenon, grandmothers ensured cultural continuity by telling stories to their small grandchildren and thereby conveyed to them the history of their society and about what life was like in the olden days. In other words, they provided the roots for future generations. For example, in the Philippines, where grandmothers occupy a key role in society, there is still a dearth of literature on the topic. Yet there exists a popular saying 'that from womb to tomb the grandmother shares her wisdom with successive generations.' A scientific enquiry into the health care messages that Filipino grandmothers pass onto their grandchildren found that many practices thus conveyed were beneficial. For example, it was discovered that grandmothers advised their pregnant daughters and daughters-in-law to use guava leaves as a vaginal wash to prepare for a clean delivery. It was then scientifically proven that a decoction of guava leaves provides a good disinfectant. However, some messages turned out to be harmful, for example, when grandmothers advise pregnant women to refrain from eating squash for they may deliver a bald baby. Yet, when squash was tested it became apparent that it provides an important source of vitamins. Therefore, this practice deprived pregnant women of an important source of vitamin A .[11]

The total content of socialisation packages that grandmothers in different societies pass on to their successive generations need to be documented. Some of the beneficial traditional cultural practices, such as, the breastfeeding of babies, have been abandoned by young mothers to the detriment of their child's development. Hardly any of the beneficial traditional practices which grandmothers conveyed to their successive generations have so far been promoted by governmental health care personnel.

Thus there is not only a need for developers and public health authorities to target their publicity on grandmothers but also for developers and public health authorities to find out in detail what knowledge and practice grandmothers convey to their successive generation so that they can adopt and promote the beneficial messages that may emerge from such a piece of research.

Of course, in order to bring about change where elders are responsible for the transmission of traditional values and practices, the senior generation has to be convinced of the need for change in the first place. Hence the need to educate them too. This may seem a cumbersome and circuitous strategy. But the existing focus on individuals in the productively most active period of their lives presents a shortcut which, in many instances, has failed. It is high time we gave grandmothers an opportunity to improve the quality of life of succeeding generations (Epstein 1993).

Yet there are hardly any signs of change in this context up to now.

Endnotes

[1] I herewith acknowledge my gratitude to all my doctoral students' preparedness to share their research experiences and data with me. I am particularly indebted to Monica Das Gupta, George Mkangi, Joseph Sennyonga, Naveed-i-Rahat Jaafri, Aida Vitayala S. Hubeis, Masliana Bangun, Jharna Nath and Rajni Palriwala.

[2] See *Maragoli*, the documentary film based on Dr Joseph Sennyonga's study of the Maragoli people of Kenya.

[3] I am indebted to Dr Aida Vitayala S. Hubeis for this case study, which she collected when she was a PhD student member of the 'Action-Oriented Study of the Role of Women in Rural Development' that I directed at the University of Sussex from 1978 to 1982.

4 I am indebted to Nafish Bedri for sharing with me some of the research work she did in Sudan for her doctoral degree.

5 For this section I am indebted to Dr Judi Aubel for letting me have access to the draft of her forthcoming publication titled, 'Literary Review of Grandmothers: The Learning Institution; The Role of Senior Women in Promoting Child Education, Health and Development in Developing Countries'.

6 *Impact of AIDS on Older People in Africa: Zimbabwe Case Study*, 2002.

7 This section is abstracted from HelpAge International 2002: 26–27.

8 I am indebted to Dr George Mkangi for this case study, which formed part of his doctoral thesis.

9 The figures are extracted from HelpAge International 2002.

10 I gratefully acknowledge the help of the Plan International Togo Country representative who kindly collected for me this and similar stories from young Togo school children.

11 Source: Personal Communication from Fortuna, Sandy M. Pedrito 1999.

References

Abel, Judi. Literary Review of Grandmothers: The Learning Institution; The Role of Senior Women in Promoting Child Education, Health and Development in Developing Countries. Forthcoming.

Bedri, Nafish. 1992. Unpublished PhD thesis. London University.

Epstein, T. Scarlett. 1962. *Economic Development and Social Change in South India.* Manchester: Manchester University Press.

————. 1973. *South India: Yesterday, Today and Tomorrow.* London: MacMillan.

————. 1993. Grannies Hold the Key. In *POPULI,* July/August.

————. 1998. *Village Voices—Forty Years of Rural Transformation in South India.* Delhi: Sage Publications.

HelpAge International. 2002. *State of the World's Older People.* London: HelpAge International.

————. 2004. *Ageing and Development.* Newsletter, no. 8, June.

Hubeis, Aida Vitayala S. 1982. Role of Women in Rural Development in Indonesia. Unpublished PhD thesis. University of Sussex.

ILO. 2004. *More Women Are Entering the Global Labour Force than Ever Before, but Job Equality, Poverty Reduction Remain Elusive.* Department of Communication File, press release.

Impact of AIDS on Older People in Africa: Zimbabwe Case Study. 2002. Switzerland: World Health Organization.

Mkangi, George C. 1978. Unpublished PhD thesis. University of Sussex.

8

Cooperatives and Industrialisation in Rural Areas
The Indian Experience

B. S. Baviskar and Donald W. Attwood

INTRODUCTION

In this chapter, we describe and analyse how cooperatives have helped to promote industrialisation of rural areas in some regions of India. We also try to account for the different degrees of success or failure of these agro-industrial cooperatives. This subject is important, because of the well-known fact that in developing countries, failed cooperatives far outnumber the successful ones.

The body of this chapter consists of three main sections. The first, presents an overview of the growth of Indian cooperatives in general and agro-industrial cooperatives in particular. In the second section, we outline some patterns of success and failure as well as some of the common (and erroneous) explanations for these patterns. The third section presents our analysis of the real factors which have contributed to the varying degrees of success or failure of these cooperatives. We argue that three major factors play a significant role. First, the political economy of a region, including its landowning structure and caste system, creates relatively favourable or unfavourable ground for the cooperatives to flourish. Second, the nature of the commodity and the level of investment needed for processing it influence the behaviour of producer members in terms of their loyalty and participation. Third, because cooperatives are a state (and not a federal) responsibility, the policy of a given state government to allow autonomy and freedom or to interfere in the working of cooperatives strongly determines their chances of success or failure. In the concluding section, lessons are drawn for the healthy development of cooperatives in the process of industrialisation of rural areas.[1]

ORIGINS AND GROWTH OF COOPERATIVES IN INDIA

The cooperative movement originated in early nineteenth-century Europe, a product of the social movements and communitarian experiments which characterised this period. The movement was, in part, a response to the needs of urban workers, addressing their needs as consumers. A famous example was the Rochdale Society, founded in England in 1844. With this and other models for inspiration, cooperatives of various types soon spread to other European countries and other areas of the world. Their animating spirit was often that of the Rochdale pioneers, who instituted the principles of democratic control, open and voluntary membership, and distribution of surplus among the members in proportion to their transactions with the society.

India's cooperative movement started officially in 1904, with the enactment of the Indian Cooperative Societies Act. This was largely in response to the plight of small farmers exploited by unscrupulous moneylenders. Thus, the initial focus was on the formation of societies supplying agricultural credit to needy farmers.

After independence in 1947, the central and state governments began promoting a greater number and variety of cooperatives. Like many other newly independent countries, the Indian government saw great potential in cooperatives as instruments for increasing production and reducing poverty. Soon, cooperatives emerged in diverse fields and large numbers. No longer confined to agricultural credit, they expanded to include marketing and processing. Supply of inputs (such as seeds and fertilisers) to farmers was channelled through cooperatives. And cooperatives spread to urban areas in the form of consumer cooperatives, housing cooperatives and urban cooperative banks. In India today, practically no field of economic activity is untouched by cooperatives, and almost all sections of the population are involved with them in one way or the other. There are over 500,000 cooperatives all over the country with more than 12 million members. They handle 188 billion rupees as share capital, and Rs 2,271 billion as working capital. They provide employment to several million people.

One of the most significant developments associated with the spread of cooperatives is the boost they gave to industrialisation of the rural areas. Most of these cooperatives happen to deal with agricultural processing. Agricultural processing industries by their very nature tend to be located in rural areas close to the sources of their (bulky) raw materials. It makes economic sense to process sugarcane, milk, cotton, tea, oilseeds, and other commodities close to where they are produced, both to facilitate access to fresh produce and to save on transport costs. Especially with perishable commodities, such as sugarcane or milk, it is vital to process them quickly near the farm.

State governments in India have promoted or encouraged agricultural processing cooperatives wherever conditions were considered favourable. During the period of the centrally planned economy (c.1950–91), cooperatives often received preferential treatment in the granting of industrial licenses. Moreover, governments also helped in the collection of share capital, in acquiring large loans for plant and equipment, in providing inputs at concessional prices, and in exempting cooperative from paying taxes for specified periods. In certain cases, such as milk and oilseeds, massive international aid was sought and accepted for establishing cooperative processing units.

Of course there was a certain rationale behind these policies. Wherever agricultural processing was in the private sector, farmers were exploited in a number of ways. They were invariably given low prices for their produce, were cheated when their goods were weighed, and were never paid on time. Besides, there was no guarantee that a private company would buy whatever the farmers offered. Companies bought when it suited them and refused to buy when it did not. And of course, they pocketed the surplus which accrued from the value added to the finished product. As a consequence, farmers had to bear most of the risks attached to growing such commodities for the market.

Processing cooperatives were expected to free the farmers from the clutches of such intermediaries. Once farmers formed their own processing cooperative, it was expected that they would attain greater security as a result of guaranteed purchase by the cooperative of their crop. Moreover, the farmers would also gain a share in profits arising from the value added by these processing units. Since the cooperative (in theory) would be the farmers' own organisation, the problems of cheating in weighing and late payment would be eliminated.

There were also broader expectations attached to these cooperatives. It was rightly thought that they would provide additional employment and income to the rural people, thus slowing the exodus to urban centres. These industries would enable local people to acquire new skills. It was also assumed that cooperative processing industries would enjoy industrial peace due to harmonious relations with their workers. Owing to their close family and other ties to the farmer-members of the cooperative, locally recruited employees would feel a stake in its efficiency and survival. This would make them more responsible and productive as employees. Agricultural processing cooperatives were also expected to accelerate economic growth in their areas through multiplier effects arising out of the demand for auxiliary industries and services.

Given these expectations, it is not surprising that agricultural processing industries have proliferated in the rural areas of different regions of India. Let us take the case of sugar cooperatives. India produces between12 to 20 million tonnes of white sugar annually, often the largest amount among all sugar-producing countries. More than half of this output is produced in the cooperative sector by over 315 cooperative sugar factories. In the case of milk, nearly 200 district-level cooperative dairy unions process and market 30 per cent of India's milk production. Thanks partly to the contribution of dairy cooperatives (based in nearly a hundred thousand villages), India is not only self-sufficient in milk and milk products, it is also an exporter in this field. In 2004 India produced 88 million tonnes of milk, being the second largest producer of this commodity in the world. The story of oilseeds processing cooperatives is similar. Just fifteen years back India was an importer of oilseeds, and both the farmers and consumers were at the mercy of oil kings—the private mill owners and traders of edible oil. The entry of processing cooperatives and their marketing strategies have made the country self-sufficient in oilseeds and brought many benefits to the farmers. On a smaller scale, there are scattered achievements in the cooperative processing of cotton, tea, fish, and a few other commodities.

VARYING DEGREES OF SUCCESS AND FAILURE

There has been significant growth of industrialisation in India's rural areas largely through the expansion of agricultural processing industries. But even an ardent supporter of cooperative enterprises could not claim that they are all healthy and successful. Any objective observer of India's rural landscape will admit that few cooperatives meet their own declared objectives. Many suffer from apathy, political and bureaucratic interference, inefficiency, and corruption.

On the other hand, some types of cooperatives in certain regions, for example, the sugar cooperatives of Maharashtra and dairy cooperatives of Gujarat, have been successful, at least for a generation. How was this possible? Why do some cooperatives work, but not others? With a team of Indian and Canadian colleagues, in 1985 we organised a research project to address this question. We published a full account of our exercise in *Finding the Middle Path* (1995). Here we review and update some results of that study.

In India, some patterns of cooperative success and failure are so obvious that they have generated a variety of folk explanations, most of which may be described as circular or tautological. To illustrate, we may consider the cooperative sugar factories of Maharashtra state in western India—a set of industrial enterprises that were highly successful from about 1955 to 1990.[2]

It was commonly said that these cooperatives succeeded, because they were supported and subsidised by the state. But so were cooperatives in all other states, and most of them were failures. As we shall see, our analysis shows that state support was more generally a cause of failure than success.

Likewise, it was commonly said that the sugar cooperatives were economically successful because they were politically powerful. But how did they become so powerful? If they had been inefficient and unhelpful to their members, they would not have attracted much political support. It would be closer to the truth to suggest that these cooperatives were powerful because they were successful.

It has also been said that these cooperatives were successful because they offered high prices for the sugarcane supplied by their members. But the ability to pay high prices to their members is a measure of success and itself calls for explanation.

Some people said that these cooperatives were successful because they were blessed with good leadership. But many other regions produced good leaders in the late colonial movements for independence and social reform. If these regions could produce good political and social leaders, why not cooperative leaders as well?

People sometimes try to escape one tautology by invoking another. For example, they may answer the previous question by saying that people in western India are imbued with a 'spirit of cooperation'. But what does this mean, and where does this spirit come from? It is just as likely to be a consequence as a cause of effective organisation.

HYPOTHESES CONCERNING COOPERATIVE PERFORMANCE

In our quest to explain success or failure among India's rural cooperatives, we arrived at nine tentative hypotheses. Given the constraints of space, we boil the most important down to the following four hypotheses:

1. Regions with a broad stratum of peasant proprietors are more likely to nurture successful cooperatives. Likewise, regions with numerically large, middle-status farming castes are more likely to nurture such cooperatives.
2. Perishable products requiring expensive processing equipment tend to encourage vertical integration and thus successful cooperation.
3. Heavy investments in equipment encourage leaders to be concerned with capacity utilisation and thus with participation by small producers.
4. Cooperatives flourish in regions where they have greater autonomy from state control.

The first set of hypotheses is concerned with regional political economies, focusing on the economic, social, political and historical environments which affect the performance of cooperatives. The next two (hypotheses 2 and 3) concern internal design principles of industrial organisation. They particularly concern the implications of dealing with perishable products involving investments in heavy capital equipment. The last hypothesis is a matter of regional state policy. Thus (i) the agrarian political economy of the region; (ii) constraints affecting the equipment, capital investment, and organisation needed to process a commodity; and (iii) the role of the state appear to be crucial factors determining success or failure. Let us briefly consider how these factors work.

The Agrarian Political Economy of the Region

A region's agrarian political economy is shaped by its structure of landownership and its caste system, both of which are very complex—and their interaction adds to the complexity. Agrarian systems in India range from wet rice cultivation supporting dense populations in coastal plains to dry land farming, especially of sorghum and millet, supporting much thinner populations in the semi-arid plains and plateaus of the interior. In the humid, densely populated coastal regions, economic and caste inequalities tend to be more extreme, meaning that land is concentrated in fewer hands, that landless labourers and sharecroppers make up a large share of the rural population, and that these workers tend to belong to low-status castes widely separate in status from the landowning castes.

Extreme economic inequality inhibits the formation and maintenance of effective cooperatives. There are several reasons for this. For example, powerful rentier elites tend to be more interested in maintaining power than improving production. They have little interest in promoting new economic institutions and often see cooperatives as threats to their power. In addition, they can monopolise, distort, or block any channels leading to external agencies offering credit or other support for nascent cooperatives. This comes out clearly in the contrast between West Bengal and Maharashtra. West Bengal is a humid region of high population density with an agrarian structure long dominated by rentier landlords. In this state, cooperatives seem to be scarce and ineffective. Maharashtra, on the other hand, is a semi-arid region with relatively open and flexible stratification in the villages. The region is dominated by peasant proprietors, mostly with small holdings. Maharashtra is also a region where cooperatives (and many other voluntary organisations) have flourished for a long time.

Cooperative performance hinges not simply on a negative factor (the absence of extreme inequality) but on a positive factor that follows from this absence: the presence of a large stratum of middle peasants, that is, of medium and small-scale proprietors who cultivate their own land. What makes this a positive factor? Small and medium-scale farmers tend to have precisely the skills and interests which are crucial to cooperative performance. When presented with new opportunities their customary skills, habits and values make them formidable innovators. They know how to work hard, increase output, manage assets and cope with risks (landless labourers also know how to work hard but have less experience with managing assets). These abilities contribute to their success as enterprising farm families; and they also have abilities needed to establish new organisations for solving local problems. Thus, agrarian regions which nurture a broad, middle-farmer stratum should be able to nurture innovative and successful cooperatives— though not all of them do.

On the other hand, societies ruled by landed oligarchies are often rigidly stratified by caste, race or ethnicity. Such societies are not likely to provide fertile grounds for cooperation. Examples of this problem may be found in many parts of rural Latin America.[3] Within India, states like Bihar and West Bengal perhaps come closest to this extreme.

In India, regional caste systems and agrarian structures are often closely interconnected. In Maharashtra, rural society is dominated by a very large, middle-status caste. The Maratha caste includes a majority of the rural population and encompasses a wide range of large and small farmers as well as agricultural labourers. Most villagers are small Maratha farmers, placing them in the middle in two respects: in terms of caste status, and in terms of wealth and occupation. Thus, caste divisions do not reinforce class divisions as strongly as they do elsewhere.

Caste, like ethnicity, provides a cultural identity, and this identity can strengthen the ideological basis for cooperation. Maharashtra has a long history of rural opposition to urban interests, a history which pre-dates the rise of the influential sugar cooperatives. Since the turn of the century, Marathas have tended to see themselves as economically exploited and politically neglected by urban elites. This sense of cultural identity and ideological opposition was a major impetus behind the rise of the cooperative movement. It also helped propel the Marathas to dominance in state politics after independence in 1947.

On the other hand, there are regions where middle-status castes are numerically small, where the largest castes are found at the bottom of the status hierarchy. In such regions, big landowners and small cultivators belong to very distinct levels of the caste system. Thus caste divisions reinforce economic ones and inhibit cooperation between classes. In West Bengal, for example, much of the land was owned by a tiny elite of high-caste landlords, closely connected to urban elites. Their lands were cultivated by low-caste tenants, sharecroppers and labourers. The absence of a numerically large and economically secure middle-farmer caste, created a polarised system of status and power. It also means that the people with hands-on experience in agricultural production lack the assets to initiate technical and organisational improvements.

Moreover, the elite values of high-caste landlords imbue them with contempt for those who work the land. This acts as a barrier to the transfer of technical knowledge concerning potential improvements in agricultural and agro-industrial production. High-caste landlords act as rent collectors, not as enterprising managers. Ignorant of the technical options, they have little interest in cooperative organisations which might help to implement new options. Thus, social barriers perpetuate technical and organisational barriers.

The demography of caste in India's regions is highly variable; but it is crucial to the politics of cooperation, affecting not only the local distribution of power but the whole character of state politics.

Organisational Factors

Among the various organisational factors influencing cooperative performance, we found that the nature of the commodity and the level of capital investment needed for its processing are important. It is obvious that each crop has its own technical characteristics: that is, each one requires that certain operations be done in certain ways and at certain times. The same is true when the crop is processed for the market. Each crop has specific technical requirements, and some crops lend themselves more readily than others to cooperative processing.

Sugarcane and milk share two important technical characteristics: they are both perishable and bulky. It is more profitable to process them for urban markets than to sell them locally in the villages; but large-scale processing for sale in distant markets requires heavy industrial machinery. In order for this machinery to be profitable, it must be used at full capacity. If the supply of raw material falters, the machinery will stand idle, and overhead costs will eat up profits. Farm and factory operations must therefore be closely coordinated to insure a steady supply of perishable raw material to the factory. This coordination is best achieved when farm and factory are vertically integrated in a system of common ownership.

In many parts of the world, the sugar industry has come to terms with these requirements through a particular type of organisation: the central mill, which owns and manages a big plantation. With farm and factory under common management, a full and steady supply of cane throughout the harvest season can be assured. In western India, this solution has been applied in reverse: several thousand small cane growers own and manage each cooperative sugar factory. Their goal is to gain high prices for their sugarcane from the cooperative. They know that the cooperative can only do this if it receives a steady cane supply throughout the harvest season. Therefore, the farmer-members consent to a highly centralised harvesting system, scheduled and managed by the sugar factory. Both types of ownership structure (the central mill and the cooperative) have been used successfully in different periods in Maharashtra.[4] In both cases, vertical integration is a solution to intrinsic problems of high uncertainties and high transaction costs in the market between cane growers and processors.

Similar constraints apply in the case of dairy processing. For milk to reach a large but distant urban market, it must be chilled and processed in modern plants, since milk is highly perishable. As in the case of sugar, a large dairy plant can only run at a profit if the milk supply is fresh and reliable. This means that some form of co-ownership and co-management of farm and dairy plant will make for greater efficiency. Once again, the technical characteristics of the farm product encourage cooperative processing and marketing.

Most farm products are not as perishable as milk or sugarcane; so in most cases, it is unlikely that technical factors will encourage cooperatives to become large, complex, and stable in their organisation. In Gujarat, for example, cotton cooperatives sometimes fragment, reunite, or close down intermittently, since there are many options concerning how much capital equipment to employ and on what schedule. This is because cotton is not as perishable as sugarcane and milk. It can be stored by individual farmers who may hope for higher prices if sold after the harvest season. This, of course, means that cotton ginning cooperatives cannot rely on a steady supply of raw material. Their operations are inherently unstable.

In studying the successful sugar and dairy cooperatives of India, we observed that the leaders tended to be large farmers, while the great majority of members were small or middle farmers. It seemed intuitively important that the large farmers, with their skills and resources, be committed to these cooperatives—or at least, that they not be committed to undermining them.

As noted, some farm products encourage the use of heavy equipment and require close co-ordination between production and processing. What does this imply about the relationship between large and small farmers? If large farmers have to invest heavily in large-scale equipment in order to process their raw material, they will be strongly motivated to achieve full capacity utilisation. If the machinery were forced to stand idle, owing to an irregular and inadequate supply of raw material, it would be costly to the owners, who would be paying interest on the capital investment.

In a cooperative processing plant, the urgent need to achieve full capacity utilisation implies that leaders will be motivated to recruit other farmers as members and retain them as loyal suppliers. This means that a cooperative sugar factory cannot afford to cheat its smaller and weaker members when it comes to weighing their cane and paying for it. If the small farmers, who constitute the vast majority of members, believe that they are being cheated, they will either stop growing cane, sell it to another factory, or else process it themselves, into crude brown sugar (*gur*) as they often do in Uttar Pradesh. In other words, the leaders of the cooperative know that they must encourage steady participation by the smaller members. The only way to do this is with an open and honest system of cane supply and payment.

Stated simply, a heavy investment in equipment gives leaders a strong incentive to promote efficiency, which also encourages them to promote equity in the sense of fair terms for small farmers who supply the raw material. The same logic applies to dairy cooperatives. However, it must be emphasised that two limiting conditions apply to this observation. First, if the plant is heavily subsidised, that is, if the leaders do not have to invest much of their own capital, the hypothesis is weakened. Dairy cooperatives established under 'Operation Flood', India's national dairy development scheme, illustrate this limitation, since most of the capital is raised by external agencies, including foreign aid donors.

Second, if local leaders lack effective ownership—that is, if they lack managerial control—heavy investments may not make much of a difference. It is not enough simply to invest; local leaders must also have the means to make the investment pay. As we shall see in the next section, if they lack managerial control, they cannot make an organisation operate efficiently. Studies of 'cooperative' sugar factories in northern India show that when local leaders lack such control, they tend to act in flagrant opposition to the interests of the organisation. In these cases, as in many others throughout India, managerial control is vested in government bureaucrats, not in the 'member-shareholders' of the 'cooperative'. If there is no hope of improving an organisation through your own actions, nor through alliances with your peers, then the most practical course of action is to steal as much as you can for your personal benefit.

We emphasise here the importance of class analysis in understanding the basis for cooperation. In other words, the potentially divergent interests of large and small farmers must be taken into account. Under the conditions spelled out here—that is, when large farmers need to invest in heavy processing equipment and are allowed to manage this equipment themselves—they seek to encourage equitable participation by small farmers.

Class differences are often invoked to explain why cooperatives fail. To our knowledge, they have not been invoked to explain why some cooperatives succeed. Yet it is necessary to explain the political economy of success as well as failure.

The Role of the State

In India, as elsewhere in the developing world, cooperatives have often emerged not as a result of initiative by their members but as a result of promotion by the government. Governments promote cooperatives through various means: spreading propaganda, sending out officers with quotas and deadlines, and offering subsidies. The latter may include credit at low interest rates, tax holidays, monopoly licences to engage in a particular business, or import/export quotas. As a result, members join not because they value the organisation, but because they want the subsidies. Many cunning people set up bogus cooperatives to take advantage of these subsidies. The moment the subsidies disappear, so does their interest.

We have found many examples of cooperatives founded and managed entirely by state governments in India. Tea processing cooperatives in Tamil Nadu and fishermen cooperatives in Kerala are examples. In such cases the members' commitment and loyalty tends to be low, and the cooperatives suffer from a variety of problems. When cooperatives emerge because of local initiative, they tend to last longer and respond dynamically to members' interests. Leaders and members may work hard to ensure that these cooperatives survive. However, they have no such stake in a government-promoted cooperative. The failure of the latter will be considered the government's failure and few will care.

A real cooperative is managed by its member-shareholders, who elect leaders to make policy decisions. These leaders and members have a real stake in the efficiency of the cooperative, and they are usually best qualified to judge which management decisions and technical staff will benefit the cooperative. Managers appointed from the state bureaucracy lack these qualifications.

As India has a federal constitution, rural development policy is in the hands of state governments. Legislation regarding cooperatives and agriculture comes mostly under the jurisdiction of the states. There is much variation in state politics and rural development policies.

Our hypothesis is that cooperatives flourish in those regions where they have greater autonomy from state control. In all regions, state governments lay down laws and regulations for cooperatives. In some states (particularly Maharashtra and Gujarat), locally elected leaders are allowed to manage at least some kinds of cooperatives within this regulatory framework. However, in other regions, such as Tamil Nadu, Haryana, Punjab and Uttar Pradesh, state-appointed officials are in charge of the day-to-day management of most or all 'cooperatives'. This almost invariably leads to corruption, inefficiency and wastage of scarce resources. 'Cooperative' sugar factories have been established in northern India—in UP and Haryana, for example—yet these organisations are actually managed by state officials. As a result, the cooperatives are inefficient and corrupt, and the members sell much of their sugarcane to private small-scale enterprises making crude brown sugar (*gur*) or open-pan white powdered sugar called *khandsari*.[5]

The problem is that state officials generally have no stake in the efficiency of these enterprises. They have no share in the ownership or the potential profits. Why, then, should they make extra effort, or indeed any effort, to promote efficiency? They can be compelled to work efficiently only if the owners (the members, as shareholders) have the power to hire and fire or otherwise discipline them. But when state officials are delegated to manage cooperatives, the members usually have no voice in determining who is hired or on what terms.

Our results show that local initiative and autonomy are crucial for cooperative success, and their absence generally causes wastage of resources, rampant corruption, technical inefficiency and institutional paralysis. This lesson is so obvious, as one compares cooperatives from one region of India to another, it hardly seems to require emphasis. Yet the countryside is littered with 'cooperative' schemes demonstrating official determination to go on doing things wrong. One must ask then: what causes this persistence on the wrong path?

In some regions the state government encourages autonomous management, and the results are often positive; in other regions, no such autonomy is tolerated, and the results are usually pathetic. The intriguing question, then, is not why cooperatives fail in these latter regions, since the reasons are generally obvious. More interesting is the second order question: why are some states willing to encourage autonomy while others are not?

Different political economies in these regions provide some explanation for the varying degree of autonomy enjoyed by cooperatives. Genuine cooperatives, after all, empower their members to improve their economic condition, which in turn enables them to demand a greater share in political power. In some regions, the rise of a strong rural middle class may be seen as a threat to those in power.

In some cases, political ideology may play a role in stifling cooperatives. Since the 1970s, West Bengal has been ruled by a leftist coalition dominated by the Communist Party of India (Marxist). The supreme importance of party loyalty in communist ideology may prevent state leaders from promoting rural organisations which might become somewhat autonomous from the party. Also of course, cooperatives are reformist, not revolutionary.

On the other hand, in regions dominated by numerically large, middle-status farming castes, there may be common interests among those elected to govern the state and those wanting to promote cooperatives. Under such conditions, cooperatives may enjoy greater autonomy from state control because of common political interests. For example, the Marathas are now dominant in Maharashtra state politics, and they are also actively involved in cooperatives; thus, there is a greater possibility of favourable policies for cooperatives. In the absence of such common interests, those in power in the state are likely to interfere in the working of cooperatives.

Even so, there are other states, such as Karnataka, Haryana and Punjab, dominated by middle-status farming castes but lacking notable achievements in cooperative industrialisation. In such cases, our hypothesis is not very helpful, and we are forced to fall back on the specific political history of each region in order to explain why state policies are unfriendly to cooperative autonomy. There is no room here for a detailed analysis, but we have made an attempt at this in *Finding the Middle Path*.

CONCLUSION

Industrialisation of rural areas offers the potential to reduce poverty and stimulate economic growth. It is also likely to check the exodus of people migrating to urban areas, providing much-needed employment and income to rural people. Moreover, it will enable them to acquire new technical and organisational skills. Agro-based industries will also help stabilise the farm economy by providing higher returns to farmers as a result of improved marketing and processing facilities.

Rural industrialisation logically begins with agro-based industries, since they provide the crucial advantage of access to raw materials. Once the foundation has been laid, other industries are likely to follow in due course owing to availability of infrastructure and skilled human resources.

Such industries should be more beneficial to farmers and others if they are in the cooperative sector. Past experience shows that private companies exploit the farmers in a variety of ways. Nor can the public sector deliver the goods. It is generally inefficient, corrupt, and indifferent to farmers' needs and concerns. We suggest that cooperative processing industries are likely to be the best instruments for the development of rural areas.

However, the performance of cooperative processing industries has not been very encouraging. Excepting for a few regions, such as Maharashtra and Gujarat, cooperative industries have performed poorly. In other regions, state political and bureaucratic interference has done tremendous harm to local cooperatives. In the emerging climate of liberalisation and globalisation it should not be too difficult to reduce the destructive role of the state and allow greater autonomy to cooperatives.

But, it must be admitted that the cooperative sugar factories of Maharashtra have left behind their days of impressive efficiency and innovation. For political reasons, too many licences were issued for new factories. Given the available water resources, Maharashtra can support at most 100 modern sugar factories, but there are now more than 165. This means that most factories cannot obtain a full and steady supply of cane during the harvest season. As noted above, declining capacity utilisation means higher costs and lower earnings for a factory, which means that it pays lower prices for sugarcane supplied by the members. As a result, the loyalty and commitment of the members declines.

Other new problems arise from changes in state politics and central government sugar policies. These changes unfortunately led to massive corruption in many of the cooperative sugar factories of Maharashtra.[6] Corruption was always present to some extent, but it was held in check by various mechanisms, including democratic governance and intense competition with neighbouring factories— competition that once motivated factory leaders to focus on technical and economic efficiency, not on lining their pockets.[7]

With India's shift to reduced state management of the economy, many of the inefficient and corrupt sugar factories in Maharashtra may be allowed to die. This will provide an opportunity for the remaining cooperatives to put their houses in order. In other regions, the long-standing political habit of buying up 'sick' private factories and moving them into the public sector or into the 'cooperative' sector (but under state management), may also die out as the states are forced to put their fiscal houses in order.

In our view, cooperatives have an important role to play in the industrialisation of rural areas, but we must understand the nature and process of cooperation to realise their full potential. This is the lesson to be derived from the Indian experience.

Endnotes

[1] Parts of this chapter are based on our book (Baviskar and Attwood 1995). The statistical data are taken from *Handbook of Cooperative Statistics*, Government of India, New Delhi, 2004.
[2] See Baviskar (1980), and Attwood (1992).
[3] See Almy (1988).
[4] See Attwood (1992).

[5] See Batra (1988, 1995).
[6] See Baviskar (2007).
[7] See Attwood (1989).

References

Almy, Susan W. 1988. Vertical Societies and Cooperative Structures: Problems of Fit in North-eastern Brazil. In *Who Shares? Cooperatives and Rural Development*, ed. D. W. Attwood and B. S. Baviskar, 46–68. Delhi: Oxford University Press.

Attwood, D. W. 1989. Does Competition Help Cooperation? *Journal of Development Studies* 26(1): 5–27.

————. 1992 *Raising Cane: The Political Economy of Sugar in Western India*. Boulder: Westview Press.

Batra, S. M. 1988. Agrarian Relations and Sugar Cooperatives in North India. In Attwood and Baviskar, *Who Shares?* 91–111.

————. 1995. Dominant Classes and Cooperative Leaders in Western Uttar Pradesh. In *Finding the Middle Path: The Political Economy of Cooperation in Rural India*. ed. B. S. Baviskar and D. W. Attwood, 323–41. Boulder & Oxford: Westview Press.

Baviskar, B. S. 1980. *The Politics of Development: Sugar Cooperatives in Rural Maharashtra*. Delhi: Oxford University Press.

————. 2007. Cooperatives in Maharashtra: Challenges Ahead. *Economic and Political Weekly* 42(42): 4217–21.

9

Patidars as Metaphor of Indian Diaspora

Pravin J. Patel and Mario Rutten

THE PATIDAR DIASPORA IN BRITAIN

People of Gujarati origin constitute one of the largest groups of Indians in Britain. According to a 1991 estimate, there are 84,000 Indians in Britain. Approximately, 48 per cent of them are Hindus, and an overwhelming majority of them are Gujaratis (Vertovec 2000: 88). An equally large number of Indians in Britain originate from the Punjab region (Jain 1993: 36). Among the Gujarati Hindus in

This essay is a revised version of the paper presented at an international workshop on 'Globalization of India and Indianization of Globe' jointly organised by the University of Oxford and London School of Economics and Political Science, at the London School of Economics, London, 14–16 February 2003, which was later published as a working paper by Sardar Patel University in 2004. This paper is based on an international research project 'Long Distance Familism: A Study of Patels of Central Gujarat Settled in UK' jointly undertaken by Pravin J. Patel and Mario Rutten, and sponsored by the Indo-Dutch Programme on Alternatives in Development (IDPAD). The fieldwork for the study was conducted in central Gujarat and Greater London. In central Gujarat, 313 families were surveyed, and in Greater London we had surveyed 159 families who were related to the households surveyed by us in central Gujarat. Pravin J. Patel is at present with Sardar Patel University, India, and Mario Rutten is with Amsterdam University, the Netherlands.

The authors are grateful to B. S. Baviskar, Tulsi Patel and Javed Khan for their useful comments on the previous draft of the paper.

Britain, the Patidars, popularly known as Patels, of Gujarat constitute one of the largest communities.[1] According to a conservative estimate of the membership of associations of all the Patidar marriage circles in Britain, there were about 30,000 Patidars from central Gujarat living in Britain in the early 1990s (Lyon and West 1995: 407). Not surprisingly, therefore, 'Patel' is one of the most famous Indian surnames abroad along with 'Singh', the surname of those Indians whose families originate from Punjab.

The Patidars of central Gujarat have emigrated in large numbers. Central Gujarat, also known as Charotar, is the heartland of the state, which includes two most affluent and advanced districts, namely, Anand and Kheda.[2] The Patidars have gone abroad from almost every village, out of about 1,000 villages in this area. And, more than half of the Patidar families have emigrated from many of these villages. These Patidars, a middle-ranking agricultural caste of central Gujarat, are highly status conscious and upwardly mobile.

The Social Origins of Patidar Diaspora

The emigration of the Patidars began during the British period, particularly in the late nineteenth century. First, they migrated to East Africa, and then they moved to almost every corner of the world, wherever they found greener pastures. One of the most prominent general explanations of emigration found in the literature of the subject, which is mainly an economic explanation, also known as 'the push-pull theory', refers to adverse economic factors pushing out people from their place of origin and pulling them towards the lands of opportunities. In consonance with this theory, scholars like Pocock argue that members of this agricultural community left their native place under the compulsions of some natural disasters such as famines, droughts and plagues (Pocock 1972).

However, a deeper examination reveals that these natural disasters and the 'push-pull factors' do not fully explain the Patidar out-migration. In this connection, we will examine the significant role played by social factors such as the social structure in which the Patidars were located and their prevalent social customs.

Social Structure, Social Customs and Patidar Diaspora

The Patidars of central Gujarat constitute about 15 to 20 per cent of the total population of the area (Rutten 1995). Although they do not constitute a numerical majority in the area, they have acquired .economic, social and political dominance in the state as well as the region since the late nineteenth century during the British regime (Hardiman 1981). In other words, to borrow a term from Srinivas (1992[1959]), they are 'a dominant caste'; for they are a landowning caste, having the ownership of the means of production. The owner of a piece of land also has authority, like a ruler, over the others who worked on that land. Besides, the institution of the Jajamani system also socially defined and legitimised the interdependence of the castes of a village community. Thus, landowning in India has been traditionally associated with higher status as well as greater authority. Therefore, land in India, besides being a means of livelihood, also has been a source of social prestige, status, power and pride. To be without land, conversely, implied being without all these socially coveted attributes, since persons without land were either landless labourers or those who worked for others like servants without having much autonomy.

In this context, we will discuss some important social customs of this status-conscious community. One is the custom of patrilineal rule of inheritance of property by which only sons inherited property, mainly the agricultural land and the ancestral house, from their fathers. Besides, in contrast to the practice of primogeniture, the property of a person was equally divided among the sons inheriting it. Consequently, the land was so divided from one generation to another that by the end of the nineteenth century, it became uneconomical in providing reasonable sustenance for quite a few Patidar families. In the meanwhile, formal education, introduced by the British, became one of the major means of maintaining their prestige and dignity, acquiring respectable white-collar jobs in the modern organised sector, and enjoying status and power equivalent to that of a landowner. However, since such occupations were available only in urban centres, the educated Patidar youth started moving towards the newly emerging cities of British India, leaving behind their not-so-educated brothers back home to look after the land. In addition, other social customs like hypergamy and dowry also gave impetus to movement outside the village. The customary practice of hypergamy encouraged a girl's marriage with a boy from a family with higher status. This custom generated a competition in this highly status-conscious community whereby they got their girls married into higher-status families, enhancing the importance of the traditional custom of dowry.

Dowry was a custom prescribed for the members of the community to indirectly give girls their share of their father's property at the time of their marriage in the form of marriage gifts, both in cash and kind. As noted earlier, only boys in a family had a right to their father's property under the custom of inheritance. However, over a period, the custom of dowry was vulgarised as a result of the practice of hypergamy and the consequent status-seeking competition among the parents to get their daughters married into higher-status families. Nevertheless, an unintended consequence of the practice of dowry was that it encouraged the members of this community to earn more money and save as much as possible to display their status by spending lavishly in the form of dowry, and also in the form of conspicuous consumption, such as wedding feasts and other marriage-related extravagances like elaborate electric decorations and expensive music bands at their daughters' weddings.

Therefore, some educated members of such families were encouraged to search for better employment opportunities outside their villages so that they could earn enough and arrange the marriages of the girls in their families to suitable boys enjoying equal status or preferably those from families with a higher status. Otherwise, it was considered disgraceful for the whole family if their girls remained unmarried for want of dowry, or, still worse, they were compelled to marry into lower-status families. But, owing to the slow growth of the Indian economy in the colonial period, there were not enough jobs for moderately educated Indian youths. Incidentally, around the same time, plenty of jobs were available in East Africa where the British laid the railway lines, and the native African population was not educated enough to take up these positions. As a result, many young and educated boys from the Patidar community started going to East Africa in search of better prospects. In East Africa, initially, most of them took up jobs in the railways and other civil services. There were so many Patidars in the East African railways that there was a time when it was known as 'Patel Railways'. Employment in such jobs provided them a much more secure and reliable source of earning in comparison with agriculture back home. With almost the same amount of labour, they could earn much larger sums of money to enable the whole family to maintain its status with dignity. Moreover, some of these enterprising migrants also started doing business when they found it more profitable. After having settled down in this new land of opportunity, they started encouraging their family members and other relatives to join them. Thus, a chain migration from India to East Africa began.

However, in the 1960s, when these African countries started becoming independent and initiated the process of Africanisation of their economy and polity, these migrants were forced to leave and move towards Britain, for they were already considered British subjects and entitled to a British passport. Therefore, we find a sizable number of Patidars in the UK today. Most of them decided to settle down in the UK, though they were not used to the hostile climate of their newly adopted country, for they saw no prospects for themselves in India.

Interestingly, there are differences within the Patidar community in Britain, between those who migrated from the East African countries and those who migrated directly from India. Those Patidars, who entered Britain from East Africa, especially from Kenya, Uganda and Tanzania, are twice-migrant families. In our sample of 159 households studied in Greater London, 72.7 per cent of the total number of household members migrated to Britain from East Africa(this figure includes those who came to Britain after a temporary stay in India following their departure from East Africa). The remaining 27.3 per cent consists of those who migrated directly from India to Britain without any previous migration history.

The 'East African Asians', in general, are associated with higher educational and occupational backgrounds than those who migrated directly from India (Modood et al. 1997). The 'East African Asians' had a longer and deeper acquaintance with the English language, and also with urban, middle-class 'European' (albeit colonial) lifestyles. These traits, in turn, are equated with higher status. Steven Vertovec (2000: 90–1) also discusses the difference between these 'East African' Gujaratis and the 'Indian' Gujaratis. In general, as he emphasises, 'East African' Gujaratis are viewed as having a higher education, better occupational background, greater wealth and higher status as compared with those who migrated directly from India. Though it would be difficult to prove the validity of all such traits, they remain common stereotypes that suggest that those Patidars who migrated from East Africa were better prepared for successful adaptation to Britain.

ADAPTATION OF PATIDARS TO BRITAIN: ECONOMIC ACTIVITY

Many of the first-generation Patidar migrants in Britain turned to small private businesses such as grocery shops, corner shops selling confectionery, tobacco, and newspapers, or small sub-post offices. Partly, this preference for small businesses is related to the fact that these first-generation migrants had great difficulty, upon their arrival in Britain, in finding middle-class occupations similar to the ones they held in East Africa or India. Others were already owners of shops or trading companies in East Africa and preferred to remain their own masters than to work under someone else. However small their businesses, these Patidars considered it better to work long hours in their own shops than to work as blue-collar workers in private or public companies.

This preference among the British Patidars for managing their own enterprises is based on a strong feeling of self-reliance among them in general. Their long history as independent peasants in Gujarat has created an attitude of self-reliance and an insistence on autonomy. Whenever possible, they do their utmost to avoid situations in which they are subordinated to others.

This attitude had already deterred them in Gujarat from getting into the government bureaucracy or into the salaried ranks of big private companies on a large scale, their preference being independent profession or business (Rutten 1995). Even though the younger generation from the richer Patidar families in Gujarat stands a relatively good chance of finding a job in government or a private company, most of them still prefer to manage family-owned businesses than to work under someone else.

This desire to establish oneself as an independent entrepreneur employing others instead of being employed is still a typical characteristic of members of the Patidar community in Gujarat today. Among the more wealthy members of this community, the prospect of spending one's working life as a government officer or as a salaried employee in a private company is rejected almost with contempt or considered as the last option. The phrase *nokeri kare chhe* ('he is in service') is used to express the low status of a salaried job and of the person performing it. If the person in question happens to be a relative who belongs to one of the wealthier families in the village, it is often explicitly stated that this is a temporary expedient only, which can be thrown aside as soon as the person has enough experience to set up a business of his own.

The predominance of small businesses among the Patidar migrants in London is confirmed by a study, in the early 1990s, by Michael Lyon and Bernice West. According to their findings, about 90 per cent of the businessmen belonging to the Patidar community of London are involved in independent retail business such as corner shops. Nearly 70 per cent of these Patidar firms in London sell newspapers, confectionery and tobacco. About 20 per cent of them own grocery or off-licence liquor shops, while about 10 per cent of those Patidars who are independent businessmen are professionals like pharmacists, accountants, opticians, and dentists (Lyon and West 1995).

According to Lyon and West, shops owned by the Patidar migrants are spread all over London. About half of these families combine their shop with their family residence, with the shop on the ground floor and a residential apartment above it. In many cases, both husband and wife run the shop by rotation. Especially among the first-generation Patidar migrants from India, there are some who are not fluent in English, even though their clients are mostly whites, blacks and non-Gujarati Asians. In most cases, they are able to make a small profit because of their willingness to work very long hours, usually from about six o'clock in the morning to eight o'clock in the evening. In almost all these families, the children start helping their parents in the shop once they have joined secondary school.

Since the 1980s, however, these corner shops, groceries, and small post offices have started losing business. To operate a corner shop or small grocery on profit has become increasingly difficult owing to the rise of supermarkets in the major cities of Britain. These supermarkets have come up in large numbers in London and are able to remain open for even longer hours by employing people in different shifts. Moreover, since they buy their goods in bulk, they are able to sell at lower prices as compared with the small shops. An additional advantage is that the supermarkets are in a position to sell a larger variety of products, as a result of which they offer the average customer an opportunity to buy all required goods in one single place, which is often easily accessible by car. For more than a decade, most families in Britain have changed their shopping patterns. Now, they prefer to buy the bulk of their daily necessities from a supermarket. For all these reasons, the supermarket, often part of a larger supermarket chain, has gradually pushed the corner shops and small groceries out of business. As a result, many Patidar owners of these shops have a difficult time making a living and are only able to do so by working even longer hours and by creating additional sources of income through family members, working outside.

The small post offices that have seen most of their business disappear over the past decades have met with a similar fate. To a large extent, this is due to the fact that post offices no longer have a monopoly over selling stamps and, even more important, they have lost their role in the disbursement of social security benefits through the weekly payment of cheques. In general, the technological revolution in banking and modern mass communication have marginalised the utility of post offices. Since the mid-1990s, there is a clear tendency among the Patidars owning post offices to close down their business. Some have changed their business by opening shops selling ethnic-oriented goods such as Indian clothes or spices. Considering the importance of retaining Indian culture among the migrant population in London and the personalised customer-oriented relations of the owners, these shops are likely to survive for some years to come.

However, the Patidar owners are also increasingly facing competition from other Indian or South Asian communities in this business.

All these changes have resulted in the fact that the small shops owned by the first-generation Patidar migrants have become economically less viable. Over the years, many of their children, who were born and brought up in Britain, do not intend to continue the family business. They prefer to find employment in private or government companies. To a large extent, members of this second and third generation have started entering professional occupations. Notwithstanding these changes, the first-generation Patidars in Britain is still associated with the ownership of small corner shops, groceries, or post offices.

Adaptation of Patidars to Britain: Social Life

The social life of first-generation Patidar migrants is profoundly influenced by their village life in Gujarat, where they had lived and studied during their formative childhood years. Moreover, many of them grew up during the patriotic period of the national independence movement, which made them even more conscious of their pride in Indian culture and heritage. The social, religious and cultural bonds with their home village and with other Patidar migrants from the same region, when they first lived in East Africa and later on in Britain, further cemented those ties with their villages of origin. Therefore, the social identity of the first-generation Patidar migrants is deeply embedded in strong family ties, in their linkages with their places of origin, and with their relatives and friends in Gujarat, which are still quite powerful.

Type of Household

A manifestation of the emphasis on traditional family values among the Patidars in London is visible in their family structure. About 62 per cent of the respondents of our sample from Britain live in nuclear households, mainly because many of their relatives are back in India. Those who have their family members in Britain do not live together partly owing to constraints of housing space and partly owing to the fact that their children prefer to live separately. However, it is significant that still about 38 per cent of the respondents live in joint households (table 9.1).

Table 9.1.   Type of households in Greater London

Type of Household	No. of Household	Percentage Households
Nuclear Household	98	61.6
Joint Household	61	38.4
Total	159	100.0

Interaction within the Community

A characteristic feature of the Patidar community is that they remain attached to Indian culture and to their Gujarati background in terms of their social relations. There are many social activities that take place throughout the year, especially among the first-generation Patidars who live a retired life in Britain. But, mostly, these activities are confined to the Gujarati community, dominated by Patidars of central Gujarat. In summer, for instance, an elderly group of Indians in Wembley organises regular outings. In most instances, these are one-day trips of sightseeing in England, although they also involve holiday tours of several weeks through various countries in Europe.

Following our participation in one of the one-day trips/outings, we have made the following observations, which will illustrate the point

> . . . on a Sunday of the summer of 1999 about 150 elderly first-generation migrants, the large majority of them belonging to Patidar community of central Gujarat, hiring three coaches went to Brighton for a day on the beach. All 150 participants were Gujaratis. It is obvious that they are enjoying their life in Britain. One of the reasons is that they are economically secure, due to their pensions, social security, free medical help, and the fact that their children are well settled and are able to support themselves.
> . . . they organize these kinds of outings quite frequently. Usually, they try and keep them low budget by carrying vegetarian food from a Gujarati caterer and hiring coaches from an Indian travel agent. During these trips the participants are mostly from the first-generation migrants. Many of them know

each other from their stay in Kenya or Uganda and originate
from the same region or even from the same village in Gujarat.
To a large extent, they are of equal status in terms of economic
position and social standing. Having a similar life history and
common past experiences, they prefer to be in one another's
company. This is further strengthened by their shared problems
of relating to their children and grandchildren who were born
and brought up in Britain.

. . . the Patidar women seem to have retained many traits of
their traditional Indian culture. All of them wear Indian saris, are
religious, and are strictly vegetarian, preferring to eat Gujarati
dishes only. In this preference for Indian culture, however, they
have at the same time been able to adapt themselves to the new
culture in which they are living. Many women, for example, have
work experience in Britain, they have started to take an interest
in what are typical British hobbies, such as gardening, they can
drive, and make use of modern equipment in their kitchens.
Following the fact that these women have worked outside their
homes after their arrival in Britain, they have introduced a few
new habits in the management of their household. Contrary to
what they were used to in India and in East Africa, they have
started the practice of cooking Indian food of different variety in
large quantities, which are then kept in the freezer to entertain
unexpected guests and relatives, or to share with the households
of their daughters and sons.

Village-based and *Gol*-based Associations in Britain

Most of the older generation members have retained their Patidar
identity by organising themselves on the basis of their village of
origin and marriage circle (known as *gol* in colloquial Gujarati). These
village-based associations and organisations of village circles (gols)
in Britain bring out directories, giving details of all the members of
each Patidar family of the concerned village or gol. These directories
are mostly used as a resource to establish contacts with one another
and also to help arrange marriages of their children. In addition, the
village associations and marriage-circle associations arrange several
social functions, such as, those to celebrate Navratri, Diwali, and
other important Indian festivals.

One of the most important concerns of the Patidar community
in Britain is the marriage of their children. Since the traditional
method of arranging marriages through reliable middlemen is

becoming irrelevant, because of the dispersal of the community, they are compelled to introduce some social innovations. For instance, the associations of Patidars organise marriage-*melas* (a formal gathering of boys and girls along with their parents or relatives), where young boys and girls publicly introduce themselves standing on a platform, followed by an informal interaction through which they try to seek out suitable life partners. In many instances, however, this kind of traditional arrangement is found too formal and awkward by the younger generation. Therefore, weekend dinner-and-dance parties are becoming more popular, where there is dancing to the tunes of Hindi songs till late in the night. However, conservative parents become anxious about such parties and fear that the children will take undue liberties; but parents are also worried about becoming too conservative and strict with their children, especially in view of the fact that the instances of inter-religious, interracial marriages are increasing.

Religion

Many Patidars participate in religious activities in which Hindu temples are often the focal points. Although most of the active participants in these activities belong to the older generation of Patidar migrants, some temples also have youth committees in which youngsters are involved and encouraged to organise and participate in various activities.

Generally, the temples become more active on weekends when many devotees find enough time to visit and participate in the religious discourses and functions. In big temples, like that of Akshar-Purushottam Swaminarayan Temple of London, important events are organised on weekends and, often, important visitors from India are also invited to participate. Such weekend events are usually followed by a community dinner so that the devotees coming from distant places do not have to bother about cooking food at home. Besides, they also have the satisfaction of doing some sacred service (seva) by participating in one or another activity related to the temple or even by helping in preparing or serving the community dinner.

Therefore, such visits are mostly family visits which include teenage children. It is believed by most of the parents visiting such temples regularly that if their children are exposed to temples from an early age they will not only become religious but will also acquire the Indian culture (*sanskars*), which will keep them away from 'undesirable' Western influences, such as, drinking, smoking, dating, etc. Thus their religiosity seems to be rooted in their concept of traditional Indian culture and Indian family life. They want their children to be loyal, obedient, and to care of their parents. The elders want to be respected and looked after by their children in their old age and, therefore, they want to inculcate traditional family values such as being loyal to their parents and siblings, helping their relatives back home, loyal to the village in general, and Patidar community in particular.

Such weekend visits to temples also have a social purpose; they provide an opportunity to network and to meet one another's friends and relatives and thereby strengthen their social ties, which can be useful in arranging marriages of their grown-up children or sending some gifts back home, or obtaining some news from their native place.

Gujarati Language

Besides organising social and religious events, members of the Patidar community in London have started making organised efforts to teach Gujarati to the younger generation. Children of second-generation migrants are mostly able to understand functional Gujarati, but they find it difficult to speak and are often not able to read and write the Gujarati script. Of course, this problem is not confined only to the Patidar community in Britain. The Gujarati community, as a whole, has become more conscious about teaching Gujarati to their children. There are about 500 classes that teach Gujarati language all over Britain, often for two hours a week on Saturdays and Sundays. At the end of the 1990s, about 1,000 to 1,500 students appeared in Gujarati language examinations each year.

Interracial Interaction: The Case of Barham Park Veterans' Club

However, it is not as if the members of the first-generation Patidars do not at all try to integrate with British society. This point can be illustrated by the case study of a more institutional form of social activity of the Barham Park Veterans' Club of which a number of first-generation Patidars have become members over the past few years. During our stay in London, we visited this club several times. The following are some excerpts from our field notes

> Barham Park Veterans' Club was established in 1947 as a social club for British war veterans of the Second World War. The club is located on the border of a park in Wembley and consists of two buildings with a kitchen, a snooker table, a card room, and a space to play darts. At present there are about 100 members. Out of them, 40 members are white British men of which 22 are ex-servicemen, the category for which the club was originally established. The remaining 60 members are all of Gujarati origin; most of them belong to the Patidar community.
>
> Until 1990, Barham Park Veterans' Club did not have a single member of Indian origin. At that time, there was a serious danger that the club would be closed due to the fact that its membership had declined drastically over the previous years. Most of the war veterans were over seventy years of age. If they were still alive, many of them owing to health problems were unable to visit the club regularly. The board of the club therefore decided to open its membership to outsiders. Within a few years, the number of Gujarati members very quickly increased to about 60 in 1999.
>
> Most of the Indian members of Barham Park Veterans' Club are Patidars from central Gujarat. All of these Patidars have lived in East Africa, especially in Kenya and Uganda. Many of them know each other from their stay in East Africa or sometimes even from their childhood years in their home village in India. Although some of them have started to play snooker and darts and join the white British in their competition, most of the time, the Patidars stay in the card room, which is in a separate building. There they play Indian card games and exchange views, or simply sit together to talk in Gujarati among themselves. Once in a while, they organize a dinner in the club for which their wives are also invited. Although these dinners are open to all members of the club, it turns out that only Gujarati members join these dinner meetings. The informal visits to one another's house are also confined only to the Indian members. However, the British members join the picnics organized by the club mostly once in a year.
>
> Following the increase in Gujarati membership in the Barham Park Veterans' Club, Patidars have also entered into several of its committees. While there was only one Gujarati member on

the board in 1997, their membership had increased to three in 1999 already. In order to avoid a feeling of antagonism with the other white members, the Patidars have consciously chosen for a minority position in the committees and do not want to occupy the position of president of the club. This choice is also made with an eye to the local council, which, according to the Patidars, might be less inclined to continue its subsidy for a war veterans' club if people of Indian origin dominate it.

LINKAGES WITH THEIR RELATIVES IN INDIA

Various types of linkages between the Patidar families of Britain and their relatives back home are indicated: (i) through written or oral communication; (ii) through personal visits; (iii) through financial help; and (iv) investments, as discussed below.

Social Contacts through Communication

Communication through letter writing and telephone talks is quite common between the Patidars of Britain and their relatives in India. However, there is a slight difference between the preferences in the mode of communication used from the British and the Indian sides.

Communication from Britain to India

As indicated in table 9.2 most of the respondents maintain contacts with their relatives in India.

Table 9.2.   Contacts of the household members of Greater London with their relatives in their native village in Gujarat

Contacts with Gujarat relatives	No. of households writing letters	No. of households making phone calls
Never	94	18
Rarely	54	98
Regularly	11	43
Total	159	159

The telephone is the main source of communication used by the Patidars in Britain for keeping in touch with their relatives in the villages, though letter writing is also an important way of doing so. While many Patidars only rarely make a phone call to their family in the village, some phone from Britain almost every week for a few minutes. During these calls, information is exchanged about the well-being of family members on both the sides, as reflected in the following case

> Navinbhai Bhupendrabhai Patel is 40 years old. He lives together with his wife and their son in London where they have a grocery shop. Navinbhai was born and brought up in one of the selected villages and married with a girl who was a British citizen born in East Africa.
>
> Navinbhai's father, his mother, and his younger brother Yogesh and his family are still living in their ancestral house in the village. Almost every year, Navinbhai pays a brief visit to his family for about ten to fifteen days. Usually, he comes alone, leaving his wife behind in London to take care of their shop. In between his visits, Navinbhai keeps in regular contact with his relatives at home. At least once a week, Navinbhai makes a brief phone call to his father and his brother, Yogesh. These calls are generally made on a Sunday, every week. According to Yogesh, Navinbhai especially buys telephone cards with a limited amount on it, which he uses to talk for some minutes every week. During these brief conversations, the brothers exchange information about the health of their relatives on both the sides, about the educational progress of the children of both brothers, and their business undertakings. '. . . although our telephone conversations are very brief indeed, it gives us an opportunity to regularly keep in touch and to have the feeling that Navinbhai and his family are not so far away. . .', Yogesh told us after Navinbhai had made his weekly call.

Communication from India to Britain

Letter writing is the main mode of communication used by the households in Charotar to contact their relatives in Britain, though making phone calls is also an important way of keeping in touch (table 9.3).

Particularly after the increased access to telephones, owing to the introduction of public call offices (PCOs) by the Government of India, the frequency of telephone use by relatives from India has increased. However, owing to the costs involved in this mode

Table 9.3. Contacts by household members of selected
central Gujarat villages with their UK relatives

Contacts with UK relatives	No. of households writing letters	No. of households making phone calls
Never	121	182
Rarely	170	115
Regularly	22	16
Total	313	313

of communication, telephone calls from India to Britain are usually
infrequent, are of a very short duration, and often made only in case
of emergencies or for very specific purposes.

Personal Visits

A very important mode of contact between the households in Charotar
and their family members in Britain is through personal visits made
by relatives from both the sides. However, there is a difference in the
frequency, duration, and the purpose of the visits from the British
and the Indian sides respectively.

Visits from Britain to India

A relatively large number of the relatives from Britain visit India
(table 9.4).

Table 9.4. Visits to India by members of selected households of
Greater London in the last five years

Visits	No. of households	No. of household members	No. of visits
Visits made to India	14	—	—
Visits to India in the last 5 years	145	412	805
Total	159	412	805

A substantial number of relatives visit India frequently and most
of them stay for about one to three months (table 9.5).

Table 9.5.   Duration of stay in India by members of selected
households of greater London in the last five years

Duration of visits to India	Total number of household members
< 1 Month	155
1–3 Months	495
4–6 Months	133
7–12 Months	22
> 1 Year	—
Total	805

'Marriage' and 'Leisure' are the main reasons for visits to India by
relatives from Britain (table 9.6).

Table 9.6.   Reasons for visits to India in the last five years by
members of selected households in greater London

Reason for Visits to India	Total No. of Household Members
Marriage/Social	598
Religion	36
Economic	6
Leisure/vacation	126
Other	39
Total	805

In many instances, short-term visits by relatives from Britain are
often related to marriages of one of their family members. During
their visits to India, activities related to religion are very common.
Although 'religion' is not always the main reason for their visits,
many religious activities also take place during those trips, which are
mainly supposed to be for 'leisure' or 'marriage'. During their stay
in India, many Patidar migrants from Britain make tours to several
pilgrim centres in India. Many of them make substantial donations
to the temples and participate in rituals and gatherings.

Due to the substantial donations they make to local temples,
they are often given special treatment in terms of a comfortable
and prominent position. This is, of course, viewed by some local
relatives with jealousy and often ridiculed in private conversations, as
illustrated in the following case

Mohanbhai retired from his clerical job in London in 1988, while his wife Vimlaben retired from government job in 1991. Since then the two of them have been visiting Gujarat every year during winter season for two to three months. In 1994, they bought their own apartment in the nearby city of Baroda.

During their stay in Gujarat, Mohanbhai and Vimlaben spend most of their time in Baroda and from there they also make trips to Charotar to visit friends and relatives in their native village. Alongside these social visits, they take the opportunity to visit temples in Gujarat during their stay, and usually also take a tour of a few days to other religious places in India. Mohanbhai emphasizes his religious nature, and indicates that he regularly makes donations to local temples. 'Also when I am in London', he told us, 'I very often make visits to the temple. In London, I am a member of the temple of Akshar-Purushottam. Whenever we stay in Gujarat, we make it a point of going to the big temple of Akshar-Purushottam Swaminarayan (Akshardham) in Gandhinagar'.

During one of their trips to their native village, Mohanbhai and Vimlaben showed to some of their local relatives the photographs of the Yagna ritual in the village temple in which they had participated a few weeks back. While showing the photographs, Vimlaben pointed out several of her relatives and friends from the UK and USA. They were in fact easily recognizable because Vimlaben and the other women from the UK and USA were making up the first row of the audience, sitting in chairs with their plates on a table in front of them, while all the other women from the village sat on the floor behind them.

Mohanbhai explained that Vimlaben and the other women from UK and USA had been the honoured guests at the Yagna ritual in the village temple. While further elaborating on this, he took from his wallet a letter that he showed to us and his local relatives with some pride. It was a letter of recommendation from the Swaminarayan Mandir in London in which it was mentioned that Mohanbhai is a member of the Mandir in London and was allowed to stay in any of their temples in Gujarat for two days with a maximum group of 8 persons. 'In this letter, the temples in Gujarat are requested to provide me with boarding and lodging, and to enable me to pray and to have conversations with the priests', Mohanbhai told us. 'About two years ago, the Swaminarayan Mandir in London started to issue these letters in order to ensure that only genuine and honest persons can make use of the facilities of the temples in Gujarat. And because of this letter, I will get a special treatment during my stay in the temple, such as a clean private room furnished with a table and a chair,

and air-conditioning if available, dining facility on a table... they
will not prepare too spicy food for us and give us mineral water
. . . This "VIP treatment" is usually given to every NRI (Non-
Resident Indian) who visits a temple in Gujarat', Mohanbhai
told us before he and Vimlaben left the house to visit some old
school friends of Mohanbhai in the village.

Shortly after Mohanbhai and Vimlaben had left, their local
relatives started making some critical comments on what had
been discussed before. One of Mohanbhai's cousins remarked:
'This VIP treatment is given to the NRIs only because they
donate in pounds or dollars. Many of them were never very
religious when they were staying in Africa or when they came
to Britain. But now that they have retired, they suddenly have
a need for Indian culture and rediscovered religion. However,
many of them have already become too westernized. They are
not even able to sit cross-legged on the floor for a long time and
their stomachs can no longer stand our drinking water'. The
other relatives present supported the cousin in their attempt to
ridicule the NRIs' emphasis on religion, but could at the same
time also not hide their feelings of jealousy about the special
treatment the NRIs are given at local temples.

Visits from India to Britain

Relatively smaller number of the respondents stated that they visit
their relatives in the UK (table 9.7).

Table 9.7.   Visit to the UK by members of the households from
selected central Gujarat villages

Visits	No. of households	No. of household members
No. of visits to the UK	179	—
Visits to the UK before 5 years	54	69
Visits to the UK in the Last 5 years	80	128
Total	313	197

However, such visits clearly indicate that there are a substantial
number of household members from the villages who have visited
Britain recently. These visits, though less frequent, are often of a
longer duration as compared with the visits of their relatives from
Britain to India (table 9.8).

Table 9.8.   Duration of stay with UK relatives by members of
households of selected central Gujarat villages

Duration of Visit to UK	Total No. of Household Members
< 1 Month	10
1–3 Months	58
4–6 Months	42
7–12 Months	14
> 1 Year	4
Total	128

This finding is obviously because the visitors would like to extract maximum economic return from such costly trips from India to Britain, which they cannot afford to undertake frequently, whether financed by themselves or their UK relatives.

'Leisure' and 'Marriage' are the main reasons for visits to Britain by the household members of Charotar (table 9.9).

In some instances, however, these visits by household members from India to Britain are motivated by economic purposes. Some of these visitors help their relatives in their shops or other businesses.

Owing to the existing immigration regulations in Britain, entry of young boys or girls on visitors' visas with the intention of marriage is decreasing. For this purpose, the joint family or kinship linkages between Patidars in Charotar and their relatives in Britain are extremely important to support these youngsters financially and also to find them marriage partners in a relatively short period of time. However, such long-distance joint-family relations is not always free from tension. In some cases, young people from India have to work for long hours in shops against less pay. Thus, they feel that they are exploited. On the other hand, their British counterparts feel that they are obliging them by providing accommodation and employment to such inexperienced relatives, who have no work permit. However, since the early 1980s, Indian migration to Britain declined quickly as a result of regulations, which allow entrance almost exclusively through marriage and on the basis of rights of birth. Moreover, relatives in Britain are also not now very willing to accept such social obligations, which, they think, are likely to end up in some misunderstanding on either side, owing to over-expectations.

Table 9.9.   Reasons for visits to the UK by members of households from selected central Gujarat villages

Reason for visits to the UK	Total No. of household members
Leisure	71
Religion	5
Marriage	35
Birth	7
Sickness	9
Death	—
Business	1
Total	128

Financial Help

Financial help is an extension of social obligations the Patidars have towards their relatives. Not surprisingly, therefore, we find such financial exchanges from Britain to India and also from India to Britain, though varying in extent and purpose.

Financial Help from Britain to India

Nearly 60 per cent of the respondents from Britain admit that they extended no monetary help to their relatives in India. However, it is significant to note that more than 40 per cent still continue to help their relatives in India (table 9.10).

Table 9.10.   Monetary help by members of selected households of Greater London to their relatives in Gujarat

Monetary help extended	No. of Households	Percentage
No	94	59.1
Yes	65	40.9
Total	159	100.0

Much of this financial help and support is given to the aged parents, or to cover part of the maintenance of the family in the village, or to pay for part of the repair costs of the house, or to build a new house, or to contribute to marriage expenses, religious rituals, or other social occasions of the family in central Gujarat (table 9.11).

Table 9.11. Type of monetary help by members of selected households of Greater London to their relatives in Gujarat

Type of monetary help	No. of household members extending monetary help
Maintenance of Parents	19
Renovation of House	11
Social Purpose (Marriage/Death)	28
Religious Ceremonies	32
Other (Cash Gifts, Education, etc.)	21
Total	111

This kind of help does indicate that the family ties of these respondents still continue to be relatively strong.

Financial Help from India to Britain

Monetary help from the households in India to their relatives in Britain is almost non-existent as expected, for the relatives back home are economically weak in comparison with their British counterparts. However, it certainly is not totally absent (table 9.12).

Table 9.12. Monetary help to UK relatives by the household members from selected central Gujarat villages

Monetary help extended	No. of households
No	248
Yes	65
Total	313

The existence of some kind of monetary help from Patidars in India to their relatives in Britain is a very interesting phenomenon, because it indicates a transfer of resources from India to Britain. Nevertheless, in most cases, such monetary help to relatives in Britain is related to customary social matters (table 9.13).

It may be mentioned here that among the Patidars of central Gujarat, there is a custom of distributing some gifts in the form of cash and/or kind among relatives on some social occasions such as marriage and death of some close relatives. Most of the monetary help given by the Indian relatives to their counterparts in Britain is of this

Table 9.13. Types of monetary help to UK relatives by household members from selected central Gujarat villages

Type of monetary help to UK relatives	No. of household members
Maintenance of Parents	4
Repairs of House	—
Social Purpose (Marriage/Death)	49
Religious Ceremonies	3
Other: (Cash Gifts, Education, etc.)	9
Total	65

nature and is almost symbolic, since the amount involved is usually meagre, though socially significant, symbolising the recognition of continued family/kinship ties.

However, as stated by the Patidar respondents from Britain, the relatives in Gujarat help them by providing accommodation for them when they visit India or by looking after their property. Some of them also help in arranging marriages (table 9.14).

Table 9.14. Type of help extended by relatives in Gujarat to members of households in Greater London

Type of help extended	No. of household members extending help
Accommodation	106
Looking after Children	—
Business	—
Marriage	4
Looking after Property	31
Other	3
Total	144

However, some times tensions do develop among the relatives over the distribution of the ancestral property, as illustrated by the following case study

> Ramanbhai Patel belongs to one of the big villages. They are four brothers; two of them are living in India and two abroad. One of his brothers is living in Kenya and another brother went to

the UK from Kenya. In the words of Ramanbhai: 'I was working as a clerk in a school in my village, I have two sons and two daughters, we had about 40 acres of land in the village, but most of it was taken away under the land reform act by the tenants who were tilling it. Even otherwise, agriculture was not very profitable and my salary was not very high. I had to support my family and my widowed mother. My brother who is living in the UK sometimes sends money for my mother. Whenever he visits India and stays with us, he does small repairs in our ancestral house, which is a common property of all the four brothers. We two brothers who are living in India are also not very rich. We are a middle class family. Two of my brothers are married to girls who were born in Kenya and, therefore, they could go there. But one of my brothers, who is still in Kenya, is not well-off, whereas the brother who went to the UK is relatively better-off. I am the only one living in the village, looking after my mother and ancestral property. I have to spend some money as per our customs on social occasions like birth, marriage, death, etc., of our relatives on behalf of my family. I have to do this because I am living in the village. Of course, those who are living outside the village later contribute to the expenses. However, when my children grew up, I realized that it would be difficult for them in future to live a comfortable life in India. Therefore, I requested my brother who is in the UK to invite my eldest son as a visitor there, and arrange my son's marriage with a girl who has a British passport. He did oblige me. He invited my eldest son to the UK in 1976 and within six months my brother arranged his marriage with a girl from *Chha Gam* (Six Villages) marriage circle having British citizenship. Now my eldest son, who is about 47 years old, is well settled in the UK having a candy shop and a post office. After he settled down there comfortably, he started sending money to me. Out of this money, I completely renovated my ancestral house, spending about ten lakh rupees. Later, I also bought three taxis for my younger son. My younger son was working in a factory as a clerk. I asked him to take voluntary retirement and to start the transport business with these three taxis. Now we are relatively better off. We have built two houses on the outskirts of the village for both the sons and I could also arrange marriages of my two daughters in good families. My younger son has a son and a daughter. Both of them go to English medium schools.'

However, this does not mean that there are no tensions in Ramanbhai's family. As a matter of fact, as there is co-operation on the one hand in the family, there is conflict also on the other hand. For instance, Ramanbhai says:

'But what is the use of this prosperity? As my economic position improved, my brother started demanding his share in the ancestral house in which I am living and which I have rebuilt by spending a lot of money sent by my eldest son from the UK. And this has caused a considerable tension in our family of four brothers. Now, I am economically better off but socially unhappy.'

Investment

As far as investment is concerned, it is obviously a one-way traffic. The Patidars from only the British side invest in India; the Patidars from India obviously do not invest in Britain.

Investment from Britain in India

Interestingly, more than 75 per cent of the respondents still have a share in their ancestral property (table 9.15).

Table 9.15. Share in ancestral property by members of selected households in Greater London

Share in ancestral property	No. of households	Percentage
No	37	23.3
Yes	122	76.7
Total	159	100.0

Nearly one-third of the Patidars living in Britain have invested in India (table 9.16).

Table 9.16. Investment in India by members of selected households from Greater London

Investment	No. of Households	Percentage
No	111	69.7
Yes	46	29.0
No Information	2	1.3
Total	159	100.0

Some of the 46 respondents who have invested in India, however, made more than one type of investment. Therefore, the total number of investments reported to us turns out to be 61 (table: 9.17). Those who invested did so in bank deposits or in shares. Part of these investments is related to the various schemes that have been set up for the 'Non-Resident Indians' (NRIs) by the Indian government over the past few years. The second priority in investment is landed property, most of which are investments in residential plots, or houses and apartments. Only five per cent of the investors have invested in business or factories (table 9.17).

One of the most visible changes brought about as a result of investments in residential property in almost all the villages of central Gujarat is the construction of beautiful houses, with all modern facilities, on the outskirts of these villages. This has changed the village landscape. Taking advantage of this tendency, many builders have floated expensive housing projects, even in the nearby cities and towns, with plans of luxurious houses, especially for the NRIs. The builders have advertised them in the UK and at times have collected money in foreign exchange. As a result, the real estate business and the building industry got a tremendous fillip in central Gujarat. However, these investments in property of the Patidars from Britain sometimes create jealousy and resentment among the local population, which holds their investment behaviour responsible for the enormous increase in prices of real estate over the past few years.

Thus, despite the size and frequency of monetary help and financial transfers of the Patidars from Britain, there are no strong productive linkages between the villages in Charotar and the Patidar community in Britain. Investments in business make up only a very small minority of the investments of the Patidars from Britain, though they are certainly not completely absent. In instances where they occurred, these productive investments of Patidars from Britain are made in the village or in one of the nearby towns, mostly in partnership with the family members or near relatives. When asked about their intention to invest in India in the near future, interestingly, only 35 per cent indicated their willingness to do so.

Actually, the trend of investing capital in India is, so far, not a major trend for the following reasons. First, the children of the first-generation migrants do not have long-term interests in India, and, therefore, the first-generation emigrants to the UK also seem to have adopted the UK as the place of their permanent residence, willingly

Table 9.17. Type of investment in India by members of selected households in Greater London

Type of investments in India	Total No. of households
Bank/Shares	26
Farm/Land	6
House/Plot	8
House/Flat	17
Business	3
Other	1
Total	61

or unwillingly. Thus, they are losing long-term interest in India. Second, lack of political and economic stability back home in India, as perceived by the Patidars in Britain, also does not encourage them to make major capital investments in their homeland. Third, the bureaucratic red tape and corruption experienced by some of them in India discourage them from making a determined effort to put their money in long-term investments in their region. Above all, being rational, they do not invest without any real prospect of handsome gains. Perhaps, the most important motive for their investment, in addition to the profit, is long-term security. They invest in India not merely because they love India, but they do so because they do not want to keep all their proverbial eggs only in one basket, that is, the UK. Moreover, they think that this money will be useful to them when they visit India. Owing to all these reasons, there are no strong commercial or entrepreneurial linkages between the villages in Charotar and the Patidar community in Britain, despite the size and frequency of monetary help and financial transfers of Patidar relatives from Britain.

However, lack of enthusiasm in maintaining financial linkages and of making investments in Gujarat on the part of the Patidar migrants in London is usually a part of lively discussions, both in India and Britain. Among the Patidar migrants in London, there are those who emphasise that the Indian government is more interested in their Pounds. To some, particularly those who came from Uganda, a more shocking experience than the sudden and unexpected expulsion from Uganda by Idi Amin was the lukewarm response they received from the Indian government in the early 1970s. In those days, the Indian government did not realise the importance of the Non-Resident Indians. Therefore, many of those who have settled down in the UK, after being expelled from Uganda, ironically interpret the term 'NRI', much trumpeted by the Indian government of late, as 'Non-Required Indians', and their bitterness is also reflected in their lack of enthusiasm in maintaining linkages back home in the form of investments in India.

On the other hand, many Patidars in the villages express their negative views about migrants from Britain who do not contribute as much to the development of their home village as they used to do in the past. Although they do understand the economic problems faced by the Patidars in Britain today, they strongly feel that they avoid their responsibilities by not contributing to the welfare of their home village, as indicated in the following case:

Sureshbhai's family belongs to one of the economically most well-to-do families in the village. They own about 20 acres of land and have a large cold-storage building along with one tiles factory and several other undertakings. Sureshbhai's younger brother Mahendrabhai is a regional politician who is also quite active at the local level. Among other things, he is the chairman of the educational board and secretary of the village cooperative bank

On various occasions, Sureshbhai and Mahendrabhai gave voice to their criticism about the large-scale migration to the UK and the USA of members of the Patidar community. '. . . not one of our direct relatives has migrated abroad. . .' Sureshbhai used to say with some pride. '. . . we are happy to live here and are not like all those Patidars who do anything to be able to go abroad . . .' Mahendrabhai adds to that: '. . . and when they leave this village, they forget about their native place. In the past few years, there has hardly been any financial support from the Patidars of our village who live in the UK. Until the 1960s, Patidars who migrated to East Africa from our village used to regularly make donations to the educational board and village panchayat. It was because of these donations that our village was among the first in the area to have high school. Since they migrated from East Africa to the UK, however, we have hardly received any donations from our fellow-villagers abroad. Even though they established a *samaj* (village organisations) of persons from our village living in London, this has not resulted in substantial support to the development of our village. We realize that it is expensive to live in London, but as compared to Gujarat, the Patidars in Britain hardly have any social obligations and therefore fewer expenses in this regard. I personally feel that Patidars in the UK are only after money and obsessed with saving as much money as they can. Pound has become their god. They hardly care about relatives back home, but have become misers who do not want to spend money on social obligations . . . when they are in the UK, they don't think about the welfare or development of their native village, but when they visit their village, they start to emphasize that we are all part of the same village and *samaj*. They even expect us to treat them with the highest respect because they have come from abroad. But to be honest, I don't think the Patidars in Britain from our village are part of our community anymore, they have become strangers to us, strangers who are no longer really concerned about the welfare of their native village'.

Thus, the visits and contacts, however, are not without problems. The above example indicates that there are sometimes differences of opinion between the Indian migrants in London and their relatives in Gujarat on the nature of their relationship and on the type of help rendered.

Investment from India to Britain

Although relatives from India do not invest in Britain since they are not financially capable enough to do so, these family members from the villages are often asked to help their relatives in Britain to buy and afterwards to maintain property in India for and on behalf of the latter.

CONCLUDING REMARKS

Thus, members of the Patidar community from UK maintain frequent long-distance family linkages with their home region in India. Regular visits and frequent contacts keep many of the Patidar migrants well linked to the villages in Gujarat and vice versa. During such trips, their relatives in India provide accommodation for them in their houses. Another important service which they get from their

Indian relatives is one in which their property in India is taken care of by the relatives and, in addition, they help in arranging marriages. It is, therefore, not surprising that most of the British Patidars have retained their share in their ancestral property. On the other hand, there is no dearth of instances where British Patidars have helped their relatives to migrate to Britain, or to maintain their ancestral property, or to support their aged parents, or to arrange the marriages of the family members. Therefore, the local Patidars in central Gujarat derive enormous prestige because some of their relatives live in foreign countries.

Joint Family and Kinship Ties as a Social Resource

Such linkages are facilitated by the institutions of joint family and kinship, which prescribe strong interpersonal ties and cooperation among the members of the family and the kin. The willingness and capacity to extend help to other family members and also to near and distant relatives is positively evaluated in the community. Thus, it becomes an important criterion to define some one's status in the community. Therefore, there is an extraordinary emphasis in the community on maintaining 'good relations' with one's kith and kin, whether they like one another or not, because one never knows whose help will be needed when. Such relations become useful resources both for the migrants and their relatives back home.

Lack of Capital Formation, Constant Struggle to Acquire Wealth, and Continued Urge to Migrate

The strong joint family ties demand that personal financial gains of an individual are also to be shared with the rest of the family in one form or the other, mostly on some social occasions. Therefore, the rational and calculative economic behaviour of some members of the family is socially disapproved. There are instances where such behaviour has created interpersonal jealousy, mutual distrust and family feuds. The social cost of such family tensions, caused by economic rationality, is so high that normally family members tend to avoid it by following seemingly irrational customary traditions such as lavish feasts on an extravagantly large scale or elaborate electric decoration at the time of marriage. This has some times made it difficult for the Patidars to accumulate capital on a large scale, in comparison with other Hindu castes living in the UK, such as Vanias, Lohanas, and Oswals. This is one of the reasons why they are unable to invest in a big way. However, in the absence of such a sizable capital formation, the struggle to acquire wealth remains a continuous process among the Patidar families from generation to generation. This, in turn, becomes a constant factor motivating members of the successive generations to search for better prospects any where in the world. Therefore, it has not hindered a section of them to become a substantial part of the business elite in various rural and urban areas of Gujarat. Nor is it surprising to find many Patidars now migrating from the UK to the USA.

Continued Linkages and Consequent Social Tensions

However, there are in-built tensions in such utilitarian relationships. For, within a joint family and kin group, the members are socially equal though they may differ in their material achievements. Yet, someone's ability to help others, even within the family, creates a situation of inequality by socially distinguishing the 'giver' from the 'receiver', the former being superior to the latter, both in terms of status and power. Moreover, it is a matter of self-esteem, if not pride, for the 'giver', to be able to help someone. At the same time, it is a matter of humility, if not humiliation for the 'receiver', to be in a situation of such 'inequality' among equals. Therefore, the receiver looks for the earliest opportunity to return the favour in one form or the other to be equal in the relationship. Thus, the network is not only lubricated, but the struggle to be financially equal continues.

Since all members of the joint family and kinship group are not financially equal, it becomes the responsibility of a wealthy member to spend more for the sake of the family's status. Thus, sometimes some successful members of the community feel that their success is a blessing as well as a curse. It is a blessing because they become more important and can derive a sense of pride by helping the less fortunate members of the family or kins. But, sometimes it becomes a curse, because they think every one in the network is interested in taking away their hard-earned wealth. Moreover, at times, they find that no one is satisfied with any amount of help extended by them. What is worse, some of those who derive benefit from their 'generosity' are not as grateful as they expect them. Also, the receivers of such help think that it is the duty of successful relatives to help them and should not expect any overt reward for discharging their obligations. The receivers think that they also reciprocate in their own way. In such a situation, it is not always easy to decide whether or not the reciprocal exchange is equivalent. Thus, there is a scope for developing a feeling of injustice among the reciprocating parties.

The relations dealing with family property in the village are not always without problems. The relatives in Britain are of the opinion that they not only have a right to an equal share of the family's property but also the equal right to sell it off. On the other hand, members of the households in the village are often of the opinion that they alone are entitled to the entire ancestral property, because they looked after the family's property and also after their parents and other elder relatives in the village. Besides, they think that though it may be legally correct for the British relatives to have a claim on the ancestral property, it is not morally justifiable for these 'rich' relatives to insist upon such a claim. Therefore, in several cases, relations between relatives in Britain and their family members in the village in Gujarat have become severely strained owing to conflicts over property.

Continued Traditionalism: Preference for Traditional Custom of Arranged Marriage

Despite increasing transnationalism, the first-generation Patidar migrants still remain traditional in many ways, particularly with reference to their women and also in regard to their preference for arranged marriages within the caste (Rutten 1995). This attitude, operating outside one's home territory, is seen in their approach towards the problem of getting reliable information on potential marriage partners and their families living outside India. Many of them are under the impression that it is as easy to acquire information about families living in England or the USA as it is about families living in central Gujarat. Characteristic of their behaviour is that they try to get information by using the same methods that have proven to be successful in their home area, that is, by requesting their relatives and friends to collect the information on their behalf.

The inadequacy of this method of obtaining information for arranging marriages is revealed in the increasing number of early divorces, which is becoming a cause for concern for many of the Patidar families. One of the reasons for such early divorces or unhappy marriages is because most families have to depend either entirely on matrimonial advertisements while choosing such marriage partners from foreign countries or on inadequate information obtained through distant relatives or friends. We were told about these problems several times by the Patidar families in the villages. Not surprisingly, therefore, 'Beware Before You Get Your Daughter Married in a Foreign Country', is one of the common headlines in local Gujarati dailies.

Increasing Transnationalism and Emerging Cosmopolitanism

As a result of the varying patterns of migration within the Patidar community of central Gujarat, many Patidar families in the villages are today part of a regional, national, and even international network of relationships (Rutten 1995). To a certain extent, those who have settled outside central Gujarat have become the reference group for the Patidar families in the villages. To be part of this extended social network requires an emphasis on joint family, kinship, caste, and village ties, though of a different order than before. Instead of strengthening sub-caste and marriage-circle divisions within the Patidar community, these families tend to ignore marriage gols, based on sub-caste, and tend to emphasise the solidarity of the entire Patidar caste, based on loyalties between those families which are economically well off and belong to the upper social stratum in society. Some of them even go a step forward and consider themselves as members of a larger community consisting mainly of Patidar and other upper-caste families, whose freedom of movement is not limited to the village, sub-castes, and kin ties but which operate on a regional, national, or even international level. The local, regional, national and international migrations of relatives of the Patidar families from the villages have broadened their horizons by providing them with new social contacts and experiences. Many of them consider these new contacts as nothing more than an extension of their network in central Gujarat and act accordingly, displaying an unlimited faith in their own strength and superiority. Some of them even accepted intercaste, inter-religious, and also interracial marriages in their families.

Ambivalence

Thus, we find a strong sense of ambivalence among the first-generation migrants. For instance, on the one hand, they are becoming modern and transnational, and, on the other hand, they retain many of their traditional attitudes. Similarly, their attitudes to the country of their origin and the country they have adopted as their new homeland also reflect such ambivalence. For instance, they love India immensely since it is their motherland. At the same time they cannot hide their hatred for the economic backwardness, political instability, rampant corruption and nepotism found in the country. Likewise, they admire the generosity and liberalism of an average Briton, the British political and economic system, and the respect for law and justice found in Britain. Yet, they are extremely critical of the instances of racism and discrimination experienced by them in their day-to-day life. In the same way, they are proud of their children's achievements in their studies and in their occupational lives but feel frustrated by their insistence on their individualism.

Thus, at the beginning of the twenty-first century, the Patidar community in India and Britain seems to be at the crossroads in every sphere of life. On the one hand, it is becoming transnational and extending its links to different countries of the world: first from India to East Africa, then to Britain, and thereon to the USA, Canada, Australia, New Zealand, etc. On the other hand, however, it is struggling to maintain its traditional culture in Britain by reclaiming the younger generation and by redefining its linkage with relatives in the home region of central Gujarat. This continuing process of both intimacy and antagonism between the two sides of the transnational family, which is quite noticeable in the way in which they interact and influence each other, is not a new phenomenon for most of the Patidar migrants in London. Especially for those who lived part of their life in East Africa, this has been part of their daily existence as migrants who maintain intense and frequent linkages with their relatives in their home villages.

The future of such relationships will depend upon two factors: (i) the net balance of the cost-benefit relationship; and (ii) the attitudes of the second and third generations. At present it seems these linkages will not last with the same intimacy and intensity for more than 20 or 25 years, as the net balance of the cost and benefit is not considered favourable by relatives from both the sides. In most cases, the parents who were the binding factor have passed away. Besides, the first-generation migrants are on their way out, and the second and third generations have very little interest in India, except from curiosity. In this context, it seems that the expectations of the Government of India from the NRIs regarding huge remittances are either unrealistic or are based on sentimental but essentially non-rational considerations such as patriotism.

Endnotes

1 The term 'Patel' originally was used as social title conferred upon certain revenue- collecting individuals in India during the feudal period. Therefore, though the term is quite commonly used these days as a surname in Gujarat and also, to some extent, in other parts of India, it is a generic social category encompassing several social groups of different religions. Therefore, it is not uncommon to find individuals of diverse religious communities, such as Hindus, Muslims and Parsis, using the same surname 'Patel'. Moreover, within a religious community, all 'Patels' are not of the same social group and of equal status. For instance, all Hindu Patels of Gujarat are not socially alike or equals, not to mention all the Hindu Patels of other parts of India. Even within Gujarat, the Patels of central Gujarat, or the area popularly known as Charotar, the Patels of south Gujarat, the Patels of north Gujarat, and the Patels of Saurashtra, though all are Hindus, constitute socially distinct and unequal groups, having nothing much in common except the surname. Each of these groups is a separate endogamous unit following its own customary laws regarding marriage and other social practices.

The Hindu Patels of central Gujarat are also known as Patidars or Leuva Patidars.

2 The major part of central Gujarat, lying between two rivers, Mahi to the south-east, and Vatrak to the north-west, is popularly known as Charotar in Gujarat. Formerly it constituted one administrative district, known as Kheda district, and recently it is divided into two districts, namely Kheda (near Vatrak river) and Anand (near Mahi river).

References

Hardiman, D. 1981. *Peasant Nationalists of Gujarat: Kheda District, 1917–1934.* Delhi: Oxford University Press.

Jain, Ravindra K. 1993. *Indian Communities Abroad: Themes and Literature.* Delhi: Manohar Publications.

Lyon M. H. and B. J. M. West. 1995. London Patels: Caste and Commerce. *New Community* 21(3): 399–419.

Modood, T., R. Berthoud, J. Lakey, J. Nazroo, P. Smith, S. Virdee, and S. Reishon. 1997. *Ethnic Minorities in Britain: Diversity and Disadvantage.* London: Policy Studies Institute.

Pocock, D. F. 1972. *Kanbi and Patidar: A Study of the Patidar Community of Gujarat.* Clarendon: Oxford University Press.

Rutten, M. 1995. *Farms and Factories: Social Profile of Large Farmers and Rural Industrialists in West India.* Delhi: Oxford University Press.

Srinivas, M. N. 1992 [1959]. 'The Dominant Castes in Rampura. In *Social Stratification,* ed. Dipankar Gupta, 307–11. New Delhi: Oxford University Press (originally published in *American Anthropologist* 41, 1959).

Vertovec, Steven. 2000. *The Hindu Diaspora: Comparative Patterns.* London: Routledge.

10

The Socio-Cultural Context of Informed Consent in Medical Practice

Aneeta A. Minocha

I

The doctrine of informed consent in medical practice has evolved during the past few decades. It has developed a firm footing in Western medical thought and practice. However, the problems in its applicability in many Western as well as in more traditional societies continue to be discussed and debated. Essentially, the doctrine rests on the premise that every individual has the right to control his mind and body and, therefore, has a right to decide what can or shall be done to him. In the medical context, the doctrine of informed consent implies that the person, that is, the patient, is vested with the right to decide which diagnostic and treatment procedures should be used to manage his illness. His formal permission or consent is necessary before the physician undertakes his medical treatment along the lines chosen by the patient.

In this doctrine, the permission given by the patient has to be an informed one and is based on his right to know and to decide. It is legally binding on the treating doctor to inform his patient about the disease, its prognosis, and the various possible lines of treatment. He must tell the patient about the different therapeutic alternatives for the treatment of his disease, the risks and side effects they carry, and their expected outcomes. Also, he must let the patient know about the consequences of not accepting any medical aid and letting the disease follow its own course.

Informed consent thus involves much more than the earlier practice of the patient filling up and signing a form giving his written consent to undergo medical treatment at his own risk. Such a procedure was considered by all concerned to be a mere formality without having much implication for the treatment process. The consent was given in the context of an asymmetrical power relationship between the patient and the doctor wherein the former submitted to the latter's directives. As a matter of fact, it was assumed by all that having chosen his physician, the patient could just rely on the doctor of his choice for taking all the decisions on his behalf and looking after all aspects of the illness and its management to the best of his ability. In contrast to this, in the doctrine of informed consent, the emphasis is on the patient's active role in decision-making which is to be governed by principles of rationality and of equality between him and the doctor. This means that the patient should first receive all the information from the doctor and comprehend all the significant aspects of the treatment options before he takes his decision in favour of any one of them and records it in a legal language.

Several countries of the West have accepted the doctrine of informed consent and have enacted laws spelling out the physicians' duties and the patients' rights in the medical relationship. The doctrine of informed consent challenges the traditional paternalistic model of the patient-physician relationship in which the physician took the important medical decisions for the patient, who acquiesced and subordinated his own ideas and wishes to those of the physician with the confidence that being the expert the doctor knew best.

A major paradigm shift is visible in the new doctrine in so far as it emphasises the patients' active participation in medical decision-making and his overall control and power with respect to the doctor. The doctrine reverses the earlier model and redefines the role, expectations and social responsibility of the doctor toward his patient. It views the patient as an independent, autonomous, rational and empowered person, who, armed with the necessary information, is competent as well as free to take his own decisions and assume the responsibility for all the consequences of these decisions. The new doctrine, therefore, endows the patient with considerable power and legally defined rights vis-à-vis the physician. It thus questions the Parsonian model of relationship resting on the patient's subservience to the paternalistic medical establishment. A significant aspect of this new doctrine is that the exercise of the above-mentioned rights becomes possible and worthwhile only when the patient has obtained information about all aspects of his medical condition from the doctor, so that he can evaluate and weigh the risks and benefits of various alternative treatment regimes as suggested by the doctor.

The notion of the patient's right to choose a medical therapy for his ailment has emerged in the context of the increasing tendency towards pluralism in medical systems, therapies and techniques, which provide several alternatives. There is a range of acceptable modern and traditional, alternative and complimentary medicines which are available today and which are no longer dismissed as being non-scientific. Moreover, a plurality of agencies and institutions, such as the doctor's clinic, multi-specialty hospitals, government and privately run institutions, polyclinics, etc., with different levels of complexity of organisation, different patterns of administrative control, fee structure, etc., are available to the patient to choose from, making choice between them a complex proposition (Minocha 1980). Also, newer technologies, such as minimally invasive techniques, self-diagnostic instruments, safer drugs and techniques, etc., have made the exercise of choice still more complex. Since medical advances and breakthroughs in medical care and techniques are advertised in the media and popular literature, many patients are familiar with their extraordinary and quick healing capabilities. Such a vast range of possible alternatives make it inevitable to exercise choice. However, individual doctors may not be acquainted with and equipped to offer all the desired options. The medical institutions also may be lacking even the basic infrastructure, tools and trained personnel to offer what the patient wants. The lag between information about options which the patient possesses and their availability is likely to create confusion, if not misunderstanding and distrust, between the doctor and the patient.

With the expansion and dissemination of medical knowledge, a process of demystification of medical knowledge and of its practitioners, especially doctors, have taken place, more so in the recent past, especially among the educated classes, who now have access to this information through the press and the electronic media. Medical information is no longer considered to be esoteric, and, therefore, incomprehensible to the lay person, nor is the doctor any more put on a high pedestal of nobility and professional dexterity. He can be questioned about his work, held responsible for his errors, and taken to a court of law and punished. All these developments have made it conceptually possible for the layperson to obtain information, critically evaluate it, and then plan his actions accordingly. It is beside the point that the information available through the media is often inaccurate, exaggerated, or misunderstood. The lay person has also been made aware of his rights as a patient, which can be upheld legally. The patient is motivated to get his dissatisfactions and complaints addressed legally and to obtain monetary compensation if something goes amiss in his medical contract with the doctor. In other words, conceptually at least, the patient can now participate knowledgeably and actively in his treatment on an equal footing with the doctor. It is important to note that in the new paradigm, the patient also has to own responsibility for undesirable consequences resulting from the medical treatment carried out as per his choice and consent. He cannot blame the doctor exclusively for such outcomes.

II

Medical sociologists and anthropologists have helped in creating the awareness that the patient-physician relationship and the mutual rights and obligations it entails are deeply embedded in culturally defined values and norms of society. It follows from this that the doctrine of informed consent becomes meaningful and operational only when a culture valorises and upholds the individual's autonomy, freedom of choice, and free will. Only in the context of such values can the individual exercise his free choice between alternatives and assume responsibility for his decisions and actions. It would not be wrong to say that the evolution of the doctrine of informed consent is closely linked to the socio-cultural and intellectual movements, under the influence of modernism, which characterise contemporary Western, industrially advanced societies. These intellectual developments have helped in the evolution of the concept of the rational, independent, empowered, and autonomous individual, free to take his own decisions in all spheres of his life.

As an intellectual movement, modernism arose as a reaction to the erstwhile Victorian ideas, beliefs, norms and modes of thought and action. The new ideas and ideologies were accompanied by significant scientific and technological developments and breakthroughs. The ideational changes gradually ramified into all segments of the society and penetrated into all fields of intellectual endeavour. Consequently, there were remarkable alterations in values, beliefs and attitudes in almost all spheres of life in society. Most importantly, the concept of the individual underwent significant changes. The 'individual' became the bearer of several rights. The distancing of the individual from religion was accompanied by his increasing alienation from fellow human beings and/his own heightened sense of autonomy, individuality and freedom. The modern man, with his faith in human intelligence, relied on science and technology as sources and means of acquiring information to achieve his goals and to explain the external world to himself rationally and meaningfully. He also became a more reflexive and private human being, capable of assuming responsibility for all his decisions and actions. All these intellectual developments made the modern man assume control over his self, his body and his mind. He was vested with the freedom to exercise his personal choice in all matters of vital concern.

The modernist thinkers laid stress on the multifaceted nature of events and emphasised that there were varied ways of visualising and intellectually comprehending the world. Persons could assign their own specific meanings to events and processes and carve out their unique ways of self-realisation. All these intellectual developments, along with technological innovations providing greater control over the processes of life, helped in framing world views in which life and death found new social meanings and interpretations. The individual assumed greater control over his own body and mind to do whatever he wanted with them, without interference, and the way he deemed it fit. The idea of quality of life made inroads into the medical sphere, and the individual obtained the right to opt for a better quality of life, or to reject its mere prolongation, to be lived in suffering and pain and without serving any useful purpose.

It was inevitable that such profound intellectual currents in the West would influence the medical establishment and force it to re-examine its beliefs and convictions about managing issues of life and death and evolving conceptualisations of persons, processes, norms, roles and relationships in the medical field. Subsequently, a new perspective on the patient, per se, as well as on his relationship to the doctors and others in the medical establishment, emerged in lieu of the Parsonian conceptualisations. In the new paradigm, the patient, far from being a passive and submissive recipient of the doctor's orders, was now viewed as an empowered, informed, and discerning person endowed with several rights to protect his own interests, likes, and dislikes vis-à-vis the doctors. A few charters listing patients' rights were drafted (for example, American Hospital Association 1992; Active Citizenship Network 2002). Chief among the rights was the patients' right to select a line of medical treatment or refuse treatment altogether. But this right, as mentioned earlier, was to be exercised in a rational manner after being informed by the doctor about the various options in treatment regimes, their respective side effects and outcomes. The patient was to be told also about the outcomes, including death, if he chose to delay his treatment or decided to completely forego it. These rights redefined the doctors' role and made it obligatory on him to inform the patient about all aspects of his disease and its management and obtain from him a 'consent' for carrying out a line of treatment as selected by the patient. All these changes constituted the context in which the doctrine of informed consent gradually evolved in the West.

This doctrine assumes that the patient is rational and intelligent and is therefore able to comprehend and accurately weigh the various treatment options against each other after obtaining all the relevant information. In other words, the patient ought to know what is best for him medically, and be able to look after his own interests and use his discretion to take his own decisions about every aspect of his illness. The patient's right to choose a line of action was further extended by the advocates of euthanasia, another novel concept that includes an option for termination of one's life if, in the patient's perception, his/her life became unbearable. In this new scenario, therefore, the doctor has lost much of his erstwhile dominant position of control, and the patient emerges as a rational, free and empowered person vis-à-vis the doctor.

The relatively novel and overarching framework of human rights, considered most sacred in civil society today, especially in industrially advanced societies, has influenced drastically the individual's self-perception as well as the other's perception of him. Several human rights have been formulated which tend to enlarge the domain of self-chosen actions by a person, including his right to die and administering his own death. The individual has the human right to manage his body, his self, and, therefore, his destiny in a rational mode as per his wish, instead of depending upon others for this or others forcing their opinions on him. The autonomy of the individual has been upheld by many scholars. According to Kuczewski and McCruden (2001), for example, the concept of patients' autonomy is a product of Western culture, which values individual freedom and self-determination. The point that is being made here is that informed consent has to be understood and practised only in a specific cultural milieu in which the individual is perceived in a particular manner.

III

Since informed consent is culturally bound, scholars have started doubting its universal validity. Issues concerning the suitability and applicability of the doctrine in the context of different cultural values, beliefs and practices, especially of non-Western societies, have been raised. Asai (1996), for instance, has discussed the barriers to informed consent in Japan. In the more traditional societies, larger units such as family and community tend to overpower the individual without leaving much scope for him to assert and express his individuality. Below, we delineate some of the issues involved in the translation of the doctrine into the doctor-patient relationship in a non-Western society such as India.

In any society, the practice of the doctrine involves three components broadly defined as:

1. The patient whose informed consent is to be elicited.

2. The physician who is to obtain consent from the patient by facilitating the patient's opinions by giving all the relevant information and removing doubts.

3. The dominant socio-cultural and other relevant features of the society, including the health infrastructure and people's general knowledge about health, medicine and disease, which facilitate or hinder the practice of informed consent.

At the outset, the first question relates to what the patient and doctor mean by 'consent'? Does it simply mean a 'yes' from the patient who gives the 'go ahead' signal to the doctor to pursue a chosen line of treatment, or does it convey to the patient that he is also being made responsible for any untoward happenings while the treatment selected by him is being carried out. This is a serious responsibility, and many a patient may not be comfortable with it. Further, having taken his own informed decision, is the patient confident about it? What if the patient is able to guess that his decision is not what the doctor would have preferred? Is it expedient for the patient to deviate from the expert's opinion? On the doctor's part, having obtained the patient's consent, does the doctor feel relieved that he has passed on the responsibility of the outcomes to the patient? Does this free him from the tension of the likelihood of being dragged to a court of law? Does the doctor think that after giving his consent, the patient is likely to be more compliant and to continue the treatment? The important question here is, for whose benefit does informed consent work? For the patients' or the doctors'?

The doctrine makes one presume that in any given case of treatment, the doctor has explained the treatment options in all detail to the patient's satisfaction and that the patient, having comprehended all the information, has rationally and voluntarily taken his decision on the line of treatment he desires and requires. All these assumptions need examination.

An important question pertains to the patient being clear about everything he is consenting to. Is he giving a 'blanket' permission to the doctor to proceed along the selected line of treatment, say a surgical intervention, or is he giving his clearance to a particular procedure of this intervention, for example, blood transfusion, which carries its own risks? If it is a 'blanket' permission, then before it is recorded, the doctor would have to do a lot of explaining of all possible situations or exigencies that may emerge, with their risks and dangers in the course of the entire treatment and of the likely techniques for dealing with them. Such details about all the contingent situations and the risks involved may both scare and confuse the patient making it difficult for him to decide confidently. But, if the explanation is given whenever an unexpected exigency takes place in the course of the treatment's requiring an unanticipated procedure, then providing the explanations and obtaining the consent at that stage may unduly delay or obstruct the ongoing treatment. In such a situation the patient may not get a true choice since some procedures cannot be initiated, reviewed and undone midway.

In some ailments, no real alternatives in treatment are possible, and the patient will be left to either go in for a given treatment or forego it altogether. In the latter case there may be significant consequences, if, after some time, the patient changes his mind about his decision and agrees to a procedure rejected by him earlier. But this change of mind may come too late when the suggested treatment procedure may have lost its utility and effectiveness.

Evidently, the physicians' ethical and professional obligation to provide relevant information and explanations to the patients in order to help them make up their mind about management of their ailments is not an easy one to carry out. This job is facilitated if the patients have some general knowledge about the modern system of medicine. Many Indian patients do not understand the functions of procedures such as drawing blood samples, measuring blood pressure, various invasive and non-invasive techniques and procedures, the use of anesthesia, X-ray, ultrasound, endoscopy, etc. (Minocha 1996; Gopal 2004). The doctor would have to explain these to the ignorant patient, who may be hearing about them for the first time and does not understand how they are carried out. In other words, the doctor would have to first educate the patient about modern medicine and then inform him about particular treatment options in order to translate the doctrine of informed consent into action. This may, however, consume a lot of his professional time which he may not like.

The above remark is not to undermine that good clinical practice does involve the doctor's listening to the patient's anxieties, answering his queries, explaining procedures and allaying his fears. A good clinician will do this in any case; but it is a different matter when it becomes a legal obligation for the doctor to run through all the information for the patient before he opts for a particular line of therapy in order to obtain his legal written consent.

In a study of women patients in a general hospital in New Delhi, (Minocha 1996), I observed that most of the patients were not acquainted with such elementary things as to why blood samples were drawn, and repeatedly too, how blood for transfusion was obtained, what was a surgical operation like, etc. However, the patients did show an interest in knowing about the different facets of their treatment and sought information from whomever they considered 'patient-friendly', be it a nursing sister, ward orderly, or a *safai karamchari*. The enterprising ones speculated and arrived at their own explanations, rightly or wrongly. The doctor's job therefore becomes complicated and onerous, or easier for that matter, depending upon the patient's prior exposure to and experience and understanding of the therapeutic system.

It was observed that the patients in the hospital felt much more at ease with the non-medical functionaries at the lower echelons in the ward, and they turned to them for satisfying their curiosity about modern medicine. It was a different matter that the answers they got did not give a very accurate factual picture, since these functionaries themselves did not know a great deal and tried to interpose their own ideas about folk remedies in answering the patients' queries.

The doctor's explanation about the risks involved in the treatment and the probability of a risk materialising are not without difficulties. The doctor can at best inform the patient of the likelihood of any adverse effect. But its statistical probability may not be understood easily. The patient may not understand the implication of such expressions as, a big or small chance, one in a hundred chance, one in a ten thousand chance, etc., of something going wrong. The question in his mind would be whether he is the *one* in the hundred or ten thousand, etc. To help the patient, the doctor may consider it expedient to reassure the patient in terms of the unlikelihood of his being the one. Such a reassurance may help the patient to make up his mind in favour of a particular option. However, in such a case, the patient's consent would be based more on the doctor's reassurance than on comprehending the information he provides. The element of reassurance from the doctor greatly influences the Indian patient, who wants to get well after having made a big effort financially, and otherwise, to obtain the services of a doctor. His keenness to get treated and recover surpasses his desire to be fully informed about the probabilities.

The next question is: how much information is the patient able to comprehend in order to make a rational decision? Given his limited familiarity with the medical system and his psychological state of anxiety and apprehension, the patient may misunderstand his own prognosis, or overlook the finer points of the treatment, or misjudge the gravity of the risks involved. In fact, the patient may be left with more doubts, confusion and anxiety after listening to the doctor, having picked up a few meaningful words here and there without understanding the implications as well as the context of the advice. With this situation in mind, Kuczewski and McCruden (2001) have emphasised the importance of the patient's cognitive capacity to make his treatment decisions.

This takes us further to the question of how much the doctor should tell the patient. If the patient poses his questions and his doubts intelligibly, the doctor may be able to answer these to the former's satisfaction. But, if the patient is quiet, passive, and unresponsive, the doctor may be clueless about the patient's need to know and his ability to understand. He may not be sure if the patient has heard him right before making up his mind. Obviously, one has to have some background knowledge about the system and how it works to be able to ask intelligent and relevant questions about particular therapies, etc. In its absence the patient may remain tongue-tied, not knowing how to frame his questions. Being aware of his own ignorance, the patient may feel diffident and shy about articulating his worries before the doctor. Some apprehension may also be experienced by the doctors on this score. Not knowing the depth of knowledge a particular patient possesses about modern medicine, the doctor may not be able to decide where to begin, what to presume, and what to explain in order to carry out his ethical obligation of informing the patient before obtaining his/her consent. Informed legal consent apart, even otherwise, providing information is necessary for eliciting the patient's compliance. For instance, in the study of women patients new to modern medicine, mentioned earlier, it was observed that a few had run away from the X-ray table for fear of being injured when they saw the 'big machine' approaching too close, because, reportedly, nobody had informed them how X-ray machines worked vis-à-vis the patient (Minocha 1996). Patients' ignorance about modern medicine became evident to me in our conversations in hospitals. I noticed their puzzlement, and some amusement, over their observations that they were told to have their bladder full for some tests (ultrasound) and empty for some others (bone scan), because they were unaware of how the machines worked differently in the two cases. In their study of Indian patients, Sriram et al. (1991) noted that, in the doctors' opinion, illiteracy of the patients was the main constraint in providing information in order to obtain consent.

Evidently, in more literate societies, where people have had exposure to modern medicine for generations, the task of the doctor to inform the patient becomes easier and faster. Far from being passive recipients, the patients can critically evaluate whatever they are told and discuss their doubts with their doctors. Asai writes about his patients in USA '. . . enjoying their right to and responsibility for autonomous medical choices. They wanted to know, they wanted to decide, and they were usually willing to take responsibility for the outcomes of their decisions' (1996: 91).

IV

It is doubtful that in many traditional societies the patients would be able to appreciate why at all, in the first place, their explicit consent is required before initiating the treatment. What are its implications for the patient, the doctor, as well as the treatment? As it is, most Indian patients reach the doctor quite late when the disease has almost reached a state of being irreversible. Their only interest is to get the treatment started immediately and come out of the illness alive. They are not motivated to seek information about the nitty-gritty of the disease and its management and would be willing to sign on any paper so that the treatment is initiated at once. In such a mental state, any discussion on 'informed consent' would be lost on the patient and his relatives, who are more likely to become confused and anxious about the 'delay' in treatment that this may cause.

Most Indians are used to the traditional therapeutic systems in which the healer tries to build the patient's confidence in his healing skills by the display of his intuitive capability in arriving at a diagnosis and by giving assurances of speedy healing and recovery (Marriott 1955; Carstairs 1955). In contrast, the long explanations given by the doctor to evoke the patient's participation in selecting a treatment option, and statements on what can go wrong, as envisaged by the informed consent stipulations, would make the patient sceptical of the doctor's competence and self-confidence. According to them, a self-confident doctor need not ask too many questions or give explanations of his work. For them the patient-healer relationship is more of a fiduciary type resting on the former having faith in the latter's craftsmanship, his medications, his diagnostic and treatment procedures and in his intentions. True to this type of relationship, Japanese doctors want, according to Asai (1996), their patients to take their advice because they know best and have the patients' interests in mind.

The patient's role is culturally defined in all societies. In traditional societies such as Japan and India, dependency role of patients is well recognised. Women patients in India are especially dependent on male relatives when negotiating the external impersonal domain, such as the hospital, and in dealing with strangers. It is the family members who take important decisions on their behalf, especially if the decisions are to rest on possessing technical knowledge. During her illness, a woman is expected to let others assume responsibility for her welfare. Even male patients are expected to play the dependency role. In such a social context, the assertion of his autonomy and individual rights by the patient, as envisioned in the doctrine of informed consent, would not carry much sense. Any discourse on a sick person's rights would look a bit incongruous in such a cultural matrix. As mentioned earlier, it is only within the context of an overall ideological framework, which values free, autonomous, rational, and responsible individuals, that a fertile ground for the nurturing of all types of human rights, especially patient's rights, can exist. In an elaborate paper on the cultural dimension of medical ethics, Kuczewski and McCruden (2001) argue that the conception of patient autonomy is a Western cultural one, which emphasises self-determination and the individual's freedom.

V

An interesting question is: how does the patient handle the information received from the doctor? How does he evaluate and weigh the different alternatives before according his consent to one of them? It is more likely that the patient's parameters for evaluation of the information received would be influenced by his own wishes, preferences and circumstances, which need not be strictly medical in nature. Different patients may have divergent yardsticks and these may be at sharp variance with those of medical personnel.

My observations of patients in different regions in India (Minocha 1996; 2004) show that for any sickness the patients use a variety of medical and non-medical parameters to evaluate the information, to make the choice of therapy and decide on the timing of its initiation. Some of these yardsticks/parameters are:

1. Number of hospital days required, if hospitalisation is necessitated, and the number of days required for recuperation.
2. Cost of the treatment, loss of wages or income, and other opportunities to be lost.
3. The pain and discomfort to be experienced.
4. The probability of complete or partial recovery and return to normal life.
5. The side effects of the treatment.
6. The reputation of the doctor as a person and as a medical expert, and his training and competence to carry out the procedures.
7. The timing of the procedure. For example, surgeries may have to be postponed till after a festival, children's school examinations, delivery of a pregnant relative, marriage in the family, and other important social events.

Evidently, different patients, and for that matter the same patient for different diseases, would take cognizance of the above-listed parameters before giving or withholding consent. Moreover, the patient's age, gender, social position, and perceived usefulness, and importance to others would influence his own as well as his relatives' evaluations and viewpoints on the above parameters. For example, an elderly woman may not wish to spend a great deal in getting herself medical treatment, because she has lost her social usefulness according to herself as well as her family members, whereas the very same person may mortgage property to pay for the treatment of a male bread-winner of the family. There may be other important social reasons for rejecting or receiving treatment. In a hospital in Delhi, for example, the father of a teenage girl facing leg amputation told the doctor that he would prefer his daughter to be dead instead of her losing a leg. 'What will I do with a daughter who is physically not whole? Who will marry her? She would be a burden for the family. Who will look after her after I am dead?' (communicated to the author by the doctor).

In other words, it is in terms of the patient's socio-economic characteristics that the information provided by the doctor is received, understood, evaluated and acted upon. Medical considerations may or may not be an important part in this calculus. As an illustration of this, illiterate women patients in India are not considered intellectually competent to receive communication on technical matters from the doctors. It is only her male relatives who would try to articulate queries and receive the information and take decisions on her behalf, depending upon their own intellectual competence. It is also not necessary that the others in the reference group will try to safeguard the patient's own interests, desires and wishes, and not let their own inclinations affect their judgement. The above case of the girl facing amputation exemplifies this. Moreover, it is not always certain that the male relatives of illiterate and ignorant women patients will themselves have the necessary exposure to modern medicine to be able to comprehend the doctor's information about the patient's disease, its prognosis and management. Given these constraints and limitations, it is probable that the consent accorded by the patient or the relatives, in consultation with each other, would not be a truly medically informed one and rational.

To a great extent, it is actually the family's decision whether to get the patient any treatment at all; which medical system to resort to, be it allopathy, homeopathy, ayurveda, folk therapies, etc.; which agency to get treatment from, for example, a private practitioner practising from his clinic, or a doctor working in a government hospital, etc.; how to finance the treatment and reorganise the household dislocated by the illness. Such decisions are taken over time, after eliciting the opinions of others in their reference groups, especially of persons who profess to know about modern medicine and its efficacy, on the one hand, and the needs of the patient, on the other.

Moreover, owing to his ignorance, the patient may feel diffident when interacting with the doctor and in posing questions to him. In a study of a hospital for women in New Delhi, Minocha (1996) observed that the patients, who were mostly illiterate and without much exposure to modern medicine, felt shy when talking to the doctors on their own initiative, because, in their perception, the doctors were culturally and socially quite different from them. Therefore, they were not very much at ease while interacting with them. However, they felt close enough to the para- and non-medical staff to seek answers from them and satisfy their curiosity. But, this category of staff were themselves not adequately informed and could not give accurate information on various aspects of surgical interventions and conservative treatment. The information they did give was often coloured by their own perspectives and opinions about what ought to be done in particular illnesses, including magical and shamanistic interventions. Many a time the patients sought answers from visitors of neighbouring patients in the ward. That is to say, the patients had several sources for obtaining 'information', including persons who were themselves not knowledgeable enough about the therapeutic system and did not know the correct answers. The information collected from various sources was therefore often contradictory.

In the practice of the doctrine of informed consent, much will depend upon the nature of the rapport between the patient and the doctor and their mutual expectations, perceptions and stereotypes. In the study of the Delhi hospital mentioned above, there was stereotyping of the patients by the doctors and vice versa. The doctors categorised the patients as ignorant, illiterate, and not able to easily comprehend technical matters. On their part, the patients thought that the doctors, because of their professional education and superior social background, urban affiliations, etc., were quite different from them and were, consequently, disinterested in satisfying their curiosity and incapable of understanding and appreciating the patients' perspectives. They held the doctors in awe and did not feel free enough to engage in a dialogue with them for fear of being reprimanded for their ignorance. Also, the patients usually saw the doctors on their ward rounds and presumed that they were always in a hurry to move on to the next patient and, therefore, having little time or inclination to listen to patients individually and talking to them at length. The standing posture of the doctors also discouraged the patients from addressing them. They preferred to have the doctors sitting comfortably and giving them their focused attention. The point I wish to make here is that building a rapport between the patient and the doctor is a must to achieve a comfortable dialogue, as demanded by the doctrine of informed consent, to the satisfaction of the two parties and resulting in the patient giving his consent which is really informed.

VI

As mentioned earlier, the doctrine of informed consent in Western countries emerged almost as an adjunct to the ideas of rationality in human thought and action, individuality, and freedom of choice. In contrast, in most Asian societies, the individual's identity is situated within the matrix of his family, friends, neighbourhood and community. Important decisions are seldom taken unilaterally by him. It is considered more prudent to discuss matters of importance with relevant others in the reference group before arriving at decisions. Quite often, such decisions are taken in the family on behalf of persons who are expected not to raise many queries but submit to the collective wisdom of the reference group. This is especially true of sick persons who are expected to depend upon others for the management of the illness. This passivity is a characteristic especially of women patients who are expected to exhibit this cultural trait in many other spheres of life. The sick person in India, therefore, is not autonomous, nor independent, nor culturally empowered to take his own unilateral decisions and assume responsibility for any consequent adverse outcomes. It is regarded as inelegant and asocial for a person to pretend to be an independent human being.

There is ethnographic evidence to show that the attention of the Indian patient as well as of his well-wishers is focused on the psycho-social aspects of the illness, such as why the illness happened to him; what could have gone wrong in his thought and behaviour towards others for which he is being punished by falling ill; is he the victim of evil dispositions of others towards him, etc. Such queries are quite central to their minds. This is in contrast to the biomedical discourse which the doctor considers more relevant to the medical management of the patient. He may, therefore, brush aside these social concerns and move on to his job of informing the patient about the medical aspects in order to elicit his informed consent. The patient, on his part, may not evince keen interest in what he perceives as the technical nitty-gritty of the treatment process on which he believes the doctor is an expert and alone competent to decide matters. He would rather relegate these matters to the doctor. In their study of 148 patients, Sriram et al. (1991) found that patients felt that the details of the investigation and prognosis need not be always told to them. The primary interest of the patient and his well-wishers is in his getting cured and returning to his normal routine at the earliest. How the doctor achieves this for him, what therapeutic route he takes, which procedures he decides to adopt, is not their job to deliberate upon. Having reposed their faith in the doctor's acumen, they wish to follow his instructions without much debate and delay. They are not enamoured by the patient's legal rights to know, to seek full information, and to freely choose before the treatment is initiated. These rights are extraneous to their immediate concerns. This is, however, not to say that they are not curious about what is going on and in what the doctor intends to do by way of establishing a prognosis and planning the treatment. But, to consider information-seeking as a legal right which has to be exercised before starting the treatment is not what impresses them the most. The point that is being made here is that whereas the doctor is professionally trained and oriented to deal with biomedical facts about the disease and its medical management, the patients are very much involved with the psychological and social dimensions of the illness, its causes and its management, and the after-effects of the cure. They prefer to relegate the technical matters to the doctor.

This takes us to the related question of whether, indeed, the patient wants to have the type of information envisaged in the doctrine of informed consent and whether he wants to or can handle it to be able to enact his rights. This is notwithstanding the question whether he wishes to decide matters at his individual level. My observations reveal that not all patients desire to be informed and not many feel capable of handling the information received. Indeed, it is not easy for most patients to accept a bad prognosis dispassionately. It has been noticed that some patients get so anxious about a bad prognosis or the likelihood of a prolonged treatment that they run away from it altogether, thereby denying a fair chance to the treatment. The patients may also visit other practitioners or quacks who give unwarranted assurances with confidence. Some patients are reported to go to religious mentors to seek their permission and blessings before undergoing the treatment. Some others wait for a more astrologically auspicious time for it.

The doctors are professionally ordained to evoke the patient's psychological will to recover. This involves giving him some reassurances of recovery, which keeps the patient going and boosts his morale during difficult moments. Thus, while there are patients who are capable of handling bitter truths, others may have to be managed more tactfully by the doctor. In short, the practice of the doctrine of informed consent should enjoin the doctor to anticipate the patient's mental make-up and decide what should be told to him and what details are to be withheld in his own interest. Illness being a sensitive as well as an emotive issue, the doctor cannot subscribe to a uniform pattern of behaviour for all patients. This makes the doctors' job of informing patients a challenging one.

VII

The doctrine of informed consent rests on the premise that information is a prerequisite for more rational decision-making. That is to say, information empowers the person and promotes rationality. It presumes that once in possession of medical information, the patient, by using his reasoning faculty, would opt for the most rational and, therefore, the most suitable treatment for his illness. Conversely, he would reject other modes of therapeutic action. That is to say, selection and rejection of the therapeutic options available should be a rational act based on the weighing of pros and cons in the context of the medical information provided. This line of reasoning implies that if non-medical considerations become important in decision-making, it is less rational. One may, however, argue that even if he keeps the social and economic considerations uppermost in his calculations, the patient may still be rational in arriving at decisions in so far as they help him in making a prudent choice.

Since the volition exercised has legal implications, the question arises whether the patient should record his decision along with its rationale. It is likely that many persons would find it difficult to record the reasons with precision. But, if it was to be made mandatory it would give legal protection to the doctor in so far as the recorded statements will give some indication of the thoroughness with which the doctor had informed the patient and will help in protecting him legally. In this context, since the patient is to be made dependent on the doctor for obtaining information, he is also made vulnerable to the latter's influencing him to go in for his own preferences. The doctor is expected to help the patient in decision-making without any self-interest and guiding him towards opting for the appropriate therapy. However, this guidance by the doctor to the patients to opt for a particular treatment may turn out to be more on commercial considerations and driven by market forces and not merely a professional judgement, thus violating ethical norms.

An important dimension of obtaining and giving informed consent is the understanding the patient has of why his consent is being sought at all and why he is being given, unasked, so much information about the ifs and buts of the treatment proposed for him. He is likely to wonder how this information will benefit him and what implications his consent would have on the treating doctor and on his interaction with the patient. This issue is important because informed consent is a new imposition on the classical fiduciary doctor-patient relationship in which the mutual rights of the role partners remained hidden, in an implicit form, while faith and trust take the upper hand. The patient was hardly aware of his rights as a patient and the doctor perceived his client's rights in the relationship, if any, as implicit. The rationale of converting the fiduciary relationship into one of legal rights and obligations, as in informed consent, may not be easily understood and appreciated by the patients. On his part, the Indian patient, at least, puts his trust in the doctor's expertise and good intentions, having once decided on getting his technical services. It is, therefore, difficult for him to appreciate why he, a lay person, has to himself choose the course of medical action and not the expert doctor. Also, why does the doctor have to do so much explaining on the different aspects of the treatment, focusing on all that can go wrong. Moreover, why is the patient being asked not only to decide matters but also to put his signatures on lengthy documents as if to make his decisions more legally binding?

Notwithstanding the above, my field experience suggests that the average Indian patient does desire information about his illness and its treatment, and reassurance from the doctor about recovery. This alleviates his anxiety and encourages him to follow the doctor's instructions with some understanding. What is difficult for him to appreciate is that seeking detailed information is his legal right, almost a duty, which has to be performed before getting the treatment.

VIII

In many ways, informed consent may be viewed more as an aid to the doctor practising defensive medicine than as a patient's legalised privilege to get the best treatment possible. The doctor can confidently presume that having given his consent, the patient is more likely to be compliant and morally obliged to follow the doctor's instructions and less keen to drag him to a law court. By shifting of the responsibility of untoward happenings onto the patient who has given his consent, the doctor can feel professionally more secure. It can give him legal protection if the matter goes to court because of any charges of medical negligence or malpractice on his part.

The chief merit of the doctrine of informed consent is believed to be that by involving the patient in his own treatment he is given a sense of participation in the treatment process. Instead of being a passive recipient of medications, etc., the patient becomes a consciously active participant. It follows that the patient's compliance, which was presumed in the earlier paradigm, now has to be deliberately evoked by the doctor. The doctor is obliged to empower the patient by imparting information to him so that he can make well-considered rational decisions. Having done so, the patient would be able to assume responsibility for his decisions and not blame the doctor for unexpected outcomes unduly. In other words, the doctrine safeguards the interests of both.

On close analysis, the assumption underlying the doctrine of informed consent, that information leads to empowerment which enables rational choices, becomes somewhat problematic. In this context one may ask what is the place of emotions in decision-making in an emotionally charged situation of a serious illness? When the doctor himself falls sick, does it make us expect that the informed and knowledgeable doctor will necessarily make for himself rational decisions uninfluenced by his emotions? Are the patients, or for that matter, doctors not influenced by their own emotions. Thus, there is the example of a gynecologist who refused to get a biopsy for a lump in the breast because she was scared to be told that it may be a confirmed malignancy. Indeed, she knew too much about what a confirmed malignancy entailed that she became 'irrational'. One may however agree with her decision, as it emerged from the exercise of her freedom to choose. But, was it a rational one in the given medical circumstances? Does it therefore leave scope for emotions to play a legimate role in important medical decision-making? Indeed, one may argue that what appears emotional and therefore irrational consideration for some may appear quite rational to many others. Emotion and rationality may not be therefore always poles apart in sickness and health. Due weight should therefore be given to the importance of emotion in medical decision-making.

In India, the ideas enshrined in the doctrine of informed consent, though not legally binding yet, continue to percolate into the medical and lay discourse. Many a doubt could be raised about the applicability of such a doctrine to a highly illiterate traditional society such as India, having limited exposure to modern medicine. In such a society the sick person is treated as someone dependent on others, with the family playing a crucial supportive role in the treatment as well as in the patient's interaction with the doctor. The concepts of individual autonomy and freedom of choice in the medical domain, by and large, still remain extrinsic and alien to the Indian thought process. As for Japan, Asai contends that 'Imposing informed consent on people who do not want medical information and decision-making is ethically wrong and paradoxically paternalistic' (1996: 91).

The problems involved in obtaining informed consent from unconscious or critically ill and mentally challenged patients are of a different nature and need to be addressed separately. I have not discussed them in this paper. This paper examines the doctrine of informed consent in terms of various dimensions of its application. It delineates the socio-cultural and other constraints, which tend to influence the translation of this doctrine into the patient-physician relationship in the Indian context.

References

Active Citizenship Network. 2002. *European Charter of Patients' Rights*. Basic Document. Rome.

American Hospital Association. 1992. *Patients' Bill of Rights*. Chicago, http//:www.aha.org.

Asai, Atsushi. 1996. Barriers to Informed Consent in Japan. *Eubios Journal of Asian and International Bioethcis* 6(4): 91–93.

Carstairs, G. M. 1955. Medicine and Faith in Rural Rajasthan. In *Health, Culture and Community*, ed. B. D. Paul. New York: Russel Sage Foundation.

Gopal, Reema. 2004. Multipurpose Workers in the Context of Primary Health Care. PhD thesis. University of Delhi.

Kuczewski, Mark, and Patrick J. McCruden. 2001. Informed Consent: Does It Take a Village? The Problem of Culture and Truth Telling. *Cambridge Quarterly of Healthcare Ethics* 10(3): 34–46.

Marriott, M. 1955. Western Medicine in a Village of Northern India. In Paul, *Health Culture and Community*.

Minocha, Aneeta A. 1980. Medical Pluralism and Health Services in India. *Social Science and Medicine* 14B(4): 217–24.

———. 1996. *Perceptions and Interactions in a Medical Setting: A Sociological Study of a Women's Hospital*. New Delhi: Hindustan Publishing Corporation.

———. 2004. Health Services and Their Utilization: A Sociological Case Study. Report submitted to the Indian Council of Social Science Research (unpublished).

Sriram, T. G. et al. 1991. Informed Consent: A Study of Experiences and Opinion of Utilizers of Health Services from India. *Social Science and Medicine* 32(12): 1389–92.

Part IV
Disciplinary Concerns

11

Empirical Meaning and Imputed Meaning in the Study of Kinship

André Béteille

I

I would like to begin by considering whether there is a uniquely advantaged point of departure in the systematic study of kinship and marriage. There appear to be two important candidates in the field: first, what has for long been conventionally known as the 'elementary unit of kinship' comprising parents and their unmarried children, and, second, what, according to the terminology established by Lévi-Strauss, is called the 'atom of kinship' comprising a woman, her brother, her husband, and her son. It appears to be widely believed that the second unit is more economical and gives us a wider and deeper insight into the nature of kinship than the first. I shall argue that this is a mistaken belief.

The idea that the elementary unit comprising parents and unmarried children contains within itself all the primary elements of kinship has been in currency so long that it is difficult to attribute its original use to any single author. Yet, there was a time when it was necessary to assert that the elementary family had a central place in primitive as well as modern societies, for anthropologists of the nineteenth century did not generally believe that it had such a place in the societies about which they wrote. Most of them, from Morgan to Durkheim, believed in the evolutionary priority of the clan over the family, which they assigned to a later stage in the evolution of society. This perception began to change only after World War I, and a major turning point was the publication of *Primitive Society* by Robert Lowie (1920) in which the older argument about clan and family was effectively demolished.

The work of Lowie (and his contemporaries) cleared the ground for serious studies of the elementary family, and these received a fresh impetus from the field investigations conducted by Malinowski and his pupils in the London School of Economics in the 1920s and 1930s. At the same time, it has to be stressed that the 'elementary unit of kinship' with which I am concerned is not the same thing as the elementary or nuclear family. The former is primarily a conceptual device designed for understanding the nature of kinship, whereas the latter is a particular type of domestic arrangement, more significant in some societies than in others. The elementary unit of kinship as conceived here is a useful point of departure for the study of kinship in all societies, including those in which the extended or the compound family is more typical than the simple or nuclear family.

The analytical utility of the elementary unit of kinship became a commonplace of British social anthropology through the writings of Radcliffe-Brown (1950). As Dumont (1971) has pointed out, it made its way into the popular handbook of the Royal Anthropological Institute known as Notes and Queries in Anthropology. But it is in the writings of Meyer Fortes that we see the most comprehensive use of this analytical device. Although in his later writings Fortes was inclined to stress the influence of Radcliffe-Brown, we cannot ignore the lasting influence on it from the apprenticeship with Malinowski.[1] It was the 'biographical approach', first proposed by Malinowski (1930), that animated Fortes's work (1949a, 1949b, 1953) on the domestic domain with its stress on the genetic processes of growth and development.

The elementary unit of kinship, as defined by Radcliffe-Brown and elaborated by Fortes (1969), consists of three basic relationships, between spouses, between parents and children, and between siblings. It can easily be shown that, no matter which relationship one starts with, one can reach the other two: marriage leads to parenthood and is sustained by it; siblings are offspring of the same parents who, as husband and wife, are their begetters and bearers. But, although the three relationships are held together in a complex web of interactions, they are necessarily distinct by virtue of the rule of incest. Finally, each relationship is made up of a number of different strands that may appear in various combinations.

Clearly, the elementary unit of kinship cannot take into account directly all relations of kinship and marriage, although it provides points of entry into the entire range of such relations. It does not tell us anything directly about in-laws, but indicates that an in-law is the wife's sister or the husband's brother. It takes the grandparent into account in so far as he or she is the mother's father or the father's mother. And, so on for siblings of spouses, spouses of siblings, parents of parents, and children of children.

An alternative to the elementary unit of kinship as described above was proposed by Lévi-Strauss (1963) in an ambitious paper in which he urged anthropologists to profit from the methods developed in linguistic analysis.[2] It was the forerunner of a new type of structural analysis that sought to displace the type of structural-functional analysis that had become characteristic of the work of Radcliffe-Brown, Fortes, and others. Followers of Lévi-Strauss were to appropriate the term 'structural' or 'structuralist' for their own style of analysis, using the term 'empiricist', usually in a pejorative sense, for the older type of kinship analysis presented as an arrangement of rights, obligations, sentiments and interactions.[3]

As appears from more than one commentary (Dumont 1971: 37; Barnes 1971: 117), there is a certain ambiguity in the use of the phrase 'elementary' in Lévi-Strauss' accounts of kinship structure. The 'elementary' unit that constitutes the 'atom of kinship' in his paper of 1945 is not the same as the 'elementary' structure of kinship which is the subject of his treatise of 1949. The 'true *atom of kinship*' is significant everywhere since it contains the code for the basic disposition of attitudes in all societies irrespective of rules of descent or of marriage. The 'elementary structure of kinship', on the other hand, is a feature of some societies and not of others that are characterised by 'complex structures'.

It is not altogether clear as to how the two concepts—the atom of kinship and the elementary structure of kinship—stand in relation to each other. One might say that the later formulation superseded the earlier one, and it is indeed striking that the atom of kinship does not feature as such in the treatise on elementary structures. At the same time, Lévi-Strauss not only included the 1945 essay in an important collection of his papers but made revisions in it in 1957 before its republication in 1958 (Lévi-Strauss 1963) nearly a decade after the publication of *The Elementary Structures of Kinship*.

There is clearly some relationship between the two formulations of Lévi-Strauss since they both put their stress on alliance, the exchange of women, and the relations between bride-givers and bride-takers; but he himself does not make that relationship clear. My present concern is limited to a consideration of the atom of kinship and its claim to universal significance, independently of any general theory of kinship and marriage. Just as one may consider the elementary unit of kinship without a bias for any theory of descent, so should it be possible to discuss the atom of kinship without entering into the merits of any theory of marriage alliance.

The alternative model proposed by Lévi-Strauss and designated by him as the 'atom of kinship' consists of four positions and four relationships. The four positions, as indicated earlier, are: a woman, her brother, her husband, and her son; and the four relationships are those between husband and wife, brother and sister, father and son, and mother's brother, and sister's son. The two models may be diagrammatically represented as follows:

It will be seen at once that a great advantage of the 'atom of kinship' is that it is able to represent directly a relationship between in-laws which the elementary unit of kinship is not able to do. However, it must be pointed out that the relationship between in-laws represented in the model is of one particular kind, that is, between brother and sister's husband or husband and wife's brother. The economy of the model requires the in-law relationship to be represented in this particular form and in no other form. If we had the woman's sister *instead* of her brother or the husband's instead of the wife's brother, the model would lose its cogency; if we included them *in addition*, it would lose its economy.

A look at the two models together will bring out a striking difference between them. Whereas the elementary unit of kinship

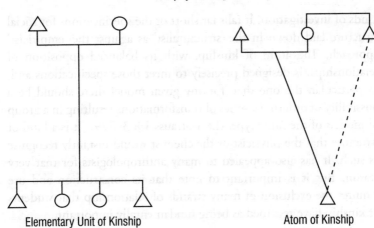

Elementary Unit of Kinship　　　　　　Atom of Kinship

is symmetrical gender-wise, having two males and two females, one at each level of generation, the atom of kinship is not. In the form presented by Lévi-Strauss, it has four positions of which one is occupied by a female and the three others by males. The addition of new positions to restore the symmetry of gender would, again, jeopardise the economy of the model, whereas additional positions can easily be incorporated in the other model, say, more children of either sex to indicate the significance of birth order, without any damage to its basic analytical purpose.

A second manifest limitation of the atom of kinship, related to the first, is its very inadequate representation of the sibling relationship. It does not in fact have a proper place for the sibling relationship as such, but only for one between siblings of opposite sex. This follows directly from the requirement of the model that the relationship between siblings should balance the relationship between spouses. Now, in a very broad sense, all societies require that spouses should be of opposite sex, but there can be no such requirement for siblings. But the requirement of the model leads to the bracketing out the relationships between brother and brother, and between sister and sister in order to highlight the relationship between brother and sister.

The elementary unit of kinship hardly corresponds to what would be called a model in the advanced sciences. It is a rough-and-ready device, useful in ordering some kinds of data and in furthering some kinds of investigation. It falls far short of the specifications for social structure laid down in the 'structuralist' as against the 'empiricist' approach. The atom of kinship, with its balanced opposition of relationships, is designed precisely to meet those specifications and, in particular, the one that 'for any given model there should be a possibility of ordering a series of transformations resulting in a group of models of the same type' (Lévi-Strauss 1963: 279). It is a kind of structure that the physicist or the chemist would instantly recognise as such. It has also appealed to many anthropologists for that very reason. But it is important to note that its construction and use requires the exclusion of many strands of relationship that students of kinship have regarded as being fundamentally important.

II

A model is constructed with a purpose, and we must briefly examine the work that the atom of kinship has been set to do. One of the objectives of the original formulation of Lévi-Strauss was to show that although the relationship between mother's brother, and sister's son stood in opposition to the relationship between father and son, the content of neither relationship had much to do with what Radcliffe-Brown (1952) regarded as crucial, namely, the rule of descent. It has to be agreed that Lévi-Strauss was on the whole successful in undermining the thesis that these relationships are invariably determined by the rule of descent.

If the relationship between mother's brother and sister's son is not governed by the rule of descent, what is it governed by? It is governed, according to the requirement of the model, by the relationship between father and son. And what is that governed by? That, in its turn, is governed by the relationship between mother's brother and sister's son. What we need to know in order to predict the nature of either relationship is not the rule of descent, but the nature of the other relationship. It is the same with the two relationships at the same generational level, between brother and sister on the one hand, and between husband and wife, on the other. It is noteworthy that in the model, relationships on the same generation level are not governed by relationships between adjacent generations: one cannot tell from the relationship between either husband and wife or brother and sister what the relationship will be between mother's brother and sister's son or between father and son.

Radcliffe-Brown's mistake seems to have been to depend too closely on the rule of descent in explaining the specific features of a dyadic relationship, in this case the one between the mother's brother and the sister's son. As is well known, the avunculate had intrigued anthropologists for a long time when Radcliffe-Brown came on the scene. The conventional explanation till then was that it was a residue of a past rule of matrilineal descent. But he put his case much too strongly, and it is now not very difficult to show that descent need not always be a factor governing the relationship between mother's brother and sister's son.

Over and above the rule of descent, Radcliffe-Brown used a number of other principles of varying degrees of generality, such as the equivalence of siblings, the sex principle, the generation principle, and so on. He also pointed out, in my view quite perceptively, that the true opposite of the relationship between the mother's brother and the sister's son was not the one between father and son, but the one between the father's sister and the brother's son; I shall return to this point shortly. In trying to account for the facts of kinship, Radcliffe-Brown was inclined to invoke a variety of principles in a somewhat ad hoc manner. He failed to provide any rule by which those principles might be combined. Here the models proposed by Lévi-Strauss have a clear advantage, for he specifies rules regarding not only the internal components of the model but also the transformation of one model into another.

But the very looseness in the conception of the elementary unit of kinship gives it a certain advantage of flexibility. It enables one to move virtually across the entire space of kinship by adding one relationship to another while operating with only the three primary relationships. Thus, there was no difficulty, within the framework provided by the elementary unit of kinship, for Radcliffe-Brown to compare and contrast the relationship of the mother's brother to the sister's son not only with the relationship between father and son but also with the one between father's sister and brother's son. It is difficult to see how this can be done within the more finely balanced model of the atom of kinship. What would happen if, instead of taking a woman, her brother, her husband and her son, we took a man, his sister, his wife and his son? Would we then have a different model of the same type or models of two different types? The relations at the same generation level would be analogous in the two models, but that does not appear to be the case with the relations between adjacent generations. It is quite clear that the second model will not be able to do the same kind of work as the first and might for that reason fail to qualify as the atom of kinship.

Some believe that the great advantage of the atom of kinship is that it incorporates the rule of incest by showing that the husband has to be someone other than the brother (or son). But that rule could be made equally explicit by taking either a woman, her brother and her husband, or a man, his sister and his wife. The problem with the second alternative will not be with ego, spouse and opposite sex sibling but with the displacement, from the viewpoint of the lower generation, of the mother's brother by the father's sister. Nor does it sound convincing to say that a sibling must be introduced in the parental generation to make the incest rule explicit. The incest rule is accommodated within the elementary unit of kinship by the proposition that its three component relationships are mutually *irreducible*. This simply means that any one of the three relationships excludes the other two. One's sibling cannot be one's spouse, and one's spouse cannot be one's sibling; one's parent (or child) cannot be one's sibling; one's spouse cannot be one's child (or parent). It is only these three relationships that are primary. The relationship between mother's brother and sister's son is not primary in the sense that it is not excluded by the three other relationships: mother's brother and sister's daughter may also be husband and wife as in south Indian kinship.

The elementary unit of kinship merely recommends that in approaching any kinship system, we should start with and keep constantly in sight three basic and irreducible relationships: between spouses, between parents and children, and between siblings. It tells us very little about the contents of these relationships in any given society or culture, which it leaves to empirical investigation. It is completely open as to whether the emotional tone of the relationship between spouses, between siblings of the same or opposite sex, or between a parent and a child of either sex is likely to be 'positive' or 'negative'. Indeed, the whole emphasis in the work of Fortes and others has been on exploring the complexity, the flexibility and the richness in these relations, taken singly or in combination. The parent-child relationship hardly declares its meaning until we know whether the parent is a father or a mother, the child a son or a daughter, the son an elder or a younger son. In this scheme, to say that the emotional tone of the relationship with the sibling must be identical with or opposite to the emotional tone of the relationship with the spouse would make very little sense. They are likely to be similar in some respects and dissimilar in others, and it is up to the investigator to observe, describe, and interpret the similarities as well as the differences.

III

The atom of kinship, unlike the elementary unit, is a true model in the sense that its terms are so arranged that one can generate a series of models through appropriate transformations. Its terms are four relationships arranged in two pairs: (i) between husband and wife and between brother and sister; and (ii) between father and son and between mother's brother and sister's son. But, while one term in any pair governs the other term in the same pair, it tells us nothing about either of the terms in the opposite pair. Thus, we can tell from the brother-sister relationship about the husband-wife relationship, but not about the relationship between either father and son or mother's brother and sister's son. To the extent that it showed that the avunculate is unrelated to any rule of descent, the model served its original purpose. But it remains incomplete in so far as it fails to establish any link between the two pairs of terms, whereas it was Radcliffe-Brown's purpose to explore how relations within the generation affect those between the generations both within and outside the elementary unit.

In the atom of kinship, values are imputed to the four terms or relationships that are its constituent parts. It is the distribution of these values that gives the model its distinctive character; in talking about transformations, one is talking in effect about their redistribution among the basic terms. The values are specified in a particular way so that a term can have either a positive or a negative value but not both at the same time. The model is so constructed that the terms are always balanced in regard to their values. Thus, of the four terms in the model, two must carry positive and the remaining two negative values; moreover, each pair must have one term with a positive and the other with a negative value.

How should we decide what kind of value—positive or some other—to assign to any primary relationship within the domain of kinship? The whole tradition of field-based studies in kinship has been to look for the answer in the empirical material of fieldwork. This has generated a certain natural misgiving about clear and categorical answers to such questions. We can see this easily as we move from Radcliffe-Brown to Fortes, for the data become increasingly rich and complex. Radcliffe-Brown's own initial formulation on the avunculate took off from the available empirical material, which at the time lacked the richness of the material made available by anthropologists of the next generation such as Firth (1936), Fortes (1945, 1949a) and Evans-Pritchard (1951). But his own comparison of father, mother's brother, and father's sister was intended at best to provide a limited empirical generalisation and not a model for universal application.

The imputation of positive and negative values to the terms in the atom of kinship raises problems of a more fundamental nature. As Barnes (1971: 172) has pointed out, the model is tightly constructed and does not have any room in it for representing variations in the strength or intensity of the positive and negative values. Lévi-Strauss was in fact using the same kind of empirical material as colleagues across the channel, but he brought to its use a different kind of inventive skill from theirs. For him, the atom of kinship was not so much an empirical generalisation as a model designed 'to make immediately intelligible all the observed facts' (Lévi-Strauss 1963: 280).

Lévi-Strauss demonstrated the use of his atom of kinship by presenting five forms of the model, each with a matching ethnographic example. The examples were carefully selected so as to undermine the assumption of an association between the relationship of the mother's brother to his sister's son with any rule of descent. But while it settled, or appeared to settle, one question, it raised many others about data, method and theory.

The first question relates to the kinds of facts that we will require in order to test the adequacy of the model. Here, the five ethnographic examples actually presented by Lévi-Strauss must be regarded as illustrative rather than exhaustive. Towards the end of his paper, Lévi-Strauss points out, first, that the system of basic attitudes comprises four terms and not just the two he had represented by a plus and a minus sign; and, second, that a single relationship between two individuals might be governed not by a single attitude as shown in the model, but by a 'bundle' of attitudes. But at this point, where we begin to enter deep water, his discussion virtually ends.

One may notice that in adding, towards the end of his paper, two new attitudes to the ones dealt with in the ethnographic examples, Lévi-Strauss has altered the meanings of the first two attitudes. To begin with, the + sign denoted 'free and familiar relations' and the - sign, 'hostility, antagonism and reserve' (Lévi-Strauss 1963: 44). But when the system of signs is made complete, the + sign denotes 'rights' and the - sign 'obligations' (Lévi-Strauss 1963: 49); the two other signs now denote mutuality =, and reciprocity ±. This at once sets a puzzle for the student of kinship as a social system, for he will find it difficult to understand how any social relationship can be defined, save in the extreme case, solely in terms of either rights or obligations.

The concluding part of the discussion appears to open up the very questions that one had thought had been settled with the five examples in the model. We are now no longer clear whether the emphasis is to be on relations viewed in terms of 'rights', 'obligations', etc., or in terms of 'bundles of attitudes'. There should be no difficulty in principle in taking account of rights and obligations as well as bundles of attitudes, and, indeed, it is standard practice to do so in all anthropological studies of kinship based on fieldwork. The problem will be in devising an algebra by means of which all of that can be accommodated into models governed by strict conditions of transformation.

What is not fully clear from the representation of the atom of kinship is why the model can carry only some combinations of signs and not others. Why, for instance, can the relationship between brother and sister not carry the same sign as that between husband and wife? Or the relationship between father and son the same sign as that between mother's brother and sister's son? But if any of the four relationships can carry either of the two signs (+, −), or perhaps one of the two other signs (=, ±), it is difficult to see what purpose the atom of kinship serves other than being an aid to observation and description. In that case we are back to the three irreducible relationships of the elementary unit of kinship with the addition of a new term that merely extends the range of observation and description. That extension, however, can be made in a number of different ways, and not only in the way proposed by Lévi-Strauss. By extending it laterally, we get two new relationships, between wife's brother and sister's husband, and between mother's brother and sister's son. If one made a vertical instead of a lateral extension, one would also get two new relationships by adding a single position: between father-in-law and daughter-in-law, and between grandparent and grandchild. The advantage of a lateral over a vertical extension does not make itself immediately apparent from the viewpoint of kinship studies in general. The atom of kinship can serve as a model only if the distribution of signs in it is governed by some rule. This means that we must know not only which combinations are excluded but also the rule which governs their exclusion.

If we look at the two relationships at the same generation level in the atom of kinship, it certainly appears plausible that they should bear opposite signs. The same thing is after all meant when we say that in the elementary unit of kinship, siblingship and marriage exclude each other. But whether their mutual exclusion (or opposition, or contrast) is made clearer by assigning plus and minus signs to them is a different matter, particularly where the same signs are made to do work with other and very different kinds of relationships.

It was Radcliffe-Brown who had pointed to the contrastive nature of the relationship between father and son, and between mother's brother and sister's son, but his observations were confined to a particular range of societies and were not meant to apply to all human societies. Assuming that there is a contrast at this level in some, or most, or even all societies, is it at all the same kind of contrast as in the first case? Are such contrasts perceived in the same way by the actors themselves, or are they merely phenomena of the *unconscious infrastructure* (Lévi-Strauss 1963: 33) that the model brings to light?

IV

As is well known, students of kinship have been divided on many matters relating to approach and method. One important division of long-standing has been between those who have examined kinship within the framework of social structure and those who have related it to the framework of culture. This division goes back to the famous debate in the years immediately preceding World War I between Rivers and Kroeber (Schneider 1968), and it has reappeared in one form or another in the last several decades. The issue has been complicated by the appropriation of the term 'structure' by those who, in the context of the Rivers-Kroeber debate, take their orientation from culture rather than social structure.[4] From the time of Radcliffe-Brown onward, students of kinship as social structure have taken some of their central ideas from the discipline of law, whereas the cultural analysis of kinship has been much influenced by lingustics; Kroeber himself assigned great importance to language and psychology in the understanding of kinship (Kroeber 1909).

As Fortes (1969) has pointed out, Radcliffe-Brown's paper of 1935 on 'Patrilineal and Matrilineal Succession' had a marked influence on subsequent studies of the principle of descent and the constitution of kin groups. It was a landmark in a series of contributions in which a particular conception of social structure assumed pre-eminence in the analytical study of kinship, especially in Britain. It is true that Radcliffe-Brown's concept of 'social structure' (and the related concept or 'social function') draws much on the organic analogy. What must also be noted is the frequent application of legal ideas in his writings on social structure in general and kinship structure in particular. It is no accident that the essay on patrilineal and matrilineal succession was written for a law journal.

The specification of rights, duties and obligations is central to all discussions of kinship structure in the writings of Radcliffe-Brown and those directly influenced by him. In this conception, a social structure is nothing but an arrangement of positions whose occupants are related to each other by a variety of rights and obligations. This is so whether we are considering dyadic relations, or complex networks of interpersonal relations, or relations between enduring groups. It is of course recognised in this view that one has to deal also with beliefs, sentiments, values, and so on, but what is of central importance is the distribution of rights and obligations. It is difficult to accommodate in this scheme relations defined solely by rights or solely by obligations, except of course as limiting cases. Brother and sister, wife and husband, father and daughter, men and women, adults and children, generally speaking, all have rights and all have obligations, although, of course, they do not all have the same rights or the same obligations.

The definition of social structure in terms of rights and obligations gave a certain rigour to the study of kinship and linked it most fruitfully to the study of politics. Apart from the analysis of the rights and obligations of persons occupying various positions in various systems of relationship, the juristic approach influenced the conception of the corporate group, particularly in the writings of Meyer Fortes (1969: 276–310) whose work on the nature of descent is regarded as definitive. Some students of kinship, following Gluckman (1955) have adopted the case method, commonly used in legal studies, to show how rights and obligations are manipulated and redefined in various contexts of social action (Van Velsen 1964).

But the application of the juristic approach and, in particular, the conception of social structure as a system of rights and obligations had its limitations. The concept of 'rights' was frequently stretched to accommodate a great variety of customs, usages and practices in a manner that sometimes appears puzzling to the lawyer. At the same time, this extension, no matter how large, could not possibly accommodate or do justice to many of the basic aspects of kinship to which other anthropologists had devoted attention for a long time.

Besides studying it as a system of rights and obligations, one may also study kinship as a system of symbolic representations. One important difference between Radcliffe-Brown and Lévi-Strauss is that, whereas for the former it was primarily a system of rights and obligations, for the latter, kinship as a social fact is above all a system of representations. There is, of course, a long tradition in American anthropology, from Kroeber (1909) to Schneider (1968b), of the study of kinship in terms of symbolic patterns, but what marks out the work of Lévi-Strauss from that tradition is the very distinctive concept of structure that animates it.[5]

The study of representations and the interpretation of their meanings may be made in a number of different ways. Despite the overlap, one must keep in mind the distinction between the cognitive and the moral aspects of the problem. As Kroeber had pointed out as far back as in 1909, a central issue in the study of kinship is that of classification in general and of identifying the criteria that may be and in fact are used in mapping out the domain of kinship. In broadly the same vein, Schneider (1968b) has tried to ask in his study of American kinship who counts as a relative, what makes a person a relative, what distinguishes relatives from in-laws, and what are the different kinds of relatives in the minds of the American people. As he has shown, to ask and answer these questions is to deal with symbols and their meanings.

The early bias of anthropological studies, clearly seen in the study of kinship from Morgan to Rivers, was towards extensive comparisons. These comparisons were often made without due caution and on the basis of very limited and unreliable empirical material. From 1922 onwards, general comparative studies of kinship have had to contend with detailed monographic studies based on intensive fieldwork. Although doubts have been raised from time to time about the value of the comparative method (Béteille 1990), our understanding of kinship in any one society would be greatly impoverished if we failed to make systematic comparisons between kinship systems in different societies. The only point to note is that comparisons have now to be made with attention to many more things—rights, obligations, norms, values, symbols, meanings, and, above all, actions—than were taken into account in the past.

Over the years, those engaged in the comparative study of kinship have devised a variety of approaches, strategies, concepts and models to give their studies greater range as well as greater depth. It is in this light that one has to view the elementary unit of kinship as well as the atom of kinship. The former merely provides certain guidelines for empirical enquiry into kin relationships without indicating much about their contents. The latter is more ambitious for it tells us that, given certain features of kin relationships, it should be possible to predict others.

Among those who stress the paramount importance of meaning in human culture, there are those who maintain that the meaning of a relationship, a role, or even an action may not be apparent to the actor himself. One might then construct a model to make the hidden or unconscious meaning apparent to the investigator. This I would characterise as the analysis of imputed meaning as against the study of the empirical meaning or the actor's meaning, characteristic of other approaches to the study of society and culture. There is a fundamental difference between the two approaches, although it is obvious that no approach confines itself solely to the one kind of meaning to the total exclusion of the other.

What distinguishes the approach of Lévi-Strauss to kinship is not simply that he is dealing with meanings rather than rights and obligations, but, further, that the meanings that he deals with are, at least to some extent, imputed rather than ostensible or empirical meanings. This follows from his bias for the code underlying the unconscious infrastructure. Once we know the meaning of the relationship between husband and wife, the logic of the model, rather than any empirical investigation, will tell us the meaning of the relationship between brother and sister. Similarly for the pair father-son and mother's brother-sister's son. The model simply closes certain possibilities and puts them beyond the reach of empirical enquiry.

Empirically, of course, one might encounter—either in one's fieldwork or among one's neighbours—a woman who has relations of 'hostility, antagonism, or reserve' with both her husband and her brother, but that is precluded by the atom of kinship. Likewise, one might actually know a boy or a man whose relations with both his father and his mother's brother are 'free and familiar', but that also is precluded by the model. It can certainly be argued that the anthropological analysis of kinship is not concerned primarily with the individual case or the ups and downs of interpersonal relationships, its primary concern being with the meanings encoded in the culture as a whole. Undoubtedly, the anthropological approach has assigned a degree of autonomy to the realm of culture or, in Kroeber's phrase, to the 'superorganic'.[6] The central task of anthropology in this view would be the analysis of the meanings encoded in a culture. In its extreme form, the individual might then be seen as a vehicle through which the meanings in the code are expressed, much as in 'les mythes qui se pensent dans les hommes'.

If we accepted such a view, whether in a moderate or an extreme form, we would still ask why a code of kinship should exclude certain combinations from the atom of kinship. It is clear from the model presented by Lévi-Strauss that all four terms in it never carry the plus sign. We may admit that this is borne out by the facts of ethnography in the examples selected by him. The view that all four of the primary terms cannot simultaneously be characterised by 'free and familiar relations' certainly appeals to common sense. But common sense is not enough: we must know what the cultural logic is that determines that the primary relationships of kinship cannot all be positive (or negative) at the same time.

We might reach the generalisation that the primary relations of kinship always come in pairs, with one positive and one negative term, on the basis of observation and comparison. But in the present case, the observations are not sufficiently firm and the comparisons not sufficiently extensive to sustain such a generalisation. However, one can also speak of generalisations in another sense where they can be deduced from certain axioms.

If we accept that the generalisations contained in the atom of kinship are based on axioms and not just observations, we must ask what those axioms are and what kind of standing they have in the study of human society and culture. In presenting the atom of kinship as an improvement on the elementary unit of kinship, Lévi-Strauss has made short work of empirical generalisations, but he has told us nothing about the axioms from which he has constructed his own models. As a result, what he has offered may look very different from the tools of enquiry used by his predecessors in the study in kinship, but it still falls far short of his own requirements of a structure laid down in his paper on the subject (Lévi-Strauss 1963: 277–323).

V

The search for latent, unconscious and real meanings has sometimes led to fruitful and surprising discoveries, but in the study of human societies it can never replace the slow and laborious investigation of the empirical or ostensible meanings that human beings give to their own everyday actions. There is a great tradition in sociological enquiry of the study of the meaning that the actor as a human agent gives to his own action, and our understanding of kinship can draw much sustenance from it.

The tradition of studying social institutions in terms of the meaning that an action has for the actor himself finds its definitive form in the sociology of Max Weber (1978). Although his training as a lawyer made him fully aware of the importance of rights and obligations, for Weber, the starting point of sociological enquiry was the meaningful orientation of the actor in the social situation. The meanings that are of primary concern here are not deduced from any model of structure or history, but the empirically observed or ostensible meanings that individuals assign to their own actions in everyday life. What is of significance in social life must be significant for the actor and not only the investigator, although it goes without saying that an action, a relationship, or an institution rarely has the same significance for all persons.

In anthropological investigations, one would expect the bias of participant-observation to lead the investigator to observe and record, if not to analyse, the meanings given by people to their everyday practice. Monographic studies of kinship by Firth (1936), Fortes (1945, 1949a) and other students of Malinowski are in fact replete with such information. As is well known, Malinowski himself constantly emphasised the need to understand things 'from the native's point of view' (1922), and he heaped scorn on his colleagues for dabbling in 'kinship algebra' (1930). His theoretical pronouncements were often unfortunate, but his general approach to the study of man had a very fruitful influence on the work done on kinship by his pupils although some of them turned against him for his dogmatic pronouncements (Fortes 1957; Leach 1957).

Weber's sociology, which had greater reach and sophistication than Malinowski's and was, moreover, largely free from its dogmatism, has been described as *Verstehendesoziologie*. As the phrase indicates, its central, though by no means only, concern was with the understanding and interpretation of meaning in social life, or, to use another phrase, to show the connectedness of meaning (*Sinnzusammenhangen*).[7] In his interpretive sociology, Weber made extensive use of ideal types, which, to be sure, are models of a certain kind, but they are models designed for describing, comparing, and classifying the actions of human agents. Obviously, there are difficulties in relating the empirical material of sociological observation to these models, particularly in comparative studies, but the model as such does not provide any substantive conclusions which can be reached only by arranging the observed facts in a systematic way.

In applying this approach to the study of kinship, we might ask whether we cannot define the domain of kinship itself in terms of its meaning. Fortes would say that the domain of kinship may be defined in terms of its meaning, what it signifies for people to view themselves as being related in a particular way. What defines kinship for him is the 'axiom of amity' which, he would say, sets apart a particular field of action and relationship in all societies (Fortes 1969: 219–49). This axiom is treated as the defining feature of the domain of kinship on the basis of the information collected from a great variety of societies. Fortes is of course aware that the axiom of amity does not exclude conflict in the actual relationships between kinsmen, and he has himself extensively documented such conflicts between parents and children, between spouses, and between siblings.

For most persons, the meaning of kinship is made real through interaction with particular kinsmen and categories of kinsmen perceived as relatives or in-laws of one kind or another. Although some persons count as kin in all societies,[8] many more persons count as kin in some societies than in others. In some societies, few distinctions are made among kinsmen, while in others many such distinctions are made. An Englishman can distinguish between his father's brother and his mother's brother as well as a Tamilian, but the distinction does not mean as much for the former as it does for the latter. Again, while the distinction might mean as much for the Bengali as it does for the Tamilian, it does not mean the same thing in the two cases: a Tamil woman may, under favourable circumstances, marry her mother's brother, but for a Bengali woman that would be out of the question.

David Schneider (1968b) has shown that the study of kinship must deal, first, with the person as a relative, and, second, with the relative as a person. It is true that his observation was made in the specific context of American culture where the concept of person has a special significance. But notwithstanding what Mauss (1979: 57–94) has said on the subject, the person is given some recognition in every society (Béteille 1991: 250–75), and nothing brings this out more vividly than examining the micro-structures and processes of kinship (Fortes 1987: 247–86).

It was with the development of intensive fieldwork and participant-observation that anthropologists began to devote serious attention to the micro-structures and processes of kinship. Earlier anthropologists had concentrated on the formal rules of kinship and marriage—matrilineal and patrilineal descent, endogamy and exogamy, levirate and sororate, and so on; and on the structure of relationship terminology and its real or assumed correspondence with the past and present organisation of kinship and marriage. Malinowski and his pupils, on the other hand, were interested is showing how it all worked to make the life of the individual, the family, and the community some sort of a coherent whole.

As an alternative to various speculative or conjectural approaches to the study of kinship, especially through the analysis of relationship terminology, Malinowski proposed his 'biographical approach'. In this approach, he begins with the infant and shows how the universe of kinship unfolds as he learns to identify various persons as kin and affines through his own growth from infancy to adulthood. In this process he learns to assign different meanings to different persons as he enters into relationship with them: first the mother, then the siblings, then the father, and the mother's brother, then various others related through the mother and the father; on marriage, with the wife and her relatives; then, with the birth and growth of his children, their relatives by marriage.

Malinowski's insights, particularly into the genetic processes of kinship, were greatly enriched by the detailed ethnographic studies of Fortes, first of the patrilineal Tallensi (1949a) and then of the matrilineal Ashanti (1949b). Fortes's writings on kinship bring together two of the most fundamental concerns of students of kinship and marriage: the study of jural rights and obligations, and the study of moral sentiments and ideas. The former derives its inspiration manifestly from Radcliffe-Brown, whereas the latter goes back to earlier influences, most notably that of Malinowski.

Fortes's interest in the politico-jural domain and the structure of descent has been matched by his concern for the domestic domain and the moral basis of kinship. As he has put it, 'In all human societies, the workshop, so to speak, of social reproduction, is the domestic group' (Fortes 1958: 2). It is here that we are able to examine in all their richness and complexity the three irreducible relationships, between spouses, between parents and children, and between siblings, that make up the elementary unit of kinship.

Each of the three relationships is made up of several strands and the relationships as well as their various strands change over time. As the concept of 'complementary filiation' shows, the term 'parent' does not have a single meaning for the child (Fortes 1969: 250–75). A child has two parents, and his orientation to the mother is never identical with his orientation to the father. Moreover, the child may be a son or a daughter, and that in turn would affect its orientation towards the parent. We are very far here from the atom of kinship in which the father-son relationship is singled out for counterposition with the relationship between mother's brother and sister's son. There the parent-child relationship is not considered for its own sake; all strands in it that cannot be counterposed with the relationship between mother's brother and sister's son are bracketed away. It tells us something about kin relationships but leaves out a very great deal that is of equal significance to the basic relations of kinship.

Understanding the meaning of the parent-child relationship requires us to take into account a great many things besides differences of gender at each of the two generational levels. From the viewpoint of interpretive sociology, it must surely matter to a mother whether her son is an only child or one of seven. The birth order of children influences to some extent the values assigned to them. As Fortes (1987: 218–46) has shown, the first born, in particular the first-born son, has in many societies a special significance that other children do not have.

The sibling relationship is a whole small world of symbolic significance in itself. Distinctions of gender and birth order mean different things in different cultures. Even a cursory examination of relationship terminology will bring this out. Most systems have separate terms for brother and sister, but in some, such as the Truk (Goodenough 1951), there is one term for siblings of the same sex and another for siblings of the opposite sex, each used reciprocally. Differences of birth order are stressed in some cultures and ignored in others. In Tamil, there is no term for brother, but only a term for elder brother (*anna*) and another for younger brother (*thambi*); and, likewise, a term for elder sister (*akka*) and another for younger sister (*thangai*); phonetically, the correspondence is by seniority rather than gender.

The same complexity is inherent in the relationship between husband and wife, which, moreover, is not static, but, like all the elementary relationships, changes over time, as the couple ages, as children are born and grow up, and as grandchildren enter the world. Where preferential kin marriage prevails, the husband must mean something different to the wife, at least in the early years of marriage, if he is her mother's brother from what he would mean to a wife who is unrelated and from a distant home.

The basic relationships of kinship are, of course, governed by rights and obligations flowing from the politico-jural domain. But there is more to the relationships between siblings, between spouses, and between parents and children than just rights and obligations, no matter how broadly conceived. And if kinship has a moral basis, underlying its jural framework, it is in these elementary relationships that we see that basis most clearly. As Fortes has put it, 'In the experience of the actor, the elementary relations of kinship thus emerge as irreducible moral relations . . . in the sense that they are felt to be axiomatically binding and to stipulate the rule of amity as the basis of kinship behavior. Thus they are maintained through the force of conscience as well as in compliance with the jural code' (Fortes 1969: 76, emphasis added).

One of the most profound insights for sociology as a whole that emerges from Fortes's study of the elementary relations of kinship relates to the fiduciary element at their core. 'There is a fiduciary element in amity. We do not have to love our kinsfolk, but we expect to be able to trust them in ways that are not automatically possible with non-kinsfolk' (Fortes 1969: 249). But then this statement takes him a little further away from Radcliffe-Brown than he might be prepared to concede. One might even suggest that he is perhaps closer to Malinowski than to Radcliffe-Brown when he says, 'it is conceivable—and I for one would accept—that the axiom of amity reflects biological and psychological parameters of human existence. Maybe, there is sucked in with the mother's milk, as Montaigne opined, the orientation on which it ultimately rests' (Fortes 1969: 251).

It should be obvious that the elementary unit of kinship has a very different purpose from that of the atom of kinship. Its purpose is not to provide generalisations about relations between terms or relations between relations, but to serve as signposts or guidelines in the empirical investigation of one of the most important aspects of social life and to relate it to other aspects of it. This investigation has to be an empirical investigation, and I believe that a great deal may be gained by asking, at the outset, questions of the following kind: what does it mean for a woman to bear a child, to be a mother? What does it mean for children to grow up as brothers and sisters in the same home? What does it mean for husband and wife to develop a relationship through the expansion and dispersion of the domestic group? It is only by keeping firmly in mind the actor's experience and his point of view while asking and answering such questions that we can connect the empirical investigation of kinship to the great tradition of interpretive sociology.

Endnotes

[1] In his Foreword to the second Tallensi book, Fortes (1949a: viii) wrote, 'I was fortunate in that both my chief teachers on this subject, the late Professor Bronislaw Malinowski and Professor Radcliffe-Brown, approached it with working hypotheses founded on the realities of field observation'. However, in the Morgan lectures (Fortes 1969), all the praise was for Radcliffe-Brown, whereas Malinowski was given short shrift; see also Fortes 1957.

[2] The paper was originally published in 1945 in the first issue of the journal *Word* and later revised to take account of some points of criticism regarding facts made by Luc de Heusch.

[3] For an interesting comment on the 'two structuralisms', see Sahlins 1976: 1–54; for an unfavourable review of the 'empiricist' position by a follower of Lévi-Strauss, see Dumont 1971.

[4] The paper presented by Lévi-Strauss at the famous Wenner-Gren conference on the current state of anthropology was titled 'Social Structure', and it was received with some surprise by the participants; see Tax 1962.

⁵ Schneider (1968a: 14) has, in my view, correctly pointed to a certain similarity of outlook between Kroeber and Lévi-Strauss.

⁶ The phrase was given currency among anthropologists in the present century by Kroeber (1952), although its original use goes back to Herbert Spencer.

⁷ In Weber's view, a sociological account is complete only when it is both adequate in terms of meaning and causally and functionally adequate (Weber 1978; Shils and Finch 1949).

⁸ The overwhelming majority of anthropologists are agreed on the universality of kinship, but there are a few exceptions; see Schneider 1984 and Needham 1974.

Reference

Barnes, J. A. 1971. *Three Styles in the Study of Kinship*. London: Tavistock.

Béteille, A. 1990. *Some Observations on the Comparative Method*. Amsterdam: Centre for Asian Studies.

————. 1991. *Society and Politics in India*. London: Athlone Press.

Dumont, L. 1971. *Introduction a deux theories d'anthropologie sociale*. Paris: Mouton.

Evans-Pritchard, E. E. 1951. *Kinship and Marriage among the Nuer*. Oxford: Clarendon Press.

Firth, R. W. 1936. *We, the Tikopea*. London: Allen and Unwin.

Fortes, M. 1945. *The Dynamics of Clanship among the Tallensi*. London: Oxford University Press.

————. 1949a. *The Web of Kinship among the Tallensi*. London: Oxford University Press.

————. 1949b. Time and Social Structure: An Ashanti Case Study. In *Social Structure*, ed. M. Fortes. Oxford: Clarendon Press.

————. 1957. Malinowski and the Study of Kinship. In *Man and Culture*, ed. R. W. Firth. London: Routledge & Kegan Paul.

————. 1958. Introduction to *The Developmental Cycle in Domestic Groups*, ed. Jack Goody. Cambridge: Cambridge University Press.

————. 1969. *Kinship and the Social Order*. Chicago: Aldine.

————. 1987. *Religion, Morality and the Person*. Cambridge: Cambridge University Press.

Gluckman, M. 1955. *The Judicial Process among the Barotse of Northern Rhodesia*. Manchester: Manchester University Press.

Goodenough, W. H. 1951. *Property, Kin and Community on Truk*. New Haven: Yale University Press.

Kroeber, A. L. 1909. Classificatory Systems of Relationship. *Journal of the Royal Anthropological Institute* 39: 77–84.

————. 1952. *The Nature of Culture*. Chicago: University of Chicago Press.

Leach, E. R. 1957. The Epistemological Background to Malinowski's Empiricism. In *Man and Culture*, ed. R. W. Firth. London: Routledge & Kegan Paul.

Lévi-Strauss, C. 1963. *Structural Anthropology*. New York: Basic Books.

Lowie, R. H. 1920. *Primitive Society*. New York: Boni & Liveright.

Malinowski, B. 1922. *Argonauts of the Western Pacific*. London: Routledge & Kegan Paul.

————. 1930. Kinship. In *Encyclopaedia Britannica*, 14th ed., 13: 403–9.

Mauss, M. 1979. *Sociology and Psychology*. London: Routledge & Kegan Paul.

Needham, R. 1974. *Remarks and Inventions*. London: Tavistock.

Radcliffe-Brown, A. R. 1950. Introduction to *African Systems of Kinship and Marriage*, ed. A. R. Radcliffe-Brown and D. Forde. London: Oxford University Press.

————. 1952. *Structure and Function in Primitive Society*. London: Cohen & West.

Sahlins, M. D. 1976. *Culture and Practical Reason*. Chicago: University of Chicago Press.

Schneider, D. H. 1968a. Rivers and Kroeber in the Study of Kinship. In *Kinship and Social Organisation*, ed. W. H. R. Rivers. New edition. London: Athlone Press.

————. 1968b. *American Kinship*. Englewood Cliffs: Prentice-Hall.

————. 1984. *A Critique of the Study of Kinship*. Ann Arbor: University of Michigan Press.

Shils, E. A., and H. A. Finch, eds. 1949. *Max Weber on the Methodology of the Social Sciences*. Glencoe: The Free Press.

Tax, S., L. C. Eiseley, I. Rouse, and C. F. Voegelin, eds. 1953. *An Appraisal of Anthropology Today*. Chicago: University of Chicago Press.

Van Velsen, J. 1964. *The Politics of Kinship*. Manchester: Manchester University Press.

Weber, M. 1978. *Economy and Society*. Berkeley: University of California Press.

12

Gendering Sociological Practice
A Case Study of Teaching in the University

Rajni Palriwala

Disciplinary reviews are periodic and necessary exercises in our intellectual projects. They usually focus on a particular theme, sub-discipline, or perspective and start from varied questions, through which the published and, at times, unpublished literature are examined. Occasionally, they may be conjoined to a study based on primary data.[1] Reviews of sociology from a feminist perspective or from feminist social science have focussed on theoretical and empirical blindness and/or conceptual confusion in the dominant paradigms,[2] or on the new analytical conclusions, advances, challenges and interests of feminist social sciences.[3] A critical aspect of the history of feminist sociology/social anthropology has been a battle for recognition, even to the point of disciplinary rupture. Thus, an issue common to most review projects has been the extent to and manner in which feminist questions, perspectives, concerns and persons have been incorporated within the discipline.[4] The answers rest on the intellectual, pedagogical, organisational and institutional dimensions taken into account. Reviews have looked at the extent to which women and feminist themes are present in articles published in professional journals, books displayed at professional fora, and at the number of women who are members or holding positions in professional associations or in faculties, even as they have examined the critique, concepts, and arguments of feminist sociological research and writings. The attempt has been to assess the shifts and continuities in the discipline through these discussions.

STUDYING CURRICULUM CHANGE

Part of such an assessment has also to be whether and how the concerns and analyses of feminists of various hues enter university syllabi. However, most reviews do not attempt an overview of shifts in course structure and the teaching of sociology in universities and colleges.[5] Teaching reflects current disciplinary content and boundaries and influences future research agendas and thereby directions in the discipline. Of course, this is not an easy task even if the varied curricula of the innumerable universities in India alone could be collected and collated.[6] As most university teachers know, there can be a gap between the written document and the practice— not necessarily negative—making the project even more complicated. Further, sociological interest lies not only in the shifts in content and style of teaching but in the dynamics which enabled or hampered disciplinary shifts and ruptures. That syllabus revision and teaching gender studies is an exercise in the widest and critical sense of politics and movements for change is almost a truism for feminists and others (though some may describe it as a political exercise in the narrow sense of a jockeying for position and pelf). An understanding of this process requires that more actors and agents are interrogated— students, teachers, 'academic officials', among others.

In this paper, I make an attempt in this direction through one case study, that of the Department of Sociology, University of Delhi, where A. M. Shah was a professor for many years and encouraged the study of women and gender. I explore the dynamics of the engendering of a syllabus through a narration of the process in this department, primarily in the years 1987–91, based largely on the first-hand experience of a then new and temporary faculty member, along with material from interviews of different generations of students, group discussions and folklore. The narration may be seen as a coded transformation of the story of the politics of and struggle to change gender relations and transform society beyond the university, an experience which parallels it, is structured by it, and feeds into it.

In reviewing the process of curricula change and looking at the shifts and inertias, the successes and failures, a number of interacting features emerged and can be delineated. (i) The structure of the university in terms of a series of committees through which new or revised courses must traverse.[7] This tiered system is entailed in the federal structure of the university (DU henceforth) in undergraduate teaching, is an academic review and monitoring mechanism, ensures a semblance of democratic functioning, and can become a bureaucratic nightmare. The cumbersome procedure also means that individually initiated changes can come to fruition most easily in MPhil/research courses (where the number of committees is at the minimum as discussed below). At the graduate and undergraduate levels, radical syllabi changes are possible only if a number of colleagues in the discipline, the department, and elsewhere in the university are sympathetic to the concerns and are carried along— in other words if there is a movement within the discipline. There are few shortcuts to this. (ii) The discipline of sociology in terms of articulated boundaries—with other disciplines, between academic versus activist, applied versus theoretical, published and unpublished work, and the closures of professionalisation. This of course directly feeds into and is determined by the validation of issues and the content of the discipline, which is explicated and embodied through teaching syllabi. (iii) The specificities of a department in terms of theoretical and political orientations of individuals who make it up and the institutional culture and history, which may or may not amount to a 'school'. (iv) The strength, spread, visibility, and nature of the women's and other movements outside the university and among various sections of the university community. Owing to limitations of space, this last aspect is unfortunately the least discussed in this paper.

INITIATING SYLLABUS CHANGE IN THE UNIVERSITY

The Department of Sociology in DU was set up in 1959 under the headship of M. N. Srinivas with an MA programme. An undergraduate programme was introduced in 1964. An MLitt programme was also started but was replaced by the MPhil in 1976, which included course work. In 1981–82, a course on 'Women in Indian Society' was offered as part of this programme jointly by the Sociology and History Departments of the university. Before this paper was introduced in the Department, there had been an occasional dissertation—MPhil, MLitt, or PhD—which had looked at aspects of middle-class women's lives or women-related concerns of social reform and, in the immediately prior period, the registration of two doctoral students whose research questions pertaining to rural women were explicitly rooted in current streams of feminist thought and theorisation.

The MPhil 'Women' paper had been designed and was run at the initiative of a research associate in sociology and a professor in history, both of whom were women, one who was at the entry point of recruitment to the faculty and the other in a senior position. Given the total intake in the MPhil programme, a respectable number of students, largely from the Department of History, opted for it. After a few terms (about two to three), it was not offered for some time, though, like most of the existing courses, it was retained as an optional paper in the restructured MPhil, in which two compulsory papers were introduced. The 'Women' paper was subsequently revived and taught by two other members of the sociology faculty in separate years—again a research associate and a professor and, again, both of them women—with different relations to feminism and the political edge of women's/gender studies, and the orientation they gave to the course. Except for once, there were always keen takers, though in varying numbers. In one term, the lone student who opted for the course refused to change her option, though it was suggested that she might find it either too hard or not rich enough in discussion as she would have no classmates.

It may also be mentioned that this cooperation between the History and Sociology Departments also saw the formation of a Gender Studies Group in the mid-1980s. It consisted largely of teachers and research students from these two disciplines and emerged as a response to the need that research students had expressed for a group interested in gender studies in which they could discuss their work. For a couple of years it was active in holding discussions and workshops where students, faculty and visitors presented their research. The GSG was reborn later in the early 1990s—at the initiative of some MA students in sociology and with a more activist orientation.

That the first teaching paper in the Department was at the MPhil level—the highest degree to include course work rather than the lowest, the BA—was not surprising. It is very easy in DU to introduce a new course in the MPhil programme. Officially, only the Department's MPhil committee has to pass it and the printed syllabus does not carry a reading list, which signals that MPhil papers are research oriented, flexible, and can be constructed afresh each year by the teacher and students. Unofficial practice, as in the Department, may require that the Staff Council vets and passes a new course and that the proposer circulates a suggested reading list on which discussions in the committee will be based. There is a strong notion that each course becomes part of the public documentation and profile of the Department, likely to remain forever on the books for which all faculty members are held 'accountable'. Furthermore, in subsequent years, teachers other than the original designer may offer the course. This is seen to necessitate a collective discussion and 'approval'.

In the oral histories of the Department and in oft-reiterated views of its institutional culture, the MPhil is the point for experimentation, innovation and specialisation in syllabi. The MPhil committee can allow for a catholicity not possible in lower-level degree courses, which are taught separately at a number of colleges with diverse faculty but a common examination. Thus, not only women/gender but also courses on agrarian structure, development, environment were first offered in the MPhil programme. The point at which themes can be introduced is where sociological research is 'young'—or where faculty introduce previously untaught interests, where disciplinary boundaries may be transgressed, where the Parsonian division of subsystems or the original course divisions into 'system, structure, change, problems' are put aside. It is here that one can move beyond the classics in heretical directions. The naming of the Department as a Centre of Advanced Study in Sociology by the UGC also means that it has to ensure that it is at the cutting edge of the discipline, important to the self-image of the Department.

The introduction of the MPhil course on women was not before its time. Since the publication of *Towards Equality* in 1974, the International Year of Women in 1975, and the renewed women's movement in India from the late 1970s, issues of growing gender and class inequalities, women's rights, and violence against women (rape, dowry deaths) were in the public domain again. The ICSSR had instituted doctoral fellowships to encourage research in women's studies, which had directly led to the registration in the Department of the two doctoral students mentioned earlier. Not only was the struggle for a women-sensitive academics about a decade old internationally, many studies and documents had been published in India.[8] An Indian Association of Women's Studies (IAWS) had been formed in the same year as the course was begun, and courses had already been initiated in other universities. Its path of entry into the formal teaching programme and the changing levels of student interest in the MPhil 'Women in Indian Society' course indicated the acceptance of 'women's studies' in Indian social sciences, but as an empirical specialisation rather than a remaking of any of the disciplines.[9] One sees here the legitimacy given to a theme by the active support and position of individual teachers[10] and of the creation of intellectual interests within academia by social movements outside it.

DESIGNING GENDER

Already registered in the Department as a doctoral student, I joined it as a research associate in the mid-1980s, after earlier short stints as an ad hoc lecturer during which the Department had completed a long overdue revision of the BA (Honours) syllabus, in which women/gender did not figure anywhere. Others who had been engaged with gender in their work were no longer in the Department. While the number of PhDs or MPhil dissertations which was women-/gender-/feminist- focussed could still be counted on the fingers of one hand, the issue was visibly present in discussions in the public arena, in movements, in academia at large, and in sociology. By this time, Srinivas, the founder of the Department, but no longer in Delhi, had written a couple of academic papers on women in India, as had other faculty members. Women formed a large percentage of the faculty (though not of professors) and an even larger percentage of the students at all levels, underlining the absence of a necessary link between the presence of women and a gender-sensitive/feminist sociology.

Discussions on revising the MA papers had started and immediately there were contentious issues, as is bound to be. Some detail is necessary here, if we are to understand the problems and possibilities of the engendering process. First, leaving aside the first step in revision, which is what I focus on, the remaining steps (outlined earlier) before a new course gains approval and becomes part of the university's curriculum can take up to a year or more. Redesigned courses and papers as well as new papers can only be taught to students admitted to the university in the year after the entire procedure has been completed. This of course not only means that by the time a course is taught in a mushrooming area of research, much new and exciting work has been published which is not part of the official course readings. It also means that for the department faculty 'unofficial' change in their teaching and suggested reading list is easier and can be continuous, so that the urgency to change the written, authoritative document is experienced in an attenuated manner. The printed syllabi, however, have to guide the examinations which 'must be in course', thereby putting a break on radical change.

As I have mentioned earlier, the syllabi are repeatedly described as public documents. The MA and BA course structures can be read not only as a take on the state of the discipline but as a charter for sociology's future in the university and the country, that is, the Department's manifesto. It gives status and legitimacy to the sociology practised by individuals and the Department as a unit. Every faculty member, even those who say that they eschew politics and that their academics is non-ideological, feels s/he must have her/his say on arriving at the manifesto, particularly since any and all may have to uphold it and teach any part of it subsequently. Given the university structure, a consensus has to be arrived at. Thus intellectual engagement, academic commitment, and democracy are equally significant when syllabi are discussed in DU, making it a slow process. Further, experience made it clear that there had to be a specification of both collective and individual rights and responsibilities—in this case of the Staff Council and the individual designer/subcommittee. At times these were pitted against each other, not least because of differences in theoretical approach and views on sociology of the individual members. In such a context, changing syllabi can be educative like research seminars, a consciousness-raising exercise, and a lesson in democracy, hegemony, and hierarchies in universalistic institutions.

In the revision process which developed, the most contentious issues and papers were the compulsory as against the elective papers, the number of compulsory as against elective papers, and which papers were to be compulsory and which were to be elective, as well as who had the right to revise an old paper or design a new one. Simultaneously, it was oft asserted that if courses on which consensus could not be arrived at were not to be stopped, colleagues should propose as many new electives as they wished. Of course, the more eminent and senior you were in the Department, the more likely that the course would be accepted in the form you had designed, despite serious misgivings on the part of other colleagues. Or the more junior you were, the more necessary it was that either you carried more than the majority with you or the course was seen as peripheral and yet desirable, with nobody else ready to do the job. As is well known in institutions and universities, the numbers and position in the faculty of advocates of one or another sociology do influence the directions in which sociology will be pushed.

These battles raged, and first and second drafts of individual courses were discussed. As a junior faculty member I would mumble about gender and, along with other newly joined faculty members, assert the desirability for more and newer electives. Many of my colleagues, including professors designing courses on stratification, development, and India, recognised that 'Women' had to find a place in the MA course of the Department and would talk to me about it. Finally, the professor coordinating syllabus revision asked me if I would design an elective course on women and I jumped at the suggestion. I deliberately did not get into issues of the course title as it would mean a discussion on perspective—women or gender—and ignored the pointer that it was to be an elective paper. I was asked to name two colleagues to join my subcommittee. By now, I had realised that strategy was important. I asked for a colleague whose research focus at that time was not on gender and who was even more temporary than me, but who had taught courses on women, gender, and feminism elsewhere. The second name I proposed was one of the two senior professors who I knew had strong views, as all professors do, and who would raise objections. I decided that I would prefer to engage with them in the subcommittee rather than the departmental forum and thereby work out my arguments for the course I proposed. Also of importance, I knew that the senior professor would ensure that my design was not so out of keeping with the Department's sociological philosophy that the course would be killed at the start.

The institutional culture was my starting point. The closest there is to a DU 'school' of sociology or a sociological philosophy can be described through nine elements which make a disciplinary orientation, culture, or style. These are: (i) an emphasis on ethnography (and on intensive fieldwork at the doctoral level); (ii) on the classics, which are to be read in the author's own words, albeit translated; (iii) the difficulty if not impossibility in demarcating sociology from social anthropology in a postcolonial time and context. This was important for there was more of gender in anthropology than in sociology; (iv) that the comparative and an India-focus are both important; (v) an emphasis on sociological debates rather than 'facts' in the teaching (more at the postgraduate than at the graduate level); (vi) that undergraduate and postgraduate courses are best structured through the device of the four subsystems reified by Parsons; (vii) only readings labelled as sociology or social anthropology and (viii) published work may be included in the official syllabus; and (ix) finally, that on these points, especially iii–vii, there may be dissension and debate, which, however, may only be aired or allowed a marginal space in practice.

These elements are extracted from the discussions on various courses during the syllabus-revision process. They became most apparent to me when designing, presenting and defending the gender paper through the subcommittee, the department council, and the committee of courses. It was an intense learning and socialisation process. I give only some of the details regarding the process and the debates. I tracked down and looked through a vast array of gender/ women courses in sociology and social anthropology and in women's studies departments in India and in other countries and talked to colleagues working on courses elsewhere (cf. Uberoi 1989). Not only was it necessary to distil all this, there was a need to delicately balance the above nine elements and make a break with them. Feminist and Marxist work had been questioning the canon and what was designated as the classics, the four subsystems, and the boundaries of disciplines—it was also not finding it easy to be published (Delamont 2003; Rege 2003). The social construction of gender as a possible title was rejected at a very early stage within the subcommittee itself. The simple title of 'Gender and Society' reflecting the move from the description of women to that of relations between and among women and men was settled on. The ban on unpublished material was turned into a tool to help us delimit what was already too vast a field for such a general paper.

From the start, there was a consensus that the course must be comparative and rich in ethnography, theory, and debate. It would not only be consistent with the other MA papers, this also seemed necessary if the paper was to arrive at some sort of feminist pedagogy. The teaching of gender and women had started in the Department with an MPhil course oriented to the empirical/substantive in India. In designing the MA course, I wished to move from the study of 'facts', to encourage critical thinking regarding the common sense on gender among the students who opted for it, about the world around them, their own lives, and the sociology they had done so far. We felt that to further this, we needed to include materials which integrated the comparative and theoretical with the ethnographic and picked up on themes, concepts, and authors that they would have tackled in other courses in their MA programme. Thus, we framed the course to start from the point of looking at the history of the discipline as a sociology/anthropology of men. It would then broadly trace developments from women's studies to gender studies, articulating and making visible women in society and turning to the study of gender relations. Selected readings, such as that by Douglas (1970) on purity and danger or by Uberoi (1971) on men, women, and property in Afghanistan, were not necessarily feminist. Encouraging critical thinking also meant that the course should demand hard work and excellence from the students, rather than allow them to float through it! Despite continuous pruning, the final approved course was thought to have rather a too long reading list, including some work by students, some of whom had hoped to opt for an easy and marketable elective (see below).

Needless to say, there were queries about the logic of topics and the justification for readings. Why was there a topic on feminist politics when there was none on feminist economics or culture? I delineated how other topics incorporated feminist analyses of economics, family, and culture. I argued that De Beauvoir, a philosopher rather than a sociologist, was included in the reading list on the grounds that *The Second Sex* was a classic for any study of gender in contemporary social sciences. This perhaps formed a real break in one element of the Department's sociology. Ethnographies on India, such as Sharma's study on women, work, and property, were not questioned. The authenticity of Mead's ethnographic comparison of gender and personality in three societies had been aggressively questioned in recent years[11] and had become a point of contention. However, the necessity of including a reading by her in a course which introduced students to the social anthropology of gender and the comparative dimension of that particular book finally made it acceptable. That there had to be a balance of classics and contemporary readings allowed the inclusion/exclusion of some readings as did the argument that they should/would be covered in other courses.

GENDERING THE MA PROGRAMME

Pedagogical concerns meant a continuing insistence that a gender paper cannot be the only place where gender enters the syllabus and that it had to be an issue in compulsory papers in particular. Despite my socialisation into the department pedagogical practice and growing realisation of its sacred cows, the apparent encouragement of discussion I perceived here made me rush in where angels feared to tread. Undoubtedly, the extent and quality of scholarship on women/gender that was by then available, the questioning of the silences on women in the social sciences, institutional measures such as the ICSSR Programme for Women's Studies, research committees in international professional bodies, the increasing visibility of women's issues in public life, and a long history of excellent and vocal women academics were arguments supporting my contentions.

Women/gender was included as sub-topics or readings in a few papers. Was the inclusion merely tokenism? Women (and class) were a minor sub-topic in one of the two papers on India. Broadly, these two papers divided the sociology of India into two—India as the land of caste, tribe, village, family, and religion and India as a nation in the making. It was in the latter paper that a sub-topic on 'Women in Indian society' had been included. Its wording had been revised in response to comments in the department committee, but not the readings. Gender and race were the two sub-topics under 'Natural differences and social stratification' in a paper titled 'Social Stratification' and framed around occupation. The readings listed— statistical and positivist—was in keeping with the overall structure of the paper, which it was decided could not be tampered with. In the development paper there was no topic, but a chapter from an empirical macro-study on women and the environment had been included. Kinship, a natural for engendering, had neither topic nor reading, and with other battles being fought over that paper, the issue of gender could not be raised. Another surprise was the continuing absence of gender in the paper on political sociology. The elective on population could not but have age and sex as a sub-topic of elements of population analysis, but no reading which had emerged from feminist sociology or demography was included. And the elective on the sociology of science, another area in which feminist scholarship had raised critical issues, remained silent on the matter, as did all the other papers, compulsory and elective. Wanting to ensure that the gender paper was passed with some feminist scholarship forming its core, the battle over the inclusion of gender in other electives was not always pushed very hard.

One aspect became evident. It is at the point of working out the frame and the principles which will organise the topics and readings of a paper that gender has to be part of the discussion. Thus, the orientation of the stratification paper made the particular reading chosen seem the most suitable. The silence in the political sociology paper can be related to its framing in terms of state and local political systems, a perspective which had been gender-blind, though feminist analyses of these concepts were available. The absence was furthered by the idea that movements and resistance were more appropriately discussed in a separate paper, in keeping with a perspective that system, structure and change are to be treated as distinct fields of study.

A vital issue in looking at the MA programme is the implications of the division between compulsory and elective courses. One of the factors which opened the doors to a course on gender and society in the late 1980s, in the design of which temporary members of the faculty were primarily involved, was that it was an elective course. On the one hand, it thereby became part of our charter and showed that we were at the cutting edge of sociological scholarship and teaching. On the other hand, it did not threaten the non-gendered interests and concerns of other members of the faculty. In any case, there had been a long and bitter discussion over many weeks as to the compulsory-elective combination, the numbers having been finally settled. Which courses would be compulsory had now to be decided. In a short and sharp exchange, my request that the gender course be made compulsory was rejected. This had as much to do with views on the centrality or otherwise of the study of gender to sociology, a valuation of the scholarship on gender, and contending claims. What was gender to replace? The theory or India papers, methodology, one of the subsystem papers, or symbolism, stratification or development, the three specialisations which were included in the compulsory list? All were more basic and central to the MA programme it was averred. Further, the scholarship in gender studies, it was argued, did not as yet match that which any of these other papers could call on.

Did this mean that the sociology of gender was marginalised or that it was able to retain its critical edge? Neither and both! A few years later there were sharp attacks on the declining standards in universities following feminisation and the lack of rigour in feminist scholarship (Béteille 1995; Gupta 1995). These pieces, by two male sociology professors, one an eminent and senior scholar and member of the Department, who had written on gender, and the other also well known and associated with it, have many implications. As others have commented, the backlash against gender and feminist studies seen worldwide suggests that even as feminist scholars feel they have a long way to go, things have moved. Whether owing to the specific efforts of scholars in academia or the wider impact of the movement, sociologists have to take account of work by women and feminists. Yet the backlash can also have negative effects on our labours. Attacks by important people in the discipline affect new and aspiring entrants to the profession, to the study programmes, and to those who administer them. Undoubtedly, by and large a woman sociologist still has to be better than a man and much more 'professorial' before she will be considered for an equivalent post. Even now, when research proposals are examined, questions regarding the absence of a gender dimension can be labelled as group and identity claims, rather than as issues of epistemology and methodology.

TEACHING GENDER

What a written syllabus means in terms of pedagogical practice depends not only on what is in the public document, but on the orientation and interests of the teacher, official pedagogical instruments and the under-life of the institution. As emerged from the practice of teaching in subsequent years, even a token sub-topic can pave the way for further questioning and provide more space to do so than a reading not attached to a topic. It does not necessarily get sucked into a larger unchanging discourse. A topic can be given more time within the span of a course than a visual impression of the written outline conveys. Thus, in the papers on India and stratification, as more faculty members developed an interest in or a concern with gender, it became one of the lenses through which they discussed many topics and one of the points of view in the various debates which ran through the substantive and theoretical issues in each paper. This was also the case for the kinship paper where, though gender was not mentioned in the topics, the debate on nature/culture was central and topics on political/jural and personal kinship gave an entry point to a teacher or students who wished to look at the growing field of kinship and gender. In the papers on development, on population, and on education, gender/feminist studies could again seep beyond its stated space, but was rarely articulated as fully formed separate examination questions. This influenced the attention students gave to the issue.

The shift in interest and the growing visibility of the scholarship in the sociology of gender emerges if the tutorial topics that students were asked to work on are examined in the papers mentioned earlier. The tutorial programme in the Department is intensive, more so since continuous internal evaluation was begun about a decade earlier. It is a critical pedagogical instrument and central to the self-valuation and image of the Department. Each semester, students write essays after discussing the topics in a group of four to six classmates and a tutor. The lecturer in each course suggests the topics with readings, which an individual tutor may modify or add to. Through the tutorial topics, readings, and discussions, teachers introduce new writings, issues, perspectives and debates beyond the bounds of the printed syllabus which determine the annual examination. Student seminars are another pedagogical tool which can and were put to use in this manner.

The significance of the theoretical and pedagogical orientation of the teacher means that the reverse can also occur—a course may be bleached of its gender content or feminist interrogation. Despite being a sub-topic or reading, there may be no lectures on it, leave aside its influencing the rest of the paper. The students may be asked to read up on it on their own and pick up mixed signals on the relevance of the topic or reading, depending on their own orientations. Examinations are critical to the attention they give to readings and topics, and if they pick up the signal that 'there won't be a question', they may leave it aside. Student interest in gender has also grown and waned over the years, but their demands on particular courses seem to take into account the interests of the teacher. Thus one year, in teaching the paper on India, I had not suggested a student seminar on gender. Some students, however, pointed out that they had heard that in previous years I had done so and that they would like to make a presentation. The teaching of sociology in general and gender in particular is tied to responses from students as discussed further below.

WHY STUDY GENDER?

Gender has been a concern expressed by a range of students, but not necessarily their focus, partly, it seems, because the idea has percolated that it is a sub-question in any area of research. In the

MPhil programme, I have been finding over the years that while students may not choose an elective on women, they choose ethnographies on gender or with a strong gendered theme for their seminars and term papers within a rubric of theoretical orientations in sociological research in India. Most of them would actually read the gendered ethnographies which others were to analyse than those on other themes! They did not wish to specialise in gender, but wanted an acquaintance with gender theory and ethnography. This of course supported what has long been my pedagogical contention. Rather than depending on separate women's studies courses and programmes alone, making the themes and perspectives part of existing disciplinary and more general programmes and courses can go further in fighting the silence on women and gender and encouraging a critique of intellectual work and social relations. However, not only is that the more difficult exercise, as the experience of introducing a gender course and gendering other courses in the Department illustrated, it depends on the interests and orientation of both teacher and student.

The number of students opting for the gender course in MA has varied greatly. In recent years, enrolment has been relatively high. As the number on the faculty interested in gender issues increased, so have the number of MPhil courses with a gender content, and the sum of those opting for one or the other are a good part of the total intake.[12] It is important to recall that at all levels in DU, the majority of students in sociology are women, more so than their proportion in the university as a whole. This is also true for the faculty. Both in the faculty and in study programmes, however, the balance shifts as one moves up the hierarchy of positions (research associate to professor) or courses (MA to PhD). Thus, it is not surprising if most students who opt for an MA elective on gender are women. Parallel to this, as far as I have been able to ascertain, except for the first year and perhaps one other year, the proportion of boys in the course have been in accordance with or more than that in the class as a whole.

Students in their final semester of the MA and in the MPhil expressed a variety of reasons for their choices and of their experiences of the MA programme and the gender course. MPhil students, in particular, mentioned the teacher as an important factor in their options. One MA student said he had chosen the gender elective as he had thought it would be 'scoring,' and because it was an important area in sociology. He compared the 'gender' studied in this paper as against that in the compulsory ones such as in the India paper. He said the latter was more empirical and on women, whereas in the elective the focus was more on relations between men and women and it was more 'ideological'. He confessed, however, that he had attended few classes and this was his take on the topics and readings as printed in the syllabus. While he was very comfortable with the fact that the majority of the teachers in the Department were women, he felt that they were stricter evaluators than the male teachers! Some students chose the gender elective for personal and intellectual reasons. One girl spoke of how she had perceived gender discrimination in her family. The gender paper had helped her to understand much more about gender relations and structures in her everyday life, clarifying aspects she had been 'sort of aware of'. This was a view expressed by a number of women students and was reflected in the deathly pall which fell in the classroom one year as we discussed de Beauvoir's critique of the idea that love marriage expresses gender equality or emancipation. For a couple of students, the MA course confirmed for them that they would like to undertake research in gender studies. A number spoke of how male classmates had changed over the two year MA programme with the discussions inside and outside the classroom. However, some pointed out that there were those who continued to make a division between women as 'girlfriend or good wife material'![13]

For a number of students, the paper was not practical enough—as they felt was true for most of the MA programme. Among the latter were students who had come to MA sociology in search of a course on social work. For some, this was a response to the constant interrogation of their everyday lives and assumptions in the gender course and the MA programme as a whole, leaving them with few certain answers or those which were difficult to live by. One student said she had not chosen the gender elective as gender was discussed in other compulsory and elective courses, such as the papers on kinship, India, stratification and urban sociology. Not only did she feel that she could read about it on her own, she participated in discussions in her hostel organised by women's organisations and the union, as well as activities of the GSG in the Department. She chose electives on themes which she felt had been little touched on otherwise in the programme. Furthermore, given that two of her other electives were 'heavy', she wanted some which did not involve as many readings as did the gender paper!

Thus, choices are made on a number of grounds. Intellectual engagement, personal interest, toughness and scoring possibilities, future plans, and employment possibilities all play their role, as do developing significations of 'gender', informal ratings of teachers and their position in the academic hierarchy. Discussions with their 'seniors', oral histories, and local mythologies are important in their assessments on 'scoring and toughness' and teacher ratings. Intellectual engagement and personal interest are linked to what students have studied in previous programmes and papers and to extra-curricula discussions around them. While there seems to be no clear connection between the presence of gender in earlier papers and programmes and their opting for electives on the theme, explicit running down of gender issues as serious and central to the discipline does dissuade uncommitted students from opting for the elective.

The impact on the teaching programme made by active feminist groups within the campus is more complex. On the one hand, they help create an awareness and build discussions around gender, become support groups for students and teachers interested in researching and teaching gender, and take up feminist issues within the campus. On the other hand, given the other factors which influence the choice of electives, students may opt for the vibrant extra-curricula discussions on gender along with formal courses on other specialisations. Furthermore, the greater visibility created by activists for gender issues can be seen as threatening to some who become sharper in their ridicule. Choices made by students of study programmes are clearly linked to past life experiences and future aspirations too, and this is undoubtedly tied to the direction and strength of the women's movement outside academia—both in the direct impact on the nature of research undertaken by feminist or anti-feminist scholars and in opening up questions and validating concerns.

Time and again, students have said of others that they made a choice for or against a particular course because of its marketability, because it was scoring, or because it was not tough. The marketability of the gender course has grown with the expansion of the NGO and development sector and the shift from voluntary to paid activism in the women's movement. Sociology students who choose not to continue in academics or teaching are going into journalism, publishing, NGOS, and market research—all areas which have been impacted by the women's movement and where various institutions have leapt into the spaces created by the movement. On the one hand this is disturbing—the critical edge of gender studies had to be blunted if it was so easy or chosen instrumentally. On the other hand, whatever the reason for which students chose a course, could they be left unaffected by the constant interrogations of lived assumptions and sociological certainties which the readings made explicit? Would it not ensure that feminist and gender concerns spread into fields beyond academia and committed activism? A twist to this is that since attendance is not compulsory, students can miss much of the critical thought, debate, and discussion. Thus, marking examination scripts can be very hard on the spirits!

Hopefully Not a Conclusion

This narrative could now elaborate on the recent changes in the undergraduate programme in sociology, in order to examine the impact of gender teaching in the MA programme and also the influence of the growing feminist scholarship within the discipline. However, I will be very brief on this. The overall structure of the programme remains the same—India, theory, method, subsystems, stratification—but with the introduction of four elective courses, including one on gender and society. Gendered topics have been brought into the introductory and kinship papers as well as a number of others, particularly those in which the theme was introduced many years ago in the MA programme—India and stratification. Thus, gender concerns have spread across the syllabi and teaching of sociology in DU. Certain bastions seem to remain—such as the study of the sociological masters—partly because the departmental style dictates that commentaries are not part of the written syllabus unless it is by a thinker in her/his own right. This is also to do with the continuing difficulty of accepting the theoretical power of a feminist thinker, especially within sociology,[14] and the growing number of those who may be considered contemporary 'masters' (cf. Delamont 2003).

The case study of DU sociology demonstrates that sociology has changed over the last two decades. However, if efforts to engender sociology are to move forward, they have to begin from the point when teaching programmes and papers are being framed, rather than being added later on. Generally, gender-sensitive and feminist sociological writings are still asked to prove themselves as twice as good and rigorous—on the basis of pre-gendered criteria—to be included in reading lists. As with any attempt to change an existing structure, it requires extra labour from advocates of the change and a readiness to take on more than one's share of responsibilities. Personal and intellectual interest in gender studies has grown and diffused among many of the faculty as well as the student body, whose profile has changed. The enjoyment by a subsequent generation of young women of openings made possible by earlier collective struggles has much to do with the ebbs and flows in feminist interrogation. The hope that as a specialisation it will enable employment and the fear that it will mean marginalisation in the discipline are simultaneously present, with contradictory pulls in making student choices. This has much to do with the environment within and outside the Department and particularly the ongoing processes and debates within the institutional context of the university. Finally, gendering sociology means pushing debates over the modes of apprehending and theorising social relations and culture, the central concepts of the discipline, and indeed of the relationship between sociology, the university, and society.

Endnotes

[1] Of the last genre, A. M. Shah's *The Household Dimension of the Family in India* is a premier example. Over the years, students have returned to this

book time and again for its classification and analysis of fieldwork data and through this its review of the then state of the art within this area of study and the elaborate critique and clarification of the various concepts used in this literature.

2 See Acker (1973), Oakley (1972), Millman and Kanter (1975), Smith (1974) for early feminist critiques of sociology, and Lutz (1990), Rapp (1970), Rosaldo (1980), Strathern (1987), and Collier and Yanagisako (1989) for discussions of anthropology. Dube 1997 and Palriwala 1994 review what gender studies can draw on in a specific area—kinship in South (and Southeast) Asia. Rege (1994) and Uberoi (1993; 1994) look at Indian developments in gendering sociology.

3 Barrett (1980) and Moore (1988) were widely read 'review' texts which pulled together themes and debates in feminist sociological and anthropological research (in the 'west') respectively. Delamont (2003) is a more recent review of feminist sociology.

4 Delamont (2003) and Rege (2003) make this the central query of their reviews.

5 While teaching was not the main focus of either Delamont (2003) or Rege (2003), both these overviews carry critical discussions regarding sociology as a profession, as institutions and teaching departments which are relevant for issues raised here.

6 Uberoi (1989) and a number of unpublished papers by sociologists, such as N. Desai, and presented at conferences focus on the theme of the teaching of gender sociology or womens' studies through individual case studies. These are among the examples which an overview could draw on as Rege (2003) does to an extent.

7 Starting from the first step, the general body of teachers in the discipline for undergraduate courses or the Staff Council of the university department for graduate papers, the Committee of Courses and Studies, the Faculty of Social Sciences, the Academic Council Standing Committee and the Academic Council. Recently, another tier has been introduced before the last but one—the 'peer review'—consisting of three persons within the discipline, but outside the university.

8 A large number of studies had been commissioned by the Committee on the Status of Women in India (CSWI) and many of them were published in various collected volumes.

9 From the mid-1980s, and after, a number of UGC- or ICSSR-sponsored centres for women studies and women's development centres were set up inside and outside the university structure. However, almost none was engaged in teaching or syllabi development in the first decade, and in Delhi they did not have a direct impact on teaching in the universities.

10 That one of the original designers of the first MPhil course on 'Women' was a professor was important.

[11] Freeman (1983) queried Mead's presence in the fields she discusses (1935) and suggested that her ethnography and analysis were fiction.

[12] Thus, in recent years a course on masculinities and another on reproductive rights, sexuality and power have been introduced and taught.

[13] Not only is this a reflection on those male students, it is a commentary on the dynamics of interaction between young women and men—where current or future sexual engagement appears as the master principle.

[14] As seen in the superficial reading of feminist texts reflected in Gupta (1995).

References

Acker, J. 1973. Women and Social Stratification: A Case of Intellectual Sexism. *American Journal of Sociology* 78 (4): 936–45.

Barrett, M. 1980. *Women's Oppression Today.* London: Verso.

Béteille, A. 1995. Feminism in Academia: Changes in Theory and Practice. *Indian Journal of Gender Studies* 2(1): 111–13.

Collier, J. F. and S. Yanagisako. 1989. Theory in Anthropology since Feminist Practice. *Critique of Anthropology* 9(2): 27–37.

Committee on the Status of Women in India. 1974. *Towards Equality.* Delhi: Government of India.

Delamont, S. 2003. *Feminist Sociology.* London: Sage.

Douglas, M. 1970. *Purity and Danger.* Harmondsworth: Penguin Books.

Dube, L. 1997. *Women and Kinship: Comparative Perspectives on Gender in South and Southeast Asia.* Tokyo: United Nations University Press.

Freeman, D. 1983. *Margaret Mead and Samoa: The Making and Unmaking of an Anthropological Myth.* Cambridge, Mass.: Harvard University Press.

Gupta, D. 1995. Feminification of Theory and Gender Studies. *Economic and Political Weekly* 30(12): 617–20.

Lutz, C. 1990. The Erasure of Women's Writings in Socio-cultural Anthropology. *American Ethnologies* 17(4): 611–27.

Mead, M. 1935. *Sex and Temperament in Three Primitive Societies.* New York: William Morrow.

Millman, M., and R. M. Kanter, eds. 1975. *Another Voice: Feminist Perspectives on Social life and Social Science.* Garden City, N. Y.: Anchor Press/Doubleday.

Moore, H. 1988. *Feminism and Anthropology.* Cambridge: Polity Press.

Oakley, A. 1972. *Sex, Gender, Society.* New York: Harper Colophon Books.

Palriwala, R. 1994. *Changing Kinship, Family, and Gender Relations in South Asia: Processes, Trends and Issues.* Leiden: Women and Autonomy Centre, University of Leiden.

Rapp, R. R. 1970. Anthropology: A Review Essay. *Signs* 4(3): 497–513

Rege, S. 1994. If this is Tuesday, It Must be Social Roles: Sociology and the Challenge of Gender Studies. *Economic and Political Weekly* 29(19): 1155–56.

————. 1995. Feminist Pedagogy and the Sociology of Emancipation in India. *Sociological Bulletin* 44(2): 223–39.

————. 2003. Introduction to Feminist Challenge to Sociology: Disenchanting Sociology or "For Sociology"? In *Sociology of Gender: The Challenge of Feminist Sociological Knowledge*, ed. S. Rege. Delhi: Sage Publications.

Rosaldo, M. Z. 1980. The Use and Abuse of Anthropology: Reflections on Feminism and Cross-Cultural Understandings. *Sign* 5(3): 389–417.

Smith, D. 1974. Women's Perspective as a Radical Critique of Sociology. *Sociological Inquiry* 44(1).

Strathern, M. 1987. An Awkward Relationship: The Case of Feminism and Anthropology. *Signs* 12(2): 276–92.

Uberoi, J. P. S. 1971. Men, Women, and Property in Northern Afghanistan. In *India and Contemporary Islam*, ed. S. T. Lokhandawala. Simla: Indian Institute of Advanced Study.

Uberoi, P. 1989. Some Reflections on Teaching the Sociology of Gender. *Samyashakti*, 4–5: 279–99.

————. 1993. Reciprocity in Social Science: Gender Issues. *Indian Journal of Social Science* 6(3): 243–58.

————. 1994. Sociology, Gender, Family Studies: Regressive Incorporation. *Economic and Political Weekly* 29(2): 1686–87.

13

Why Are Children's Voices Largely Unheard in Household Ethnographies?

Shanti George

In my analysis of the village households as well as of the literature, I kept in view a very well-known fact: the household is the site for play of some of the deepest emotions and sentiments in human life. A basic aim of the study of the household is, therefore, to grasp the nature of these emotions and sentiments. This aim required me to recognize, first, that every member of the household, male or female, old or young, is important and, then, that the terms, concepts, methods and techniques I use should help achieve the aim. I do not claim I achieved it but I submit I took steps in that direction.

I

The rich tradition of ethnography at the Department of Sociology of the University of Delhi was one of the features that drew me there, first as a student in the late 1970s and then as a member of faculty in the 1980s. The figure chiefly responsible for instilling this tradition, Professor M. N. Srinivas, had by then moved on, but Professor A. M. Shah—and the faculty and students that he worked closely with—maintained strongly the imperative of detailed and vivid ethnographic analysis. I cannot, alas, say that I have been part of

The epigraph to this chapter is drawn from the Introduction to *The Family in India: Critical Essays* by A. M. Shah (New Delhi: Orient Longman, 1998), 3.

this. I did not produce any memorable doctoral monograph on a village, or a small town, or a factory, or a school or a prison. I did not even stay at the Department of Sociology. Instead—as part of the process of establishing a household—I wandered away, first to southern Africa and then to western Europe (and more recently, to work on West Asia). I am not therefore one of Professor Shah's many exemplary students and colleagues, but a maverick can also reflect profitably on his teachings.

Professor Shah's teaching and writing have long affirmed the household as a unit of analysis in ethnographic study[1] and the quotation above vividly evokes the complexity and multi-dimensionality of households. Shah modestly states that he made efforts to capture this, if depicting it fully was not easy to achieve. One generation on, and of the other gender, I have to confess that I have not until now fully apprehended what Shah has so clearly set out above. I was aware—as most researchers in the mid-and late 1980s were, especially women researchers—that households comprised adults of both genders and that gender positions influenced perceptions strongly, so that households did not manifest some simple monolithic view of the world around. At the same time, I did not adequately grasp the equally basic fact that households are composed of people of different ages, and that this generates a dynamic of differential power and access that is no less central to the 'politics of the household' than are gender variables.

Conventional approaches to the politics of the household have been well summarised by O'Laughlin (1999: 8):

> The . . . assumption underlying many household studies is that within the domestic domain there is such a strong degree of interdependence, pooling of resources and commonality of interest that we can ascribe agency to the groups formed there. It is common in development studies to talk about the interests, activities and strategies of households—to assign them agency. It is assumed that there is a natural division of labour by sex and age within domestic groups such that the structure of authority within domestic groups makes it possible for the head of the household to know and represent the interests of the household.

II

Looking back on the ethnographic studies I carried out with care and pleasure in rural settings in southern and western India and in southern Africa in the 1980s, I am struck by how I tended to treat children as extras in a cast that I otherwise strove to represent faithfully, taking pains for example to report on the perceptions and experiences of both women and men, both the affluent and the poor, and both those who had access to power and those who had not. I was not, however, the only one to treat (or rather ignore) children in this way. Few ethnographies, even today, produce a script in which children are routinely present as actors in their own right—unless the subject of the study is explicitly about children. If ethnographies similarly only illuminated women's interests and perceptions when the subject was 'gender,' there would be an outcry against such 'gender-blindness'. 'Generation-blindness', on the other hand, seems to go unremarked.

Following the general prescription that 'discretion is the better part of valour', I shall refrain from a general critique of generation-blind ethnography and therefore from citing the work of other analysts. Instead, I shall criticise my own ethnographies for their myopia, and for assuming that only people above the age of fifteen or twenty are able to exercise agency in the lives of themselves and of others. The advantage in doing this is not just politic, in not annoying and embarrassing others. It is epistemically useful in that I know and can examine some of the reasons for my generation-blindness that may well have relevance to others who shared these reasons in those places and times, and possibly to analysts in other places and times (such as the present) who still evince generation-blindness.

III

The need to listen to multiple voices—the voices of both genders and from various social classes—was well understood when I first embarked on fieldwork in a village in central Kerala in 1984. Direct experience underlined this, then and later, as in the example below.

Late one afternoon in March 1988, I arrived at the gate of a household in the village of Chakkupallom in the Kerala hills. As part of an international research team that was spread all over Kerala, I had selected ten households for close study after a more general survey of the area, and this one represented the upper end of the socio-economic scale.[2] Forty-two-year old Damodaran—the undisputed head of a household that spanned the families of two younger brothers in addition to his mother, his wife, and his five children—received me cordially. No women generally came through the front door of the house, but I was an honorary male, even if clad in a saree, because I was highly (in Chakkupallom terms) educated and paid, and had been introduced there by respected people from established agencies.

After some polite initial conversation, I embarked on the questions intended to cover various central issues in the research. As one of the members of the research team who could speak Malayalam, I did not need to be accompanied by a translator. My questions were about the various livestock that belonged to the household, and Damodaran answered them dutifully. His mother brought me a glass of tea and a saucer of homemade *neyappam*, listened silently to our conversation awhile and was then called away by a neighbour.

Not long into the conversation, I became aware of a contrapuntal set of responses—that sounded far more elaborate and authentic— to my questions. These came from the next room. It was the voice of a middle-aged woman, whom on subsequent visits (this time entering through the back door) I found to be Damodaran's wife. He had little interest in the milchstock, because they were women's work, whereas men were busy with land and draught animals. All the same he courteously hazarded answers to my questions. I maintained eye contact with him and nodded, but my ear was cocked towards the next room and my pen busily scribbled down verbatim all the detailed information and opinion poured out in the invisible woman's voice.

I later realised the combination of factors that had allowed me to tap this rich source of data. The woman had only come to take an unseen sounding of the conversation, because her curiosity had been piqued by the appearance of a woman (and a city woman at that) at their front door. She had only stayed to listen because I was speaking Malayalam and not English. She had been provoked by my questions into answering, because they were about the cows whose care and produce she coordinated. A male visitor may not have drawn her away from her busy routine, she would not have understood if English had been spoken and it is possible that she only spoke up in response to a woman's voice. Possibly, also, she sensed my interest even from the next room, for when Damodaran had finished his brief answer, I always pretended to be scribbling it down until the woman had completed her more extensive one.

Over the years, I have told that story many times in order to communicate the importance of listening carefully to multiple actors. Only recently, however, have I realised that my practice has not lived up to such preaching, especially with regard to another category of people, namely, children. An illustration follows (George 1994: 88).

Another of the ten households, far less well off than Damodaran's, was headed by sixty-four-year-old Pappachan. His wife Chellamma was fifteen years younger, and their three sons in their twenties lived with them as did their teenaged daughter, Sherly. Pappachan was engaged in managing their landholding and the three sons earned intermittently from the trades that they had learned. Chellamma and Sherly had gradually built up a small herd of milch animals that they maintained with much labour and from which they earned an income by selling milk.

Sherly is the only person under twenty in my written account of Chakkupallom[3] who is distinguished by name, probably because of her high profile in the household's dairying. She is one of the few people below adulthood whom I quoted in some detail

> Chellamma could not tend a cow, a buffalo, a pregnant heifer and a male calf by herself, and her lieutenant was her daughter Sherly. When I first visited their house, Chellamma was out and Pappachan answered my initial questions. Sherly took me to see the cattle, which were grazing at a little distance, and then out of earshot of her father she confided proudly: 'Mother and I have assembled all these animals, from the money from the cow's milk, we bought the buffalo, and with the money from the milk of both cow and buffalo we bought the heifer.' In consequence, Sherly's studies were neglected. She spent little time on homework, and sometimes stayed back from school to help with the cattle. The family did not think that Sherly would have done well in school anyway. 'She has no great aptitude for study. Her marks were never good.'

Re-reading this a decade later, I am struck by the similarity in the two situations, between the invisible woman giving her testimony and Sherly waiting until her father could no longer overhear our conversation to share her pride in what she and her mother had achieved through dairying. A key epistemological difference was that I took down the invisible woman's testimony with some effort (whilst giving her husband the impression that I was listening to him) and returned another day to talk to her more fully—but I did not pursue the discussion with Sherly, at that opportunity or later, even though she was similarly brimming over with ideas and information about an enterprise that she was closely involved in.

I regret this now, of course. I strove for rich ethnographic renderings that were textured with multiple perceptions and voices, but there were clearly perceptions and voices that I ignored, notably those of people below the age of 'majority.' I followed local tradition in this, treating offspring who lived with their parents as 'children' (even if they were in their twenties), and only those at the apex of households as having voices to be harkened to. I went to lengths to incorporate minor voices into my narratives about rural settlements, literally, as when I once walked through fields in a village in Zimbabwe to get to the home of the poorest and most marginal person there, an old woman without family.[4] Yet there was a whole category of minor voices that were easily accessible but that I wrote out of scripts, although I sometimes quoted them as second hand, when their parents reported what they had said. These were the voices of those that the law considers 'minors.'

Some of the reasons for this screening out of young voices will be explored below. Here I note—again with regret—the casual manner in which I dismissed the costs to Sherly's formal education of her involvement in dairying. I did not ask her what she felt about this, although her enthusiasm for the dairy enterprise was obvious and it is quite possible that she found this more meaningful than attending school. I reported

> The family did not think that Sherly would have done well in school anyway. 'She has no great aptitude for study. Her marks were never good.'

I quoted her parents and described them as 'the family.' Was she not part of 'the family'? Would she have given the same estimate of herself?

I apologise to Sherly, across the years, and apologise also to her peers for not talking to them seriously and instead merely presenting their parents' perceptions of them. This is not to say that their own perceptions would necessarily have differed sharply but they may well have. They deserved to be listened to in their own right. We can adopt O'Laughlin's position here on the issue of gender in households, of 'household' as a 'useful, historically appropriate, analytical and descriptive concept' (1999: 35), but one that should not assume unitary interests across genders and generations nor subsume female under male or child under adult.

IV

The irony is that children were far from invisible in my fieldwork sites, whether in Kerala or Gujarat or Mashonaland (in Zimbabwe). They were a different kind of social actor in the little rural universes I moved through in the course of my research. I should clarify that here that the 'children' I refer to in the paragraphs below were people between the age of about five (when they were considered old enough to leave the homestead and trail along with groups of those somewhat older) to around twelve years, after which they assumed a quasi-adult status. It was between these ages that children were likely to materialise spontaneously in a group anywhere in a village where something unusual and/or interesting was going on, not least something as unusual as a person—who looked and spoke differently—asking questions (to adults) about their everyday lives.

These children articulated very easily the amusement that my different appearance, accent, and interests provoked in these rural settings. They laughed at and commented on the way I looked and spoke with an openness that inhibited adults could not match, although these adults derived considerable relief from the children's frank expressiveness, saying to each other 'What are these kids laughing about?' and exchanging amused glances. Accurately, the Malayalam word used in Kerala was not kids but 'calves' (*kadavangal*). Since my research was on livestock, I was tickled by this usage and the notion that children could act as a bridging category between the human and animal world, but I did not, alas, go on to consider seriously what kind of social actors children were.

It was especially ungrateful of me to treat children as extras in the cast when I wrote up my ethnographies, for they often played roles crucial to my fieldwork, for example, that of translator. When pursuing research in eleven settings in rural and peri-urban Gujarat in 1986, for example, the household data I amassed was greatly enriched by the fact that it was the school summer holiday and children were at home and available to translate from Gujarati into Hindi (a language that they studied at school and that their parents were less exposed to). Children were generally not only available but very willing indeed, easily entering into my conversations with their parents or relatives or neighbours and facilitating exchange. I thank these children—again across the intervening two decades— and apologise for not seeing them as more than transmitters of adult views and experience.

That the status of 'child'—in comparison with that of 'adult'—has opportunities as well as constraints was clear (although not to me at the time because I focused only on adults). I shall illustrate this from the study of eleven settings in south Gujarat just mentioned.[5] As customary in that area at that time (i) different areas of a village were inhabited by people who belonged to particular castes, (ii) relationships between castes varied between villages and within villages, and (iii) the current state of these relationships was manifest in the ease with which people moved—or did not move—between residential sections associated with different castes. In one (extremely unusual) village, for example, relationships were so positive that a man from an ex-untouchable caste walked easily with me across physical caste boundaries to a rich high-status household and sat there for a while with me. There were, in contrast, villages where relationships between castes were very tense indeed and adults did not cross the spatial boundaries (although these were clearly demarcated only in the mind, and actual walls were rare).

Children, however, enjoyed greater freedom than adults from these social and physical constraints. When I asked directions to another section of the village, the adults with whom I had been conversing hesitated—between the perceived constraints on crossing boundaries and their sense of the village's obligation to a visitor—and they then asked the children (who were as usual hanging around and taking in all that was happening with great interest) to guide me to where I wanted to go. It might even be the case that children had already crossed these boundaries in one direction—from where they 'belonged' to where something interesting was going on—and would then be identified from among the young bystanders and asked to take me to their section of the village. And then quite often a number of children would accompany me and my new guides across boundaries again, from where we had been and where they 'belonged,' to the new site of my investigations. The defining characteristic of the village where caste relations were most tense was that even children did not cross boundaries. Instead, children from one caste group handed me over to the children from another caste at the undrawn but clearly understood borders between residential sections.

I happily availed of these services and even used the 'permeability' of boundaries between caste-based residence as indicating the degree of tension between castes in a village. I never thought, however, to ask children about their perceptions and experiences as we walked through a village together, treating them only as friendly and often amusing guides. In fact, children accompanied me wherever I went, whether asked to or not, making it impossible for me to retire behind a suitable bush to ease a full bladder. I developed formidable bladder control during these periods of fieldwork, for which I must acknowledge further indebtedness to children in these areas.

Looking back, I wonder that I did not avail better and more respectfully of the resources that children could have provided in the locales where I did fieldwork. Their sparkling intelligence was more than evident. My maiden fieldwork effort—in a village (Muttam) in central Kerala in 1984, mentioned earlier—involved a list of about twenty questions about livestock that was intended to guide me through semi-structured interviews in the more than two hundred households there.[6] Over the weeks of this endeavour, a flock of children attached themselves to me and soon mastered my list of questions. When I glanced surreptitiously at the list to remind myself which question came next, the children would prompt me from memory, often correctly. On occasions when I waited at the bus stop, children would beguile their time and mine by reciting my list of questions, frequently imitating my accent. I say children, but most prominent in this enterprise were boys around the age of nine to eleven. The difference from girls, I suspect, was not so much in comprehension as in expression, in a setting where girls would be inhibited to express themselves so freely.

Boys of about nine to eleven or slightly older would parody the questions I asked about livestock, thereby demonstrating (i) their grasp of the sort of question I would pose, despite (ii) the complete incomprehensibility to them of what I was about, and (iii) their keen sense of humour. As I walked through the village, for example, one of them would call loudly to another in Malayalam, with a sideways mocking glance at me, 'So you there, tell me, is your hen white or is it black?'

And, yes, I must acknowledge, twenty-one years on, for not cottoning on right then and there to how smart and aware children are about what is going on around them—yes, indeed, the joke was on me.

Girls sometimes did interact directly with a visitor to their village. When I compared the permeability of boundaries between the residential areas inhabited by different castes in eleven rural settings in south Gujarat, I made a casual reference to 'two teenaged Anavil girls' who 'came to the Halpati hut where I was and then accompanied me to Koli and Darzi residences', adding that these two girls were 'on vacation from the city' (George 1994: 411). Recreating the event from notes made at the time (in 1986), the actual event was as follows. After talking to families in the high-ranking Anavil Brahman section of the village, I asked the way to where the less exalted lived, notably the Halpati caste of bonded labourers, now nominally freed by law yet living in great poverty. My Anavil host politely despatched one of his servants to guide me to this section and this escort left me there (he was nonplussed as to the purpose of my activities). Some time later, the two Anavil teenaged girls turned up in the squalor of the Halpati section, probably for the first time in their lives. They waited until I had finished my discussions there and then escorted me to the residential areas of the Koli and Darzi castes. I thanked them before I left on my journey home but did not think of them as anything other than pleasant companions. Polite small talk elicited the information that they studied at a college in the nearby city of Surat and were home for the vacation.

I surmise now that—as college students—they were aware of research and had listened to my conversations and had watched my note-taking in the Anavil section of the village where they 'belonged.' They had observed me leave with the servant for the Halpati section and afterwards seen him return alone. They must have conferred and then told their families that it was not right to leave an educated woman from the city on her own in the village and that they would accompany me around. This was not conduct typical of genteel young women belonging to a high caste, but the tertiary education that was new in their generation must have given them some authority in the eyes of their relatives. Of course, no Anavil girl would have come alone to the Halpati section, however educated. These two young women were kind enough to volunteer as my escorts. They would very likely have had interesting perceptions to share had I encouraged them to do so. But I dismissed them in my report with a sentence, rather than reflecting about them in the manner that I have just done.

Thinking back some more, I realise that what I have described of Anavil girls in Gujarat was unlikely to have a parallel in Kerala, where young women tended to be more inhibited and more socially restrained (which was then also my feeling as a relatively young woman living in both settings). This was the case even though female education is notably higher in Kerala than elsewhere in India. Had I thought seriously about the two kind Anavil girls, I might have extended my comparative analysis profitably.

In an integrated presentation of my fieldwork in various settings, the acknowledgements read(George 1994: xviii)

> My primary debt is to the rural households (258 in Kerala, 772 in Gujarat and 107 in three areas of Zimbabwe) who have provided the material for much of this book. If I have been able to articulate some of these households' problems and concerns, that will be a small return for their patience and hospitality.

I did not articulate the 'problems and concerns' of younger members of households. In omitting to do so, I had blithely ignored some of those who had shown the most patience and hospitality towards me in various research settings.[7]

In Zimbabwe, I was less dependent on children as translators and as guides, because of the different rural landscapes there as well as differences in style of research. Not knowing local languages (in contrast to my fieldwork in Kerala and Gujarat), I relied on Sylvia Kuimba as my collaborator and translator. In Kerala and Gujarat, as in many other parts of India, villages are dense residential areas inhabited by various castes, with agricultural land stretching away beyond. In Mashonaland and Manicaland, where my research in Zimbabwe was carried out, dwellings were more spread out among fields, and Sylvia drove the two of us around from one homestead to another. I did not therefore need children to volunteer as my translators or guides as in India.

In Zimbabwe, I came across the occasional household inhabited only by people below the age of twenty, yet I glided over children's perceptions as I had in India. In the rural setting of Majuru in Mashonaland, Sylvia and I interviewed fifty-one of a total of sixty households in 1989.[8] Among the households described as marginal to the village was one that consisted only of two school girls, whose mother was dead and whose father lived in 'town' (the nearby capital city, Harare) with his second wife and their children. I am embarrassed to note that my formulation of this scenario at the time treated the two girls as appendages of their absent father, even though I had met them and not him.

> . . . the father lived in Harare with his second wife and their children, while his two school-going daughters by his first (deceased) wife lived in Majuru.

So much for consciously avoiding partiarchal presentations! Apparently I was sensitive enough to avoid doing this when it came to 'grown' women but not in the case of women who were 'minors'. My field notes on the household inhabited by the two schoolgirls are sketchy indeed compared with the long scribblings about other households. The only similarly sketchy notes are about a household in which an eighteen-year-old man lived alone. Obviously I did not consider these 'real' or 'proper' households, to be given the same attention as those inhabited by 'full' adults. Single-person households where the single person was a recognised adult was treated in much more detail in my notes than these two were.

At least the age of the eighteen-year-old who lived by himself was mentioned. Elsewhere in my account of Majuru I used the term 'boys' to refer without specification of age to young men whom I subsumed as under the authority of their fathers or uncles

> The Kunaka herd consisted largely of cows, heifers and female calves, with only one ox. But the Kunaka boys, especially the second brother's sons, had a talent for 'turning oxen,' that is, of breaking them to the plough, a dangerous and difficult occupation. There were young oxen to be 'turned' in each agricultural season, and in the process the Kunaka boys managed to plough the fields of all the patrilineage's households, and indeed sometimes hired themselves out along with the oxen they were turning for additional income. The patrilineage's human resources thus saved members from having to hire oxen for their fields.
>
> (George 1994: 110)

> The donkeys were also hired out for ploughing, escorted by the Tagarira boys.
>
> (George 1994: 117)

'Boy'—with its connotation of immature male—was a spectacularly inappropriate word to describe young men who were physically and psychologically able to handle strong and unruly oxen and donkeys. The usage here is comparable to 'boy' as addressed to an African-American man in order to diminish his status. The least that I would do here if writing this again would be to substitute the more accurate and respectful word 'youth.' I then went on to refer collectively to these useful and productive young men as 'the patrilineage's human resources,' without inverted commas, faithfully echoing their fathers' and uncles'—and probably their mothers' and aunts'—perceptions of them. Strange for someone who considered herself a self-consciously progressive 'new researcher' and who would never have referred to adult women as a 'patrilineage's human resources'!

I similarly used 'girl' to describe any adolescent female. In fact I did not use the word 'adolescent,' preferring the more euphemistic 'teenaged,' which focussed on these females' chronological age rather than on their developmental status. I thereby missed making some critical linkages. One such related to Baviskar's identification of the presence of an 'able-bodied' woman (1988: 353) as essential to a household's ability to maintain a milch buffalo or cow (in addition to having the finances to buy the milch animal, a space to keep it, and fodder to feed it, the latter in turn implying some access to land). Since I apprehended and presented Sherly and her female peers as 'teenaged girls,' I did not classify them within the category of 'able-bodied' young women. In fact their families had a closer appreciation of the point made by Baviskar (without having read Baviskar!), for the use of these young women's labour to tend milchstock was constantly under review by their parents.

To illustrate this, we return to Chakkupallom, but not to Sherly, instead to two of her peers, yes, two 'teenaged girls,' sisters. I did not record their names but acknowledged their existence in a kinship diagram as two circles descending from the bar that represented their parents' marital tie. (In good colonial anthropological tradition, as embodied for example in *Notes and Queries of the Royal Anthropological Society*, females appear in kinship diagrams as circles and males as triangles.) Why take down children's names? Streamline the data collection process, avoid unnecessary detail. I was radical enough at the time to note the name of these two girls' mother, namely Shoshamma, and not only that of the 'household head,' their father Varghese. Here are Shoshamma's musings about her daughters, whose labour was crucial to the household, apparently more so than her sons

> My sons aren't good at studies. The older boy failed in the eighth standard. My daughters are better. The elder of the two now at home studied up to the tenth standard, but failed there. It wasn't her fault. I was away at the time, nursing my sick mother. My daughter couldn't look after the house and study at the same time.

It would be hard to say no if some agency were to offer us a loan for a cow. But there are other uses for a loan. We thought of taking a loan to buy a sewing machine. My daughter—who failed tenth standard—now learns tailoring from a girl in the neighbourhood who was trained somewhere outside. If we get a sewing machine, our daughter will have paid work. Her younger sister can learn tailoring by helping her, and when the older one marries, the younger one can earn some money in turn from the sewing machine. So you see, it would not be only a question of using the loan for a sewing machine or a cow, but whether my daughters should look after a cow—as with this one [referring to a cow temporarily brought into the household]—or work at a sewing machine. But the main question is whether we should risk taking a loan for either cow or sewing machine.

(George 1994: 68)

I may have devalued children in my research, but the households I studied were fully aware of how critically dependent on their offspring parents would be later on in life—especially those whose other resources were very constrained. In Chakkupallom, too, I listened to Eliamma, ageing like her husband Daniel and dependent on agricultural labour

We don't have sons, only four daughters, of whom one remains to be married. We can't expect any help from our daughters in our old age, and we worry about how to support ourselves when my husband is too old for agricultural labour. Already he feels the strain of the work. If we had even one son.

(George 1994: 66)

Elliamma and Daniel had taken a loan to buy a cow 'to provide an income for them in their old age when agricultural labour was no longer possible' (George 1994: 94). Despite their anxious care, the cow died before the loan was repaid. It was not insured ('We didn't know that insurance was needed. We don't have sons to find out such things'). Elliamma described the cow's death thus

I rose early and ran to see how she was. She lay as if sleeping.
I called out to her, *Molle* [daughter].

(George 1994: 94)

V

Why did I not take children seriously, even when they were so integral a part of my fieldwork experiences? The obvious answer is that the theoretical and methodological orientations of the time did not extend to children. These orientations had already stretched to cover the perceptions of non-hegemonic groups—attempting to go, for example, beyond 'Brahmanical' views of rural society in India— and of the subordinate gender, beyond 'patriarchal' presentations of household or village life. Their coverage did not then reach out to the viewpoints of the subordinate generation.

Do they now? Even in these days of explicit recognition that children have rights, twenty years after an international convention was signed, has all this been translated into theories and methodologies that give form and meaning to such recognition? Is 'every member of the household important' nowadays when social scientists go about their investigations? Including younger members?

A clue to a potentially useful vein of analysis lies in my casual description of Sherly, quoted earlier

> Chellamma could not tend a cow, a buffalo, a pregnant heifer and a male calf by herself, and her lieutenant was her daughter Sherly.

My depiction of an adolescent girl as subordinate to a parental 'commanding officer' resonates with what are long well known as 'subaltern studies' in South Asia

> The term 'subaltern' is used to denote the entire people that is subordinate in terms of class, caste, age, gender or office, or in any other way.
>
> (Sen 1987: 203)

These lines were published around the time that I carried out field-based research in the various settings described in this paper. Such ideas as then articulated clearly included age as one axis of subaltern status, and yet there was little acknowledgement that children are a subaltern category. I wonder if there is adequate acknowledgement even today, outside the relatively new and still very limited field of what is called 'children and youth studies.'

Even had I been far ahead of my time and sensitive to the protagonism and agency of children, I doubt if I could have adequately incorporated their perceptions and experiences in my fieldwork. Why? Children in the settings that I investigated were frankly intrigued by and curious about me, and open in their monitoring of my activities. But the adults were also intrigued and curious and also monitored me, conferring with each other. Had I engaged in extended and probing discussions with children in these settings, there is no doubt that adults would have approached to listen intently (just as children came to audit my conversations with adults) or would have questioned children sharply as to what I had been asking them about—or both.

For all that ethnographic research attempts to be low-key, unobtrusive, and non-threatening in its approach to the people that it studies, it represents an encounter between those who are 'other' and is therefore inevitably tinged with some suspicion. As a mature but still relatively young woman, who strove to dress and speak and behave appropriately and unthreateningly (and who was introduced by locally respected people and organisations), I was accepted fairly easily in all the settings where I carried out fieldwork. My inquiries concerned the trivia of everyday life and especially livestock, not subjects that might be considered as trespassing on the deeply private or intimate—although investigations into relationships around livestock inevitably threw penetrating light on relationships between people. My education and formally employed status usually allowed me some privileges as an honorary male, for example talking to men, as in the conversation with Damodharan described earlier in this paper. There were—all the same—moments when I seemed to threaten established relationships and situations and met with the attitudinal equivalent of closed doors, even if briefly.

A few times that this happened concerned daughters-in-law. In Chakkupallom, for example, one of the households that I visited was the residence of Annamma, a woman in her mid-thirties, who had invested much time and labour in her milch cow and liked talking about it.[9] She had married into the village and into a large family there, and lived next door to her parents-in-law. I once ran into her husband's father on my way to Annamma's house, and it was clear that he was not enthusiastic about my spending time with her. I might not have very much to do with my time except ask people fairly obvious things about their livestock, as an idle over-educated woman who generally spent her days at a desk, but Annamma did have a lot of work to be distracted from. I might put ideas into her head, as a woman of about the same age but living a very different life. I might do something that unsettled the delicate system of extended family relationships to which Annamma was pivotal, as the wife of the eldest son. I might stir up feelings that she presently kept a lid on, for example, regret that she had recently moved out of a larger house that had then been sold to finance the marriage of her husband's sister.

I think that similar negative reactions might have emerged if I had spoken at length and in depth to children in these settings. Children were similar to daughters-in-law in that they were members of families and households who were seen as open to subversion by outsiders. In the case of daughters-in-law, this was explicitly made clear to me by a woman in Muttam in central Kerala during my fieldwork there in 1984. She lived with her family in a fragile hut in an informal settlement that had sprung up abutting a disused road, and the household relied on casual labour of various kinds to eke out a fairly minimal existence. She explained to me that she had found a wife for her son from a village at considerable distance from Muttam, expressly because she wanted to keep household matters relatively private. On a day when we only have rice for one meal—she elaborated—and not enough for two, or have to eat rice without curry, a local girl would 'trumpet' the news around the village, whereas a daughter-in-law from relatively faraway who lacked close ties within Muttam would keep this information to herself (George 1984).

Households have their sensitivities and there are certain features and events that they would like to keep to themselves. The same applies to larger human units, such as villages, and there is concern about those who might 'tell,' daughters-in-law, for example, who may not be adequately bonded into units that they were not born into, or children who in their innocence might reveal information to a prying outsider that others in the household or the village would like to maintain as classified information. People with a strong interest in their neighbours' affairs have long been known to cross-question their children—or other people's children or anybody's children—in order to elicit details about situations to which their adult size and status deny them access.

Children do tell (and this increases both their value as 'informants' and the ethical questions about drawing on information from this source). I only knew how I was perceived and referred to in Majuru village in Mashonaland because—as I was leaving a homestead once—a child called out 'Has the *murungu* gone?' and Sylvia translated this for me with some amusement. *Murungu* literally means a 'speaker of English,' and was obviously the term by which I was locally described. Yet none of the more than fifty adults with whom we spoke at length let this slip, not even in so slight a manner that Sylvia as a native speaker and a skilled investigator could pick up. Children do ask why the Emperor has no clothes on. They break tacit conspiracies of silence, often because they are not aware of them.

Many attitudes that apply to women are parallelled in the case of children. Why would someone talk to women when they can talk to knowledgeable men who wield authority within households? And, why would someone want to talk to children if they can talk to knowledgeable adults who wield authority within households? People who talk to women must presumably be looking for weak spots in families and households to exploit in some way. And, people who talk to children must be looking for weak spots in families and households to exploit in some way, presumably. In my case, as a woman, it was understandable that I would talk to women.[10] My conversing with children might have aroused disapproval in the same way as a male ethnographer speaking extendedly and intimately with woman.

If I had carried out fieldwork in the traditional anthropological manner advocated and exemplified by Shah, residing around the clock in the setting studied for up to twelve months, this problem might have been overcome, because I would gradually have been accepted and even taken for granted. But my fieldwork was never carried out on a residential basis, and never amounted to more than some weeks at a time in a particular setting. I remained a daily visitor of whom local people were always conscious and whom they carefully monitored.

Conventional male ethnographers have not infrequently taken advantage of their wives' co-residence in the setting under study to gain access to the experiences and perceptions of women in that setting. There have also been ethnographer couples who together wove rich multi-voiced accounts of life in a particular place and time. Could children contribute similarly?

Certainly much that I know about family life and school environments in the western European country where I now live has come from the vivid accounts of my daughter, who has grown up in this country, is a native speaker of the language, and thus has an understanding of how various people here think but is also able to take some critical distance from local ways through association with her non-native parents. Her existence and presence have also allowed me access to situations that I could not have entered without such legitimisation. However, especially from the time when she was around eight years of age, she has been able to illuminate for me mainly the world of young girls and I have not had similar privileged access to the parallel world of young boys (since I do not have a son).

There is increasing discussion of children as researchers, but many questions of ethics, procedure and methodology remain to be answered. Of course, similar questions in the case of adult ethnographers are far from fully resolved. As for household, village, and other ethnographies, we have not yet succeeded in rendering these sufficiently polyphonic with regard to gender and class position. Let us add to our efforts by striving to hear children's voices, perceptions and experiences as well as the viewpoints of various categories of adults, remembering that 'every member of the household is important.'

Endnotes

[1] See Shah 1973.
[2] See G. George et al. 1988.
[3] See George 1994, chapter 8.
[4] See George and Kuimba 1989.
[5] See George 1994, chapter 11.

⁶ See George 1984; also George 1994, chapter 8.
⁷ Baviskar (1995: x) is a refreshing contrast, in thanking a named list of children prominently in the Acknowledgements of a book based on fieldwork in the Narmada Valley.
⁸ See George and Kuimba 1989.
⁹ See George 1994: 74–79.
¹⁰ Not all analysts agree on the effectiveness of information-gathering by women ethnographers from women in specific settings. See Kishwar 1998 for some interesting viewpoints.

References

Baviskar, A. 1995. *In the Belly of the River: Tribal Conflicts over Development in the Narmada Valley.* Delhi: Oxford University Press.

Baviskar, B.S. 1988. Dairy Co-operatives and Rural Development in Gujarat. In *Who Shares? Co-operatives and Rural Development*, ed. D. W. Attwood and B. S. Baviskar. New Delhi: Oxford University Press.

George, G., S. George, P. J. Raj Kamal, R. Sukumaran Nair, J. Philip, U. Shankari, B. Strebel, N. R. Unnithan, and S. Walty. 1988. *Case Study: A Multidisciplinary Field-Level Research on Cattle Holding in Six Villages of Kerala.* Department of Geography at the University of Zurich (commissioned by the Swiss Development Corporation/Intercooperation and the Kerala Livestock Board).

George, S. 1984. Diffusing Anand: The Implications of Establishing a Dairy Co-operative in a Village in Central Kerala. *Economic and Political Weekly* 19(52–53).

————., and S. Kuimba. 1989. *Development and Participation: The Dairy Development Programme in One Village of the Chikwaka Communal Area.* Harare: Norwegian Ministry of Development Co-operation and the Agricultural Development Authority of Zimbabwe.

————. 1994. *A Matter of People: Co-operative Dairying in India and Zimbabwe.* New Delhi: Oxford University Press.

Kishwar, M. 1998. Learning to Take People Seriously. In *Anthropological Journeys: Reflections on Fieldwork*, ed. M. Thapan. New Delhi: Orient Longman.

O'Laughlin, B. 1999. *In Defence of the Household: Marx, Gender and the Utilitarian Impasse.* Working Paper 289. The Hague: Institute of Social Studies.

Sen, A. 1987 Subaltern Studies: Capital, Class and Community, in *Subaltern Studies V: Writings on South Asian History and Society*, ed. Ranajit Guha. New Delhi: Oxford University Press.

Shah, A. M. 1973. *The Household Dimension of the Family in India: A Field Study in a Gujarat Village and a Review of Other Studies.* Delhi: Orient Longman; Berkeley: University of Callifornia 1974.

————. 1998. *The Family in India: Critical Essays.* New Delhi: Orient Longman.

Epilogue
A. M. Shah—Man and His Work

N. R. Sheth

Arvindbhai Manilal Shah (AMS hereafter) bears a rare combination of scholarly and personal qualities. His academic achievements are marked by depth, detail and determination. His work and lifestyle are characterised by simplicity, straightforwardness, grit and native wisdom.

AMS and I have had a long, binding personal and academic relationship. We were classmates during the initial two years of college at Baroda (now Vadodara). Then I lagged behind by a year. He introduced me to Professor M. N. Srinivas, to sociology, and to a Gandhian way of living and thinking informed by personal sensibility and discretion. The four of us who shared with him student lodgings for a couple of years went through a variety of experiments in group-living guided by ideas of elegance without ostentation. Our endeavours were largely directed by AMS's prudent leadership. We used to call him (in his absence) *bapuji* (father figure) to express our sense of uneasy respect or disapproval emerging from the way we were mentored and disciplined. These feelings, however, only served to cement the bonds of fraternal love we built among ourselves. The bonds have survived all vagaries of growing up.

Over the decades I have often heard expressions of mixed feelings of discomfort, respect and regard from AMS's students, juniors and associates in a variety of roles. On balance, the mix of awe and respect seems to add up to a special regard for an incisive intellectual capability and clarity enlightened by sterling personal character. Those who turn off from such a character may be losers in the field of academic bonding. A leading British social anthropologist many years ago summarised for me his impression of AMS in the phrase, 'competent, but difficult to talk to'. Or did he mean 'difficult to talk to but competent'? If you have worked with or known AMS over a longish stretch of collaboration and social relationships, you are most likely to have observed and shared the human tenderness and sensitivity dotting his more transparent toughness of deportment. Empathy occasionally reveals his childlike softness.

AMS was born and grew up in a middle-class Bania trading family in a small town in Gujarat. An aptitude for books and reading was among the traits he inherited from his grandfather and father. A paternal uncle, exceptionally well-educated and talented in literary taste for his time and social space, served as a singular source of intellectual and cultural inspiration for AMS at a young age. He learnt lessons in and imbibed the values of accuracy, meticulousness, hard work, frugality, and dignity of labour. He went to a school where teachers worked on subsistence allowance in place of graded salary structures. The town he lived in was graced by progressive leaders, who employed distinctive vision and effort to introduce futuristic models in education and library services. Such a noble exposure to forces of familial and social influence created in him a set of ideals of life and work dedicated to a Gandhian ethos with adequate space in it to inject one's own equations on work, ethics and merit.

AMS ran into Srinivas and sociology in 1951. While he had opted for economics as his subject of specialisation for his first degree at the M.S. University of Baroda, he was advised by a teacher to choose cultural anthropology as a minor subject. This unfamiliar subject was slated to be taught by Srinivas who was due to join the university and launch a new department of sociology. AMS was drawn towards sociology (and anthropology) for its academic novelty as well as for the intellectual opportunity to comprehend and relate to the kaleidoscope of human society. The emerging interest in the new discipline got progressively embellished by the exceptionally inspiring scholarship and interpersonal qualities enshrined in Srinivas's academic identity. Srinivas had a natural inclination to take deep interest in the learning process as well as personal life of his students. He exercised freedom in relation to mandatory syllabi and books to energise students with new perspectives on society, self, and the field of learning. As providence would have it, AMS had the distinct benefit of a one-on-one teacher-student relationship with Srinivas during his undergraduate period. His learning in content and form was enriched by Srinivas's stimulating informal and interactive style. At the same time, Srinivas had the opportunity of sizing up AMS's potential and promise as a competent researcher with exemplary personal and social qualities.

This mutual discovery of merit paved the way of an extraordinary opportunity gained by AMS in building a career as a professional sociologist. He was asked by Srinivas to join him in his fieldwork in Rampura village in Karnataka for two months during the summer of 1952. This turned out to be a unique experience for AMS in adding value to his personal, social and scholastic character. The advantage of working and living in the field with the 'master-craftsman' of fieldwork served to instil in him interest and skill in the various aspects of field research with its fascination and challenges. As a companion of Srinivas's over two months, he gathered a good deal of moss in the praxis of sociology and the intellectual world at large. Exposure to Indian society beyond Gujarat and the Gandhian ethos persuaded him to redefine some values such as social service and simplicity. He gave up the determination he had made earlier to wear only khadi clothes. His views on social reality and the Gandhian way of life turned less dogmatic and more informed by expanding horizons of knowledge and experience.

The intellectual gains of the summer of 1952 were strengthened and enlarged during the next summer when Srinivas persuaded the university to offer to AMS a grant for independent fieldwork in a tribal area in Gujarat. AMS had a fair knowledge of the place and people he chose for study. He returned with precious insights in the structure and dynamics of caste, tribe, village and family. He went through a similar spell of fieldwork in the same area during the following year. The scholar's intellectual fervour and the nourishment it received from a gifted guru resulted in publication of two papers in 1955 by the time he obtained his postgraduate degree. This rather uncommon achievement laid the foundation of a firm and well-acclaimed career in sociological research which was still a field of many unchartered destinations with not many dedicated recruits to tread along the sketchy, bumpy roads. Much of the work in progress in this area was in the hands of Western scholars.

AMS has a place among Indian sociologists, who brought the discipline onto the base of intensive fieldwork in the participant-observation mode. By this time the old distinction between sociology and social anthropology had got blurred in the Indian context. At Baroda, the fusion of experience and wisdom of Srinivas and I. P. Desai soon melted the two disciplines into the more comprehensible identity of sociology. Early scholars like AMS could therefore keep their feet grounded in the phenomenal reality of the field they traversed rather than getting embroiled in drawing or defending cultivated borders of academic disciplines.

The scope for expansion of vision and work across academic borders knocked on AMS's door of intellectual aptitude just as he began his doctoral work. While he initiated fieldwork for a village study for PhD, he was commissioned for collaboration in a research project undertaken by veteran anthropologists Robert Redfield and Milton Singer at the University of Chicago. AMS's assignment was to study a specialist caste of geneaologists (Vahivancha Barot) spread across the Gujarat region as well as a village community in the region. This work drew him into a variety of issues and probabilities regarding the geneaologists, their client groups, and the social order surrounding them. As he encountered recorded information of immediate concern, he increasingly realised that the present can be adequately understood only if one could lay hands on the past of people and groups. This led to vigorous search for records of tradition of which there was no dearth in Gujarat. He then cultivated an appetite for the study of tradition and looked for recorded history wherever it could be found—private collections, libraries, government archives and museums.

Since then, AMS has reflected and written considerably about a close connection between sociology and history. He regards sociology as contemporary history and vice versa. He is pleased to recognise that an integrated view of sociology and history is increasingly accepted by historians. His continuing efforts in bringing history and sociology together have enriched both the disciplines. His latest book on the history of his village contains lessons for historians as well as sociologists. Some other sociologists have used historical sources. But AMS has mastered and practised the craft of historiography with lasting effect.

Pursuit of sociology at Baroda in AMS's time offered a special advantage to students and teachers. The work and professional stature of Srinivas enabled him to attract reputed Indian and foreign scholars to visit the new department of sociology and meet local scholars through seminars and informal gatherings. Srinivas also inspired senior students to actively participate in and even to lead seminars. This meant a continuing opportunity for students to expand their disciplinary and social capital regarding the subject of their choice and the state of the art from multiple perspectives. An important driving force for self-development indeed!

Meanwhile, the sociology department had begun to grow. AMS was appointed as lecturer in 1958. As he was settling down with his twin responsibilities as teacher and fieldworker, he was blessed with an exceptionally invigorating developmental opportunity for his age and professional seniority. He was invited to spend six months each at the University of Chicago and the Centre for Advanced Study in the Behavioral Sciences at Stanford in the USA during 1960–61. Both these institutions offered him facilities to work on his research in progress. He enjoyed faculty status at the University of Chicago which facilitated access to senior teachers and researchers. As Chicago had multidisciplinary centres of learning and research, AMS's exposure to American scholarship stretched far beyond the conventional field of sociology and anthropology. He gave several seminars and attended conferences at various academic centres in the US. He could also interact with a large number of senior and reputed scholars in sociology and other social sciences. This led to maturation of his perspective on sociology and its place in the wider field of social and behavioural sciences. As in the case of history, he found sociology's borders with economics, political science, etc., more fluid than was propounded by purist scholars within the disciplines.

AMS left Baroda in 1961 to join the Delhi School of Economics (DSE) as a lecturer and worked there till he retired as professor in

1996. When he moved to Delhi, the Department of Sociology in the DSE was on its way to an ambitious comprehensive futuristic plan of postgraduate education, research and development of inter-institutional bonds under the leadership of Srinivas. The location and reputation of DSE, supported eminently by Srinivas's professional clout, attracted scholars and dignitaries from various parts of the world. This gave AMS and his peers continual opportunities to strengthen and widen their base of information and vision. The Department eventually grew in size and academic output stimulated by recognition as a Centre of Advanced Study under the University Grants Commission's scheme for promotion of excellence. The DSE faculty included seasoned economic historians whose work and ideas contributed to widening and deepening of AMS's perspective on the sociology-history connection. The growth in perspective was not one-sided.

The association with DSE was long and stable. AMS spent an academic year (1976–77) as visiting fellow at the Institute of Development Studies at Sussex in England. He was also invited as a visiting academic for three months in 1988 by the University of New England in Australia. Apart from these assignments, he visited several institutions in various countries to participate in seminars, conferences, and specific academic gatherings. These engagements progressively widened the sphere of his academic recognition and influence.

At Delhi, AMS inspired and guided research output of a large number of PhD and MPhil students as well as visiting scholars from other countries. His devotion to his responsibility as a teacher and the time and energy he invested in his students were truly exemplary. His students came from various segments of urban, rural and tribal cultures across the country. Their research interests covered a wide spectrum of themes in social systems and dynamics in the changing Indian and global environment. AMS took a holistic interest in his students' academic and personal growth. He mentored them as a friend but with a disciplinary streak in the relationship. This enriched his own repository of knowledge and outlook in fields as diverse as kinship, caste, village, religion, education, industry, health, political processes and voluntary organisations. The width of his span is well represented in his published contributions. A large part of his publications obviously relate to his chosen field: kinship, family, caste, village, religion, and the force of tradition in society. However, he has also contributed papers on themes of contemporary concern such as family planning, elections, reservations, communalism and education. Of course, his most outstanding contribution to Indian sociology is in the domain of family studies. He brought clarity in looking at the Indian family. His distinction between family and household is very valuable. His analysis of family has moved far beyond the traditional dichotomy of nuclear and joint family. His knowledge and insights have led to a significant reinterpretation of the notion of developmental cycle within kin groups.

AMS worked with Srinivas to enhance understanding of Indian institutions in international perspective. He has written several important papers on Srinivas which help to widen and clarify knowledge on Srinivas and his work at different stages in his career. This has led to a reexamination and reinterpretation of concepts such as division, hierarchy and sanskritisation in the light of additional knowledge of social reality and progress in conceptualisation. A five-volume Festschrift in honour of Srinivas was co-edited by AMS and two other colleagues. But he bore a large and heavy part of the responsibility, including interfacing with authors and publishers. A large volume of his published output in association with or in relation to Srinivas and his work spans a wide spectrum of Indian sociological themes and issues. These include rural communities, religion, caste in its myriad forms, fieldwork, status of sociology, untouchability and reservations. He has formed a habit of locating subjects of unconventional scholarship and doggedly pursued them to enlighten the world of scholars. Many years ago, he chanced upon a journal called *Indian Journal of Sociology* which was brought out in the early years of the past century. Since then, he has striven unceasingly to collect information on its origin, growth, patronage, value and life span. He has published whatever information he has on it for its historical value to current sociology. He is still pursuing his intention to know and disseminate more on this journal. It is an intellectual treat to watch him passionately soliciting clues on the unknown journal.

AMS has played a major role in the growth of sociology as a profession. The Indian Sociological Society was in a state of indifferent health along with its journal *Sociological Bulletin*. Srinivas initiated its revival in 1967 along with other senior sociologists. AMS was appointed secretary in 1967 and again during 1970–72. He worked hard and succeeded in updating records and straightening accounts. The office moved from Mumbai to Delhi and AMS spent considerable time and effort in rejuvenation of both the society and the journal. The society had lost valuable documents on financial assets, registration and taxation owing to negligence of officials in the past. AMS struggled at length to put the house in order. The financial condition of the society changed from loss to profit. The backlog in publication of the bulletin was cleared with perspicacity. It became more regular and richer in its quality, content, and readership. AMS worked on the bulletin's editorial board for ten years between 1967 and 1993. He was also president of the society during 1991–93 and earned much appreciation for his handling of various affairs in a straightforward, transparent manner. AMS edited, along with Srinivas and M. S. A. Rao, a three-volume survey of research in sociology and social anthropology sponsored by ICSSR. He worked with Srinivas on a special project of publications titled, 'Studies in Sociology and Social Anthropology', which published a series of books with the collaboration of Hindustan Publishing Corporation.

The virtues of transparency, integrity, and administrative acumen inevitably drew AMS into positions of academic administration. He was head of DSE's Department of Sociology during 1971–76 and again in 1979. He immediately succeeded Srinivas in this role, which was a source of both honour and anxiety. He was director of DSE during 1973–75 and dean of Delhi University's Faculty of Social Sciences during 1973–76. He was a member of the executive council of the university during 1973–74. He was chairman of the managing committee of the Central Institute of Education during 1974–76. He was also involved in management and problem-solving tasks in various academic institutions in Delhi and elsewhere. A hallmark of his success was the trust of colleagues in his ability to work in a spirit of selflessness. As director of DSE, he managed to recover some long-lost fixed deposit receipts. He spent much time and energy on this task regardless of the response from people around him. The interest of the institution was what mattered to him. Personal recognition was inconsequential. He declined offers of some coveted academic positions. He looked upon achievement of good work as a reward in itself.

AMS's scholarship provides a unique example of combination of perseverance and patience. In achieving desired goals of perfection or completeness, he has been willing to struggle as long as he must, whether the work is academic or administrative. His pioneering work on early nineteenth-century village records, rooted in his doctoral research, was published after about four decades of its initial draft. A volume on election studies compiled by AMS in the 1970s was published in January 2007. The five volumes of Festschrift to Srinivas took altogether about fourteen years to see the light of the day.

AMS retired in 1996 with a remarkable achievement. Immediately after retirement, ICSSR awarded him national fellowship. This helped him to pursue his research and writing backlog. He has been writing and publishing steadily on his old themes as well as new trends and events that pose intellectual challenge. His recent contributions on education and religion are important both sociologically and socially. In the field of religion, AMS's new analysis serves as a valuable contribution to the understanding of sects which have conventionally received poor attention from sociologists. He continues to get agitated about an issue or event and then looks for leads and information. When he enters a new field, he aims at acquiring mastery over it. He maintains meticulousness in collection and analysis of data and sharp logic of argument. In pursuing academic work, his aim is to enhance knowledge and strengthen scholarship.

AMS has maintained professional contacts with old friends in India and abroad. He has been chairman of Centre for Social Studies at Surat since 2001 and tries hard to energise its programmes and faculty. His family obligations compel him to shuttle between Vadodara and Delhi. Vadodara gives him peace. Delhi provides opportunities to learn from and help peers and quietly serve the profession. He has health problems but employs all his personal assets of self-discipline and calmness to manage them. He continues to show streaks of aloofness and intellectual pride. He continues to induce fear and discomfort along with respect among juniors. But those who notice these also notice the sterling intellectual and human wealth accumulated since childhood. He is occasionally seen as opinionated and impatient, especially with Marxist views and predispositions. But, without doubt, he will continue to pick up ideas, hunt for information, write, confer, and actively serve the profession. May he live long and carry on the work he seems to have integrated with his own art of living.

Glossary

adeeb-fazil	Urdu examination equivalent to the BA degree
akka	elder sister
anna	elder brother
aqiqah	initiation rite
bari	marriage gifts for the bride from the bridegroom's family
bhutna/uptan	traditional face-pack
bismillah	initiation into the learning of the Quran
burqa	veil which covers a woman from head to ankle
chachi	wife of father's younger brother
chalas	feasts hosted by close relatives of bride and bridegroom soon after the wedding
chouthi	fourth day feast hosted by the parents of the bride
dahej	Hindi word for dowry
dastarkhwan	rectangular piece of cloth on which food is served
doli	palanquin
fitra	alms
gajra	flower string
halwai	trained sweet maker
iftari	snack with which fast is broken, it generally consists of some dates, cut fruits mixed with herbs and lemon juice
izzat	honour
jahez	dowry for the bride
karambhumi	place of work
khala	mother's sister
kochu	a starchy tuber
lajja	shame
mangni	engagement
maun	observing silence

mehndi	henna
mehr	promised bride-price fixed at the time of nikah; dowry
mohalla	neighbourhood
moksha	salvation
moolahs	educated and respectable Muslim clergy
namaz	prayer five times a day as prescribed by Islam
nikah nama	marriage certificate
nikah	marriage according to Islamic rites
paigham	marriage proposal
paltawa	return gifts
pan	betel nut
pandit	Brahmin priest/scholar
phuphi	father's sister
pindi	big round sweet balls made out of finely ground wheat
qazi	priest who performs the marriage rites
Quran	religious text of the Muslims
Ramzan	the most auspicious month for the Muslims
roza	fast during the month of Ramzan
ruqaah	bio-data
sadhvi	religious acsetic
sanchak	marriage gifts for the bridegroom and his close relatives from the bride's family
satta bazaar	forward trading or betting
sawab	religious merit
sawaiyan	vermicelli
seva	service
shagird	disciple/student
sharm	modesty
sipara	a chapter from the Quran
talaq	divorce
tayi	wife of father's elder brother
thalis	big round plates
thambi	younger brother
thangai	younger sister
ustaniji/ustanji	respected lady teacher
vakils	advocates
walima	feast hosted by bridegroom's family the day after the wedding
zakat	giving two and a half percent of one's income/assets as charity to the poor, especially during the month of Ramzan

Publications of A. M. Shah

Books

1973. *The Household Dimension of the Family in India: A Field Study in a Gujarat Village and a Review of Other Studies.* Delhi: Orient Longman. Berkeley: University of California Press, 1974.

1988. With I. P. Desai. *Division and Hierarchy: An Overview of Caste in Gujarat.* Delhi: Hindustan Publishing Corporation (Gujarati translation, Surat: Centre for Social Studies, 1993).

1998. *The Family in India: Critical Essays.* Delhi: Orient Longman.

2002. *Exploring India's Rural Past: A Gujarat Village in the Early Nineteenth Century.* Delhi: Oxford University Press.

Edited Books

1973–75. With M. N. Srinivas and M. S. A. Rao. *Survey of Research in Sociology and Social Anthropology.* 3 vols. Bombay: Popular Prakashan, on behalf of Indian Council of Social Science Research.

1979. With M. N. Srinivas and E. A. Ramaswamy. *The Fieldworker and the Field: Problems and Challenges in Sociological Investigation.* Delhi: Oxford University Press. Second edition, with Preface by Shah and Ramaswamy, 2002. Paperback, 2003.

1996a. With B. S. Baviskar and E. A. Ramaswamy. *Social Structure and Change.* Vol. 1: *Theory and Method: An Evaluation of the Work of M. N. Srinivas.* Delhi: Sage Publications.

1996b. With B. S. Baviskar and E. A. Ramaswamy. *Social Structure and Change.* Vol. 2: *Women in Indian Society.* Delhi: Sage Publications.

1996c. With B. S. Baviskar and E. A. Ramaswamy. *Social Structure and Change.* Vol. 3: *Complex Organizations and Urban Communities.* Delhi: Sage Publications.

1997. With B. S. Baviskar and E. A. Ramaswamy. *Social Structure and Change.* Vol. 4: *Development and Ethnicity.* Delhi: Sage Publications.

1998. With B. S. Baviskar and E. A. Ramaswamy. *Social Structure and Change.* Vol. 5: *Religion and Kinship.* Delhi: Sage Publications.

2007. *The Grassrooots of Democracy: Field Studies of Indian Elections.* Delhi: Permanent Black.

Papers, Articles, Notes

1955a. A Dispersed Hamlet in the Panchmahals. *Economic and Political Weekly* 7(4–5, Annual Number), January 26: 109–16.

1955b. Caste, Economy and Territory in the Central Panchmahals. *Journal of the Maharaja Sayajirao University of Baroda* 4(1): 61–91.

1956. Social Change in a Multi-caste Village. In *Society in India,* ed. A. Aiyappan and L. K. Bala Ratnam, 161–80. Madras: Social Sciences Association.

1958. With R.G. Shroff. The Vahivancha Barots of Gujarat: A Caste of Genealogists and Mythographers. *Journal of American Folklore* 71(281): 246–76. Reprinted in *Traditional India: Structure and Change* (1959), ed. Milton Singer, 40–70. Philadelphia: American Folklore Society.

1959. Social Anthropology and the Study of Historical Societies. *Economic and Political Weekly* 11(28–30, Special Number): 953–62.

1960. With M. N. Srinivas. The Myth of Self-Sufficiency of the Indian Village. *Economic and Political Weekly* 12(37): 1375–78. Reprinted with revision in *Conspectus of Indian Society: Essays in Honour of Professor R. N. Saksena* (1971), ed. Rajeshwar Prasad, G. C. Hallen and Kusum Pathak. Agra: Arvind Vivek Prakashan.

1961. A Note on the Hijadas of Gujarat. *American Anthropologist* 63(6): 1325–30.

1963. With R. G. Shroff and A. R. Shah. Early Nineteenth Century Village Records in Gujarat. In *Contributions to Indian Economic History,* ed. Tapan Raychaudhury, 89–100. Vol. 2. Calcutta: Firma K. L. Mukhopadhyaya. Also in *Journal of Gujarat Research Society* 14(2): 126–34.

1964a. Basic Terms and Concepts in the Study of Family in India. *Indian Economic and Social History Review* 1(3): 1–36. Reprinted in *Family Strategies in India: Some Studies* (1982), ed. G. C. Hallen, 183–209. Meerut: Rohini Publications.

1964b. Political System in Eighteenth Century Gujarat. *Enquiry,* New Series 1(1): 83–93.

1965. Appraisal of Louis Dumont, Hierarchy and Marriage Alliance in South Indian Kinship. *Current Anthropology* 7(3): 340.

1968a. With M. N. Srinivas. Hinduism. *International Encyclopedia of the Social Sciences.* Vol. 6. New York: Macmillan and Free Press: 358–66.

1968b. Eunuchs. *Encyclopaedia of Social Work in India.* Vol. 1: 295–97. Delhi: Publications Division, Government of India.

1968c. Changes in the Indian Family: An Examination of Some Assumptions. *Economic and Political Weekly* 3(1–2, Annual Number): 127–34.

1968d. Family and Kinship among the Pandits of Rural Kashmir: A Review Article. *Eastern Anthropologist* 21(3): 305–17.

1969a. Study of Changes in the Indian Family. In *Trends of Socio-Economic Change in India, 1871–1961.* Vol. 7: 275–84. Simla: Transactions of the Indian Institute of Advanced Study.

1969b. Urgent Research in Social Anthropology: Some Points for Discussion. In *Urgent Research in Social Anthropology.* Vol. 10: 156–57. Simla: Transactions of the Indian Institute of Advanced Study.

1969c. Record of Discussion. In *Social Mobility in the Caste System in India: An Interdisciplinary Symposium, Comparative Studies in Society and History,* Supplement III, ed. James Silverberg, 116–17, 120–21. The Hague: Mouton.

1970. With Aneeta Ahluwalia. Role of Sociology in Medical Education and Research. *Economic and Political Weekly* 5(17), April 25: 705–10.

1972. The Indian Journal of Sociology, 1920. *Sociological Bulletin* 21(1): 62–67.

1974a. Historical Sociology. In *Survey of Research in Sociology and Social Anthropology,* ed. M. N. Srinivas, M. S. A. Rao and A. M. Shah. Vol. 1. Bombay: Popular Prakashan, on behalf of Indian Council of Social Science Research.

1974b. Roles–Visible and Invisible—of Sociologists in India. In *Sociology and Social Development in Asia: Proceedings of the Symposium,* ed. T. Fukutake and K. Morioka. Tokyo: University of Tokyo Press.

1975. Record of Discussion. In *Responses to Population Growth in India,* ed. Marcus F. Franda, 109–11, 151–52, 177, 218, 255–56. New York: Praeger.

1976a. Impressive Achievements. Interview on 'Progress, Bottlenecks'. *Link,* January 26: 45–46.

1976b. Lineage Structure and Change in a Gujarat Village. In *Dimensions of Social Change,* ed. M. N. Srinivas, S. Seshayya and V. S. Parthasarathy 339–67. Delhi: Allied Publishers.

1976c. Foreword to *Politics of a Small Town: A Sociological Study* by Khadija Ansari Gupta. Delhi: Impex India.

1978. Foreword to *Industrial Relations in India: A Sociological Perspective,* ed. E. A. Ramaswamy. Delhi: Macmillan.

1979. Studying the Present and the Past: A Village in Gujarat. In *The Fieldworker and the Field: Problems and Challenges in Sociological Investigation,* ed. M. N. Srinivas, A. M. Shah and E. A. Ramaswamy. Delhi: Oxford University Press.

1980. Mysore Narsimhachar Srinivas. In *Sociology in India: The Profession and Its Pioneers,* ed. Brij Raj Chauhan, 17–18. Meerat: Sociology Workers' Sangam.

1981. With E. A. Ramaswamy. Human Fertility and Culture: Some Sociological Observations. In *India's Population: Problems and Prospects. India International Centre Quarterly* 8(3–4, Special Number): 227–33.

1982. Division and Hierarchy: An Overview of Caste in Gujarat. *Contributions to Indian Sociology* 16(1): 1–33.

1986. Towards a Sociological Understanding of Ancient India. A review article on Romila Thapar, *From Lineage to State: Social Formations in the Mid-First Millennium B.C. in the Ganga Valley. Contributions to Indian Sociology* 20(1): 118–33.

1987a. Social Change: Far-reaching Implications. *The Hindustan Times*, 15 August.

1987b. Untouchability, the Untouchables and Social Change in Gujarat. In *Dimensions of Social Life: Essays in Honor of David Mandelbaum*, ed. Paul Hockings. Berlin: Mouton de Gruyter.

1987c. History and Sociology. *Seminar* 338, October: 19–21. Reprinted in *Theory and Ideology in Indian Sociology: Essays in Honour of Professor Yogendra Singh*, (1996), ed. Narendra K. Singhi. Jaipur: Rawat.

1988a. The Rural-Urban Networks in India. *South Asia* 11(2): 1–27. Reprinted in *Country-Town Nexus* (1991), ed. K. L. Sharma and Dipankar Gupta 11–42. Jaipur: Rawat.

1988b. The Phase of Dispersal in the Indian Family Process. *Sociological Bulletin* 37(1–2): 33–47.

1988–89. A Sociological Approach to the Eighteenth- and Nineteenth-Century History of Gujarat. *Journal of the Maharaja Sayajirao University of Baroda* (Social Science) 37–38(2): 111–19.

1989a. The Parameters of Family Policy in India. In Christian Academy, *The World Community in Post-Industrial Society*. Vol. 1: *Changing Families in the World Perspective*, 249–59. Seoul, Korea: Wooseok. Also in *Economic and Political Weekly* 24(10), March 11: 513–16.

1989b. Caste and the Intelligentsia. *The Hindustan Times*, March 24.

1990a. Reservations: Double Talk on Castes. *The Hindustan Times*, September 7.

1990b. With M. N. Srinivas and B. S. Baviskar. Kothari's Illusion of Secular Upsurge. *The Times of India*, October 17.

1991a. We Need Efficiency More Than Mandal. *The Times of India*, January 15.

1991b. M. N. Srinivas. *The International Dictionary of Anthropologists*. New York and London: Garland.

1991c. The Family, Socialization, and the Rights of the Child. In *The Citizen Child: Socio-cultural Perspectives*, ed. S. C. Bhatia, 31–33. Delhi: University of Delhi, Department of Adult, Continuing Education.

1991d. Caste, Marriage and the Intelligentsia. In *In Search of India's Renaissance*. Vol. 2. Chandigarh: Centre for Research in Rural and Industrial Development.

1991e. Job Reservations and Efficiency. *Economic and Political Weekly*, July 20: 1732–34. Reprinted in *Caste: Its Twentieth Century Avatar* (1996), ed. M. N. Srinivas. Delhi: Penguin.

1991f. With Gay Ochiltree et al. *Broken Families and the Issue of Child Socialization*. Bangkok: Unesco, Principal Regional Office for Asia and the Pacific.

1992a. *The Judicial and the Sociological View of the Other Backward Classes*. I. P. Desai Memorial Lecture. Surat: Centre for Social Studies. Reprinted in *Caste: Its Twentieth Century Avatar,* ed. M. N. Srinivas (1996), Delhi: Penguin.

1992b. Reservation: For Whose Benefit? *The Hindustan Times*, February 3.

1992c. Defining the OBCs. *The Hindustan Times*, March 16.

1994. Some Reflections on Sociological Research and Teaching in India. *Sociological Bulletin* 43(1): 1–8.

1996a. Is the Joint Household Disintegrating? *Economic and Political Weekly* 31(9), March 2: 537–42.

1998a. A further note on The Indian Journal of Sociology, 1920. *Sociological Bulletin* 47(1): 128.

1998b. Can the Caste Census Be Reliable? *Economic and Political Weekly* 33(39), September 26: 2498–99.

1999a. Changes in the Family and the Elderly. *Economic and Political Weekly* 34(20), May 15: 1179–82.

1999b. The Family in the Census of India. *Sociological Bulletin* 48(1 and 2): 235–37.

2000a. Foreword to *Female Infanticide and Social Structure: A Socio-Historical Study in Gujarat during the Nineteenth Century* by L. S. Vishwanath. Delhi: Hindustan Publishing Corporation.

2000b. In Memory of M. N. Srinivas. *Contributions to Indian Sociology* 34(1): 93–104.

2000c. An Interview with M. N. Srinivas. *Current Anthropology* 41(4): 629–36.

2000d. Sociology in a Regional Context. In Symposium on 'Situating Sociology'. *Seminar* 495 (November): 45–49.

2000e. Family Structures. In *Routledge International Encyclopedia of Women*, ed. Cheris Kramarae and Dale Spender. Vol. 2: 691–95. New York: Routledge.

2000f. Changes in Family and Their Impact on the Elderly. *HelpAge India Research and Development Journal* 6(2): 32–38.

2002a. Foreword to *Collected Essays,* ed. M. N. Srinivas. Delhi: Oxford University Press. Revised edition in *The Oxford India* (2009). Delhi: Oxford University Press.

2002b. The 'Dalit' Category and Its Differentiation. *Economic and Political Weekly* 37(14), April 6–12: 1317–18.

2002c. For a More Humane Society. In 'Society under Siege', a symposium on 'The Breakdown of Civil Society in Gujarat'. *Seminar* 513 (May): 58–60.

2002d. With E. A. Ramaswamy. Preface to *The Fieldworker and the Field*, ed. M. N. Srinivas, A. M. Shah and E. A. Ramaswamy. 2nd ed. Delhi: Oxford University Press.

2003a. Tribes—so-called—of Gujarat: In the Perspective of Time. *Economic and Political Weekly* 38(2), January 11: 95–97.

2003b. Discussion: The Matter of Facts. *Economic and Political Weekly* 38(42), September 20: 4491–92.

2005a. Family Studies: Retrospect and Prospect. *Economic and Political Weekly* 49(1), January 1: 19–22.

2005b. Sanskritisation Revisited. *Sociological Bulletin* 54(2), January-April. Reprinted in *M. N. Srinivas: The Man and His Work* (2007), 129–45, ed. P. K. Mishra, K. K. Basa and H. K. Bhat. Jaipur: Rawat.

2005c. Higher Education and Research: Roots of Mediocrity. *Economic and Political Weekly* 49(22–23), 28 May: 2234–42.

2005d. Communication: Reservations and Efficiency. *Seminar* 551(July): 86–87.

2005e. Parashuram: Icon of New Brahminism. *Economic and Political Weekly* 41(5), February 4: 390–91.

2005f. With Yogesh Atal et al. Intensive Studies in Village: In Retrospect and Prospect. *Eastern Anthropologist* 58(3–4): 304–11.

2006a. Some Further Thoughts on Sanskritisation: Response to Nirmal Singh's Rejoinder. *Sociological Bulletin* 55(1): 112–17.

2006b. Sects and Hindu Social Structure. *Contributions to Indian Sociology* 40(2): 209–48.

2006c. *The Indian Sociologist*, 1905–14, 1920–22. *Economic and Political Weekly* 41(31), August 5: 3435–39.

2006d. Caste Bubble. *The Times of India*, November 28.

2007a. M. N. Srinivas in Baroda. In *M.N. Srinivas: The Man and His Work*, ed. P. K. Misra, K. K. Basa and H. K. Bhat, 41–61. Jaipur: Rawat.

2007b. M. N. Srinivas, Max Weber, and Functionalism. *Sociological Bulletin* 56(1).

2007c. Caste in the Twenty-first Century: From System to Elements. *Economic and Political Weekly* 42 (44): 109–116.

2007d. Purity, Impurity, Untouchability: Then and Now. *Sociological Bulletin* 56 (3), Sepember–December: 355–68.

2008a. With Pravin J. Patel and Lancy Lobo. The Heady Mix: Gujarati and Hindu Pride. *Economic and Political Weekly*, February 23.

2008b. Violation of the Norms of Academic Discourse: A Rejoinder to T. K. Oommen's Disjunctions between Field, Method and Concept; an appraisal of M. N. Srinivas. *Sociological Bulletin* 57(3): 388–402.

In Gujarati

1967. With R. G. Shroff and P. C. Shah. *Bharatnu Gramjivan.* Translation of *India's Villages,* ed. M. N. Srinivas. Bombay: R. R. Sheth.

1969. *Amukh* (Foreword) to *Adhunik Bharatman Jnati ane Bija Lekho.* Translation of *Caste in Modern India and Other Essays* by M. N. Srinivas. Translated by Purushottam C. Shah. Bhavnagar: Bhashantar Nidhi.

1983. *Prastavik* (Introduction) to *Gujaratna Vikasata Samudayo: Azadi Pachhina Samaj Daramyan Ashprushyoni Sthitiman Ferfar* by Urmila Patel. Ahmedabad: Mangal Prabhat.

1984. *Vibhajan ane Unchnich-kram: Gujaratna Jnati-Vibhagonun Vihangavalokan. ARTHAT* 3(1): 11–39.

1986. *Gujaratman Ashprishyata, Ashprishyo ane Samajik Parivartan. ARTHAT* 5(2): 1–12.

1993. With I. P. Desai. *Vibhajan ane Unchnich-kram: Gujaratna Jnati-Vibhagonun Vihangavalokan.* Translation of *Division and Hierarchy: An Overview of Caste in Gujarat.* Translated by Arjun Patel and Ramesh Shroff. Surat: Centre for Social Studies.

1994. *Bharatman Samajshastriya Samshodhan ane Adhyapan Sambandhi Ketlak Vicharo. ARTHAT* (13:4): 4–12.

2004. *I. P. Desai: Mari Drishtiye. ARTHAT* 23(1), March: 1–14.

2007a. *Ucch Sikshan ane Samshodhan: Nimnatana Mool. ARTHAT* 24(1–2): 1–22.

2007b. *Harijan Santo: Samajshastriya Paripreksyama. SHABDASAR* 6(March): 12–14.

2008. With Pravin J. Patel and Lancy Lobo. *Nashilun Mishran: Gujarati ane Hindu Gaurav. Naya Marg,* April 16: 21–24.

Contributors

MOHINI ANJUM, Formerly Professor of Sociology, Jamia Millia Islamia, New Delhi.

DONALD W. ATTWOOD, Professor of Anthropology, McGill University, Montreal, Canada.

B. S. BAVISKAR, Senior Fellow, Institute of Social Sciences, New Delhi; Formerly Professor of Sociology, University of Delhi.

ANDRE BÉTEILLE, Professor Emeritus of Sociology, University of Delhi; Formerly Chairman, Indian Council of Social Science Research.

BISWAROOP DAS, Visiting Professor, Gujarat Institute of Development Research, Ahmedabad; Formerly Director, Centre for Social Studies, Surat.

ALPHONSUS D'SOUZA, Associate Director, North Eastern Social Research Centre, Guwahati.

T. SCARLETT EPSTEIN, Director, Practical Education and Gender Support (PEGS), Hove, UK; Formerly Professor of Social Anhropology, University of Sussex, UK.

SHANTI GEORGE, independent researcher, The Hague, The Netherlands; Formerly Reader in Sociology, University of Delhi.

LANCY LOBO, Director, Centre for Culture and Development, Vadodara.

ANEETA A. MINOCHA, Formerly Professor of Sociology, University of Delhi.

RAJNI PALRIWALA, Professor of Sociology, University of Delhi.

PRAVIN J. PATEL, Formerly Professor of Sociology, M.S. University of Baroda, Vadodara; and Vice-Chancellor, Sardar Patel University, Vallabh Vidyanagar.

TULSI PATEL, Professor of Sociology, University of Delhi.

RAGINI P. SHAH, Reader in Sociology, M.S. University of Baroda, Vadodara.

N. R. SHETH, Formerly Director, Indian Institute of Management, Ahmedabad.

MARIO RUTTEN, Professor of Sociology, University of Amsterdam, The Netherlands.

L. S. VISHWANATH, Formerly Professor of History, Pondicherry University.

Index

Advani, L. K., *Rathyatra* of, 148
agrarian structure, 208–9
agricultural processing industries, 204
agriculture(al)
    female participation in,
        113, 114, 116, 197
Ambedkar, B. R., 153
American kinship, 297
Aqiqah (initiation), 41, 42–43
'atom of kinship', 283, 285–88,
    290–92, 294, 299, 303, 305
'axiom of amity', 301, 304
Ayodhya issue, 157

Babri Masjid, demolition of, 149
Bajrang Dal, 150, 154
Bangladesh
    gender-based inequality in,
        58, 59, 64
    Grameen Bank's loan to women,
        14–16, 59, 60, 82, 84, 87,
        88, 188
    household and seclusion in,
        61–64
    hunger/starvation in, 77–80,
        86, 87
    patriarchal structure in, 15–16, 86
    poverty in, 60, 64
Bangladeshi women

child bride, 66–70
    divorced and widowed, 70–74
    economic pressure on, 77, 80, 88
    employment of, 59, 80–81, 83,
        84, 86
    empowerment of, 87
    oppression of, 85
    resilience and resignation by, 74–77
    seclusion of, 77–84
    status/position of, 62, 64, 84, 85, 88
Banias, 107, 108
Bedi Khutris, 109
Bharatiya Janata Party (BJP), 153, 166
    anti-Muslim propaganda by, 160
    in elections of, 2002 and 2004,
        147, 167
    religio-political discourse of,
        153, 162
    rise as a political power, 154, 155
    support to Gujarat riots, 158
Bhave, Vinoba, 183
bishops, 18, 133, 136–37
bismillah, 41, 43–45
bride-price, 3, 116, 117
    (*mehr*) among Muslims, 46
    among Rajputs, 111
    see also dowry
burqa, 33, 34, 40, 52–54

Canon Law, 132–35, 143
caste
  and agrarian system, 209
  and cultural continuity, 199
  female infanticide, 118, 120
  hierarchy, 3, 210
  relationship between, in Gujarat,
    338–39
  system in India 2, 154, 199
Catholic Christians
  as messenger of God, 136, 144
  'confessions' by, 135, 139
  cultic/ritualistic role of, 135, 139
  educational activities of, 141
  on cause of justice, 142–43
  preaching by, 135–57, 139
  role of, 131, 132, 135–36
  social services and welfare
    programmes by, 14
  vow of celibacy by, 136, 141
Catholic Church
  as denomination, 131
  as ecclesia, 131
  dimensions of, 132
Catholic priests
  Decons, 133
  hearing of 'confessions', 135, 139
Congress party, 147
  in Gujarat, 153–54
cooperatives, 203, 207–8
  and indutrialisation in rural areas,
    20–21, 202
  dairy, 205, 212, 213
  government/state support to,
    204, 214–17, 218
  management of, 212, 213–15
  member-shareholders of, 213–15
  organisational factors of, 211–14
  origins and growth in India, 203–6
  success and failure of, 206–7
cooperative banks, 203–4
culture(al)
  and development, 189–92
  continuity, 198–99
  role in female infanticide, 120–21

curriculum change, study of,
  309–13, 314

dairy processing orgaisations, 212
Delhi School of Economics (DSE),
  360
  Department of Sociology, 356–57,
    359
Delhi University
  Department of Sociology, 310,
    313–14, 331, 332
  ethnography study, 331, 333
  federal structure, 310
  feminist groups, 325, 327
  gender and women study, 311–12,
    317
  History Department, 311
  MA in gender studies, 317, 320,
    323, 324, 326
  MPhil Programme, 311, 312,
    313, 317, 323
  syllabus change, 310–13
demography(ic), changes, 196–98
  perspective, 118–22
Desai, I. P., 2, 13, 355
Diocese of Mangalore,
  commitment to education, 141
  laity in, 143, 144
  on causes of justice, 142
  priests in, 138
divorce of Muslim women, 34, 55,
  70–71
doctor
  legal protection to, 276
  -patient relationship, 276
  role, expectation and social
    responsibility of, 258
dowry
  and harassment for,
    in Bangladesh, 71
  among Lewa Patidars, 107
  among Muslims, 51–52
  among Rajputs, 100
  custom, 3, 120, 223

Patidar diaspora in Britain, 220–25
  activities of, 225–28
  attachment to Indian culture by, 227, 229–30
  family and kinship ties of, 228, 234–45, 249, 250, 251
  investments in India, 241, 245–49
  marriage practice among, 232, 237, 241, 252, 253
  NRI status of, 239, 246, 248
  religious activities of, 231–32, 238
  social life of, 222–25
  village-based associations in Britain, 230–31
patient
  -doctor interaction, 258, 272
  right to choose medical therapy, 259, 262
  stereotyping of, by doctors, 272–73
  women, and use of modern medicine, 266, 268, 272
priesthood.
  common, 133, 134
  hierarchical structure of, 17–18, 133
  ministerial, 133
  official, 133, 134
  role of, 132–37
  training of, 134
purdah
  among Bangladeshi women, 59, 60, 78, 85–86
  among Muslim women in South Asia, 61
  and mobility of women, 62
  and orthodoxy, 15
  and public space, 61
  and status of women, 63

Radcliff-Brown, 25, 111, 112, 284, 285, 288, 289, 291, 292, 294, 295
Rajput(s), female infanticide among, 16–17, 96, 99, 100, 109, 122
  hypergamous hierarchy

marriage practices among, 103, 105
matrilineal kinship among, 96
polyandry among, 96
social structure of, in Kathiawad, 102, 104
Suryavamshi, high position of, 109–10
Ramjanmabhoomi, 149
Rashtriya Swayamsevak Sangh (RSS), 148, 154
  anti-Muslim propaganda by, 160
religion(ous), 3, 15, 17, 18, 78, 98, 173, 183, 237, 319, 358, 360
  as social institution, 172–73
  communalism, 17
  discourse, 154
  state, 131

Sangh Parivar, 153, 154, 155, 160
  NRI support to, in Gujarat, 163
sex ratios, in north and south India, 112
sexuality, 62, 66, 88
Shah, Arvindbhai, 1–7, 98, 111, 309, 331, 349
  academic achievement of, 13, 352
  Chairman of Centre for Social Studies, Surat, 360
  at Delhi University, 8, 9, 356–57
  and Gandhian ethos, 352, 354
  and M. N. Srivas, 353
  on historiography, 35–36
  students of, 8–10
  works of, 352, 358
social anthropology, 24–27, 97
Srinivas, M. N., 2–5, 12, 13, 27, 71, 99, 310, 313, 331, 352, 354, 355, 358, 359, 360
  and A. M. Shah, 353

UNAIDS, estimate on HIV/AIDS deaths in sub-Saharan Africa, 194
  Report on parents with HIV/AIDS in Tanzania, 194–95
University Grants Commission, 357

ustani(female teacher), 44–45

Vajpayee, A. B., 151, 171
Vishwa Hindu Parishad, 150, 154
    and communal riots, 157–58
    anti-Muslim propaganda by, 160
Vivekananda, Swami, 18, 153, 174,
    177, 183

Weber, Max, 18–19, 173, 300
West Bengal, agrarian structure and
    caster in, 208–10
women
    as separated, abandoned, widowed
    and divorced, 70–74

Bhagini Mandir, home for mentally
    retarded, 179–80
in agricultural work, 113, 116
movement in India, 313, 325, 326
position in the family, 45, 197
property bill on, 16
status of, 11, 41
study on, 26, 58–59, 268, 308,
    309, 311, 313, 316–19, 323,
    328
subjugation of, 115
see also Bangladeshi women,
    Muslim women

Yunus, Muhammad, 59